CAPE COD

AND THE

ISLANDS OF MARTHA'S VINEYARD AND NANTUCKET

Upper Cape refers to the east-west stretch of the Cape nearest the mainland, from the Canal to near Cotuit. The *Mid-Cape* covers the section roughly from Cotuit to Dennisport. The *Lower Cape* extends from North Harwich to Provincetown on the curl at the tip of the Cape.

FODOR'S MODERN GUIDES

are compiled, researched, and edited by an international team of travel writers, field correspondents, and editors. The series, which now almost covers the globe, was founded by Eugene Fodor in 1936.

OFFICES
New York & London

FODOR'S CAPE COD AND THE ISLANDS OF MARTHA'S VINEYARD AND NANTUCKET:

Area Editors: Steve Connolly, Kevin Fielding, Gary Holmes, Wilson Jones, Keith Liggett, Christie Lowrance, William Scheller, Brian Shortsleeve

Editor: Cynthia Nelson

Editorial Associates: Mary Beth Brewer and Stephen Brewer

Illustrations: Ted Burwell

Maps and Plans: Dyno Lowenstein and Jon Bauch

FODOR'S

CAPE COD

AND THE
ISLANDS OF MARTHA'S VINEYARD
AND
NANTUCKET

FODOR'S MODERN GUIDES, INC.
Distributed by
DAVID McKAY COMPANY, INC.
New York

All the following Guides are current (most of them also in
the Hodder and Stoughton British edition).

CURRENT FODOR'S COUNTRY AND AREA TITLES:

AUSTRALIA, NEW ZEALAND
   AND SOUTH PACIFIC
AUSTRIA
BELGIUM AND
   LUXEMBOURG
BERMUDA
BRAZIL
CANADA
CARIBBEAN AND BAHAMAS
CENTRAL AMERICA
EASTERN EUROPE
EGYPT
EUROPE
FRANCE
GERMANY
GREAT BRITAIN
GREECE
HOLLAND

INDIA & NEPAL
IRELAND
ISRAEL
ITALY
JAPAN AND KOREA
JORDAN AND HOLY LAND
MEXICO
NORTH AFRICA
PEOPLE'S REPUBLIC
   OF CHINA
PORTUGAL
SCANDINAVIA
SOUTH AMERICA
SOUTHEAST ASIA
SOVIET UNION
SPAIN
SWITZERLAND
TURKEY
YUGOSLAVIA

CITY GUIDES:

CHICAGO
LONDON
NEW YORK CITY
PARIS

ROME
SAN FRANCISCO
WASHINGTON, D.C.

FODOR'S BUDGET SERIES:

BUDGET BRITAIN
BUDGET CANADA
BUDGET CARIBBEAN
BUDGET EUROPE
BUDGET FRANCE
BUDGET GERMANY

BUDGET ITALY
BUDGET JAPAN
BUDGET MEXICO
BUDGET SPAIN
BUDGET TRAVEL IN AMERICA

USA GUIDES:

ALASKA
CALIFORNIA
CAPE COD
COLORADO
FAR WEST
FLORIDA
HAWAII

NEW ENGLAND
PENNSYLVANIA
SOUTH
SOUTHWEST
USA (in one volume)

SPECIAL INTEREST:

CIVIL WAR SITES

CONTENTS

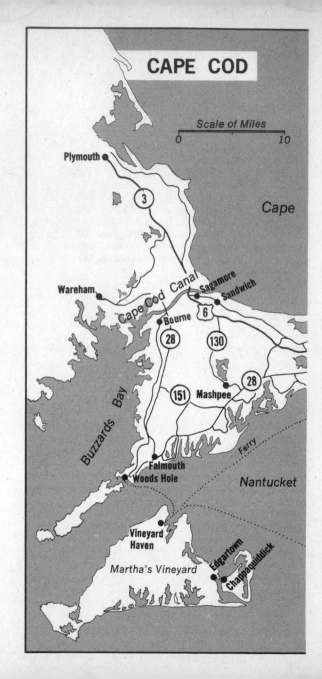

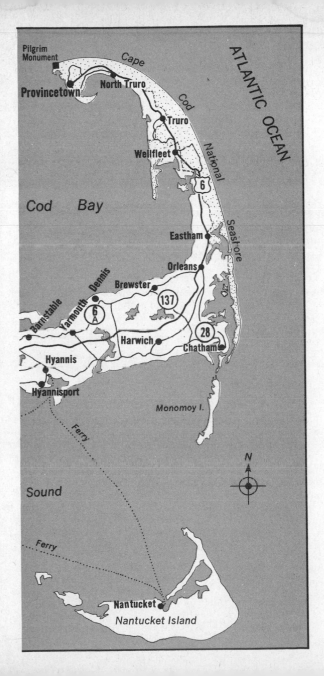

FOREWORD

Cape Cod and the islands of Martha's Vineyard and Nantucket offer something for just about everyone's taste—sunny beaches, antique stores, beautiful sailing, hiking and biking trails, whale-watching tours, old sea captains' homes, and much more.

Fodor's Cape Cod and the Islands of Martha's Vineyard and Nantucket has been written to help you enjoy as fully as possible all the attractions the area has to offer. Background text provides history and walking tours and Practical Information sections offer up-to-date listings. We have also included a chapter on Plymouth, Massachusetts, as well as a chapter on the Cape's creative past and present, and a special cruising guide to the area waters.

Occasionally we will mention a house that is worth noting for its architecture or its age. Many of these are private homes—please respect the occupants' privacy. Places that are open to the public will also be covered in the Practical Information sections in each chapter.

The selections and comments in this guidebook are based on the editors' and contributors' personal experience. We feel that our first responsibility is to inform and protect you, the reader. Errors are bound to creep into any travel guide, however. We go to press in the late fall of the year, and much change can and will occur on the Cape and the Islands even while we are on press and during the succeeding twelve months or so when this edition is on sale. We cannot, therefore, be responsible for the sudden closing of a restaurant, a change in a museum's days or hours, a shift of chefs (for the worse), and so forth. We sincerely welcome letters from readers on these changes, or from those whose opinions differ from ours, and we are ready to revise our entries for next year's edition when the facts warrant it.

Send your letters to the editors at **Fodor's Modern Guides, Inc., 2 Park Avenue, New York, NY 10016.** Continental readers may prefer to write to Fodor's Modern Guides, 9–10 Market Pl., London W1N 7AG, England.

FACTS AT YOUR
FINGERTIPS

by

WILLIAM G. SCHELLER

William G. Scheller, a freelance writer, lives in Newburyport, Massachusetts. He is editor of Appalachia, *the journal of the Appalachian Mountain Club, and the author of* Country Walks Near New York *and* Train Trips: Exploring America by Rail.

 FACTS AND FIGURES. Cape Cod, which is most frequently compared in shape to an outstretched arm bent at the elbow, extends eastward from the shoulder of Massachusetts for roughly 35 miles. The Cape then takes a sharp left turn and juts northward for an equal distance, turning back toward the mainland as it reaches its tip at Provincetown. The

1

body of water embraced by the arm is Cape Cod Bay. To the east is the open Atlantic; to the south, Nantucket Sound. At no point is the Cape's width greater than 20 miles. Seven is more typical, and at Truro, on the "wrist" of the Cape, ocean and bay are barely a mile and a half apart.

You will hear the terms Upper, Mid, and Lower Cape. Contrary to what you might think, Upper refers to the east-west stretch nearest the mainland. We have defined the Lower Cape—the part you sail down to—as the area from North Harwich to Provincetown. The Mid-Cape, of course, is in between, covering the section roughly from Cotuit to Dennisport.

There may have been some question once about where Cape Cod begins, but that was settled early in the twentieth century with the building of the Cape Cod Canal, which joins Buzzards and Cape Cod bays about 15 miles south of Plymouth. The Cape, then, is an island, its 15 towns, dozens of villages, and over 160,000 year-round residents linked with the mainland via the Bourne and Sagamore bridges.

When Cape Codders talk about the "islands," though, they are referring to Martha's Vineyard and Nantucket. The triangle-shaped Vineyard lies just six miles off the Cape's south shore. But Nantucket, which looks on the map like something that has been flung out to sea, is more than 20 miles from land, 30 miles by ferry from Woods Hole.

Topographically, Cape Cod and the islands are creatures of the last great Ice Age, which ended some 10,000 years ago. The spine of the Upper Cape and the foundations of Martha's Vineyard and Nantucket are glacial moraines. Between the moraines and the sea stretch the outwash plains, created out of finer fragments by the slowly melting glaciers. These constitute the south shores of the islands and the Cape. Much of what remains, particularly Nantucket's Great Point, and Monomoy, Nauset Beach, and the Province Lands on the Cape, are fragile expanses of barrier beach, incessantly buffeted by winds and tides.

The traveler approaching Cape Cod from the north begins to notice a change of scenery not long after leaving Plymouth, especially if the route chosen is the coastal 3A rather than 3, the inland expressway. The land flattens; trees grow shorter and scrubbier in response to the bay breezes and salt air. This is cranberry country; a good part of the Massachusetts crop is grown in Plymouth County. On the other side of Cape Cod Canal, the bogs and pinelands continue, interrupted by dozens of glacial ponds. Here, along the Upper Cape, there are three main routes of markedly different character. Rte. 6 is the central highway; its scenery is indistinguished but it will get you downcape in a hurry. Rte. 6A hugs the bay, and strings together a handsome collection of old, neatly painted seafaring towns. Rte. 28 is the south shore road; it leads to such popular resorts as Hyannis, Bass River, and Dennisport, but offers little relief from development until it reaches Chatham.

To head down the Lower Cape to Provincetown, you will take Rte. 6, or else you will walk along the beach. But as you pass through towns like Eastham, Wellfleet, and Truro, be sure to turn off onto side roads—some little better than dirt tracks—that meander over heath-covered hummocks and past hidden ponds. Finally, you reach the dunes of the Province Lands, the sandy expanse that marks the northern extremity of the Cape Cod National Seashore and the spectacular 39-mile Great Beach, which Thoreau described so succinctly in his book *Cape Cod*.

The physical appearance of Martha's Vineyard and Nantucket is similar to that of the Cape. The character of the Vineyard is a bit more tame, with rolling farmland, protected harbors, and the genial old settlements of Vineyard Haven, Oak Bluffs, and Edgartown. Only out towards the cliffs of Gay Head, at Chilmark, and at windswept Chappaquiddick does the real rawness of the sea intrude. Nantucket is a different matter: there is only one year-round town, Nantucket, and it presides over an island quilted with moors, wildflowers, and the world's largest cranberry bog. Nowhere on Nantucket can you forget that you are out on the North Atlantic.

What man has built on Cape Cod, Martha's Vineyard, and Nantucket is largely in harmony with the natural environment, especially on the Lower Cape and islands. Here you will find the traditional Cape Cod house—now as popular across the continent as the California ranch home—along with some Georgian, Federal, and Victorian creations and a profusion of the weather-scarred outbuildings beloved by amateur artists. Nothing is more quintessentially Cape Cod than the sight of wild pink roses against shingles bleached silver-gray by a century of salt wind.

For the past 60 years, Cape Cod has been courting tourists, and many have come back to stay. It is not surprising, then, that the Cape's ethnic mix has become quite varied, particularly in the more populated areas around Hyannis, Yarmouth, Falmouth, and Provincetown. But the bedrock strain is Yankee, and the most significant minority are the Portuguese. Provincetown—particularly in winter, when most of the tourists are away—has the flavor of an old English fishing village, with strong Portuguese overtones.

If New England's climate and the grudging character of its soil can be said to have forged a distinctive personality, nowhere is it more pronounced than in the native Cape Codder. Like all regional temperaments, that of the Cape and islands has been diluted by television, tourism, and migration, but the true type can occasionally be recognized. It is a weathered personality, patient and independent, and its passing will be lamented.

The economics of Cape Cod, Martha's Vineyard, and Nantucket have long since become a simple matter of tourism and fishing. A subsistence agriculture was once widespread, with corn and other vegetables the principal crops. But yields from the sandy soil were never abundant, and today only cranberry bogs and small market gardens survive. The fishery is also diminished, although the Provincetown fleet still heads out to George's Bank, and Chatham is a scalloping center. Whaling was developed on the Cape, and reached its greatest fame in Nantucket, but of course all that is memory.

WHEN TO GO. Since so much of Cape Cod's attraction has to do with water sports, summer has been the traditional tourist season. There's a great deal to be said for a summer vacation on the Cape or islands. Thermometer readings are nearly always lower than on the mainland, especially at night, and offshore breezes dispel the still, muggy air that makes many American cities unlivable between June and September. Temperatures for swimming are generally ideal throughout the Cape Cod summer, with visitors offered a choice between the warm, placid bay and the bracing ocean waves along Nauset Beach and the National Seashore. Summer is also the time for theater, special events, clambakes, and church suppers.

More and more, though, travelers are discovering the off-season Cape. Numbers are part of the reason. On a typical summer weekend, the combined population of overnight visitors and day-trippers can reach nearly half a million. This doesn't make Cape Cod Coney Island, but if you want real solitude and can't afford a place of your own, summer isn't the best time to go. (Nantucket is a partial exception.) Money is another factor. It is common for Cape Cod resorts and motels to offer substantial savings to off-season visitors; generally, these rates apply between Memorial Day and Labor Day.

The display of autumn colors on Cape Cod and the islands is not nearly as lavish as it is in the interior of New England, since evergreens make up a good part of the tree cover. But the Cape in the fall is far from drab. Dunes, sea, and sky stand out sharply in the clear October light, and the Lower Cape's cover of heather, gorse, blueberry, bayberry, boxberry, and beach plum resembles, in Thoreau's words, "the richest rug imaginable spread over an uneven surface." Spring, provided you don't show up early enough for the harsh winds of March, is equally beautiful, with birds and wildflowers bringing the land back to life.

Only the hardiest travelers used to go to the Cape and islands in midwinter, but "off-off-season" tourism is now on the rise. Twenty years ago, it was difficult to find anything beyond the basics in food and lodging on Cape Cod in winter. Nowadays, the choices are broader, although winter is still the only season in which advance room reservations are not essential. What will you find out here in December and January? Peace and quiet, mostly, along with a climate and landscape reduced to elemental simplicity. It doesn't get as cold as it does on the mainland, nor does it snow as much, but there are damp Cape winds that can find the marrow of your bones. If you go, take a room with a fireplace and find a tavern that serves hot grog.

PLANNING YOUR TRIP. A travel agent won't cost you a cent, except for specific charges like telegrams. He gets his fee from the hotel or carrier he books for you. A travel agent also can aid those who prefer to take vacations on a "package tour"—thus keeping your own planning to a minimum. If you prefer the convenience of standardized accommodations, remember that the various hotel and motel chains publish free directories of their members that enable you to plan and reserve everything ahead of time.

If you don't belong to an auto club, now is a good time to join one. Two such are the *American Automobile Association*, 8111 Gatehouse Rd., Falls Church, Virginia 22042; and the *Amoco Motor Club*, 3700 Wake Forest Rd., Raleigh, North Carolina 26709. In addition to its information services, the AAA has a nationwide network of some 26,000 service stations that provide emergency repair service. The *Exxon Travel Club*, 4400 Dacoma St., Houston, Texas 77092, provides information, low-cost insurance, and some legal services; and the *National Travel Club*, Travel Building, Floral Park, New York 11001, offers information, insurance, and tours.

The three major publishers of U.S. road atlases are Rand McNally, Hammond, and Grosset. Some of the major oil companies will send maps and mark preferred routes on them if you tell them what you have in mind. Try: *Exxon Touring Service*, P.O. Box 307, Florham Park, New Jersey 07932, or 4400 Dacoma St., Houston, Texas 77092, or *Mobil Oil Corp, Travel Service*, P.O. Box 25, Versailles, Kentucky 40383. In addition, most states have their own maps, which pinpoint attractions, list historical sites, parks, etc. City chambers of commerce are also good sources of information. Specific addresses are given under *Tourist Information* in the individual chapters that follow.

Plan to board the pets, discontinue paper and milk deliveries, and tell your local police and fire departments when you'll be leaving, when you expect to return. Ask a kindly neighbor to keep an eye on your house; fully protect your swimming pool against intruders. Have a neighbor keep your mail, or have it held at the post office. Consider having your telephone temporarily disconnected, if you plan to be away more than a few weeks. Look into the purchase of trip insurance (including baggage), and make certain your auto, fire, and other policies are up-to-date. Today most people who travel use credit cards for important expenses such as gas, repairs, lodgings, and some meals. Consider converting the greater portion of your cash into travelers' checks. Arrange to have your lawn mowed at the usual times, and leave that kindly neighbor your itinerary (insofar as possible), car license number, and a key to your home (and tell police and firemen he has it). Since some hotel and motel chains give discounts (10%–25%) to Senior Citizens, be sure to have some sort of identification along if you qualify. Usually NARP or NRTA membership is best. (See below at the end of the Hotels and Motels section.)

TIPS FOR BRITISH VISITORS. Passports. You will need a valid passport and a U.S. Visa (which can only be put in a passport of the 10-year kind). You can obtain the visa either through your travel agent or directly from the *United States Embassy*, Visa and Immigration Department, 24 Grosvenor Sq., London W1 (tel. 01-499 3443).

No vaccinations are required for entry into the U.S.

Customs. If you are 21 or over, you can take into the U.S.: 200 cigarettes, 50 cigars or 3 lbs of tobacco; 1 U.S. liter of alcohol; duty-free gifts to a value of $100. Be careful not even to try to take in meat or meat products, seeds, plants, fruits, etc. And avoid narcotics like the plague.

Insurance. We heartily recommend that you insure yourself to cover health and motoring mishaps with *Europ Assistance*, 252 High St., Croydon CR0 1NF (tel. 01-680 1234). Their excellent service is all the more valuable when you consider the possible costs of health care in the U.S.

Tour Operators. The price battle that has raged over transatlantic fares has meant that most tour operators now offer excellent budget packages to the U.S. Among those you might consider as you plan your trip are—

American Express, 6 Haymarket, London SW1.

Thomas Cook Ltd., Thorpe Wood, Peterborough, PE 3 6SB.

Cosmos, Cosmos House, 1 Bromley Common, Bromley, Kent BR2 9LX.

Jetsave, Sussex House, London Rd., East Grinstead RH19 1LD.

Page and Moy, 136–138 London Rd., Leicester LE2 1EN.

Speedbird, 200 Buckingham Palace Rd., London SW1.

Air Fares. We suggest that you explore the current scene for budget flight possibilities. There are no transatlantic flights directly to the Cape; Boston is the nearest city taking international flights. All the main transatlantic carriers have standby tickets, available a short time before the flight only, as well as APEX and other fares at a considerable saving over the full price. Quite frankly, only business travelers who don't have to watch the price of their tickets fly full-price these days—and find themselves sitting right beside an APEX passenger!

Hotels. You may have need of a fast booking service to find you a hotel room in the area you'll be visiting. One of the very best ways to do this is to contact *HBI-HOTAC*, Globegate House, Pound Lane, London NW10 (tel. 01-451 2311). They book rooms for most of the large chains (Holiday Inn, Hilton, Ramada, etc.) so you can have a multiple choice with only one contact. HBI-HOTAC specialize in booking for business firms, but they also deal with the general public.

Information. For more information on Cape Cod, you can contact, in **England:** *The London Convention Bureau*, 26 Grosvenor Gardens, London, SW1 WOD; in **France:** *The Paris Convention Bureau*, 127 Champs Elysées, Paris 75008.

PACKING. What to take, what to wear. Make a packing list for each member of the family. Then check off items as you pack them. It will save time, reduce confusion. Time-savers to carry along include extra photo film (plenty), suntan lotion, insect repellent, sufficient toothpaste, soap, etc. Always carry an extra pair of glasses, including sunglasses, particularly if they're prescription ones. A travel iron is always a good tote-along, as are some transparent plastic film bags (small and large) for wet suits, socks, etc. They are also excellent for packing shoes and spillable cosmetics. All members of the family should have sturdy shoes with non-slip soles.

Clothing for a Cape or islands trip can be kept reasonably informal. Men should bring along one jacket, dress slacks, and tie, and women should bring a dress or pants outfit suitable for evening wear, especially if plans include a meal at one of the better restaurants. Otherwise, casual skirts or slacks for women, and (depending on the season) khaki or corduroy slacks for men, should round out the traveling wardrobe. Jeans are acceptable at many, but by no means all, of the Cape's eating places. Don't forget bathing suits and shorts in summer, along with light sweaters for cool nights. In fall and spring, a heavy sweater and windbreaker or parka shell, or a tweed jacket, should suffice. Bring a heavy woolen outercoat or insulated parka in the winter.

A list of handy things to have along in the car might include: 1) a first-aid kit, with plenty of Band-Aids; 2) a supply of tissues, a roll of paper towels, and a roll of toilet paper; 3) a moist washcloth in a plastic bag; 4) insect repellent; 5) a bottle opener and a can opener; 6) a whiskbroom; 7) a jackknife.

INSURANCE. In planning your trip, think about three kinds of insurance: property, medical, and automobile. The best person to consult about insuring your household furnishings and personal property is your insurance agent. For Americans, he is also the person to ask about whatever special adjustments might be advisable in medical coverage while traveling. Foreigners visiting the United States should bear in mind that medical expenses in this country can be astronomical compared to those elsewhere, and that the kind of protection that some countries (Britain, for example) extend not only to their own nationals but to visiting foreigners as well simply does not exist here.

Every state has some sort of Financial Responsibility law establishing minimum and maximum amounts for which you can be held liable in auto accidents. Most states require insurance to be offered, and 17 states require you to have it in order to register a car or get a license within their jurisdictions. In any case, it is almost essential to have third party coverage, or "liability insurance," as claims can run very high for both car repairs and, particularly, medical treatment. Insurance premiums vary according to place and person; they are generally highest for males under 25 and for drivers who live in large urban areas.

One possibility is the *American Automobile Association* (AAA), which offers both group personal accident insurance and bail bond protection up to $5,000 as part of its annual membership (fee $40, renewal $35). The AAA can also arrange the validation of foreign driving permits for use in the United States. Foreigners should consider getting their insurance before leaving their own countries since short-term tourists will find it difficult and expensive to buy here. For the AAA, write to *AAA*, 8111 Gatehouse Rd., Falls Church, Virginia 22047.

If you are over 50, write to the American Association of Retired Persons/ AIM, 215 Long Beach Blvd., Long Beach, California 90802, for information about its auto insurance recommendations and other travel services.

WHAT WILL IT COST? This is a crucial question, and one of the most difficult to answer. We suggest that to be on the safe side in your planning, however, figure that a couple can travel in New England for approximately $99 a day for two (not counting gasoline or other transportation costs), as you can see in the table below.

If you are budgeting your trip—and who isn't—don't forget to set aside a realistic amount for the possible rental of sports equipment (boats, canoes, golf clubs, etc.), entrance fees to amusement parks and historical sites, etc. Allow for tolls for bridges and super highways (this can be a major item), extra film for cameras, and souvenirs.

After lodging, your biggest single expense will be food. You can save substantially by having only one meal a day (or less) in a restaurant. Plan to eat simply, and to picnic. This will save you money, and time, and it will help you to enjoy your trip more. That beautiful scenery does not *have* to whiz by at 55 miles per hour. Many states have set aside picnic and rest areas, often well equipped and in scenic spots, even on highways and thruways, so finding a pleasant place to stop usually is not difficult. Before you leave home put together a picnic kit.

Even in restaurants there are ways to cut costs. 1) Always stop at the cash register and look over the menu *before* you sit down. 2) Order a complete dinner; à la carte always adds up to more, unless you see someone with an enormous Chef's Salad and decide that's all you need. 3) If there is a salad bar or any kind of smorgasbord, fill up there and save on desserts and extras. 4) For children, ask about smaller portions, at lower prices. Most places are providing them now. 5) Go to a Chinese restaurant and order one less main dish than the number of people in your group. You'll still come away pleasantly full. 6) You may want to make lunch your main meal of the day—it's often a better bargain than dinner. 7) In the Dining Out section below, we suggest some chains that offer good value for your money.

If you like a drink before dinner or bed, bring your own bottle. Most hotels and motels will supply ice, but the markup on alcoholic beverages in restaurants, bars, lounges and dining rooms is enormous.

Typical expenses for two people

Room at moderate hotel or motel	$45.00
Breakfast for two (including tip)	7.00
Lunch for two at inexpensive restaurant (including tip)	9.00
Dinner for two at moderate restaurant (including tip)	24.00
Sightseeing or miscellaneous expenses	6.00
One evening drink each	4.00
Admission for two to museum or historic site	4.00
	$99.00

HOW TO GET TO CAPE COD. By car: Most travelers approach Cape Cod via either New York or Boston. From New York, the main highway to southern New England is Rte. I 95, change to I-195 at Providence and follow signs for the Cape. From Boston, take Rte. 3, the Southeast Expressway. If you are coming from the north, you can skirt Boston via Rte. 128.

Once on the Cape, follow signs for the island ferry departure points of Woods Hole and Hyannis. (For summer service from New Bedford, see below.)

By train: *Amtrak* trains connect Boston with the midwest; change at Boston for *Greyhound* bus service to the Cape. From points south, take *Amtrak* to Providence via New York, and change for Cape buses. Restoration of rail service to the Lower Cape is in the talking stages.

By bus: *Greyhound* serves Cape Cod from New York, Boston, and intermediate points. *Peter Pan Lines*, Springfield, Massachusetts, runs 1-day bus-boat trips to Provincetown via Boston (summer only). *Bonanza* also serves the Cape from Boston and Providence.

By ship: Car ferries are regularly scheduled to Martha's Vineyard and Nantucket from Woods Hole. Reservations are required well in advance. Write *Woods Hole Steamship Authority*, Box 284, Woods Hole, Massachusetts 02543. Pier parking is available for ferry passengers. Passenger ferries operate between Hyannis and Martha's Vineyard and Nantucket during the summer, and also between West Falmouth and Oak Bluffs. Passenger-only ferry service between New Bedford and Martha's Vineyard is provided from mid-May through mid-October by *Cape and Islands Express Lines*, Box J-4095, Leonard's Wharf, New Bedford, Massachusetts. The excursion boat *Provincetown* sails daily in summer between Rowe's Wharf, Boston, and Provincetown.

By air: *Provincetown-Boston Airline* flies from Logan Airport to Provincetown Airport. *Cape and Islands Airline* has flights from Hyannis Airport to Nantucket, charter to all points. *Gull Air* offers similar service to the islands.

HINTS TO THE MOTORIST. Once you cross the Cape Cod Canal, Rte. 6 is the only limited-access road. On the Lower Cape, it becomes an undivided highway with regular access. All of the Cape's major routes—6, 6A, and 28—can become heavily congested on Friday evenings (eastbound) and Sunday afternoons (westbound). If at all possible, avoid summer travel at these times—especially on holiday weekends. Shunpiking on the Cape and islands can be fun, but be sure you know what you're doing before you take a 2-wheel-drive car on a narrow, sandy road. This can be a real problem on parts of Nantucket. Incidentally, the islands are small, with plenty of bicycles available for rent. Why not consider leaving your car at Woods Hole or Hyannis?

Before a long trip, taken the precaution of having your car thoroughly checked by your regular dealer or service station to make sure that everything is in good shape. Secondly, you may find it wise to join an auto club that can provide you with trip planning information, insurance coverage, and emergency and repair service along the way. If you are a member of the NRTA/AARP, that organization has a motoring plan in cooperation with the Amoco Motor Club that offers a number of emergency and repair services. Write to NRTA/AARP Motoring Plan, 215 Long Beach Blvd., Long Beach, California 90802. Thirdly, if you must have your car serviced, look for a repair shop displaying the *National Institute for Automotive Excellence* seal. **NIASE** tests and certifies the competence of auto mechanics in about 10,000 repair shops nationwide.

Whether you are traveling through an empty wilderness or a heavily populated, well-serviced area, there are certain items of car equipment that you should have along: 1) spare tire, properly inflated, plus a jack, jack handle, wheel nut wrench, and two wooden blocks; 2) an empty one-gallon can and about five feet of hose, for getting gas; 3) a tool kit that includes an adjustable wrench, a knife, pliers, screwdrivers, and a tire pressure gauge; 4) extra spark plugs and a fanbelt; 5) an extra can of oil; 6) jumper cables and gloves; 7) an extra set of keys (find a good place to hide them); 8) road flares and a flashlight; 9) a fire extinguisher; 10) the name and address of your insurance agent, and your car insurance policy number; 11) in winter, chains, an ice scraper, small shovel, carton of dry sand; 12) trash bag.

If you get stuck on any kind of road, use the universal rule of the road. Pull off the highway onto the shoulder, raise the hood, attach something white (a handkerchief, scarf, or piece of tissue) to the door handle on the driver's side, and sit inside and wait. A special warning to women stalled at night: Remain inside the car with the doors locked, and make sure the Good Samaritan is indeed a Good Samaritan. It's easier to find telephones these days along the major highways, since their locations are being marked more and more frequently. If you're a member of an automobile club, call the nearest garage listed. Or ask the Operator for help.

Traveling by car with your pet dog or cat? Some motels and hotels accept them, but be sure to check in advance. If it's a first-time trip with your pet, accustom it to car travel by short trips in the neighborhood. And when you're packing, include its favorite food, bowls, and toys. Your dog may like to ride with its head out the window. Discourage this. Wind and dust particles could permanently damage your pet's eyes. Dogs are especially susceptible to heatstroke. Don't leave your dog (or cat) alone in a parked car on a hot day while you dawdle over lunch. Keep your dog's bowl handy for water during stops for gas; service station attendants are usually very cooperative about this. Exercising your pet periodically is a good way for you and the kids to unwind from a long, unbroken stretch of motoring.

 HOTELS & MOTELS. General Hints. Don't be one of those who take potluck for lodgings. You'll probably waste a lot of time hunting for a place, and often won't be happy with the accommodations you finally find. If you don't have room reservations, by all means begin looking early in the afternoon. If you have reservations (but expect to arrive later than 5 or 6 P.M.), advise the hotel or motel in advance. Some places will not otherwise hold reservations after 6 P.M. To get a room at that hotel's minimum rate, be sure to reserve ahead or arrive very early.

If you are planning to stay in a popular resort region at the height of the season, reserve well in advance. Include a deposit. Most chains or associated motels and hotels publish directories of their memberships and will make advance reservations for you at affiliated hostelries along your route.

A number of hotels and motels have one-day laundry and dry cleaning services, and many motels have coin laundries. Most motels, but not all, have telephones in the rooms. If you want to be sure of room service, however, better stay at a hotel. Cape motels and resorts in virtually every price category have pools; some even have indoor and outdoor pools. Small inns and guest houses, however, may not offer bathing unless they are near a beach. As for parking, it is free at virtually all Cape and islands hostelries.

Hotel and motel chains. In addition to hundreds of excellent independent motels and hotels throughout the country, there are also many that belong to national or regional chains. A major advantage of these chains is the ease of making reservations en route, or at one fell swoop in advance. If you are a guest at a member hotel or motel, the management will be delighted to secure you a sure booking at one of his affiliated hotels at no cost to you. Chains also usually have toll free WATS (800) lines to assist you in making reservations on your own. This, of course, saves you time, money and worry. The insistence on uniform standards of comfort, cleanliness and amenities is more common in motel than in hotel chains. However, many travelers prefer independent hotels and motels because they are more likely to reflect the character of the area.

Among the national non-budget hotel and motel chains, the most expensive are Hilton, Marriott, and Sheraton; the middle range includes Holiday

Inns, Howard Johnson's, Quality Inns, and TraveLodge; and the least expensive are usually Best Western, Ramada, and Rodeway. Of the many budget chains that have arisen in recent years, and whose rates are less than half those of the others, only two unfortunately operate in New England. These are: *Chalet Susse International,* 2 Progress Ave., Nashua, New Hampshire, 03060, tel. 800-258-1980; and *Econo-Travel Motor Hotel Corp,* 20 Kroger Executive Center, PO Box 12188, Norfolk, Virginia 23502, tel. 800-446-6900. Write or phone for free directories to both chains.

HOTEL AND MOTEL CATEGORIES

Hotels and motels in this guide are divided into four categories (*Deluxe, Expensive, Moderate,* and *Inexpensive*) arranged by price, and taking into consideration the degree of comfort you can expect to enjoy, the amount of service you can anticipate, and the atmosphere that will surround you in the establishment of your choice.

Limitations of space make it impossible to include every establishment. We have therefore, listed those that we recommend as the best within each price range. Our ratings are flexible and subject to change.

Although the names of the various hotel and motel categories are standard throughout this series, the prices listed under each category may vary from area to area. This variance is meant to reflect local price standards. In every case, however, the dollar ranges for each category are clearly stated before each listing of establishments.

Free parking is assumed at all motels and motor hotels. *Baby sitter* lists are usually available in good hotels and motels, and *cribs* for the children are always on hand—sometimes at no cost, but more frequently at a cost of $1 or $2. The cost of a *cot* in your room, to supplement the beds, will be around $3 per night, but moving an *extra single bed* into a room will cost from $7 in better hotels and motels.

Travelers should also be aware of the differences among **European Plan** (EP), **American Plan** (AP), and **Modified American Plan** (MAP). European Plan includes no meals. A full American Plan should include all meals, and often other services as well. Hotels or resorts on the Modified American Plan generally offer one or two meals, usually dinner only or breakfast and dinner.

Senior Citizens may in some cases receive special discounts on lodgings. *Holiday Inns* give a discount to members of the NRTA (write to National Retired Teachers Association, Membership Division, 701 North Montgomery St., Ojai, California 93023) and of the AARP (write to American Association of Retired Persons, Membership Division, 215 Long Beach Blvd., Long Beach, California 90802). Members of the AARP, the NRTA, the National Association of Retired Persons, the Catholic Golden Age of United Societies of the U.S.A., the Old Age Security Pensioners of Canada, and similar organizations benefit increasingly from a number of discounts, but the amounts, sources, and availability of these change, so it is best to check with either your organization or the hotel, motel or restaurant chain you plan to use. The *National Council of Senior Citizens*, 1511 K St. NW, Washington, DC 20005, works especially to develop low-cost travel possibilities for its members.

The closest thing America has to Europe's bed-and-breakfast is the private houses that go by the various names of Tourist Home, Guest House, or Guest Home. These are often large, still fairly elegant old homes in quiet residential or semi-residential parts of larger towns or along secondary roads and the main streets of small towns and resorts. Styles and standards vary widely, of course, and the main generalizations that one can make are that private baths will be less common and rates will be pleasingly lower. In many small towns the guest houses are good examples of regional atmosphere. Each one will be different, so that their advantage is precisely the opposite of that "no surprise" uniformity that motel chains pride themselves on. Few guest houses will have heated pools, wall-to-wall carpeting, or exposed styrofoam-wooden beams in the bar. Few, if any, will have bars. What you do get, in addition to economy, is the personal flavor of a family atmosphere in a private home. In popular tourist areas, state or local tourist information offices or chambers of commerce usually have lists of homes that let out spare rooms to paying guests, and such a listing usually means that the places on it have been inspected and meet reliable standards of cleanliness, comfort, and reasonable pricing.

There are a number of locally published directories of tourist and guest houses. Or, send for a copy of *Guide to Guesthouses, Farmhouses, and Inns*, available from Standing Orders Press, Box 183, Patterson, New York 12563.

 DINING OUT. Cape Cod's name should tell you something about the local cookery. Some old cookbooks even carry a recipe for a stuffed cod dish called "Cape Cod Turkey." While other cuisines have made inroads, the tables of the Cape and islands still groan under a tremendous assortment of traditional seafood dishes.

Many a Cape Cod meal begins with clam chowder—not the tomato-based Manhattan variety, but the New England version made with milk and salt pork. Even newcomers will soon learn to distinguish flour-thickened chowder from the superior, cream-enriched product. They'll also learn that there's more to clams than chowder. In addition to frying them and eating them on the half shell, Cape Codders bake them into something called clam pie. Wellfleet oysters are deservedly famous, and the tiny, delicate Cape scallops, although no longer as abundant as they once were, merit equal acclamation.

Almost everyone who visits the Cape orders a lobster. Although the creature they are served comes from Maine waters, the association of Cape Cod with lobster continues. The price of a lobster dinner in a restaurant has climbed here, as elsewhere, and a menu insert reading "Waiter will quote you today's price" is not uncommon. It's always cheaper to buy boiled lobster in a fish market and eat it cold at your motel—or, if you have a kitchenette, to buy live lobsters and cook them yourself. If you have access to a beach, try a clambake, adding potatoes, corn, steamers, and maybe a few crabs to the seaweed-blanketed lobsters. Ask your fish dealer for instructions.

Portuguese cookery is another Cape delight, found at its best in Provincetown. It partakes of the region's plentiful cod, haddock, and mackerel, along with the goodly amount of pork. The Portuguese do wonderful things with vinegar marinades, and have thought of a hundred or more uses for their spicy linguica sausage. Try kale soup or squid stew; finish your meal with the ubiquitous bread pudding. Another Cape dessert beloved of all nationalities is home-baked blueberry pie, made with the local crop.

Since they are the destination for thousands of sophisticated visitors, Cape Cod, Martha's Vineyard, and Nantucket are not strangers to fine international cuisine. There are French restaurants on the Cape that regularly draw Bostonians and New Yorkers used to the best of classic and nouvelle cuisine. You'll also find plenty of Italian spots and at least one excellent German establishment. Of course, you can always get a good steak—but would you order fish in Kansas City?

Unless you are staying at a resort where guests' dinner reservations are assured, it's wise to phone restaurants ahead of time. When you make your reservations, be sure to ask about dress requirements, charge policies, and children's menus.

When figuring the tip on your check, base it on the total charges for the meal, not on grand total. Don't tip on tax.

RESTAURANT CATEGORIES

Restaurants are divided into price categories as follows: *Deluxe, Expensive, Moderate,* and *Inexpensive.* As a general rule, expect restaurants in the more popular resort areas to be higher in price.

Limitations of space make it impossible to include every establishment. We have, therefore, included those we consider the best within each price range.

The dollar ranges for each category are clearly stated before each listing of establishments.

Prices do not include alcoholic beverages, cover or table charges, tip, or extravagant house specialties.

Chains: There are now several chains of restaurants, some regional, some nationwide, that offer reliable eating at budget prices. chains that operate in New England are: 1) *Arthur Treacher's Fish and Chips* (low prices, limited menu, Tuesday night special), 2) *Holiday Inns* (some offer all-you-can-eat buffets), 3) *Howard Johnson's,* which started in New England and still operate a number of franchises here. Food is predictable but inexpensive, and all-you-can-eat fish nights still turn up now and then.

DRINKING LAWS. Drinks may be ordered until 1 A.M. (2 A.M. in some towns) weekdays; until midnight (1 A.M. in some towns) Saturdays. Serving hours Sunday are from 1 P.M. (11 A.M. in some towns) until 1 A.M. Package liquor sold until 11 P.M. in package stores; no sales Sundays. Legal drinking age is 20.

TIPPING. Tipping is supposed to be a personal way of thanking someone who has taken pleasure and pride in giving you attentive, efficient, and personal service. When you get genuinely good service, feel secure in rewarding it; but when you feel that the service you get is slovenly, indifferent, or surly don't hesitate to tip accordingly. Remember that in most places the help are paid very little and depend on tips for the better part of their income. This is supposed to give them incentive to serve you well.

These days the going rate for tipping on *restaurant* service is 15% before taxes. Tipping at counters is not universal; however, most customers do leave 25¢ on anything up to a dollar and 10% on checks higher than that. There is no tipping in fast-food and take-out places. For bellboys 50¢ per bag is usual. However, if you load him down with all manner of bags, hatboxes, cameras, coats, etc., you should give him an extra quarter or two. For one-night stays in hotels or motels you leave nothing. If you stay longer, at the end of your stay leave the maid $1–$1.25 per day, or $5 per person per week for multiple occupancy. If you are staying at an *American Plan* hostelry (meals included), $2.00 per person per day for the waitress is considered sufficient, and is left at the end of your stay. If you have been surrounded by an army of servants (one bringing relishes, another rolls, and such), add a few extra dollars and give the lump sum to the captain or *maitre d'hotel* when you leave, asking him to allocate it.

For other services in a hotel or resort, figure roughly: doorman—50¢ for taxi handling, 75¢ for help with baggage; parking attendant—50¢; bartender—15%; room service—10% to 15% of that bill; laundry or valet service—15%; pool attendant—50¢ per day; snackbar waiter at pool, beach, or golf club—50¢ per person for food and 15% of the beverage check; locker attendant—50¢ per person per day, or $2.50 per week; masseurs and masseuses—15% to 20%; golf caddies—$1 or $2 per bag, or 15% of the greens fee for an 18-hole course, or $3 on a free course; barbers—$1.00, $2.00 for haircuts costing over $15.00; shoeshine attendants—25¢; hairdressers—$1.00–$3.00, depending on price of service; manicurists—50¢.

Transportation: Give 25¢ for any taxi fare under $1 and 15–20% for any above. Limousine service—25%. Car rental agencies—nothing. Bus porters are tipped 25¢ per bag, drivers nothing. On charters and package tours, conductors and drivers usually get $5 to $10 per day from the group as a whole, but be sure to ask whether this has already been figured into the package cost. On short local sightseeing runs, the driver-guide may get 25¢

per person, more if you think he has been especially helpful or personable. Airport bus drivers—nothing. Redcaps—50¢ per suitcase. Tipping at curbside check-in is unofficial, but same as above. On the plane, no tipping.

BUSINESS HOURS AND HOLIDAYS. Business hours are generally 8 or 9 A.M. to 5 P.M., but some stores, especially in the many communities used to catering to vacationers, are likely to stay open later in the evening. Evening dining hours are likely to begin at 6 P.M. on Cape Cod and the islands, with more expensive, tourist-oriented places serving until 10 P.M. or later. Restaurants drawing a predominantly local clientele generally close earlier. Phone ahead to be sure.

Most businesses, banks and many restaurants will be closed the following holidays (the dates are for 1982): New Year's Day, Jan. 1; Washington's Birthday (observance), Feb. 15; Easter Sunday, April 11; Memorial Day (observance), May 31; Independence Day, July 4; Labor Day, Sept. 6; Thanksgiving Day, Nov. 25; and Christmas Day, Dec. 25.

In addition, banks and some businesses may be closed on Lincoln's Birthday, Feb. 12; Good Friday (from noon), April 8; Columbus Day (observance), Oct. 11; Election Day (partially), Nov. 2; Veterans Day, Nov. 11.

SPORTS. The following is a brief rundown of sports that can be enjoyed on the Cape and the islands. See the individual chapters for more information. **Fishing:** From spring through fall, surfcasters head for Cape and islands beaches in pursuit of bluefish and striped bass. Deep-sea fishing is also popular; party and charter boats sail from larger port towns. Their quarry is cod, haddock, halibut, and the larger and more elusive tuna. No license needed for saltwater. For holders of Massachusetts licenses, the Cape offers fishing for trout and panfish in many of its ponds and lakes. **Surfing:** Nauset Beach, East Orleans; White Crest Beach, Wellfleet; and Coast Guard and Nauset Light Beaches, Eastham, have free surfing areas. **Sailing:** The Cape and islands abound in marinas and launching ramps for visitors with their own boats; rentals and instruction are also readily available. **Golf:** Round Hill Country Club, E. Sandwich; Checequessette Yacht and Country Club, Wellfleet; Falmouth Country Club, E. Falmouth; Highland Golf Club, Truro; Iyanough Hills Golf Club, Rte. 132, Hyannis; Bass River Golf Course, S. Yarmouth. **Tennis:** Racquet Club at Massasoit, Rte. 28, Mashpee; Falmouth Sports Center, Highfield Drive, Falmouth; Dennis Racquet Club, E. Dennis; Oliver's Tennis Courts, Rte. 6, Wellfleet; Mattakesett Tennis Club, Katama Rd., Edgartown; Raymor Racquet Club, Field Ave., Nantucket. **Bicycling** is a favorite Cape and Islands pastime. The byways of Nantucket and the Vinyard are especially suited for two-wheel travel. Be careful on major routes, and be prepared to walk your bike along sandy stretches on back roads. **Swimming** is practically what put the

Cape on the map for tourists; just remember that while the bay is warm, the ocean can be bone-chilling.

Spring and fall are good times to watch for migratory birds in woods and meadows. In winter, sporting opportunities dwindle. There is no downhill skiing, and cross-country conditions suffer from scant snowfall and scouring winds. If you find yourself on the Cape in winter with a pair of cross-country skis, try an inland golf course. **Small game** and **waterfowl hunting** are also fall and winter possibilities; parts of the Cape abound in rabbit, quail, pheasant, and grouse, and there are always flocks of ducks and geese.

ROUGHING IT. Camping opportunities on the Cape and islands are not extensive; there is no camping permitted on Nantucket and facilities are minimal on Martha's Vineyard. Myles Standish State Forest, near Plymouth, has trailer campsites and cabins. On Cape Cod, there are camping facilities at Nickerson State Park in Brewster. No camping is allowed on the Cape Cod National Seashore. For Massachusetts camping information, write the *North American Family Campers Association*, 29 Green St., Newburyport, Massachusetts 01950. Affiliated commercial campgrounds are listed by *Kampgrounds of America, Inc.*, Box 30558, Billings, Montana 59114.

The Cape and islands are reasonably well served by **Youth Hostels,** affiliates of the American Youth Hostel Association, Inc. (AYH). There are hostels in Cedarville (just north of the Cape Cod Canal, on the road south from Plymouth), Hyannis, Orleans, Truro, Nantucket, and West Tisbury, on Martha's Vineyard. To take advantage of hostels, a traveler must pay a nominal membership fee to AYH. There is no age limit. Accommodations are simple, dormitories are segregated for men and women, common rooms and kitchen are shared, and everyone helps with the cleanup. Lights out 11 P.M. to 7 A.M.; no alcohol or drugs. It is always wise to reserve ahead by writing directly to the hostel you wish to stay at. The AYH national headquarters is at 1332 Eye St., NW, Washington, DC 20005. A handy guide to hostels throughout the country is *Hosteling USA: The Official American Youth Hostels Handbook*, published by East Woods Press, 820 East Blvd., Charlotte, North Carolina 28203.

HINTS TO HANDICAPPED TRAVELERS. Important sources of information in this field are the *Travel Information Center,* Moss Rehabilitation Hospital, 12th St. and Tabor Rd., Philadelphia, Pennsylvania 19141, and *Easter Seal Society for Crippled Children and Adults*, Director of Education and Information Service, 2023 West Ogden Ave., Chicago, Illinois 60612; and the book *Access to the World: A Travel Guide for the Handicapped*, by Louise Weiss, published by Chatham Square Press, Inc. *The President's Committee on Employment of the Handicapped*, Washington, D.C. 20210, has issued a list of guidebooks for the handicapped that tells where to write for information on nearly 100 U.S. cities. The Committee also has a guide to highway rest area facilities that have been designed for access by the handicapped. And for a list of tour operators who arrange this kind of travel, write to: *Society for the Advancement of Travel for the Handicapped,* 26 Court St., Brooklyn, New York 11242.

Two publications which give valuable information about motels, hotels, and restaurants (rating them, telling about steps, table heights, door widths, etc.), are *Where Turning Wheels Stop,* published by Paralyzed Veterans of America, 4350 East-West Hwy., Bethesda, Maryland 20014, and *The Wheelchair Traveler* by Douglass R. Annand, Ball Hill Rd., Milford, New Hampshire 03055. *TWA* publishes a free, 12-page pamphlet entitled *Consumer Information about Air Travel for the Handicapped* to explain all the various arrangements that can be made, and how to get them. Available at TWA offices.

 FOR MORE INFORMATION: The classic work on Cape Cod and the Cape Cod character is Henry David Thoreau's *Cape Cod.* It is published in many editions; Apollo Books puts out a handsome paperback. Another famous account of Cape life is Henry Beston's *The Outermost House* (Ballantine paperback). A hard-to-find but worthwhile volume is Jeremiah Digges' *Cape Cod Pilot,* published by the Federal Writers' Project in Provincetown, 1937. For an understanding of how the Cape and islands were formed, and how their plant and animal communities function, read Dorothy Sterling's *The Outer Lands,* published by W. W. Norton in a revised paperback edition in 1978.

Periodicals that will help you keep abreast of local events are *Yankee* magazine and its annual *Travel Guide to New England; Cape Cod Life;* and the newspapers *Provincetown Advocate, Cape Cod Times,* and the *Vineyard Gazette.*

For specific travel information, contact the *Chamber of Commerce* listed under Tourist Information in each chapter.

TELEPHONES. All phone numbers listed have the area code 617, unless otherwise stated.

INTRODUCTION

by

BRIAN F. SHORTSLEEVE

Brian Shortsleeve has been a summer resident of the Cape since 1953, and a year-round resident since 1965. He is owner and publisher of Cape Cod Life *magazine, which is published six times a year.*

If you've heard that Cape Cod is so crowded there's no point in coming here, rest assured you've been misinformed. In certain places at certain times, it is crowded, but much depends on what you're looking for. The Cape and the Islands continue to be incomparable paradises for people seeking relief from the pressures of a hurried world. Activities available here are only as limited as your imagination. In my own perspective, all else seems to pale in light of the Cape's primary offering: a quiet walk on a beach stretching to the horizon.

If you're planning to visit the Cape and the Islands or are thinking of moving here, understand that the majority of folks who live down this way feel the particular village they call home is absolutely the best possible place to live—we like it the way it is, but we also welcome visitors and newcomers who appreciate being here. If you're coming down, know what you're likely to find and consider why you're coming. And please, be very careful of the Cape and the Islands: They're precious and fragile, and like Humpty-Dumpty, once destroyed they can't be put together again.

We have close to a dozen summer theaters offering excellent professional performances, and our piano lounges feature some of the best jazz musicians in the world. (If your idea of a vacation centers around "night life," however, you might prefer Atlantic City.) Including historical society exhibits, there are approximately 50 museums of various types, and there are more than 50 art galleries. Together, these hundred-plus establishments in two dozen villages demonstrate our pride in our history and our art. There is no risk of confusing any of these museums and galleries with the Louvre, for they are small, intimate, and personal.

Our many fine retail shops don't differ greatly from quality stores elsewhere around the country. And the views and ambiance at many of our restaurants are well worth the trip.

An evening of miniature golf with the kids is an outing. This usually includes a stop at Four Seas Ice Cream Stand, not very different now from when its doors first opened in 1937. There's a dolphin show at Sealand in Brewster, a short distance west on Route 6A from the Cape Cod Museum of Natural History. Cape Cod does not have what is commonly known as an amusement park, but in July it does have the Barnstable County Fair.

Leisure activities on the Cape: chief among them fishing, boating, golfing, antiquing, crafting, bicycling, running and walking on the beach, provide healthy fun. Successfully mastering the fine art of puttering is an enviable accomplishment. I have a good friend who often asks folks, "What is it that you do when you're not doing what you do?" A convenient distance from the business of large cities, life on the Cape and the Islands provides a fair amount of leisure time. The subtleties of life here appeal to independent types; it is a very deliberate way of life.

The Land and Its History

The forces of nature play a large role in life on the Cape. Thousands of years ago, the Cape and the Islands were formed out of the debris of a receding glacier, and they were further shaped by ocean currents. Today, the Cape's 356 ponds, many of which are kettleholes created by chunks of ice, contribute to an excellent groundwater supply system. The jagged coastline provides every town along it with at least one harbor.

The climate of the Cape and the Islands is controlled by the surrounding ocean. The average water temperature south of the Cape is close to 20 degrees warmer than in northern New England because of the proximity of the Gulf Stream. As the earth rotates in an easterly direction, warm Atlantic equatorial waters drift westerly toward the Americas. North of the equator, the Gulf Stream flows up from the Caribbean, passing close to the southeast Atlantic Coast and northward to Cape Cod and the islands, before curving eastward to spread over the North Atlantic.

The Gulf Stream is not the only weather factor following this general pattern; so do many tropical storms. When the weatherman in Boston shows a map with a giant swirling storm-cloud formation traveling 90 miles-an-hour up the Atlantic Coast, the folks in Boston say, "What a close call!" They are surprised to learn that Cape Cod is without electricity and all the boats are up on the beach. The storm may be "off the coast," but so is Cape Cod, stretching way out to sea.

In general, though, the ocean cools us on hot days and warms us a little on extremely cold days.

The earliest vegetation on the Cape and the Islands is believed to have been arctic tundra mosses, lichen, and stunted shrubs. As the climate warmed, vegetation developed into today's native grasses, shrubs, and forests. The forests were much thinned during the 1700s and 1800s by agricultural practices. Overworked soil, which was poor in the first place, saw farms all but disappear in the 20th century. The returning forests now must be protected from the overdevelopment that often accompanies population expansion.

Although deer season is popular, and we do have fox, opossum, a few bobcats, raccoons, skunks, rabbits, and squirrels, our greatest variety of animal life is found in the air and under the water. Of the approximately 725 species of birds seen in the United States, 415 are found in Massachusetts, and of these, 357 have been seen on the Cape and on the Islands.

Migratory fish spawn in the Cape's freshwater streams, and bluefish and striped bass give regular sport to saltwater fisherfolk. Annual tournaments provide competition for tuna and shark fishermen. Sea turtles, seal, porpoise, dolphin, whales and other protected species are frequently seen. The popular whale-watching trips out of Provincetown are both entertaining and informative.

There is a largely invisible universe of "developing crustaceans" in the ocean around the Cape, including crabs, lobsters, and starfish, which grow from microscopic-sized eggs and egg capsules. This animal life, so dependent on the plankton found in ocean waters, forms the foundation of a marine food chain that has survived throughout eons of our earth's history.

The sea has been a major force in shaping the history of the Cape, ever since the English navigator Bartholomew Gosnold discovered Cape Cod in 1602, naming it after the schools of codfish he found in the bay. The Pilgrims landed here 18 years later before sailing on to Plymouth, and the early settlers, finding much of the land unsuitable for farming, were able to prosper from the sea. Fishing, whaling, shipping, and passenger packet coasting to New York and Boston traditionally have drawn Cape Codders to the water. There were other early industries and businesses on the Cape, however. These included saltworks, mills powered both by wind and water, glassmaking, hide tanning, cranberry growing, freight-car manufacturing, stage coaching, railroading, and inn-keeping.

Inn-keeping on the Cape came into its own with the development of stagecoach service during the 1880s. Prior to that time, travelers by boat and horseback generally stopped at private homes. By the turn of the century, rail service had reached Chatham, and almost all of Cape Cod was accessible from Boston and New York.

Availability of transportation initially, however, had a negative impact on the Cape's population. Those of wage-earning age moved away to the cities, but Prohibition times saw certain Cape towns grow in popularity. Several Grand Old Style resorts built in the early 1900s are still favorite vacation spots today. It really wasn't until after World War II, however, when so many households had two cars, that our traveling society started to change the face of much of America, Cape Cod included.

In 1981, the Cape Cod Chamber of Commerce estimated 12 million visitors would arrive during any 12-month period. Year-round residents number over 160,000, nearly double that of the 1960s. Seasonal residents swell the count to over 400,000 during the summer. The economy is healthy and growing ever stronger; the season has stretched from March to November in recent years.

The Cape may be the main destination point for millions of visitors, but no tour of the area is complete without seeing the islands south of the Cape: Nantucket, Tuckernuck, Muskeget, Martha's Vineyard, Chappaquiddick, No Man's Land, and the several islands in the Elizabeth chain.

Nantucket comprises 30,000 acres of sand dunes, rocky soil, low rolling hills, wild roses, scrub pine, endless beach, a deepwater harbor, a 19th-century village, snug Cape-style houses, and approximately 6,500 year-round, remarkably independent residents. The Vineyard's six towns have six personalities, ranging from the largely uninhabited Gay Head with its awesome cliffs to the yachting Eden of Edgartown with its very smart homes and shops. From the ferry wharves of Vineyard Haven and Oak Bluffs, the West Tisbury Road leads past gentle farmsteads, then brings you to the fishing village of Menemsha. Details on Nantucket and Martha's Vineyard are covered in separate chapters later on.

The attractions of the Cape and the Islands are both an asset and a stiff challenge to the preservation of these fragile land masses. Early seafaring residents did little to alter the ecology of the land. Twelve million folks arriving by automobile is another issue entirely, especially those who want to drive jeeps and trucks on the beaches.

Long-term planning is now an issue in all Cape and Island towns. The popularity of our area impacts on all forms of community services; those generating the most concern are transportation, land use, water supply, and waste treatment. The best thing to happen to Cape Cod in recent years was the establishment of the National Seashore Park in 1961. Thanks largely to the urging of President John F. Kennedy, thousands of acres in five outer-Cape towns have changed but little in the last 20 years. This is not to say that no change is the answer, but rather that we need to be very careful with our environment.

Fishing, boating, golfing, antiquing, crafting, bicycling, and walking the beach all seem harmless in and of themselves. The challenge comes when these same fishers, boaters and vacationers need places to eat, sleep, and have their autos serviced. So far, we've been able to deal pretty well with the eating and the sleeping end of things. Summer traffic, however, is a huge problem. Other resort communities have dealt with it. On Mackinac Island, Michigan, all travel is by horse-drawn carriage. On Bermuda, only residents are allowed to operate automobiles. The Cape is working its way back to some rail service; maybe someday all visitors will park their cars on the north side of the Cape Cod Canal and come aboard by some sort of non-polluting public conveyance.

This area continues to be an incomparable paradise for escaping the pressures of a hurried world, but during the next few decades, the Cape and Islands resident and visitor populations will increase as sure as the tide will continue to rise and fall. Expectedly, by the year 2000 we'll still have some room for a few more folks. Hopefully, if we're careful, our very welcome visitors will still be returning, and the Cape will still offer a quiet walk on a seemingly endless beach.

CREATIVE CAPE COD—
YESTERDAY AND TODAY

by

STEVE CONNOLLY

Steve Connolly is a special feature and news writer for the Cape Cod Times, *and the author of* The Proprietary Lands of Plymouth Colony and Cape Cod.

It is said that Cape Cod has been discovered three different times in its rich history: first by the Vikings; second by the Pilgrims; and lastly by the hordes of artists, thespians, and writers who colonized it to their own creative liking in the 20th century.

Prior to this century, few noted creative people visited Cape Cod or stayed on it for any appreciable length of time. Of those who did, the most famous were poet-writer Henry David Thoreau, novelist Herman Melville, and Broadway and London actor Joseph Jefferson.

Herman Melville came to Cape Cod in the 1830s as a young able-bodied seaman aboard a Nantucket whaling schooner. He gathered most of the material for his *Moby Dick* characters on the whaling docks of Nantucket.

Thoreau made four separate trips to the Cape between 1849 and 1857. His book, *Cape Cod*, is a classic. It provides us with a view of the Cape's geography, natural environment, and what people were like during the mid-1800s.

Thoreau initially went to Cape Cod to "get a better view of the ocean"—what he found there was something much greater.

"I got the Cape under me, as much as if I were riding it bareback," Thoreau wrote afterwards. "It was not as on the map or seen from the stagecoach; but there I found it all out of doors, huge and real, Cape Cod!"

It would be four decades before other creative outsiders fully came to appreciate Thoreau's Cape Cod.

Joseph Jefferson was the first well-known entertainer of his day to actually build a summer home on Cape Cod. He loved the Cape and came here often in the summertime when he was not performing in New York or in London. In 1889, he built a magnificent Victorian mansion in Bourne on Buttermilk Bay. It still stands today.

One of his most frequent guests there during the summertime was President Grover Cleveland. Both were ardent sport fishermen. One summer, when Jefferson and President Cleveland were fishing at nearby Mashpee, an officious game warden surprised both anglers without their fishing licenses. As local legend has it, the game warden didn't believe that President Cleveland was the important person he claimed to be, and it took a lot of theatrics by Jefferson to keep both of them out of the Mashpee jail. They escaped with only a light fine.

Historically, the first real influx of creative individuals to Cape Cod occurred between 1898 and the First World War. The pathfinders of this movement were the artists from New York's Greenwich Village and from Europe. The founding father of the artists' migration to the Cape was the late impressionist painter and New York art teacher Charles W. Hawthorne, who founded the Cape Cod School of Art at Provincetown in 1899. What attracted Hawthorne to Provincetown was the undisturbed natural beauty and clear, spacious light of Cape Cod. Like other artists who were to follow him, Hawthorne was also captivated by Provincetown's small, southern European-styled fishing village atmosphere and its lively Portuguese and Cape Verdean people.

By 1916, five schools of art were flourishing in Provincetown. In addition to Hawthorne's school, there were George Elmer Brown's West End School of Art, E. Ambrose Webster's A Summer School of Painting, William and Marguerite Zorach's A Modern School of Art, and George Sensany's classes in color and monochrome etching.

For the next 45 years Provincetown was without rival as America's foremost art colony. During this renaissance period Provincetown blossomed, with such famous artists as Edwin Dickinson, John Noble, Blanche Lazzell, Max Bohm, Abraham Walkowitz, Karl Knaths, Frederick Waugh, Ross Moffett, Edward Hopper, Hans Hoffman, Samuel Edmund Oppenheim, Jackson Pollock, and painter-writer John Dos Passos.

World War I was less than a month old when the writers joined the artists at Provincetown in the summer of 1914. The small, quaint fishing village on the tip of the Cape was never to be the same again. Almost overnight it became an extension of Greenwich Village and Paris's Montparnasse district rolled into one.

Among some of the most noted writers at Provincetown that summer were: John Reed (*Ten Days That Shook the World*), Mary Heaton Vorse (*Footnote to Folly*), Hutchins Hapgood (*A Victorian in the Modern World*), Harry Kemp (Poet of the Dunes), Susan Glaspell (*Allison House*), and radical writer Max Eastman.

Like the artists before them, the writers came to Provincetown to pursue their art as well as to escape the summertime pressures of urban life. The war raging in Europe also weighted their decision to come to the Cape. Provincetown, as Hapgood put it, seemed far enough removed from reality to forget about it. Also, the cost of living was cheap in Provincetown. Many of the artists rented inexpensive rooms ($6 per week) from local residents; others bedded down in deserted Coast Guard shacks on the dunes. Some writers found lodging on the beach. "Worse come to worse," writes Evelyn Lawson in her book *Theatre on Cape Cod,* "while finishing a novel or play, one could live on fresh fish, clams, mussels with an occasional lobster donated by a friendly fisherman as his contribution to the arts."

In the summer of 1915, a few of these writers, led by George Cram Cook, John Reed and Mary Heaton Vorse, formed a local theater group called "The Provincetown Players." All the plays this group produced that summer were performed at a fish house on Mary Heaton Vorse's wharf off Commercial Street.

The following summer the "Players" moved uptown to larger quarters on Lewis's Wharf and were joined by a young, unknown playwright named Eugene O'Neill. Of the 19 original plays produced that summer by the Provincetown Players, O'Neill wrote six. Most notable was his classic *Bound East for Cardiff*. O'Neill and "The Players" charted a new, historic course in American Theater, bringing serious indigenous American plays to Broadway for almost the first time.

Mary Heaton Vorse's son, Heaton, 79, fondly recalls that time. "They were a very colorful group," says Vorse, who still resides in Provincetown at his late mother's home on Commercial Street. "But, they weren't just a group of amateurs putting on plays on social subjects. They were successful, professional writers who wanted to see what they could do in the dramatic field."

The creative seeds planted by Provincetown's artists and writers soon spread to other parts of the Cape. Most influential, for example, was the germination of small, amateur community theater groups, followed shortly thereafter by professional summer stock playhouses.

Of the amateur theaters, most notable is the Barnstable Comedy Club, which was founded in 1922, and is still in existence. It is considered by local theater critics to be the best amateur group on the Cape.

Novelist Kurt Vonnegut is one of the Barnstable Comedy Club's more famous alumni. During the late 1950s and early 1960s, Vonnegut acted in many of its productions as well as had some of his early plays (*My Name Is Everyone* and *Epicac*) produced by the group, to which, a few years ago, he gave "permission to make dramatic use of anything whatsoever of (his) throughout all Eternity without charge and without notification."

The genesis of Cape Cod's professional summer stock theater was the result of one person—the late Raymond Moore. On July 4, 1927, Moore opened his Cape Playhouse in Dennis and presented *The Guardsman,* starring Basil Rathbone and Violet Kemble Cooper. The rest is history.

Until his death in 1940, Moore brought to the Cape Playhouse such stars as Bette Davis, Henry Fonda, Robert Montgomery, Ethel Barrymore, Lloyd Nolan, Ruth Gordon, Shirley Booth, Humphrey Bogart, Eve Le Gallienne, Uta Hagen, Sylvia Sidney, Gertrude Lawrence, and Arthur Treacher. Today the Cape Playhouse continues to offer its summer audiences the best of Broadway, Hollywood and London.

Falmouth's contribution to summer stock theater parallels Moore's Cape Playhouse. The old University Players Guild, the precursor of today's Falmouth Playhouse, opened its first production at the Elizabeth Theatre in the summer of 1928. The Guild also attracted its share of Broadway's best talent. Stars such as Margaret Sullivan, James Cagney, Orson Wells, Josh Logan, and James Stewart made regular appearances there until they went to Hollywood.

In fact James Stewart got his first bit-part at Falmouth's old Elizabeth Theatre in 1928. At the time Stewart was studying to be a civil engineer at Princeton. His college friend, Josh Logan, dragged him to Falmouth for the summer and got him a job there playing his accordion in a Cape tea room. Stewart played so badly that a producer at the Falmouth stock company felt sorry for him and suggested he try acting. Stewart played his minor roles so well that the same producer took him to Broadway that fall.

Curtain call for the Falmouth Playhouse did not occur until 1949, when Cape Playhouse producer-manager Richard Aldrich presented Tallulah Bankhead in *Private Lives*.

Aldrich did not stop with the Falmouth Playhouse, which today ranks alongside the Cape Playhouse as the best in summer theater on Cape Cod. The following year he and his wife, actress Gertrude Lawrence, broke new ground on the Cape when they opened the Melody Tent in Hyannis. Since 1950, the Melody Tent has offered its audiences the best in Broadway musical comedies, light operas, jazz concerts, and solo performances by such headline stars as Carol Channing, Joel Gray, Liza Minnelli, Tony Bennett, Crystal Gayle, Melissa Manchester, the Mills Brothers, Sandler and Young, Frankie Laine, and Merle Haggard. The Aldrich-Lawrence story, however, ended on a sad footnote when the great Broadway and London actress died unexpectedly in the summer of 1952. Afterwards Aldrich gradually lost all interest in theater and eventually left the business.

Creative Cape Cod is still very much alive today. The Provincetown Art Association, the colony's oldest (1914), and the Chrysler Museum (1958) offer the public the chance to view the works of past and present Provincetown artists, craftspeople, and sculptors. On Pearl Street there is the Fine Arts Work Center, which was once "Day's Lumber Yard." Great artists use to have a community studio here. The Center hasn't forgotten this tradition. For seven months out of the year it is the home for young artists and writers, as well as the classroom for distinguished visiting faculty members. Some of Center's residents have been writers Norman Mailer, John Cheever, John Hawkes, and John Irving; artists Robert Motherwell, Philip Malicoat, and Bruce McKain; and poet Stanley Kunitz.

Provincetown is still a lively and creative place to visit. The addresses are still the same. O'Neill's old room is still at 577 Commercial Street. Susan Glaspell and George Cram Cook lived at 564 Commercial Street. John Dos Passos lived at number 571 and Heaton Vorse still lives at his mother's place at 466 Commercial Street.

On the rest of the Cape proper, actors Tony Curtis and John Savage (*The Deer Hunter*) own summer homes in Dennis, as does retired actress Shirley Booth. Actress Julie Harris lives nearby in West Chatham. Writer Paul Brodeur (*The Stunt Man*) resides year-round in North Truro, while Paul Theroux (*Patagonia Express*) divides his time between London and East Sandwich.

The Islands—Martha's Vineyard and Nantucket—are quickly becoming the Cape's most popular summer retreat for many celebrities of the arts and letters.

On Martha's Vineyard, James Cagney spends six months of each year at his home at Chilmark. Art Buchwald, Walter Cronkite, Mike Wallace, and John Updike reside at Vineyard Haven. James Reston, the *New York Times* vice-president and columnist, owns the island's major weekly newspaper, the *Vineyard Gazette* (1967).

Another Vineyard proprietor is singer-songwriter Carly Simon, who owns the popular nightspot "The Hot Tin Roof," which draws top drop-in performers like her husband James Taylor. Other celebrity notables on the Vineyard include Beverly Sills, Lillian Hellman, James Cagney, and Patricia Neal.

Nantucket's celebrity roster is far shorter than that of the Vineyard, but it's growing. Anne Meara and husband Jerry Stiller are active there in community affairs; writers Nathaniel Benchley and Russell Baker have been longtime summer residents.

It is said today that if one were to throw a seashell on any part of Cape Cod and the Islands, it would probably hit an artist, writer, or a Broadway or Hollywood actor—a little exaggeration, but few other resort areas attract more artists, writers and other famous celebrities than does the Cape and the Islands.

A SIDE TRIP TO PLYMOUTH

by

CHRISTIE LOWRANCE

Christie Lowrance, an eight-year resident of the Cape, is a freelance writer who has contributed articles to both the Cape Cod Times *and* Cape Cod Life *magazine.*

From the Upper Cape, it is about 20 minutes to Plymouth, the point of origin for much Cape Cod and American history. To reach Plymouth from the Sagamore Bridge rotary, take Rte. 3 North toward Boston. Exit 6 at Rte. 44 will take you most directly into Plymouth Center, but there are a number of exits within the town. You can also reach it from the Cape via Rte. 3A starting near the Sagamore rotary. Rte. 3A is a single-lane scenic road that follows the shore through several Plymouth villages.

Plymouth gives a multilayered impression of seaside tourism, industry, old New England and ethnic influences, but it is best known for its Pilgrim history. Indeed, there is a compelling sense of the nation's history in this place, where you can walk the decks of the *Mayflower II,* and look across the water at a small armada of power boats. However long you gaze at Plymouth Rock and fantasize about what the Pilgrims saw here, you inevitably come back to the reality of a small city of 36,000 that has replaced the wilderness. The town itself is a monument to the determination of the earliest settlers.

The Pilgrims were Puritans, a group of English Separatist Protestants whose advocacy of strict religious discipline and simplified ceremony put them in direct conflict with the ruling Anglicans. One group of Puritans fled to Holland where they lived for about a decade. Under the leadership of William Bradford and William Brewster, they laid plans to achieve religious and economic freedom in the New World. After several arrangements with London financiers fell through, they finally obtained backing and a land patent from the Virginia Company of London. Although the weren't entirely pleased with the terms of their commitments, they were anxious to get underway before winter set in.

On September 16, 1620, Captain Christopher Jones put the ship *Mayflower* on course, with the Old World behind and the New World ahead. Many of the 102 passengers died on the two-month voyage across the Atlantic. Bad weather caused the ship to divert from its Virginia destination to the New England coast. Cape Cod was sighted on November 19, but after some exploration, it was decided to continue the search for a settlement. While the ship was anchored off Provincetown, 41 men in the group formulated and signed the historic *Mayflower Compact.* This unique legal document assigned leadership to the "civil Body Politick," or the majority, rather than to the minority or an individual ruler. It marked the beginning of a policy of American democracy.

It must have been a powerful moment in December of 1620 when the men, women, and children of the *Mayflower* stepped onto land and began exploring their new home in Plymouth. More than half of them died from exposure and malnutrition during the first winter. In fact, the colony would have probably been extinguished completely had it not been for the kindness of Native Americans who showed them where and how to fish and farm. A Patuxet Indian named Squanto taught them to plant corn, catch herring, and tap maple trees for the sap. In gratitude to God and their Indian benefactors, the Pilgrims planned a harvest feast of thanksgiving, which became an American tradition.

Within about five years, 10,000 others had joined the early

settlers of New England. They engaged in farming, fishing, and fur trading. Later, brick-making and shipbuilding took hold, spawning forges, lumber mills, and rigging shops. A large rope-making firm, the Cordage Company, operated from the 1820s to the 1960s. Some of its buildings are being considered for conversion to a retail shopping center, underscoring the town's recent turn to tourism, for which its extensive waterfront and historic background are ideally suited.

There are many historic attractions and monuments in Plymouth—from Plimoth Plantation to Plymouth Rock. For listings and locations, see the Practical Information section below.

PRACTICAL INFORMATION FOR PLYMOUTH

HOW TO GET THERE. By car: Plymouth is 38 miles from Boston via Rte. 3, about 44 miles from Providence, R.I., on Rte. 44, and 219 miles from New York City. **By bus:** The *Plymouth & Brockton Street Railway Co.* provides regular bus service to Boston, Cape Cod, and other areas. The depot is located at the 274-acre Industrial Park. **By air:** *Plymouth Municipal Airport* handles non-commercial charter flights or private planes. Approximately 45 minutes to Boston's *Logan International Airport.*

TOURIST INFORMATION SERVICES. *Plymouth Area Chamber of Commerce,* located on 85 Samoset St., Plymouth, Massachusetts 02360, offers information about Plymouth and nearby towns. The phone number is 746-3377. A Visitor Information Center is located downtown at North Park Ave. Plans are presently underway for $2 million visitors' information center in Plymouth to serve all of southeastern Massachusetts.

SEASONAL EVENTS. May: *Spring Flower Show* at Cranberry World Visitors Center. **June:** *Annual Renaissance Festival,* S. Carver; crafts, dance, drama, pageantry of 16th-century England. *Blessing of the Fleet,* town wharf, starts at 9 on the 27th with Memorial Service. *Fishermen's Harvest Festival* takes place same day and place, 10–4. *Summer Festival,* Edaville Railroad, S. Carver; arts, crafts, entertainment, displays. **July:** *Annual Antiquarian Fair,* 126 Water St., 10–3. *Fourth of July Parade,* starts on Court St. at the Registry of Motor Vehicles, N.

Plymouth at 9:30; also fireworks and concert. *Steam, Gas, and Antique Machinery Meet and Competition*, Edaville RR, S. Carver. **August:** *Atlantic Bluefin Tuna Tournament;* also *Bass and Bluefish Tournament*, town wharf. *Pilgrim Progress Parade*, from Cole's Hill up Leyden St. Every Fri. at 5. *Seventeenth Century English Country Wedding*, Plimoth Plantation, Rte. 3A, "a media spectacular." **September:** *Annual Plymouth International Criterium;* bike race with internationally-known competitors, starts at noon at the waterfront. *Plymouth Outdoor Art Show;* juried show draws artists from New England area, at Plymouth Art Guild on Water and Leyden Sts. *Plymouth–South Shore Power Boat Race;* production class power boats, international competitors, 100-mile circuit within Plymouth Harbor. **October:** All Hallow's Eve and Harvest Home celebrations, Plimoth Plantation, Rte. 3A. *Massachusetts Cranberry Festival and Fair*, Edaville RR, S. Carver, off Rte. 58. **November:** *Holly Day Happening;* church bazaar at St. Peters Parish Center on Memorial Dr. *Thanksgiving Day;* many activities including Pilgrim dinner demonstration at Harlow Old Fort House, 9–4; Thanksgiving dinner at Memorial Hall on Court St, First-come-first-serve for 2,000. **December:** *Christmas Festival*, Edaville RR, S. Carver; a five-mile ride through cranberry bog decorated with Christmas lights, throughout Dec.

HISTORIC SITES. *Burial Hill*, located behind the First Church; location of first Pilgrim fort and probably grave of Governor Bradford. *Cole's Hill*, Water St.; site where Pilgrims buried their dead; statue of Massasoit, a Wampanoag-chief who aided settlers. *First House and 1627 House*, Water St.; reproduction of two 17th-century buildings; open Apr. to Dec., 9–4. *Jabez Howland House*, Sandwich St.; only Plymouth house in which Pilgrims are known to have lived. *Jenney Grist Mill*, on the Town Brook; reproduction of original mill; corn, wheat, and rye ground daily, 10–5. *Plymouth Rock*, at the waterfront; generally accepted as the landing place of the Pilgrims. *Richard Sparrow House*, 42 Summer St.; oldest house in Plymouth, built around 1640.

MUSEUMS. Most of the antique homes, museums, and historical sites are open to the public from Apr. 1 to Dec. *Cranberry World*, Water St.; a history of the cranberry industry, display of implements, tour of working bog, free entertainment, art gallery; open Apr. 1 to Nov. 30, 9:30–5. *Harlow Old Fort House*, Rte. 3A; demonstrations of typical 17th-century activities; open Memorial Day to Labor Day. *Mayflower Society House*, 4 Winslow St.; built in 1754 by Pilgrim descendants; colonial and Victorian furnishings, paintings. *Mayflower Experience*, 114 Water St.; scale model of *Mayflower II*, audio-visual presentation. The *Mayflower II*, State Pier; full-scale model of the type of vessel that transported the

Pilgrims; shipboard demonstrations; open March to Dec. *Pilgrim Hall Museum,* Court and Chilton Sts.; oldest museum in the U.S., contains personal possessions of the Pilgrims; open daily yr.-round. *Plimoth Plantation,* Rte. 3A; fascinating re-creation of Pilgrim life with people enacting details of everyday life; questions answered only with information available in the 1600s; re-creation of Wampanoag Indian encampment on Eel River; special events; a must; open Apr. to Dec. *Plymouth National Wax Museum,* Cole's Hill; the Pilgrim story, re-created with wax figures; open March to Dec.

LIBRARIES. Plymouth Public Library, 11 North St. Children's library, special programs. Special collections on nuclear power, Pilgrim history, genealogy. Materials for blind and handicapped readers, bookmobile service. Branch library in Manomet, Point Rd.

TOURS. *Capt. John Boats Tours, Inc.*; boat tours, whale watches, sunset canal cruises, overnight and day fishing. *Plymouth and Provincetown Steamship Co., Inc.*; boat tour across Cape Cod Bay to Provincetown on the *Cape Cod Princess;* also canal trip, 4th of July, and whale watch; May to Oct. 12. *Plymouth Ocean Tours, Inc.*; narrated cruise, landmarks, and monuments. *Plymouth Rock Trolley;* half-hour tour of the Plymouth Rock area on Water St.; minimal charge.

SHOPPING. Go poking. There's everything from *The Good, the Bad, and the Ugly* second-hand shop to high-priced antique stores. *Jenney Grist Mill* is an interesting boutique complex at the Town Brook. *Village Landing* is a waterfront retail shopping area modeled after Mystic Seaport. The *Revere Copper and Brass Outlet* on the corner of Lothrop and Water Sts. is worth a stop. *Commonwealth Winery* on Rte. 3A North at Cordage Park offers a fine selection of premium wines and wine tasting; open daily yr.-round, except Sun.

PUBLIC BEACHES. *Plymouth Beach,* Rte. 3A. *Nelson St. Beach. Stephen's Field Beach. White Horse Beach* in Manomet partially opened to public. Parking available, $3–$5. Freshwater pond in Manomet.

HOTELS AND MOTELS. A complete list of overnight accommodations is available at the Plymouth Chamber of Commerce. Of those listed here, the categories are based on the same criteria as the Upper Cape.

Expensive

Governor Bradford Motor Inn, Water St. 746-6200. Waterfront location. Convenient to museums, shops, beaches. Pool. Yr.-round.

Governor Carver Motor Inn, 25 Summer St. 746-7100. Within historic downtown area. Pool, restaurant, lounge, meeting rooms; 82 units. Yr.-round.

Pilgrim Sands Motel, Rte. 3A. 747-0900. 64 units on Cape Cod Bay. Private beach, 2 pools, meeting rooms. Near restaurant, low off-season rates. Yr.-round.

Yankee Travler Motel, Rte. 3A. 746-3000. Pool, tennis, telephones. Near golf course, saltwater beach. Full-service restaurant and lounge. Some kitchenettes.

Moderate

Blue Spruce Motel, Rte. 3A. 224-3990. Pool, outside recreation area. Near beach, restaurant, golf course.

Inn For All Seasons, 97 Warren Ave. 746-8823. Refurbished Victorian mansion, 15 guest rooms, outdoor patio. Ocean view, restaurant, pool, recreation room. Yr.-round.

Plymouth Motel, Rtes. 3A and 44. 746-2800. Near fishing, beaches; ½ mi. from Center, historic sites. Heated pool, kitchenettes. Special off-season rates. Yr.-round.

The Sleepy Pilgrim, 182 Court St. 746-1962. Car ports, room coffee, ½ mi. from Plymouth Center

 RESTAURANTS. The following list of a few Plymouth restaurants shows their variety in terms of atmosphere and menu. All fall within the *Moderate* ($9–$15) to *Inexpensive* (under $9) price ranges. Most offer an average full dinner for less than $10.

Bert's. *Inexpensive.* Rte. 3A, at Plymouth Beach. 746-3422. Oceanfront. American menu, seafood and beef. Serves all 3 meals, yr.-round, casual. 2 lounges, nightly entertainment.

The Hungry Pilgrim Restaurant. *Moderate.* At Gov. Carver Motor Inn, 25 Summer St. 746-7100. New England cuisine, lobster in season, scrod, fisherman's platter. 3 meals served daily, yr.-round. Lounge, entertainment, dancing.

The Inn For All Seasons. *Inexpensive.* 97 Warren Ave., Rte. 3A. 746-8823. Relaxed dining with crystal and candlelight. Continental cuisine, veal specialties; crêpes, quiches for lunch. Dinner served 4–10. Sunday brunch. Nightly entertainment in lounge. Open daily, yr.-round.

McGrath's. *Inexpensive.* Water St. 746-9751. Waterfront family dining. Seafood specialties, steaks. Open yr.-round.

Plymouth Tea House. *Moderate.* 35 North St. 747-3690. Sea captain's house, waterview, 3 dining rooms, open porch. Limited dinner menu, specializes in lunch and tea. Homemade soups, desserts, scones, tea breads. Open 11:30–4:30, Tues. to Sat., yr.-round.

'1620' Restaurant. *Inexpensive.* 158 Water St. 746-9565. Waterfront location. Extensive seafood menu, scallops, lobster, bluefish in season; beef. 2 lounges, entertainment, dancing Wed. to Sat. Open daily, except Christmas. Family operated since 1933.

THE UPPER CAPE

by

CHRISTIE LOWRANCE

The world's widest sea-level canal separates the Upper Cape from the rest of Massachusetts, but the dividing line between upper and lower Cape Cod is far less tangible. The distinction does not appear to have physical or geographical origins, although some people have linked it to water supply; others say the labels were invented for the convenience of salesmen and the media.

For the people who live in the villages and towns here, however, the term Upper Cape carries an extended sense of neighborhood. It simply feels more natural to shop and do business within the Upper Cape, even though Hyannis or Yarmouth may be just as close. To drive from Sandwich to Mashpee is to cross one boundary; to drive into Barnstable is to cross two. In the Upper Cape, there is a concept of "us" among people in the four towns—

Bourne, Sandwich, Mashpee, and **Falmouth**—"them" being the rest of the Cape, Martha's Vineyard, Nantucket, and, especially, the mainland. This fine and subtle sense of regional identity is as fragile as a beach rose petal, however. It breaks down almost immediately when politicians and local officials begin to speak of "regionalization" with one's Upper Cape neighbor in the interest of providing a mutual solution to a mutual problem. Whether the proposal involves roads or dumps, the instinctive reaction is: Every man and municipality for himself. Although some respected leaders laud regionalization as the key to the future, others follow the thinking of a crusty Bourne selectman who predicted some years ago that regionalization would bring an end to life as Cape Codders knew it.

This reluctance to embrace regionalized solutions does not mean that people are uncooperative; they simply have a strong sense of independence and identity, born perhaps from such close encounters with nature. The encounters once took place on whaling ships or clam flats, or in woods that led to unseen homelands. But today the encounters are still very real, even if they involve nothing more than standing on the shore at Old Silver Beach and squinting across the bay to the distant patch of mainland that is New Bedford. Whether these encounters take place on the safe shore or on the soundless deep, they evoke a subconscious understanding of the need to resist and the ability to survive.

Although Bourne, Sandwich, Mashpee, and Falmouth are neighboring communities, the history and development of each is surprisingly different from that of the other. Within the towns are villages, and those too have their own distinctiveness. Some villages like Pocasset and Cataumet in Bourne have their own post offices and shopping areas. Others are little more than thickly settled districts, but there is generally a historic or economic reason for their existence.

Native or Newcomer?

Who comes to visit Cape Cod? Basically, it's people seeking relaxation in the sun and sand. Who lives in Cape Cod? Basically, it's the people who came to visit 15 years ago, bought a piece of property, built on it, and retired here to relax in the sun and sand. Condominium development is attracting a lot of retirees. Men and women who work in Boston are willing to commute from the Upper Cape. (Reliable bus service helps make the 60-mile trip more palatable. The commuter parking lot at the rotary by the

Sagamore Bridge has been expanded twice since it was built in the late 1970s.)

The colorful fisherman in Woods Hole might well have been a grocer in New London last year, and the colorful grocer in Buzzards Bay might have been selling life insurance in Yonkers before he got restless. It generally pays to get to know people; there are some very interesting stories to be heard. But people who wear T-shirts that say "I'm not a tourist, I live here and I don't answer questions" usually mean it. You'll still find many Cape Codders who were born and raised here. They have names like Eldred, Hoxie, Eldridge, Gibbs, or Crowell and a faint Yankee twang. They're the ones who remember when Quaker Meeting House Road in East Sandwich was a country dirt road, or when the days before the Otis/Edwards Military Reservation, before the canal, before development

It's a sign you've been here awhile if you can say, "I remember when . . . ," but it's getting easier all the time because things change so rapidly. Sandwich's population has tripled within the last 20 years, from 3,000 in the early 1960s to about 9,000 in 1980. Mashpee is the second fastest-growing town in Barnstable County, having tripled its population between 1970 and 1980. Falmouth's population has steadily increased; it's about 23,000 now, with more than twice that in the summer. Bourne's development has been more influenced by the military base than by tourism. It exploded from 3,519 in 1950 to 14,011 in 1960, but the population now is down to about 12,000.

The dynamic growth pattern on the Upper Cape might be a sweet dream for the building industry, but it's more like a nightmare for town officials who have to respond to increased demands for municipal services. They are trying to balance residential growth with commercial development by courting businesses with industrial parks, but so far there has been limited success. Planning boards try to implement zoning and restrictive bylaws to control growth. Everyone agrees the towns need to plan for the future, but whose future—the businessman, the retiree, the young family? When the party gets crowded, it's hard not to step on toes.

Growth has had an impact on water supply. With the exception of Falmouth, which has a surface water reservoir, the Upper Cape depends on groundwater sources tapped by wells. There is a large freshwater aquifer beneath the outwash plain in South Sandwich that supplies much of the water to much of the Upper and Mid-Cape. Recent drought conditions have caused Falmouth to regulate water, which is supplied by a municipal reservoir at Long Pond. Wastewater treatment and disposal is also an issue that is being examined by the four Upper Cape towns. Urbanites moving into the area don't always realize that sewer service is practically nonexistent.

Environmental awareness is crucial in a fragile area like the Cape. Evidence of a very small oil spill that occurred in Buzzards Bay more than ten years ago can still be found, and the thought of a major spill brings sweat to the brow of every property owner and motel manager on the Upper Cape. Falmouth alone has 68 miles of coast, including precious saltwater marshes and 12 miles of sandy beaches. Yet economic pressures are tremendous, as evidenced by the off-shore oil drilling debate.

Whatever decisions are made, one thing is sure: The sea and the winds and the land will ultimately dictate to man the paths that he may take. It will not be the other way around.

The Cape Cod Canal

The prominent geographical features of the Upper Cape, such as the kettlehole ponds in Falmouth, the Mashpee rivers, Bourne boulders, and the Sandwich ridge, were created by glacial activity thousands of years ago. There is one exception: the Cape Cod Canal. The seven-mile-long canal was opened in 1914. It had been under construction for 50 years and under discussion for 250 years. In 1898, one historian wryly referred to "the great ship canal, if it is ever finished."

Myles Standish and George Washington were among those who noticed how convenient a canal would be. Less than a mile lay between the waters of the Manomet and Scusset rivers. A shortcut for the treacherous 100-mile water route around Cape Cod would be a godsend to those who tried to earn a living from the sea. Many ships have been wrecked off Cape shores.

The General Court in Plymouth named a committee in 1697 to examine the feasibility of building a canal in what was then Sandwich, but interest in the project was sporadic. Aside from having to deal with such pressing matters as King Philip's War and the American Revolution, early residents were afraid the tidal differences between Buzzards Bay and Cape Cod Bay would erode and destroy the peninsula.

Serious plans were not developed until the late 1800s and weren't completed until the 1900s. It's odd to think of both colonial and 20th-century engineers standing on Bournedale hillsides discussing what a great place it would be for a canal. Once underway, the project progressed about as smoothly as a one-oared dory in the Woods Hole rip. The Cape Cod Ship Canal Company dug a 7,000-feet-long ditch before going broke. The Cape Cod and New York Company that followed it also ran into financial problems. Then August Belmont, a New York financier with Cape bloodlines, came on the scene. Ground was broken with a silver spade in 1909. The man obviously was ambitious, as well as solvent, for he started three bridges along with the canal. Two drawbridges were completed by 1913. One year later, as gates were opened and waters of two bays collided in a boiling rush, Cape Cod was officially severed from the rest of Massachusetts. Old photographs show the excitement on the faces of the men watching the dramatic moment. It must have been an impressive sight, especially since it took two and a half centuries to materialize.

The canal project always managed to defy men's predictions and expectations. Belmont thought it would make him rich, or richer, but when it was sold to the federal government in 1928, his nearly bankrupt estate had lost close to $5 million. Both Bourne and Sandwich expected to become industrially powerful from canal traffic and trade, but by the time the waterway was ready for heavy shipping, industrial enterprise on the Upper Cape had practically died. The major benefit to the two towns that border the canal is the drawing power of an endless parade of giant ocean-going tankers, sleek yachts, and stubby tugboats. People come from miles to watch, and from them another kind of industry, tourism, has developed.

The two highway bridges that span the Cape Cod Canal were completed in the 1930s. They are owned and operated by the U.S. Army Corps of Engineers, as is the railroad bridge in Buzzards Bay. A four-year repair project begun by the Corps in 1979 drove home to both residents and tourists exactly what it means to rely on two steel-bridge roadways for access to and exit from Cape Cod. Although the Corps tried to minimize inconvenience, it was practically impossible when barbers, doctors, stores, gas stations, and town halls were located on the other side of a closed bridge. The repairs sometimes meant that Bourne residents from the village of Pocasset had to drive down to Sagamore to get over to Buzzards Bay—it was like making a 10-mile U-turn.

But under normal circumstances, crossing the canal is easy and pleasant. You get a lovely view of the boats on the canal and Cape Cod Bay. Rte. 6 crosses the Sagamore Bridge and brings travelers to Sandwich, the first big town, on the northern shore of the Upper Cape.

Sandwich History

Sandwich was settled on April 3, 1637. A few people, including William Leveridge, a minister from Duxbury, were already living in Sandwich when the legendary "Ten Men from Saugus" received permission to explore and purchase lands within Plymouth Colony. Probably attracted by the forests, fish supply, salt marsh hay, and a navigable river to the Bay, some 60 families were granted permission to settle in Manomet, later renamed Sandwich for the English town on the Stour River in Kent County. Another 50 families, called "undertakers," arrived shortly after the first settlers. They came from Lynn (Saugus), Duxbury, and Plymouth.

Incorporated in 1639, Sandwich was the first town in Barnstable County and the fourth in Plymouth County. The objectives of the early settlers were bluntly summarized later: "To worship God and make money." Life was difficult. Corn had to be ground in Plymouth. There were no roads, just the clearing along the coast. Wolves were plentiful and brought a two-pound bounty. Civil law was almost as harsh as the laws of nature. Severe whipping was the penalty for working on Sunday. There was a 10-shilling fine for overdrinking and a 12-shilling fine for smoking on the highway.

Some settlers decided that laws good for the geese ought to be good for the ganders, so to speak. Thomas Dexter, the builder of Sandwich's first mill, sued Governor Endicott for hitting him, and was rewarded ten pounds in damages. With a decided contemporary flair, Dexter went on to file eight suits between 1648 and 1649, including a claim against the Town of Barnstable for rights on Scorton Creek. He won.

The Pilgrims had so many laws and rules about worshipping God, it's a wonder they had any time left for worship after enforcing them. A number of Quakers who came to Sandwich were converted within 20 years after its settlement. Judged heretics by the Plymouth leaders, the Quakers were physically and legally harassed, imprisoned, and stripped of their holdings. Heavy pressure was put on Quaker sympathizers, who were fined five pounds, the equivalent of a year's pay, for entertaining a Quaker. History books alternate between apology and indignation at the attempts at religious repression, which were officially stopped in 1661.

Christopher Hollow, a new subdivision in Sandwich, took its name from a secret meeting place in the woods where Christopher Ludlow led the Society of Friends in worship. Stephen Wing was the first Sandwich convert. His descendants maintain his farm in

East Sandwich as a museum. It is not far from a sturdy two-story Quaker meeting house that testifies to the durability of the spirit the Pilgrims tried to extinguish.

Farming, fishing, and survival were the primary occupations of the early days. Hampered by the lack of a deep-water harbor, Sandwich never participated as fully in the whaling industry as other Cape towns did, but its men shipped out to sea from New Bedford, Falmouth, and other ports. Shellfishing and day-fishing in Cape Cod Bay brought in food and money. Some Sandwich residents can still remember weir-fishing with nets off Scorton Creek.

Sandwich was an industrial town, a workingman's town, for much of the 19th century. The boxey sea captains' homes were in Falmouth; the extravagant summer mansions were in Bourne and Falmouth along Buzzards Bay. Many of Sandwiches' antique homes are former boardinghouses, duplexes, or single-family homes for the factory workers. Much of its coast is marshland rather than sandy beach. Its summer areas, mainly Town Neck and North Shore Boulevard, weren't developed until fairly recently, unlike Falmouth Heights or some of the summer colonies in Bourne. But 150 years ago, Bourne was Sandwich; when it separated, Sandwich lost its warm-water coast as well as some fine old homes.

The Boston and Sandwich Glass Company, opened in 1825, made Sandwich famous for its beautifully colored glass. Other factories in operation at the same time were the Cape Cod Glass Company, the Sandwich Card and Tag Company, and several shoe factories. Some assume the glass companies came to Sandwich for its sand, but, ironically, local sand was not suitable for glass production so it had to be brought in. The oak forests, however, were ideal for fuel. Ships filled their holds at docks along the harbor and carried Sandwich glass around the world. Much of it was ordinary housewares, tumblers, and salt shakers, but exquisite artwork was also produced.

Identifying true Sandwich glass can be tricky because it wasn't stamped, but those familiar with the merchandise can pick it out. The old Boston and Sandwich Glass Company office stamp surfaced from the back of an attic not long ago. The last time it had been used officially would have been in 1888, when the factory closed after 63 years of operation. When workers threatened to strike, owner Deming Jarves counter-threatened to put out the factory fires and close down. Unfortunately, they both carried through with their threats. There were several efforts to reopen the plant after it closed, but they were unsuccessful.

One old history refers to Sandwich as being "full of dignity and industry and checkered fortunes.'' All those qualities must have been wonderfully displayed in the 250th celebration of the incorporation of the town which was held on September 3, 1889. A committee of 40 people was appointed to look after the details, and an invitation was extended to all who had lived in the town. Bells rang from church steeples, school buildings, and factories. The streets were jammed, flags flew, and passengers on each incoming train were welcomed home. Dinner was planned for 1,000 people. Reverend Chamberlayne, the orator of the day, must have spoken for hours, judging from the text of his speech. Only polite remarks and well wishes were made about Bourne, which had separated from Sandwich five years prior.

Sandwich Center

From Rte. 6, get off at Exit 1 and proceed through Sagamore on Rte. 6A to Sandwich. At the town border on the left, look for a handsome old farm house surrounded by trees. It is the Freeman Farm, once property of John Freeman, the son of a founder of Sandwich. A short distance along Rte. 6A the road splits. The road to the left leads to the marina and canal entrance. Sandwich has the fifth largest fishing fleet in the state, and marina expansion for commercial and recreation vessels is in the works. Straight ahead on Rte. 6A is the commercial area of Sandwich, and a right turn onto Old Main Street takes you to Sandwich Center. One Cape photographer called the center ''almost too perfect.'' Indeed, the old mill wheel turning slowly at the end of Shawme Pond, the white swans paddling in the shadow of the stately Town Hall, and the old homes nearby give an timeless aura to the whole area. There are museums, shops, restaurants, churches, and pleasant walks downtown.

The site of the Boston and Sandwich Glass Company is on Factory Street, and around the corner to the left is a boardwalk over the marsh. Sometimes during a full-moon tide, the whole marsh floods. The small boxes on the marshes are for green-head fly control. The state maintains a fish hatchery open to the public on Rte. 6A near the village. Continue on to East Sandwich.

East Sandwich

East Sandwich originally developed as a farming area. You'll pass cranberry bogs and spring-fed ponds on either side of Rte. 6A. The bogs are very colorful, especially in the fall after harvest time. Skaters like the shallow waters, and ice-hockey games are often played here. Water lily "farms" in East Sandwich used to provide plants for the fish ponds of the wealthy.

Native beach plum, cranberry, strawberry, and wild grape jams and jellies have been made and sold for nearly 80 years at the Green Briar Jam Kitchen and at other places along Rte. 6A. This winding road is dotted with interesting little shops that are worth a visit. The bridge over Scorton Creek is a favorite jumping-off spot for swimmers; if you prefer, you can stay dry and just enjoy the beauty of this Cape Cod salt marsh.

You can follow Rte. 6A all the way down to Orleans. There is relatively little commercialism along the road, primarily because of the regulation of the Old King's Highway Regional Historic District. The district was formed to preserve the historical integrity of the land north of Rte. 6, which includes all of Rte. 6A in Sandwich. Some feel the district stifles architectural development and complicates the lives of ordinary citizens, but it does appear to have cut down significantly on the sights and sounds that have given a Coney Island flavor to certain sections of Rte. 28.

To see more of the Upper Cape, turn around in Orleans and make a left on Quaker Meeting House Road. Continue on to Rte. 130 and Forestdale.

Forestdale

Forestdale is a small rural village located about four miles from Sandwich Center on Rte. 130, which used to be the main road between Sandwich and Falmouth. In its earlier days Forestdale was a farming community with a lot of sheep-raising. The first record of anyone owning land in the area is dated 1706. The village was once called "Snake Pond," the name of a pretty freshwater pond off to the right of Rte. 130. The name was later changed to "Greenville," but it had to be changed again when residents got a post office, because there was already a Greenville, Massachusetts.

Some of the homes in the area date back to the 1700s. One private residence on the left of Rte. 130 has unusual half windows native to Nantucket; the building was reportedly moved to Forestdale from Wakeby Lake. The Baptist Church on the left was probably built in the 1800s. Originally it was a Methodist church and stood next to the small cemetery across the street from its present location. The small red building nearby is a one-room schoolhouse that has been renovated by community groups. Following Rte. 130 south, you will come to Mashpee.

Mashpee: History of an Indian Town

Long before the Pilgrims placed a foot on Cape sands, the Wampanoag Federation of approximately 40,000 Native Americans was well established in southeastern Massachusetts. The Federation consisted of some 30 tribes, including the Massipees, an agricultural people who farmed, hunted, and fished in the vicinity of the present town of Mashpee. Some historical writers state that the eventual acquisition of Indian lands by early settlers was just and legal. Others question whether the Indians even understood the concept of land ownership, and suggest that the Indians believed they were simply acknowledging use of land, not possession, when they signed documents presented to them by the settlers.

The arrival of white men threatened the Wampanoags' existence in other ways. European diseases practically destroyed the tribe between 1617 and 1618, leaving them with few means of resisting encroachment. Thomas Tupper and Richard Bourne of Sandwich foresaw a dismal future for these generally peaceful people. They attempted to arm them with Christianity, the English language, education, and legal standing. As a former member of the General Court, Bourne was familiar with the process of government and he had contacts; he worked hard to help the Indians obtain title to "the plantation of Marshpee." In 1670, Bourne was ordained minister of the "Praying Indians" at the plantation and built a church. Bourne's descendants and Indian pastors carried on his work.

In 1685, the General Court voted that no property in the town could be sold without the consent of the Massipee tribe. Although the Indians had obtained title to their lands, they were ill-equipped for self-government in the white society that now surrounded them. An overseer system imposed by Plymouth exploited them, virtually making them slaves on their own homelands. In the 1700s the tribe's numbers dropped critically, and by 1895 the population was only 330.

Struggle for the land and waters in Mashpee continues today. It is a radical, cultural, economic, power-centered struggle that either lies below the surface of or dominates town life. An Indian land suit was begun in 1976, in which the Wampanoag Tribal Council of Mashpee pressed for return of lands comprising much of the town. The suit made national news headlines and brought construction and real estate activity to a virtual halt for three years. The town budget and private finances were severely strained, but far worse was the strain of a town angrily divided against itself. Relief was felt throughout the whole area when the suit ended. The state Supreme Court ruled that the Wampanoag Indians in Mashpee had not constituted a tribe consistently throughout the town's history, which was the basis of the Tribal Council's right to sue. One document produced during the trial was a deed written by Richard Bourne on December 11, 1665.

There are, however, some land issues on which Indian and white residents have been in agreement. A good deal of land in Mashpee is owned by the town and the state. The Mashpee River Scenic Act was adopted by the town in 1980 to preserve the pristine qualities of one of the Cape's finest freshwater rivers. The act restricts use and development of lands 100 feet on either side of the river that quietly flows from Mashpee Lake to Popponesset Bay. Residents also voted in 1981 to have the state take by eminent domain the 432-acre South Cape Beach parcel, which includes extensive saltwater marshes, pine woods, and a beautifully unspoiled barrier beach. The intent is to preserve the area from further development by the New Seabury Corporation, which planned to expand its extensive resort complex with housing and a marina.

Few people would disagree that the 2,000-acre New Seabury resort complex has had a highly significant impact on the town of Mashpee. It has brought population growth, economic stimulation, a shopping center, and increased tax revenues. However, it has also highlighted economic differences and posed a newcomers' threat to native control of local government. The power struggle is the reverse of Falmouth's 19th-century conflict between the wealthy summer people and the sea captains. The summer people wanted to keep things as they were, while the long-time residents wanted growth and progress. Those who have lived in Mashpee for generations want to keep what they have, while the newcomers want to push the town toward changes of their own design. It is not a new conflict on the Cape, but in Mashpee it is perhaps older and deeper.

Mashpee Center

Mashpee Town Hall makes a good center point from which to tour the town; it is located about six miles from Exit 2 off Rte. 6 and about three miles past Forestdale on Rte. 130. There is a small cemetery on the left as you approach town, a bit before the Tribal Council Office. On the right, across from the yellow Tribal Council building, is the Indian Museum. At the other side of the Museum parking area, on both sides of Rte. 130, is the herring run.

Each spring, hundreds of herring return to spawn in the waters in which they were born. They swim up the Mashpee River to the herring run, where they must fight their way against the current, up ladders to the pond above, and then on to Mashpee Lake. Their young will then make their way back to the sea, eventually to return to Mashpee waters and the herring run.

If you follow Rte. 130, you can turn left at the Attaquin Park and boat ramp for a visit to Mashpee-Wakeby Lake, the biggest freshwater body on Cape Cod. To continue through the Upper Cape, turn right into Great Neck Road, or Central Avenue as it is also called, where the Town Hall, Town Library, and Baptist Church are located. Farther on is the Mashpee Rotary, which will point you to North Falmouth, Falmouth, New Seabury, and South Cape Beach, or Hyannis. There is a shopping center at the rotary.

Mashpee consists of almost 24 square miles, including 26 miles of oceanfront. The summer population is practically six times the year-round population. Unlike most towns on the Cape, Mashpee has a considerable amount of manufacturing, which accounts for half of the employment. One of the objectives of the Tribal Council, according to executive director Jim Peters, is to further economic development among Indian natives in Barnstable County. The Council plays a social service role by helping people with legal and personal problems. It also hopes to renovate some older buildings in town and to keep the Indian Museum open.

Popponesset and New Seabury

Popponesset is an older summer settlement of cottages and year-round homes. New Seabury has built a number of subdivisions, golf courses, tennis courts, and full resort facilities along the coast. At its easternmost extremity, Popponesset Beach becomes a narrow jut of land called the Spit. Parking in the area is difficult, but the Spit is a wonderful place for a walk. Pilings remain from the Popponesset Community Building and dock, which stood on the Spit before they were destroyed by a hurricane. The Spit is a slender wand of sand, dusty miller (a type of plant covered with dustlike down), beach grass, and shells. Year after year, however, winds and tides strip its ocean edge, dumping the sand in the bay behind; little landmarks become distorted, and eventually the ocean may cut through and totally erode it. This natural process is going on continually in Mashpee's numerous saltwater inlets, coves, and rivers, and throughout the Cape.

It's about five miles back to the Mashpee Rotary from New Seabury, then go on to Rte. 28 and Falmouth, the second largest town on the Cape.

Falmouth

Falmouth was the first place Englishmen landed in the New World. Bartholomew Gosnold sailed from Falmouth, England, on March 23, 1602, with a crew of 32 men. On May 14, they saw land. The natives who paddled out to meet their ship spoke some English and wore some articles of European clothing. Gosnold landed at Woods Hole on May 31, 1602. He had intended to found a colony at Cuttyhunk, one of the Elizabeth Islands, but his settlers decided not to stay there.

Some think that the Vikings may have beaten Gosnold to Falmouth; there is speculation that written references to Vinoland in Leif Erickson's day may have meant this area.

Like Sandwich, Falmouth was named for an English seaport, but its earlier name, Succanessett, was given by the Indians. In 1659, Plymouth Colony granted permission to Thomas Hinkley, Henry Cobb, Samuel Hinkley, John Jenkins, and Nathaniel Bacon of Barnstable to view and buy land at "Saconessett." Thomas Hinkley and Richard Bourne were granted the same permission to deal with the local Indians. Apparently the settlers wanted to remove themselves from the religious repression of Quakers that was taking place in Sandwich and Barnstable. Isaac Robinson led a Barnstable contingent to a settlement in West Falmouth, which remained a Quaker stronghold until about the time of the Civil War. The meeting house and horse sheds still stand along Rte. 28A, and Quaker descendants are still living in the area.

People spent their time securing a living from the land and sea; they fished and raised corn and sheep. There may have been a distinctively feisty strain in the settlers, however, for one historian writes, with some affection: "It was never a town where peace abounded—quite the reverse. Its citizens all wanted their own way, according to the Pilgrim habit, and the majority always had it, according to the law." The writer continues to say that during the relatively peaceful times preceding the American Revolution, Falmouth residents, hard-pressed for controversy, spent a great deal of time debating the merit of repairing the old meeting house, leaving it as was, or building a new one. The deeper issue was probably whether the town was ready to split and divide to create another center of town life.

Falmouth was able to find a worthy adversary for its "bellicose

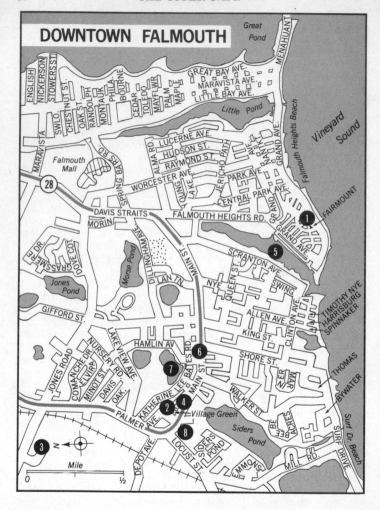

DOWNTOWN FALMOUTH

Points of Interest

1) Great Hill
2) Falmouth Historical Society
3) Falmouth Hospital
4) East End Meeting House
5) Falmouth Harbor
6) Falmouth Library
7) Shiverick's Pond
8) Katherine Lee Bates House

spirit" during the Revolutionary War. It was one of the few communities on the Cape that was attacked by the British. An English fleet had captured a Falmouth schooner, which was handily recaptured by a small group of militiamen led by Colonel Joseph Dimmick. British plans to retaliate were overheard and passed on to Dimmick. Heavy musket fire repelled landing troops, and little damage was done to the town by shots from warships anchored in the harbor. During the War of 1812, the British ship *Nimrod* sailed up to Falmouth shores, demanded that the town's cannons be handed over, and allowed two hours for delivery or evacuation. A stalwart refusal by Captain Weston Jenkins prompted heavy fire, which knocked down a few salt works and created some historic sites—the Elm Arch Inn and the Nimrod Inn still proudly show their battle scars.

The village green in the center of Falmouth was set aside in 1749 as common property for the town's 600 residents. It was used for a military training field and a meeting house lot. Now at Christmastime, it is lighted up with a beautiful display.

During the 1800s, Falmouth was involved in the whaling industry. At one point, there were 148 sea captains out of 300 Falmouth households, prompting someone to say that it was safe calling anyone over 40 "Captain." Today the homes of the sea captains contribute to the charm of this seaside town.

Shipbuilding was another Falmouth industry. The ship *William Penn* from Falmouth has an unusual story. Quakers predicted that it would have bad luck because too much work on Sunday had gone into its construction. Sure enough, a mate was killed, two boat crews were captured by hostile natives, Captain Lincoln took sick, and finally the ship was lost in a wreck on the Island of Whytbotask. So much for Sunday labor in Falmouth.

Another 19th-century Falmouth legend involves angry controversy over an East Falmouth mill, which had a dam that was blocking the herrings' path. A frustrated, aggrieved townsman loaded a cannon on the green with dead herring, fired it, and was promptly killed when the cannon exploded.

Agricultural enterprise thrived in Falmouth. Cranberries were grown commercially, forming a leading industry in the late 1800s. In 1895, about 15,000 barrels were sold. Deacon Lorenzo Eldred is credited with bringing the tart red berry to the area. Sailors from the Cape Verde Islands settled in East Falmouth and made strawberries a leading crop. One farmer alone cultivated 17 acres of strawberries, which were ideally suited to the warm climate and sandy soils. Dudley Hallett of the Falmouth Historical Society remembers the early 1900s, when back roads were filled with the scent of strawberries and truck after truck pulled up to the farms to load the crop. For three cents a quart you could pick your own.

Many acres of forestland were cleared to make pastures for cattle and sheep. Salt-marsh hay in Waquoit provided bedding. Shivericks Pond in Falmouth Center was used for sheep washing in May. There were carding mills in East Falmouth and Waquoit. Fishing, of course, was a steady industry.

The production of guano fertilizer had a brief 30-year existence in Woods Hole. Guano, or sea bird excrement, was considered ideal for fertilizer production. The Pacific Guano Company had ships returning from the Orient with empty holds stop at the Howland and Baker Islands in the Pacific and pick up loads of guano on their way back to the East Coast. The plant on Penzance Point, which is now an elite neighborhood, was never too popular with local people, who were quite pleased when competition drove the firm out of business.

During the Revolution, when salt was selling for $8 a bushel, Falmouth residents decided to make further use of their location by the sea. Materials were inexpensive, and the sun provided the labor for extracting salt from the ocean. In 1845, the 42 salt-works in Falmouth produced 24,500 bushels of salt. The last salt-works was located in Falmouth Heights on the site of the Alden Motel.

Another kind of industry got its start during the middle of the 1800s when Joseph Storey Fay perceived the potential of Woods Hole as a summering place. He ultimately bought 2,000 acres of land in Falmouth, and many wealthy Bostonians followed his lead. In 1896, the year-round population was 2,600 and the summer population was 5,000. The town as a whole has benefited from the benevolence of families like the Fays, Beebees, and Lillys, who have given it churches, sports and arts centers, and parks. They were often seen as a threat, however, by the sea captains and others in power who pushed for progress, while the summer people voted for status quo.

Second to Barnstable in population on the Cape, Falmouth had 23,640 year-round residents in 1980. It has the biggest downtown area in the Upper Cape. With 1,500 acres of sheltered bays and harbors, as well as 1,740 acres of freshwater ponds and 68 miles of coast, it's not hard to see why Falmouth has been popular with both early settlers and modern travelers. The town covers 44.5 square miles. Facilities include Falmouth Hospital, which has an emergency room and coronary care unit, and eight public schools.

Waquoit

Coming from Mashpee along Rte. 28, the first Falmouth village you come to is Waquoit. It is one of the eight or nine depending on what you count villages that came into being as Falmouth grew and expanded; today the villages comprise the town. Waquoit developed as a farming settlement, for it was rural and had a lot of open country. Marshes provided a plentiful supply of salt hay. There was a saw-and-grist mill on the Moonowist River at one point, as well as a yarn and cloth mill in the area. Small sloops put into Waquoit Bay to get herring for bait for fishing on the Grand Banks, where the shellfishing has always been good.

The Waquoit Congregational Church was organized with 18 members on February 2, 1848, it's on Rte. 28 on the right, There are some nice old homes and pretty views of Waquoit Bay along the road, which reaches East Falmouth after a few miles.

East Falmouth

East Falmouth is a fairly large area, centered around an intersection on Rte. 28. Roads off to the right go back to the farmlands that remain. The village developed around farming, primarily strawberry and cranberry crops, but much of the land has been sold for housing subdivisions. Many of the Cape Verde sailors who left the sea for farming in Falmouth eventually owned large amount of land; the generations that followed them have retained interest in their island heritage. To the left of Rte. 28 are deep inlets and long fingers of land that are pretty heavily settled with summer cottages and year-round homes.

The East End Meeting House, built in 1797, is located on Sandwich Rd. Around 1840, it was turned so its gables faced the main road, and a steeple and bell were added. For a lovely drive to Falmouth, take the Shore Road, which begins at Central Avenue.

Teaticket and Falmouth Heights

Rte. 28 goes from East Falmouth to Teaticket. Teaticket has many stores and shops. There is no obvious break between Falmouth Center and this village, whose name comes from the *Tataket,* the name of an Indian tribe. It has its own post office.

To get to Falmouth Heights, follow Rte. 28 past the Falmouth

Plaza and go straight. It is the area to the left of the Falmouth Harbor.

Falmouth Heights is a larger, more definable area than Teaticket, but it has no post office and is not considered a village. The area affords a beautiful view of Martha's Vineyard. Early in Falmouth's history, Queen Awashonks, a Wampanoag ruler from Rhode Island, summered here on "the Great Hill" with her retinue. Thousands have enjoyed its view and sandy beach expanse since the Falmouth Heights Land and Wharf Company began promoting development in the 1800s. During that time, steamers pulled into the wharf regularly to pick up and discharge passengers. Distinguished clientele stayed at the Terrace Gables, now known as the Brothers Four, a favorite hangout of the college-aged set and anyone with a taste for live rock. People who have seen the Heights through good times and bad have a deep, affectionate regard for it.

Follow Rte. 28 to the right into Falmouth Center.

Falmouth

Between Teaticket and the Woods Hole Road, Rte. 28 is lined with all manner of stores, shops, and tourist accommodations. Turn left down Scranton Avenue to get to Falmouth Harbor; you can follow the shore from there all the way down to Woods Hole along Surf Drive. Consider Rte. 28 as Main Street for now. The Artists' Guild on the right was once Yost Tavern. The waterfront lies on the left. From the Falmouth Library, you can look across at Main Street stores and see the contrast between their contemporary store fronts and their older roofs. Shiverick's Pond behind and past the library is often host to sailboats and ducks. The village green is ringed by old churches, old homes, and the Historical Society buildings.

Keep to the left of the green and turn left on the Woods Hole Road for Woods Hole.

Woods Hole

It's about four miles to Woods Hole from the point where Rte. 28 makes a right angle turn to the north. You pass Little Harbor and the Coast Guard installation just before you get to town. Make a left for the ferry or a right onto Water Street for the rest of Woods Hole. Parking is as hard to find as a miser's will, but the problem is something you'll have in common with the natives.

What Woods Hole has to offer is different from what the rest of Falmouth, or the Cape for that matter, offers. It is a scientific community that includes the Northeast Fisheries Center of the National Marine Fisheries, which was established to study fish management and conservation in the late 1800s; the Marine Biological Laboratory, which conducts research and has one of the most extensive biology libraries in the world; and the Woods Hole Oceanographic Institute, established in 1930 to study all branches of oceanography. The latter organization maintains three research vessels, including the one-man submarine *Alvin*, which retrieved a lost nuclear bomb off the coast of Spain several years ago.

In Woods Hole Harbor, the tidal difference between Vineyard Sound and Buzzards Bay can create a six-knot current that pulls huge channel buoys on their sides. The village is an interesting place to visit on foot when you have time to explore and poke in the small shops on Water Street. The Oceanographic Institute has a seasonal display on School Street. For a nice drive or bike ride, take School Street out of town. It becomes Quisset Avenue, then Sippewisset, before returning to Rte. 28. You'll pass the Woods Hole Golf Club and Quissett Harbor on the left. Take Rte. 28 for speed or Rte. 28A for scenery to West Falmouth. Before we move on to West Falmouth, however, mention should be made of the often ignored Elizabeth Islands.

The Elizabeth Islands

The Elizabeth Islands lie in a chain off the tip of Woods Hole. All except Cuttyhunk are privately owned by the Forbes family. For the most part they are uninhabited, but still interesting to see by boat. Swimming is permitted at some designated spots, but usually visitors are not allowed to venture inland on the Elizabeths without special permission.

Uncatena and Nonamesset lie nearest the mainland, and are visible from Woods Hole. Naushon, eight-miles long and the largest of the chain, is next, with its woods of oak, beech, dogwood, cedar, and many other kinds of trees. Beautiful Tarpaulin Cove, on the island's south side, has a colorful history as a hideout for pirates, British fleets, and Prohibition rum runners. You may anchor there to swim and picnic on the beach, but no fires are permitted.

The Weepeckets are tiny, rocky additions to the chain, lying north of Naushon. Pasque, just below Naushon, is a barren square mile of rocks and swamps. Farther south lies Nashawena, also known as Little Naushon. Although much of the island is low and swampy, Nashawena's landscape is distinguished by 90-foot cliffs that form a steep drop down to Vineyard Sound. Penikese, the island northwest of Nashawena, was once a leper colony; it is now the location of a work-study correctional school for young adults.

At the southernmost end of the Elizabeth chain lies Cuttyhunk, the only one of the islands that can be reached by public passenger ferry. It is also served by seaplane. Two guesthouses operate for overnight visitors (see the Practical Information section in this chapter for details). Much of Cuttyhunk is privately-owned, but there is still enough public land to attract sportsfishermen, birdwatchers, and sightseers eager to enjoy Cuttyhunk's few miles of open meadows, wild rosebushes, bayberries, ocean views, and peaceful atmosphere.

West Falmouth

The Quakers settled in West Falmouth in the 1600s, and there are some old houses and historical spots here. It remained primarily an agricultural area until development along the coast began in 1925. The big grist mill that served this area was sold to Dutchland Farm in Brockton for advertising purposes. Saconesset Homestead, built in 1678, is open to the public.

North Falmouth and Hatchville

John and Ebenezer Nye were granted land in North Falmouth around 1689. It remained in the family for several hundred years until the Silver Beach Land Company bought and developed the land. In the prosperous years that followed the first World War, many people built summer homes in the area around beautiful Old Silver Beach.

Hatchville is the area to the right of North Falmouth, south of Rte. 151. There is a post office, but no central village here. Golf clubs, riding stables, the Nickelodian movie theater, and the Falmouth Playhouse are drawing cards to the area, which developed around farming. When residents felt it was too far to go into Falmouth, they pushed for a new meeting house and the two parishes of North Falmouth and Hatchville were established. The latter was probably named for Moses Hatch, the first child born in Falmouth.

The Otis/Edwards Military Reservation

Despite the fact that the reservation consists of separate military units, it is most commonly called "Otis." Otis Air National Guard, Camp Edwards, and the Coast Guard Air Station Cape Cod take up about 14,700 acres to the north of Falmouth, in roughly the center of the Upper Cape. There are entrance gates in Falmouth, Bourne, and Sandwich. A National Cemetery was recently established at the reservation.

During the 1930s, the military maintained a small airfield at the Camp Edwards reservation. In the second World War, anti-submarine aircraft regularly patrolled the coast for German U-Boats. The field became an Air Force Base during the late '40s when the 33rd Fighter Group relocated. Other active jet air surveillance and combat units from the Air National Guard and the Air Force have followed. The base was named after Lt. Frank Otis, a well-liked ANG pilot, flight surgeon, and member of the 101st Observation Squadron, who was killed in a training mission.

Camp Edwards has been a training site for soldiers since 1930, but the equipment has changed considerably. Heavy artillery and mortar firing at the practice range bring in occasional complaints, but on the whole, the Reservation makes an accommodating, if noisy, neighbor. Its Coast Guard Air Station, for example, is practiced at plucking unlucky sailors from the sea, and the station's search and rescue territory extends from Rhode Island to Canada. The white planes and helicopters are highly visible when they set off on a mission.

Oil spill detection and abatement, drug traffic, and enforcement of the Two Hundred Mile Limit, a federally designated protective zone for U.S. fisheries, make demands on the Coast Guard's time and expertise. It also monitors the temperature of the Gulf Stream.

PAVE PAWS in an acronym for the highly sophisticated radar system at the Reservation. From the Sagamore Bridge, it looks something like a drive-in movie screen. Its purpose is to search for sub-launched ballistic missles and objects in space; the detection range is 3,000 miles.

Bourne: A Late Bloomer

By historical quirk, the oldest and the youngest town on Cape Cod were once one and the same. Bourne separated from Sandwich in 1884. There is no reacy explanation for the dramatic move. The issue of separation was put to a vote at Town Meeting and was voted down, but the dissident villages went directly to the State Legislature to have an Act of Incorporation drawn up.

Bourne appears to have had considerable economic stability before the separation; perhaps the outlying villages didn't want to support or be tied to Sandwich as it was faltering with the demise of the glass industry. The earliest Bourne residents had to walk eight or more miles to church in Sandwich each week; it was required by law. They carried their shoes to spare the leather. Business had to be conducted in Sandwich. Rivalry was surely promoted by the recorded practice in the 1800s of occasionally conducting official town meeting business after the last train of the day left with the voters from the Bourne villages.

Like marriage partners trying to keep the divorce clean, Sandwich and Bourne worked hard at projecting a polite, no-hard-feelings image. Assets were tallied. They came to $21,416.01. Debts were inspected: "School bill paid—$5,364.07"; "Pauper bill paid—$2,613,46." When the ledger was balanced, there was about $1,000 to be divided. Even maps showing the new division made it look like a geographically tidy 50-50 split.

Bourne got the warm-water coast, the summer mansions, and the blueprints of a major shipping canal. Sandwich retained rights to fishing and shellfishing in those warm waters, however, and Bourne has regretted the arrangement ever since. As recently as 1980, a Bourne hearing was held on the implementation of new shellfishing programs, and the subject of the old law was raised with obvious rancor. The new Bourne-Sandwich Shellfish Association is working toward creating better shellfish and neighbor relations.

Several tribes of Indians of the Wampanoag Federation lived in Bourne long before the white settlers came. Some way there is still evidene of the old Megansett Indian trail that led between Bourne and Falmouth, if you know where to look. E. G. Perry, writing 100 years ago, mentioned the ancient track worn deep into the earth and winding from pond to pond. The Great Rock described in legend and historical accounts supposedly marked the beginning of the trail. Located about a mile and a half from the Bourne rotary, it is now surrounded by a housing subdivision on Waterhouse Road.

Conversion of the Indians in this area was an objective of the same Richard Bourne who was influential in Mashpee. Because it fell into disuse, the meeting house that was built for his flock in Bournedale was taken down. In the late 1700s, it was transported, oak frame, cedar sills, and all, and rebuilt in South Pocasset, now

Cataumet. At that time, there were as many Indians as whites in the village. An account from 1875 says the first minister, Rev. Elisha Tupper, preached half the day in English and half the day in the Indian language. Tupper was the grandson of Thomas Tupper of Sandwich, one of four generations of preachers who served the Indians.

In 1639, nearly a decade before Sandwich was incorporated, the Pilgrims built a trading post on the banks of the Manomet River in the present village of Bourne. The intent was to establish a fur trade with Dutch settlers in New Amsterdam, but it quickly expanded to include trade with French Canadians and local Indians. Its Indian name, "Aptucxet," meant "little trap by the river." The post was closed in the late 1650s, possibly because other trade centers developed around new towns. About 300 years later, an archeological exploration of the original site unearthed an old foundation, hearthstone, root cellars, and a number of artifacts. A reproduction of the Aptucxet Trading Post was built on the site, using parts of an old house.

One historian has said that the independent spirit of the Cape Codder shows in his roads and his graveyards. A fine example of this exists in the village of Bourne, where five roads intersect. Nearby is the Old Bourne Cemetery. "The burial place of the two strangers" is its unofficial name. An unknown man died, so the story goes, and was being transported from Falmouth to Sandwich for burial, but a blizzard prevented further travel. Those in charge of the body built a fire near a stone wall to thaw the ground enough a permit a crude burial. A short time later, another unidentified man died at Perry's Tavern and, for whatever reason, was buried beside the first stranger. The owner of the land wisely decided to turn it over to the town for a cemetery.

One of the most extraordinary pieces of Bourne's history links it with the tragic journey of the Acadians Henry Wadsworth Longfellow described in his epic ballad, "Evangeline." Historical accounts mention open boats sailing up the Manomet River loaded with 70 men, women, and children. They sought the help of Sandwich residents in carrying their boats across land to Massachusetts Bay; from there, they hoped to sail on to their Canadian homeland. But they were detained, their boats sold, and their families divided. It is said that a small settlement of Canadians clung together along the Scusset River for a while, but eventually they vanished, leaving only a few wooden pilings.

Like Sandwich, Bourne was essentially rural in the early days and it became industrialized in the 1800s. Fishing and shipbuilding thrived along the coast. There were grist mills, flour mills, a comb and button factory, and lumbering. Some 4,000 cords of wood were shipped from Red Brook wharves still in existence today. Although Turpentine Road is not on Otis land, it was in Bourne when turpentine was extracted from plentiful pines and sent to Boston by packet. Industry required transportation and encouraged railroad development, and the railroad in turn brought summer people. Development of Bourne's beautiful coastline corresponds with the surge of summer colonies at Old Silver Beach and Megansett in Falmouth. Summer people didn't have quite the same impact on town life that was felt in Falmouth, though. Even President Grover Cleveland's summer home, Gray Gables, is a fairly anonymous spot.

Despite its history, which goes back to the earliest settlement of Cape Cod, there is something unfinished about Bourne. The town had been on its own for only 30 years when Cape Cod Canal was built, and this further division must have had a significant impact on the psyche of the community, driving each village to care for its own interests more deeply, at the expense of unified growth. Borune is still in its formative years.

Cataumet

As you drive up Rte. 28 from Falmouth, the first Bourne village you encounter is Cataumet. It was named for an Indian tribe that once lived in the area. There are a number of large summer mansions in the town, dating back to the 19th century; the largest one has about 40 rooms.

The broad peninsula named Scraggy Neck had 13 owners between 1846 and 1892. It sold for $1 on April 18, 1892, was bought back for $50,000, and was finally sold again for $1 to Mrs. William Eustis—all on the same day.

The Cataumet Methodist Church on Old County Road was moved from Bownedale to its present site in 1799. Kingman Marina is off Shore Road.

Pocasset

You can reach Pocasset from the Otis ANG rotary on Rte. 28, or by turning off Rte. 28 at Barlow's Landing. It is similar to Cataumet, with older homes, pretty streets, and lovely ocean views. In the Methodist Cemetery, headstones show Old Cape names such as Swift, Barlow, Nye, Burgess, Wing Dimmock, Handy, and Perry. It was once written of this town's farmers and fishermen: "Almost every man owns the soil on which he treads and the roof which covers his head . . . while there are none rich, neither are there any truly poor.''

In Pocasset, there is a golf course, mental health center, and Barnstable County Hospital.

Monument Beach

Continue on Shore Road from Pocasset to Monument Beach. The entrance to the Cape Cod Canal was originally planned for this area, until rocky ledge prevented work crews from digging any deeper. Beginning in the 1800s, Monument Beach developed as a beach colony, but not it consists mostly of permanent year-round homes. Its beach is one of Bourne's best, and the shellfishing in the area is exception.

The ever changing saltwater marshes on the right of Eel Pond are always fascinating to see. Nearby there is a historical marker where a mill was once located.

Bourne Village

From Monument, stay on Shore Road to the five-cornered intersection in Bourne Village. The Bourne Library on Keene Street used to be the town hall. It has paintings donated by the famous 19-century actor, Joseph Jefferson, who also once owned the Dutch windmill at the Aptucxet Trading Post. The trading post was a center of activity, and the original reason for the development of Bourne Village. The first Bourne public highway, no longer in existence, was probably made of planks. It was built across the Manomet River in 1823 by the Bourne family, who also maintained it.

The next stop you might want to make is Buzzards Bay. To get there, take Trowbridge Road from the Five Corners to the rotary. Cross the Bourne Bridge and go halfway around the next rotary. Keep in mind that few people from Massachusetts realize or acknowledge that rotary traffic has the right of way. It is perfectly acceptable to circle a rotary until you have enough nerve to exit.

Buzzards Bay

The main shopping area in the town of Bourne is Buzzards Bay, where you'll find restaurants, movies, bowling alleys, and bait shops. The Chamber of Commerce is located in the old railroad station. The Massachusetts Maritime Academy is situated here, accounting for the young people in uniform you may see strolling around. If you want to see a lot of happy faces in one place, be at the dock when the Academy's training ship comes in after its summer cruise. The Academy trains young men and women for the Merchant Marine and contributes to the community with excellent sporting events, special classes, and activities. From the Academy, you can get a good look at the area's first railroad bridge.

The bridge, located at Cohasset Narrows, was finished in 1848. It was strongly supported by Deming Jarves of the Boston and Sandwich Glass Company, which needed to have sand, coal, coke, and oil brought in from Maryland, Connecticut, Delaware, and New Jersey. When the new railroad bridge was built, it was the largest in the world. The platform is usually raised horizontally 135 feet in the air to permit boat traffic to pass through on the canal, but it can be lowered to seven feet above the water in less than three minutes when a train needs to come onto the Cape.

Bournedale

This is one of the old areas. There are some stores and motels, the herring run, the U.S. Army Corps of Engineers Visitor Center, and access to the Canal. During the 1800s, there was an axe factory, a drill factory, and a wagon factory in the area. A hollowware factory was built to straddle the Herring River here. However, none of these buildings is still standing.

Sagamore

Continue along the Bourne Scenic Highway to the Sagamore Bridge rotary. To complete your tour of the Upper Cape, you'll have to cross the bridge again to visit Sagamore, which is at Exit 1 off the Mid-Cape Highway. Even natives mistakenly think that the town of Sagamore is in Sandwich rather than Bourne.

The Pairpoint Glass Company and Currie's Leather Guild give tours, during which you can see their products being made. The Keith Car Company, formerly a prominent local manufacturer, was also once located in Sagamore.

In the 1800s, 500 Italian workers were brought to the Sagamore area to help build the Cape Cod canal. Many made their homes here, giving an Italian flavor to a Pilgrim settlement. This is evidenced by the food served in local restaurants and sold in Louis' Market, known through the years for its imported cheeses and meats. The canal isolated parts of the village, placing Sagamore Beach and Sagamore Highlands on one side, and Sagamore Village on the other.

PRACTICAL INFORMATION FOR
UPPER CAPE COD

HOW TO GET AROUND. By car: If you're headed for Cape Cod by car, you will have to cross over the Bourne Bridge on Rte. 28 or the Sagamore Bridge on Rte. 6. Rte. 28 is the best way to get to Falmouth and most of Bourne. Keep in mind that Bourne and Sandwich have land on both sides of the Cape Cod Canal. Rte. 6, usually referred to as the Mid-Cape Highway, will take you to Sagamore (a village in the town of Bourne), Sandwich, and on to the Mid-Cape area. Mashpee is best approached by Rte. 130 off the Mid-Cape Highway, or by Rte. 151 off Rte. 28.

You can pick up Rte. 6A in Sagamore for a pretty trip along Cape Cod Bay on the northern shore of Cape Cod, or you can pick up Rte. 28A at the Otis Rotary on Rte. 28 for a similarly pleasant drive on the Buzzards Bay side. These two roads are pastoral and relatively uncommercial.

By air: There is no commercial air service to the Upper Cape. *Hyannis Airport* is within a 45-minute drive of most places. There is a small private airfield in East Falmouth for single-engine planes. For those wishing to visit Cuttyhunk, in the Elizabeth Islands chain, there is air-taxi service from Fairhaven, Massachusetts, by seaplane. Call *Island Air Service* in Rochester, Massachusetts: 994-1231.

By bus: *Bonanza Bus Lines* has regular service between terminals in Buzzards Bay, Falmouth, Woods Hole, and Hyannis; also interstate service on *Greyhound Lines*, with stops in Boston, Rhode Island, Connecticut, and New York. *Cape Cod Bus Lines* at 11 Walker St. in Falmouth has tours with stops to Provincetown.

By ferry: The *Woods Hole Steamship Authority* provides regular year-round service to Martha's Vineyard and Nantucket. Car reservations are necessary; autos and bikes should arrive early. Pets must be leashed. If the large Woods Hole parking lot is full, there is an overflow lot on Rte. 28, with shuttle service to the dock. Contact the Woods Hole Steamship Authority, Box 284, Woods Hole, Massachusetts 02543; phone 540-2022, or, toll-free 800-352-7104 for information. For visitors to Cuttyhunk, the mailboat, *The Alert*, provides daily service out of New Bedford, Massachusetts. After Labor Day, it sails twice weekly.

By bike: There is a seven-mile bike/hike path on either side of the Cape Cod Canal. It's not difficult and you have a perfect view of the constant boat traffic. U.S. Army Corps of Engineers rangers conduct biking and walking tours. Access points to the path: on the northern side, at Scusset Beach, the Sagamore Bridge, the Bournedale herring run, and the Bourne

Bridge; on the southern side, at the Sandwich marina, Pleasant St. in Sagamore, and the Bourne Bridge.

Falmouth's *Shining Sea Bikeway* attracts cyclists, joggers, and strollers of all ages. The 3.3-mile path crosses woods, saltwater marshes, and beaches between the Falmouth entrance (parking area) on the Woods Hole Rd. and the Woods Hole entrance at the Steamship Authority parking lot. There are bike rental shops in Falmouth Heights and Monument Beach in Bourne.

TOURIST INFORMATION SERVICES. The *Cape Cod Chamber of Commerce* in Hyannis (362-3225) has information and pamphlets about Upper Cape facilities. It maintains an information booth in Sagamore at the rotary just before the bridge. *Bourne* has a Chamber of Commerce office in a renovated railroad station on Main St., Buzzards Bay (759-3122). This office is open from May to Labor Day; the business office is open year-round (888-6202). *Falmouth* has an active Chamber of Commerce in the Lawrence Academy Building off Main St. (548-8500). Each Upper Cape town has a centrally located town hall where staff can provide you with information on beaches, shellfishing, and other local resources.

RECOMMENDED READING. *Falmouth-by-the-Sea,* reprinted with additions by the Falmouth Chamber of Commerce in 1976. *History of Bourne,* by Betsy Keene, published by the Bourne Historical Society in 1937. *History of Cape Cod,* by Frederick Freeman, published by the author in 1859. *Mashpee: Land of the Wampanoag,* by Amelia Bingham, published by the Mashpee Historical Commission in 1970. *Mashpee: The Story of Cape Cod's Indian Town,* by Francis C. Hutchins, published by Armata Press in 1979. *Pilgrim Colony,* by George D. Langdon, Jr., published by Yale University Press in 1966. *Ring Around the Punch Bowl,* by George I. Moses, published by William S. Sullwold Publishing, Inc. *Trip Around Cape Cod*, by E. G. Perry, printed by Chas. S. Binner Co., copyrighted May 31, 1898.

SEASONAL EVENTS. The following activities may vary considerably in their scope and drawing power, but they all impart an essential flavor of the Cape. Sporting events are listed elsewhere.

June. *Antique Dealers Association Show*, Sandwich, Heritage Plantation, late June. *Otis Air Force Base Open House*, Bourne, late June; air shows, exhibits, special demonstrations. *Strawberry Festival*, at Aptucxet Trading Post, by Bourne Historical Society, third Saturday in June. *Strawberry Festival*, at Falmouth Village Green, by St. Barnabas Church, late June. *Thornton Burgess Society Lawn Party*, Burgess Museum on Rte. 130, Sandwich; live animal demonstrations, exhibits, music, refreshments.

July. *Antique Auto Show and Competition*, Sandwich, Heritage Plantation, mid-July. *Art Exhibit–Jury Show*, Falmouth Artist Guild, Main St. *Arts and Crafts Fair and Demonstration*, Sandwich, Heritage Plantation. *Arts and Crafts Street Fair*, Falmouth, Main St. *Barnstable County Fair*, Rte. 151, Falmouth, late July; agriculture and livestock judging, pony pulling contest, entertainment, midway. *Falmouth Historical Society Antique Show*, at the National Guard Armory on Jones Rd. *Fourth of July Events*, in most Upper Cape towns. *Indian Pow-wow*, Mashpee Center, Rte. 130; Indian dances, traditional games, canoe races, clambake, on weekend nearest July 4th. *Marine Biological Laboratory Open House*, Woods Hole; MBL labs, research facilities open, movies, food served outdoors by local restaurants, concert. *Sandwich Library Book Sale*, library grounds, Main St., sale of attic donations, sets. *Sheep Shearing Day*, Saconesset Homestead, Rte. 28A, W. Falmouth.

August. *Annual Chicken Barbecue,* by Sandwich Fire Department, at Hewlett Packard Recreation Area; games and food, last Sunday in August. *Art and Antique Auction*, by Falmouth Artists' Guild, 744 Main St., Falmouth; preview, music. *Annual 4-H Auction*, Rte. 151, Barnstable County Fair Grounds, Falmouth; professional auctioneers, new and old items. *Cape Cod Day*, New Alchemy Institute, Hatchville, Falmouth, workshops, tours, seminars on agriculture and energy alternatives. *Cape Cod Media Hot Air Balloon Race* for the Doreen Grace Fund, Rte. 151 at Barnstable County Fair Grounds, held Labor Day weekend; professional balloonists race "to somewhere"; for information, contact Richard Grace, 263-3535. *Lotus Festival*, Ashumet Holly Reservation, Rte. 151, N. Falmouth; bonsai display, Oriental dancing, kimono parade. *Quahog Boat Race*, by Bourne-Sandwich Shellfishing Association, at Basset's Island, Pocasset; boat races on 1.8-mile course, children's activities, light refreshments.

October. *Bourne Scallop Festival*, Legion Hall, Buzzards Bay, on Columbus Day weekend. *Franklinia Festival*, Ashumet Holly Reservation, Rte. 151, N. Falmouth; the Franklinia tree is the focus of activities; crafts, garden displays, dance, refreshments. *Sandwich House Tour*, by Sandwich Woman's Club; tour of interesting homes, old and new.

November and December. *Bourne Thanksgiving Parade*, Main St., Buzzards Bay. *Falmouth Christmas Parade*, Main St., Falmouth; bands, floats; early December. *Holly Days*, Ashumet Holly Reservation, Rte. 151, N. Falmouth; sale of holly and greens.

HISTORIC SITES. Old and historical buildings are often disguised by present use. The 200-year-old building in N. Falmouth known as Paul's Market, for example, looks like any other small grocery. Eben Keith was a powerful and important man in Sagamore's thriving industrial days; his impressive white clapboard house on Pleasant St., and visible from Rte. 6A, now provides office space for an optometrist.

Many buildings are gone forever, their existence identified only by a stone foundation, wooden pilings, and faded photographs. Such is the case with the famous Boston and Sandwich Glass Co., formerly located on Factory Street. A plaque, some rubble and brush mark the spot. The mile-long Keith Car and Manufacturing Co. dominated the banks of the Cape Cod Canal in the early 1900s. It was once the largest employer in New England—now the company's buildings are simply gone.

Perhaps because their function is generally unchanged, churches and cemeteries often survive the years intact. A few are included in this list of historical sites.

Bourne. *Aptucxet Trading Post*, off Shore Rd., Bourne. Originally built in 1627 for trading, especially furs, between the Pilgrims and the Dutch. Site of the first known business contract in America. Post site was reno- vated by the Bourne Historical Society in 1930. Includes displays of Indian and trading artifacts, an old saltworks operation, a Dutch windmill, and a small railroad station used by President Grover Cleveland who summered in Gray Gables. Also a Runic stone found in Bournedale. Open Apr. to Nov., 10 A.M.–5 P.M. Closed Tuesdays in Apr., May, Oct., Nov.

Burying Hill, Herring Pond Rd., off Rte. 6, Bournedale. Indian burial ground for group of 180 Praying Indians led by minister Thomas Tupper. King Saul was reported to be the last Indian buried there in 1810. The graves are unmarked; a bronze plaque in nearby park notes the site.

Cataumet Methodist Church, Old County Rd. Built in 1765 at the foot of Burying Hill as a meeting house for Indians. Moved in 1799 to Cataumet and in 1893 to its present site. The Cataumet cemetery across the street contains interesting gravestones.

Leonard Wood Homestead, 866 Shore Rd., Pocasset. Childhood home of General Wood, who commanded Teddy Roosevelt and his Rough Riders in Cuba in 1898. Governor general in the Philippines, contender for 1920 Republican presidential nomination. Not presently open to the public.

Falmouth. *The Candle House*, Water St., Woods Hole. A distinctive stone building once used as a spermaceti candle factory. It is owned by the Marine Biological Laboratory and used for storage.

First Congregational Church, on the Village Green, Falmouth. Built in 1708. Church bell made by Paul Revere has the inscription "The living to the Church I call, and to the Grave I summon all."

Friends Meeting House, Rte. 28A, West Falmouth. Built in 1775, this is the third meeting house in the vicinity. Horse shed across the street built around 1861. Cemetery nearby.

Mill Rd. Cemetery, Falmouth. Early Falmouth settlers of the 1700s and Revolutionary War soldiers buried here.

Old Indian Burial Ground, Chester Rd., N. Falmouth. No gravestones, only a marker in Nye Memorial Park.

Surf Drive Beach Markers, Falmouth. A marker at the foot of Shore St. commemorates the arrival site of the first settlers in 1660. Remains of a stone dock nearby where packets came in. Another marker at the beach notes the April 3, 1779, British attack on Falmouth, which was successfully repelled by the militia.

Mashpee. *Indian Meeting House and Burial Ground*, Rte. 28. The church was built in 1684 on Santuit Pond and moved to its present location in 1717. The lumber was sent from England to Plymouth, then carried by oxen to Mashpee. Headstones were used in the cemetery; other Indian burial grounds were at Bryant's Neck and west of Mashpee Lake. The church is open daily from 9–4 in the summer; at other times, by appointment (477-0208).

Sandwich. *Dexter Mill*, Sandwich Center. The first mill at the site was built by Thomas Dexter sometime before 1654. It was destroyed and rebuilt; the restoration work was done by the town in 1961. Working mill; ground corn on sale. Open daily during summer.

Hoxie House, Rte. 130, Sandwich Center. Reputed to be oldest house on Cape Cod (1637), although some Sandwich residents dispute it. Classic saltbox, named for 1800s owner, Abraham Hoxie, a whaling captain. Furnishings on loan by Boston Museum of Fine Arts. Open daily during summer, 10–4.

Nye House, Old County Rd., E. Sandwich. Seventeenth century home of Benjamin Nye, early Sandwich settler. Furniture, household goods, nautical instruments displayed. Open mid-May to Oct., 10–4:30, Sun., 1–4, closed Mon.

Quaker Meeting House, Spring Hill Rd., E. Sandwich. Built in 1810, following others erected on the site for the Society of Friends; the site dates to 1657. The public is welcome at Sunday services at 11:00 A.M. during July and August and for visiting on Wednesday afternoon. Headstones in the cemetery behind the church date to the 1600s.

Old Cemetery Point, Grove St., Sandwich Center. The town's first cemetery, located on the banks of Shawme Pond, has gravestones of Revolutionary War soldiers.

MUSEUMS. Falmouth. *Bradley House Museum*, Woods Hole Rd., Woods Hole. Third oldest house in the village owned by Captain Bradley who was lost at sea. Opened for Woods Hole Historical Collection in 1976. Early photographs and historical material. Open 11–4 during July and Aug., Tues.–Sat.; in June, Sept., and Oct., Wed. and Sat.

Falmouth Historical Society, Village Green, Falmouth. Includes two impressive historic homes and gardens. Julia Wood House, a hip-roofed colonial with widow's walk built in 1790. Original owner was Dr. Francis Wicks, a medical corpsman during the American Revolution and founder of Cape Cod's first hospital. Portraits, toys, colonial kitchen. Herb and memorial gardens, thrift shop in back. Conant House Museum next door. Whaling items, scrimshaw, silver, glass, china. Library and resource center. Both houses open Mon.–Fri., 2–5, mid-June to mid-Sept.

Katherine Lee Bates House, 16 West Main St., Falmouth. Home of the author of "America the Beautiful." Victorian parlor, books, manuscripts, pictures, memorabilia. June 15 to Sept. 15; closed weekends.

Saconesset Homestead, Rte. 28A, W. Falmouth. Built in 1678 by Thomas Bowerman, a Quaker who fled religious persecution in Barnstable. Home kept in the family for nine generations. Furniture, tools, documents, books, clothing. Antique shop, livestock, picnic area. Open Memorial Day to Oct., Tues.–Sun.

Mashpee. *Indian Museum*, Rte. 130, near Mashpee Center. Historical building by herring run, contains Indian artifacts, tools, clothing, furniture. Opened on request; contact Mashpee Town Hall (477-0222).

Sandwich. *Heritage Plantation*, Grove St. Prestigious rhododendron and azalea gardens, woods, walking path, on 76-acre estate of Charles Dexter. Antique car collection includes Stutz Bearcat, 1931 Dusenberg, and a 1922 U.S.-made Rolls Royce. Antique gun, flag and military miniatures in the Military Museum. Free ride on old carousel, art displays, working windmill on grounds. Special displays and activities throughout the season. Open daily May to Oct.

Sandwich Glass Museum, Tupper Rd., Sandwich Center. Most extensive collection of Sandwich glass in U.S. Special exhibits and lectures. Open Apr. 1 to Nov. 15, 9:30–4.

Thornton Burgess Museum, Rte. 130, Sandwich Center. Located at the 1756 Deacon Eldred House on Shawme Pond, which was restored by the Sandwich Woman's Club. Displays include memorabilia and books written by naturalist and children's author Burgess, who was born in Sandwich. Gift items. Summer activities for children—nature walks, wild animal demonstrations, storytime. Open daily, mid-June–Sept.

Yesteryear Doll Museum, Main St., Sandwich Center. Extensive doll collection from around the world, some dolls 500 years old. Doll houses, miniature furnishings. Collectors' shop. Museum building was formerly First Parish Meeting House, oldest parts built in 1630s. Open Memorial Day to Columbus Day, daily.

Note. Important historical and genealogical material is also kept at town archives. *Bourne*, Archives Room in the School Administration Building on Sandwich Rd., open Tues., 9–3. *Falmouth*, Resource Center, maintained by Historical Society, Village Green. *Sandwich*, Town Archives, Town Hall Annex, Main St., open daily.

 LIBRARIES. *Jonathan Bourne Library*, Keene St., Bourne. In 1887, Emily Bourne donated a library to the town that bore her father's name. The location was chosen before the Cape Cod Canal separated the site from the town in Buzzards Bay. It contains a children's library, and large-print books for the visually handicapped. A bust of Jonathan Bourne on display was carved by Gutzon Borglon, who made the Mt. Rushmore figures. Buzzards Bay branch, bookmobile.

Falmouth Public Library, Main St., Falmouth. Largest library on Cape Cod, a Massachusetts sub-regional library. Extensive children's library and reading room, special programs. Microfilm of *New York Times* from 1850 to present, *Falmouth Enterprise* from 1897 to present. Branch libraries in E. Falmouth and N. Falmouth.

Sandwich Public Library, Main St., Sandwich. Extensive reference materials, children's library and reading room, special programs. Large-print books and talking book machines. Dodge MacKnight Reading Room, displays of the artist's watercolors. Special collections, art objects, book-mobile.

TOURS. Railroad. *Cape Cod and Hyannis Railroad, Inc.* 771-1145. Revival of passenger rail service between Hyannis and Sandwich. One-hour ride with detailed commentary on countryside. Additional tours of Sandwich Glass Museum or Heritage Plantation, or walking tour of historic Sandwich.

Bus. *Cape Cod Bus Lines*, 11 Walker Ave., Falmouth, has day-long sightseeing tours to Provincetown with stops. *Gray Lines*, 29 Providence St., Boston, Massachusetts. A Cape Cod Bay and Villages tour, 8½ hrs., includes Sandwich.

Ferry. *Cape Cod Canal Cruises*, leaves from Onset, Massachusetts, daily June through Oct. Two-and-a-half-hour tour of Martha's Vineyard on the *Island Queen*, with stops. Leaves from Falmouth Harbor, on Falmouth Heights Rd. Also, an *Island Queen* Canal cruise; a three-hour cruise of five Falmouth and Martha's Vineyard harbors; a moonlight cruise with band and dancing.

SHOPPING. Many lovely and unusual gift items reflect the inspiration artists find in the Cape's natural beauty. A complete list of good shops, galleries, and stores would be impossibly long. The following places will give the reader an idea of the variety of shopping possibilities. Every Upper Cape town has at least one central shopping mall or retail area, but be prepared to do as the natives do when shopping; travel and hunt.

Falmouth is the largest town on the Upper Cape, and it has a number of long-established retail businesses. Main St. offers a potpourri of good shops, ranging from *Mrs. Weeks Yarn Shop* to *Caline's Children Shop* to *Seminara's Delicatessen.* There are interesting shops at the Queen's By-way, including some antique stores. The Falmouth Mall and the Plaza are other major shopping areas. Woods Hole has some unusual shops; most have limited hours off season. Bourne's village of Buzzards Bay has the next largest retail shopping area.

Bourne: *The Antique Mart*, 67 Main St., Buzzards Bay; collectibles, furniture, auctions; open 9–5 Fri.–Sun. year-round. *Barry's Locker*, at Kingman Marina, Cataumet; hand-carved birds, nautical gifts, and clothing. *Bournedale Country Store*, 26 Herring Pond Rd., Bournedale; handicrafts, antique toys; daily June to Oct. *Cataumet Pottery*, Post Office

Square, Cataumet; Nancy Gorbach's work, functional pottery, wind-chimes. *Jiminy Cricket*, Shore Rd., Pocasset; local hand-crafted items and international gifts. *The Old House*, 291 Head-of-the-Bay Rd.; antiques and Christmas gifts, glass, china; house more than 250 years old; closed Feb. *Pairpoint Glass Works*, 851 Sandwich Rd., Sagamore; watch craftsmen form bowls, candlesticks, vases from molten glass; factory store has firsts and seconds, cup plates; open June to Oct., 9–8 daily. *Pocasset Exchange*, 710 Old County Rd., Pocasset; antiques, collectibles, books, items on consignment; former home of owner of iron mill at the site. *Sagamore Leather Guild*, Rte. 6A, Sagamore; small leather factory; bags and belts made and sold; interesting collectibles and antiques; open year-round, 9–4. *The Stitchery*, Trading Post Corners, Bourne; quilted pillows, bed coverings, clothing, small items; fabric and quilting supplies. *Suzanne's Bakery*, 269 Barlow's Landing Rd., Pocasset; changing displays of paintings, photography, pottery, and quilting for sale, as well as fresh-baked goods.

Falmouth: *Brass Gallery*, 536 Main St.; brass furniture, articles; also repairs. *Cape Cod Candles*, Rte. 28; extensive gift assortment. *Dick Sawdo*, 97 Water St., Woods Hole; realistic ornamental carved birds; a folk art form that originated with decoy painting, earliest roots on the Cape, says Sawdo; he also sells introductory bird carving kits; by appointment, 540-3837. *Edward R. Bacon Grain Co.*, Queens Byway, Falmouth; bird seed, feeders, bird motif gifts of all kinds. *Falmouth Artists' Guild*, 744 Main St.; galleries open Tues.–Sun. during summer; art in all mediums; lessons, workshops, displays, Christmas fair, photography, prints, ceramics, summer auction. Juried annual show. *Fannie's Corner*, at back of Eastman's Hardware, Main St.; a smaller shop with nice variety of country kitchen articles. *For Arts Sake*, 1 Locust St.; art, architectural, and drafting materials; framing, graphic design service; children's area. *From Far Corners*, 22 Water St., Woods Hole; women's clothing, Greek, Indian, European imports, jewelry. *The Grain Mill*, Depot Ave., Falmouth; antiques, shop and agricultural supplies in authentic 1890 mill. *Howling Bird Studios*, Queens Byway, Falmouth and Water Sts., Woods Hole; artsy T-shirts, endangered species, Woods Hole scenes; silk-screened clothing, hand-printed clothing by local artisans. *Market Barn Gallery and Bookshop*, Depot Ave., Falmouth, Water St., Woods Hole; hardcover and paperback children's selections. Gallery on Depot Ave. displays painting, sculpture, other art mediums at 19th-century barn; open June to Sept., Mon.–Sat. *Shell Shop*, Queens Byway; assortment of shells and arrangements, local and otherwise. *Uncle Bill's Country Store*, at the Silver Lounge in N. Falmouth; antiques, penny candies, interesting articles. *Under the Sun*, Water St., Woods Hole; original leather goods, clay flounders, pottery, stained-glass ships, jewelry by Cape artisans. *Waquoit Glass Works*, 42 Carriage Shop Rd., off Rte. 28; workshop and studio; custom stained-glass windows, mirror boxes, Tiffany-style shades, small gift items; year-round, Mon.–Fri. and Sat. morning. *Wendy Terra*, 208 Main St., Falmouth; tasteful gift store; pottery, photographs, jewelry, artwork, mobiles. *Woods Hole Gallery*, 14 School St.; works of local artists, also specialize in conservation of oil paintings; closed Wed. *Woods Hole Community Building* on Water St., Woods Hole; several small galleries at the lower level, including Woods Hole Stoneware Pottery Shop, with functional tableware and cookware.

Mashpee: *Chop N' Block*, Rte. 130, Main St.; windmills and woodburning stoves and wood supplies. *Dick and Ellie's Flea Market*, Rte. 28 near rotary; a bargain hunter's must; Sat.–Sun., 8–5. *Cape Cod Bookstore*, Rte. 28 at Merry Meadow Byway; large paperback supply, and also self-service after hours; open daily year-round; indian beaded work, head bands, earrings, chokers, and wampum jewelry; call Carol Lopez at 477-0325, Meeting House Rd.

Sandwich: *Amidon Woodcarving*, 139 Main St.; handmade decorative articles, signs, lighting fixtures, figures; open June to Sept., 10–5. *Christmas Tree Shop*, Rte. 6A, E. Sandwich; Christmas items, children's favorites, bird feeders, imports; open May to Dec., 9:30–5:30. *Heather House*, Rte. 6A, E. Sandwich; attractive selection of imported and hand-made articles, country crafts. *Misty Marsh Studio*, 88 Wood Ave., Town Neck; acrylic marine paintings by Ben Neill; open year-round, 10–5. *Nina Sutton*, 23 Old County Rd., E. Sandwich; authentic Sandwich glass jewelry; by appointment, 888-1072. *Old Cranberry Barn*, 348 Rte. 6A, E. Sandwich; contemporary pottery, functional stoneware, and artwork. *Paul White, Woodcarver*, 293 Rte. 6A, E. Sandwich; American motif signs, architectural details, figure heads; one-of-a-kind custom work; year-round. *Peter Peltz*; hand-carved birds of New England; studio workshop on Rte. 6A; open year-round, 11–4. *Royal Standard Gift Shop*, Rte. 6A, E. Sandwich; extensive line of gifts, household items, glass. *Scorton Creek Studio*, Rte. 6A, E. Sandwich; hand-painted birds, scrimshaw, oils, and watercolors. *Sandwich Auction House*, 155 Tupper Rd.; antiques, furniture on consignment, inventory from S.E. Massachusetts; auction begins Wed. at 6:30 in summer, or Sat. during rest of year; previewing begins at noon. *Titcomb's Bookstore*, Rte. 6A, E. Sandwich; out-of-print and rare old books, appraisals; regional and Cape Cod books; year-round.

 SUMMER SPORTS. Baseball. Cape Cod League baseball is a hot summer interest to spectators and professional scouts; major league players like Carlton Fisk got their start here. The *Falmouth Commodores'* home field is at Guv Fuller Field on Main St., Falmouth. The Cranberry League includes the *Bourne Mariners*, whose home is Keith Field on Sandwich Rd. in Sagamore.

Boating. There are marinas, boat ramps, and boatyards in all Upper Cape towns. For current information, call the local harbormaster or Town Hall. *Bourne* has Monument Beach Marina, Parker's Boat Yard (Cataumet), Kingman Marina (Cataumet). Boat ramps at Electric Ave., Buzzards Bay; Monument Beach, Monument Beach; Eel Pond, Monks Park at

Monument Beach; Barlow's Landing, Hen's Cove at Pocasset; Parker's Boat Yard, Squeteague Beachway at Cataumet. Free mooring permits are available at the Natural Resources Office at Town Hall (759-3441). *Falmouth* has ten harbors with facilities in all. Falmouth's inner harbor has assigned spaces, and limited moorings by two commercial repair yards. Dumping trash or sewage prohibited. Town wharves located in Woods Hole, Quisset, West Falmouth, Wild Harbor, Magansett. Tie-ups range from 48 hours in Woods Hole to 30 minutes in others. Anchor-out space is limited, best bet is Great Harbor in Woods Hole. For information on all facilities, call Harbormaster, 548-9796. *Mashpee* has two marinas. The Half-tide Marina on Frog Pond Close Rd. has 47 slips and moorings, and storage, repair, gas, bait, and charter services. Relatively shallow, open year-round. Popponesset Marina is private. State-run boating access to 700-acre Mashpee-Wakeby Lake is at Attaquin Park near Town Hall. Paved ramp, no restriction on size or h.p. Other ramps at Ashumet Pond, off Rte. 151; John's Pond, off Rte. 151, no restrictions yet. Unimproved saltwater ramps at Mashpee Neck Rd. off Rte. 28 and Red Brook Rd. *Sandwich* has slips and free anchorage at the Cape Cod Marina. Showers, restrooms, marine supplies, bait, food available. Reservations necessary, call 888-2500. There are freshwater accessways at Spectacle Pond off Pinkham Rd., Peter's Pond off Cotuit Rd. (paved), and Lawrence Pond off Great Hills Pd.

Golf. *Bourne:* Pocasset Golf Club, off County Rd.; 18-hole, par 72; gas and pullcarts. *Falmouth:* Cape Cod Country Club, off Rte. 151, Hatchville; 18-hole, par 72, year-round. Falmouth Country Club, Carriage Shop Rd.; 18-hole, gas and pullcarts. Paul Harney Golf Course, off Rte. 151, Hatchville; 18-hole, par 60, gas and pullcarts. Woodbriar Country Club, Gifford St., Falmouth; 9-hole, par 3, pullcarts. *Mashpee:* New Seabury Country Club, New Seabury; private 18-hole, par 72 Blue course; public 18-hole, par 70 Green course; gas and pullcarts. *Sandwich:* Holly Ridge Golf Course, off Race Lane, S. Sandwich; 18-hole, par 72, gas and pullcarts. Round Hill Country Club, off Quaker Meeting House Rd., E. Sandwich; 18-hole, par 72.

Tennis. *Bourne:* Town courts in Pocasset and Monument Beach. *Falmouth:* Falmouth Sports Center, 33 Highfield Dr.; six indoor courts, three outdoor, two outdoor platforms. Falmouth Tennis Club, Dillingham Ave. Ext.; three outdoor Plexi-Pave, three clay, clubhouse, teaching pro; open Memorial Day to Labor Day. *Mashpee:* Racquet Club at Massasoit Crossing, Rte. 28; three outdoor courts, two indoor courts, pool, sauna; tennis pro, summer clinics; open daily, year-round. *Sandwich:* Holly Ridge Tennis Club, Country Club Rd., S. Sandwich; two outdoor courts; town courts, eight lighted courts at high school, four lighted courts at elementary school; tennis permit required, contact Community School; 888-5300.

Racquetball. *Falmouth:* Falmouth Sports Center, 33 Highfield Dr.; four courts, pro shop.

Horseback Riding. *Falmouth:* Boxberry Hill Farm, Boxberry Hill Rd.,

Hatchville. Breeding farm for quarter horses and Appaloosas, trail rides, lessons, boarding, training. Carriage Shop Stables, Carriage Shop Rd. Lessons, training, boarding, special programs for children. Cloverfield Farm, 49 Cloverfield Way, N. Falmouth. Lessons, boarding. Fieldcrest Farm, 774 Palmer Ave. Lessons, boarding, indoor arena. Haland Stables, Rte. 28A, W. Falmouth. Trail rides, private and group instruction, boarding. *Mashpee:* Maushop Stables, Old Mill Rd. Lessons, cross-country course, boarding. *Sandwich:* Meadow Spring Farm, Rte. 6A, E. Sandwich. Board, lessons, training, no rentals. Beach riding available.

Windsurfing. *Falmouth:* Windsurfing Cape Cod, 850 Main St., Falmouth. Offers instruction at the Maravista Motel, rental and sales. Reportedly takes about five hours to learn to operate a windsurfer. Open Apr. to Sept.

WINTER SPORTS. Cross-country skiing: According to one experienced skier, the Cape has an ideal terrain for cross-country skiing. He recommends those areas open for walks, as well as golf courses where permitted, abandoned railroad beds, the perimeter of cranberry bogs, and some beach areas. Equipment sales and rental in Hyannis.

Curling. Cape Cod Curling Club, Highview Dr., Falmouth. Indoor facility with three rinks, nightly games in season, Oct. to March. Summer bonspeils.

Skating. Falmouth Ice Arena, Rte. 28; public skating, figure-skating lessons, hockey leagues; skate rental, snack shop; open year-round. Gallo Ice Arena, Sandwich Rd., Bourne; public skating, hockey leagues, special events. Skate rental, snack shop; closed during Apr. and Sept.

SPECTATOR SPORTS EVENTS. *Barnstable County Swim Meet*, Sandwich High School, E. Sandwich. Held in August, for information call Craig Eldridge, Sandwich Community School, 888-5300. *Collegiate Vineyard Swim.* 25 colleges compete on a four-mile course between West Chop on Martha's Vineyard and Nobska Point in Falmouth. Held in July, for the benefit of the Doreen Grace Fund. *Falmouth Road Race*, between Woods Hole and Falmouth Heights, held in Aug. A bartender's brainstorm has grown from a local race with 90 runners to what has been called "the best non-marathon road race in the country," with thousands of participants. For information, call 540-4417 or 548-7013. *Sunfish and Force Five Regatta*, Falmouth Yacht Club. A three-day event in July. Call 548-3865. Look for tennis and golf competitions during the summer.

FISHING AND SHELLFISHING. *Saltwater fishing* is generally good in all waters around the Upper Cape, which include Cape Cod Bay (tuna, bass, bluefish), Cape Cod Canal (bass, bluefish, mackerel, flounder), Buzzards Bay (bass, bluefish, scup, tautog), Woods Hole (bass, blues, scup, squeteague) and Nantucket and Vineyard Sounds (fluke, flounder, cod, scup, bass, blues). Swordfish and marlin are caught south of the islands.

You can try your hand at shore fishing at Taylor's Point state pier by the Massachusetts Maritime Academy, or anywhere along the Cape Cod Canal from the Service Rd., which runs along both banks. Other promising spots are in Falmouth (Green Pond, Falmouth Harbor, Nobska Point, and Oyster Pond), Mashpee (Mashpee Neck Rd., South Cape Beach, Popponesset, and Waquoit Beach), and Sandwich (canal marina, Scusset Beach, Sandy Neck Beach, and Scorton Creek in E. Sandwich).

A license is required for *freshwater*, not saltwater, fishing; it can be obtained at a Town Hall or some bait and tackle shops. A non-resident 17-day license costs $11.25, seasonal $17.25. Many Upper Cape ponds and streams are stocked with trout, bass, pickerel, and perch. Try Bourne (Flax Pond), Falmouth (Mares, Deep, and Grews Ponds), Mashpee (Ashumet, Johns, and Mashpee-Wakeby Ponds and Quashnet, Mashpee, and Santuit Rivers), Sandwich (Peters, Spectacle, Lawrence, and Hoxie Ponds).

Charter and party boats are available in Falmouth. The *Patriot Party Boats* are tied up at the Harborview Fish Market Dock at the end of Scranton Ave., May to Oct., for private charter, fishing, party, or evening cruises. Other charter boats at the dock are the *Black Hawk, Peptide, Ananata,* and *Glorianna II*.

Maco's on the Cranberry Highway in Bourne is one of the few places that rents small fishing skiffs with outboards. Cape Marine on Shore Rd. in Bourne sells diving equipment and metal detectors. **Note:** Skin diving, fishing, and trolling in the Cape Cod Canal are prohibited. Activity on the canal is closely monitored and regulated by the U.S. Army Corps of Engineers.

Shellfishing permits for residents and non-residents are available at all Town Halls. Regulations and fishing areas change frequently. Permit holders are advised to know the regulations because they are enforced, and there are fines for violations. Most Upper Cape shores have quahogs, soft-shelled clams, mussels, some oysters, and blue crabs. In Mashpee there is no limit on blue crabs because they are considered predators—they are also very elusive.

 **PUBLIC BEACHES. Bourne.** Parking stickers are required, cost $1, and can be obtained at the Natural Resource Office at Town Hall. *Monument Beach*, off Rte. 28 (bathhouse, toilets, snack bar). *Buzzards Bay Beach*, Buttermilk Bay Beach near Rtes. 28 and 6. *Gray Gables*, off Rte. 28, near canal. *Pocasset Heights Beach*, Barlow's Landing Beach, off Rte. 28. *Cataumet Beach, Pocasset Beach*, on Circuit Dr., Bourne. *Sagamore Beach*, near Rtes. 6 and 3. **Freshwater:** *Queen Sewell Pond*, off Puritan Rd., Buzzards Bay.

Falmouth. $5 per day parking at Old Silver Beach, $4 parking at Surf Drive, Menauhant, Falmouth Heights. One-week permit available. Stickers for residents. Free morning swimming lessons. *Surf Drive Beach*, on Surf Drive (bathhouse, bathrooms, snack bar, life guards). *Menauhant Beach*, in East Falmouth. *Bristol Beach* at Maravista off Shore Rd. *Falmouth Heights Beach*, Clinton Ave. *Nobska Beach*, Woods Hole. *Strong Beach*, Woods Hole. *Wood Neck Beach*, Sippewisset Rd.. *Capaquoit Beach*, W. Falmouth. *Megansett Beach*, N. Falmouth. *Old Silver Beach*, N. Falmouth. **Freshwater:** Grews Pond at Goodwill Park.

Mashpee. Beach stickers at Town Hall, $5 for residents, $3 daily fee, $10 per week. *South Cape Beach*, end of Great Neck Rd., off Mashpee Rotary; a fine, unspoiled area on the warm-water side of the Cape; toilets, snack bar. **Freshwater:** *Attaquin Park* on Mashpee-Wakeby, small, sandy beach by boat ramp, no sticker.

Sandwich. Beach parking stickers for residents and property owners; a few guest passes available at motels. Stickers at Town Hall and Town Hall Annex. *Town Beach*, Town Neck Rd. to Freeman Ave., toilets, snack bar. *East Sandwich Beach*, on N. Shore Blvd.; small public parking area on beach side. *Sandy Neck Beach*, Sandy Neck Rd.; $3 parking, bathhouse, snack bar, high dunes; beautiful barrier beach. *Scusset Beach*, Scusset Beach Rd. off Sagamore Bridge Rotary; state-run, by canal, with bathhouse, snack bar, toilets. **Freshwater:** *Snake Pond*, in Forestdale off Rte. 130; life guard, toilets, picnic tables. *South Sandwich Recreation Area*, S. Sandwich Rd.; lovely sandy beach, picnic tables, gazebos, woods, trails.

Note: Cooking fires are generally permitted on beaches, but contact the Town Hall or Fire Dept. to be sure. The reduction or elimination of life guards and maintenance crews may be obvious in some areas—recreation department budgets have been taking a beating; do your part.

PARKS AND FORESTS. Bourne. *Bourne Scenic Park*, Rte. 6, Buzzards Bay; located along the canal; camping, hiking, swimming, fishing; charge for overnight or day use (see Camping). *Bourne Town Forest*, entrance by the water works on County Rd.; walking trails also on marked conservation land, County Rd. near Back River.

Falmouth. *Ashumet Holly Reservation*, Ashumet Rd., off Rte. 151; 45-acre area of woods, ponds, meadows, run by the Massachusetts Audubon Society. Rare species of trees, abundant holly. Well-marked trails. Open year-round, no smoking, dogs, or picnicking. *Beebee Woods*, at Highfield Dr.; a 500-acre gift to the town, lovely trails, no picnicking. *Goodwill Park*, Rte. 28; another gift, a 86-acre park with barbecue pits, picnic tables, large playground, swimming at Grews Pond, run by Falmouth Park Dept. *Town Forest*, Gifford Woods; adjoins Goodwill Park, trails.

Mashpee. *Lowell Holly Reservation*, off S. Sandwich Rd.; 130-acre nature reservation includes the peninsula that separates Mashpee and

Wakeby Lakes; peaceful and secluded, with trails, picnic tables, swimming.

Sandwich. *Scusset Beach State Reservation*, off Rte. 3; located on 380 acres, camping, fishing, hiking, biking, picnicking; year-round. *Shawme Crowell State Forest*, Rte. 130, Sandwich; camping, biking, hiking, horseback riding on 2,756 acres near Sandwich marina and canal; open mid-Apr. to mid-Oct. *Talbot Point Conservation Area*, Old County Rd., E. Sandwich; woods trails, picnicking. *Thornton Burgess Briar Patch*, Discovery Hill Rd., off Rte. 6A; wooded trails through area Burgess frequented as a youngster.

 **CAMPING. Bourne.** *Bayview Campgrounds*, 260 MacArthur Blvd., Bourne; open May 1 to mid-Oct.; 286 campsites with partial to full hook-ups for water, electricity, sewage; tennis courts, pool, volleyball; recreation hall, store; gas and wood for sale; public beach nearby; strictly family camping; reservations recommended; leashed pets. *Bourne Scenic Park*, Rte. 6, Buzzards Bay; canalside site, 75 acres, 465 campsites; facilities include fireplace, picnic table, bathhouses; olympic-sized saltwater swimming pool, playground; leashed pets must be attended; bottled gas, firewood sold.

Falmouth. *Old Cape Cod Forest Campground*, Thomas B. Landers Rd., off Rte. 28; long-established campgrounds, pond frontage, 130 sites, some with electricity; hot showers, rest rooms; nicely wooded area, about 4 miles from Falmouth; boating, fishing; no wood fires; near golf, riding stables, saltwater beach. *Sippewissett Family Campground*, 836 Palmer Ave., Falmouth; shaded area, 3 miles from Falmouth, 1 mile from Wood Neck Beach; 100 sites, half with water, electrical hook-up; tents, pop-up trailers, motor homes to 35'; recreation room, play area, laundromat.

Mashpee. *Otis Trailer Village*, off Rte. 151; private beach on John's Pond, boat rental, playground; 100 campsites and trailer sites, no tents; utilities available, laundry, showers, restrooms; pets allowed if well-behaved; open mid-Apr. to mid-Oct.

Sandwich. *Peter's Pond Park*, Cotuit Rd., S. Sandwich; 400 camp and trailer sites; wooded location on trout-stocked pond; fishing, swimming, boating; large playground, boats for rest; store, showers; no pets; open mid-Apr. to mid-Oct. *Scusset State Beach Reservation*, Scusset Beach Rd., off Sagamore rotary; 100 trailer and tent sites at Scusset Beach; showers, toilets, electrical hook-ups, sewage disposal; fishing pier and playground; some shaded sites; pets must be leashed; open year-round. *Shawme Crowell State Forest*, Rte. 130, off Rte. 6A; tent sites on 1,200 acres, no group sites; showers, water, toilets, sewage disposal; small trailers only, no utilities; near marina, canal, historic village; tables, fireplaces; open mid-Apr. to mid-Oct.

WHAT TO DO WITH THE CHILDREN. Anyone close to children knows that they often provide an excellent excuse to see or do something we all enjoy, but might not take time for. Such as: **Airplanes:** A tour of *Air National Guard* planes and hangars can be arranged by calling 968-4137. The ANG Museum at the Military Reservation is also open to the public. **Bowling:** Ten-pin and candle-pin alleys in Falmouth and Buzzards Bay. **Canal.** Stop at the *Army Corps of Engineers Visitors Center* on the Cranberry Highway, then drive down to the Corps' Administration Building in Buzzards Bay for a slide show, model of the Cape Cod Canal, lots of information on the three bridges. You can look in at the control room where 24-hour surveillance of canal is maintained. Call Resource Management staff, 759-4431, for group tour. **Candy.** *Trahan's*, Main St., Falmouth. Made on the spot, great selection. **Farming.** *New Alchemy*, Hatchville, Falmouth. "Farm Saturdays," older or science-minded children will enjoy the workshops on greenhouses, tree crops, chance to talk with researchers. Potluck lunch. May to Sept., 12–4:40, rain or shine. *Grazing Fields Farm*, Head-of-the-Bay Rd., Buzzards Bay. Tour of farm, stable museum, farm animals. Cows milked at 4. Open May to Sept. *Tony Andrews Farm*, off Sandwich Rd., E. Falmouth. Pick your own strawberries and peas in season. **Fish.** Herring runs on Rte. 130 in Mashpee and Cranberry Highway in *Bournedale* are fun to visit in the spring when herring come upstream to spawn. *State fish hatchery* on Rte. 6A in Sandwich raises rainbow, brown, and brook trout to release in Massachusetts streams and ponds. In-ground holding tanks, fish food for sale. **Go Karts.** Go-kart amusement park on MacArthur Blvd. in Bourne. **Nature Center.** *Green Briar Jam Kitchen*, Rte. 6A, Sandwich. Thornton Burgess Society naturalist gives tours, live animal demonstration, nature walks. Special summer classes. **Roller Skating.** *Bourne Skate Center*, 169 Clay Pond Rd., Monument Beach. **Woods Hole.** This village has some unique features, including a drawbridge on Water St., a sun dial at a little waterfront park, St. Margaret's Garden and St. Joseph's Bell Tower on Millfield St., ferry boats, sail boats, research vessels, and every other kind of boat tied up or underway, as well as a lighthouse on Nobska Rd. built in 1829.

STAGE. *Cape Cod Conservatory* at Beebee Woods Art Center, Highfield Dr.; dance instruction and recitals, year-round. *Falmouth Playhouse*, off Rte. 151, Hatchville; professional summer theater, gallery, restaurant; open June to Sept. *Falmouth Theater Guild;* community productions at Highfield Theater. *Glasstown Players;* community theater at E. Sandwich Grange Hall. *Let's Go! Theater;* instruction and performances, primarily for children, sponsored by Sandwich Community School, Sandwich High School. *Summer Dance Theater;* small group performing modern and jazz dance at Falmouth High School. *Scottish Dance Society*, Woods Hole Community Hall; lessons, exhibitions, balls. *Woods Hole Theater Co.;* community performances, workshops at Woods Hole Community Hall, throughout the year.

MUSIC. *Bourne Choral Groupe*, regular rehearsal at Bourne Community Bldg., Mon. 7–9, sing-along, Wed. at 9:30; mostly senior citizens, public welcome. *Cape Cod Festival Orchestra* gives Sandwich Youth Concert Series at Sandwich High School, outside summer performances at Shawme Pond. *College Light Opera Co.;* college music majors from Oberlin and other schools give popular summer performances. *Falmouth Town Band;* outdoor programs, July and Aug. at Falmouth Harbor, Thurs. evening. *Falmouth Interfaith Choir and Orchestra;* amateur and professional performers, fall and spring concerts. *Falmouth Music Association;* professional chamber music, four concerts yearly, St. Barnabas Hall. *Fishmonger Cafe Coffee House*, Woods Hole, has jazz, blues, local performers, twice a month. *Heritage Plantation*, Sandwich; professional jazz groups, summer outdoor programs. *Opera New England Company;* directed by renowned Sarah Caldwell, several performances yearly at Sandwich High School, including a production for children. *Woods Hole Folk Music Society;* professional groups, traditional folk music, Oct. to May, 1st and 3rd Sundays, Woods Hole Community Hall.

For a small community, Woods Hole has a rich resource in local talent and interest in classical music. Look for performances by the *Ad Hoc Musicum*, the *Marine Biological Lab Cantata Consort*, and the *Chamber Orchestra*.

HOTELS AND MOTELS. Overnight accommodations in the Upper Cape area range from plush to simple, with every variable in-between. Some places have been owned by the same family for decades; others are changing hands or just getting started. Make reservations and ask specific questions to be sure you get what you want. Falmouth has a broader range and generally higher prices than the other Upper Cape towns, where settings tend to be more "countrified." Local Chambers of Commerce have complete listings of the numerous guest houses in the area. There are two guest houses on the island of Cuttyhunk. Both operate seasonally and should be contacted for details on rates and dates. Call **Allen House,** 996-9292, or **Boswell House**, 996-9295, or write Cuttyhunk, MA 02713.

The following categories for listings are based on the average cost of double occupancy, room only, no tax: *Deluxe*, $60 and up; *Expensive*, $42–$60; *Moderate*, $30–$42; and *Inexpensive*, $18–$30. A number of establishments have indicated they will raise prices in the near future.

Air conditioning is frequently not provided in facilities near the ocean because it is not necessary, although blankets might be. The area code for all telephone numbers given is "617."

BOURNE

Mashnee Village. *Expensive.* Mashnee Rd. 759-3384. Housekeeping cottages on peninsula Buzzards Bay. Pool, snack bar, T.V. rental, free movies. Tennis, fishing, boating. Open May 15 to Oct. 15.

Bay Motor Inn. *Moderate.* Main St. on Canal. 759-3989. Pool. Restaurant within walking distance. Near recreational facilities. Open May to Oct.

Canalside Motel. *Moderate.* Church Lane, Sagamore. 888-3690. Near restaurants, fishing, bike path, Sagamore Bridge, and State beach. Pool, T.V. in some rooms.

Herring Run Motel. *Moderate.* Scenic Highway, Bournedale. 888-0084. Near small herring run, bike path, canal. Pool. Open May to Oct.

Joseph Jefferson Inn and Motel. *Moderate.* Rip Van Winkle Way, Buzzards Bay. 759-4434. Private beach, all rooms overlooking Buttermilk Bay. 19th century estate being renovated. Restaurant and bar.

Panorama Motor Lodge. *Moderate.* South Bourne Bridge Rotary. 759-4401. Pool, overlooking canal. 40 units open yr.-round. Near restaurant.

Quintal's Motor Lodge. *Moderate.* Rte. 28 at Bourne Bridge, Buzzards Bay. 759-2711. Indoor pool, restaurant, fridge in some rooms, sauna and whirlpool. Restaurant and lounge. Open yr.-round.

Redwood Motel. *Moderate.* Rte. 6 and 28, Buzzards Bay. 759-3892. Small motel, near canal, picnic areas, restaurants, beaches. Pool, courtesy coffee.

Windmill Motel. *Moderate.* On Rte. 6. 888-3220. View of Sagamore bridge. Handy to Canal Rte. 6A. Continental breakfast, outside games, pool.

Yankee Thrift Motel. *Moderate.* Rte. 6 and 28, Bournedale. 759-3883. Indoor and outdoor pool, housekeeping units. Near canal, bikepath. Off-season rates.

Ye Old Homestead Motel and Cottages. *Moderate to Inexpensive.* 829 Scenic Highway, Bournedale. 888-0333. Nice canal view. Pool, fishing, boating. Kitchenettes.

Bay Breeze Guest House. *Inexpensive.* Monument Ave., Monument Beach. 759-5069. All rooms have bay view, some with kitchen. Semi-private beach. Tennis court, library, sitting room. T.V. in lounge.

Buzzards Bay Motor Lodge. *Inexpensive.* Rtes. 6 and 28, Buzzards Bay. 759-3466. Waterfront, private beach, dock rafts. 30 units. Open May to Nov.

Carew Motel and Apts. *Inexpensive.* Rte. 28A, Cataumet. 563-3331. 5 minutes from golf course, fishing, near saltwater beach. Off-season rates.

Picture Lake Motel. *Inexpensive.* 790 MacArthur Blvd. 563-5911. Outdoor pool, picnic area. Near amusement park, Otis ANG. No pets.

FALMOUTH

Admiralty Motor Inn. *Deluxe.* Teaticket Hwy. 548-4240. Restaurant, lounge, nightly entertainment. Indoor and outdoor pool, sauna. Near town and beach. Open yr.-round. Package, group, and tour plans. 80 rooms, off-season rates.

Cape Codder. *Deluxe.* Cape Codder Rd. 540-1900 or 800-225-3114. Large, turn-of-the-century resort hotel on Buzzards Bay, with cabanas, penthouses, villa units. Oceanview restaurant and cocktail lounge, night club. Pool, beach. MAP. Lawn games, babysitting service. No air conditioning or T.V. in hotel. Recently taken over by Resorts of Distinction. Open May to Oct.

Holiday Inn. *Deluxe.* Main St. 540-2500. In-town location. Restaurant, cocktail lounge, nightly entertainment. Indoor pool, game room. Near harbor, beach, shopping. Open yr.-round. Off-season rates, package plans.

Sea Crest. *Deluxe.* Old Silver Beach, N. Falmouth. 548-3850 or 800-352-7175. A modern oceanfront resort with 234 rooms and conference facilities. 1,000-foot beach, indoor and outdoor pools, indoor and outdoor tennis courts, putting green. Sauna, steam baths. Pinball room. Restaurant, nightclub, well-known professionals. Tours, package plans, MAP.

Sheraton Inn. *Deluxe.* Jones Rd. 540-2000. Informal resort inn, restaurant, cocktail lounge, entertainment. Sauna, indoor pool, game room. Conference rooms. Near shopping, golf. MAP. Free shuttle to beaches. Open yr.-round; off-season rates.

Alden Tower. *Expensive.* Grand Ave., Falmouth Heights. 548-4443. Unobstructed view of Martha's Vineyard and Sound, across street from Falmouth Harbor. Private beach, play area, picnic tables. Pool. No air conditioning, no pets. Open yr.-round; off-season rates.

Cape Colony Motor Lodge. *Expensive.* Surf Dr. 548-3975. Oceanview, balconies. Across street from beach, near harbor, shopping, restaurant. Pool. Continental breakfast. Bike rentals. No pets. Open Memorial Day to Columbus Day.

Capewind Motel. *Expensive.* Maravista Ave. Ext. 548-3400. Privacy, exceptional grounds, 11 acres on saltwater inlet. Outdoor pool, dock and small boats. Kitchenettes, no pets. Usually yr.-round.

Coonamessett Inn. *Expensive.* Jones and Gifford Rds. 548-2300. Handsome old (1796) Inn. Gardens; restaurant and lounge with entertainment. 16 suites include bedroom, sitting room and bath; 5 apts, cottage. No pets. Fresh flowers. Near town, golf, riding. Open yr.-round.

Falmouth Marina Hotel. *Expensive.* Robbins Rd. 548-4300. Overlooking Falmouth Harbor. Pool, spacious rooms. Near restaurants, shops, island ferry. No pets. Open yr.-round; off-season rates.

Green Harbor Motel. *Expensive.* Acapesket Rd., E. Falmouth. 548-4747. Located on saltwater inlet. Private beach, boating, sundeck, boat ramp. Pools. Housekeeping units.

Maravista Motel. *Expensive.* Menauhant Rd. 548-0313. 3 buildings, 88 units. Very private beach. 2 pools, tennis, fishing jetty, playground. Windsurfing lessons. Patios or balcony, continental breakfast, efficiencies. No pets. Open May to Oct.

Mariner Motel. *Expensive.* Main St. 548-1331. Downtown, 30 units. Nice pool and picnic area. Near restaurant, shops, harbor. Water beds. Off-season rates.

Nautilus Motel. *Expensive.* Woods Hole Rd., Woods Hole. 548-1525. Formal gardens, pool, tennis. Near ferry, golf, restaurant, lounge. Open May to Oct.

Park Beach Resort Motel. *Expensive.* Grand Ave., Falmouth Heights. 548-1010. Oceanview, across from Heights beach. 50 units, balcony on second floor. Some air conditioning, continental breakfast. Pool. Near restaurant, island boats. Open May to Sept.; off-season rates.

Sands of Time. *Expensive.* Main Rd., Woods Hole. 548-6300. Restaurant, bar adjoining motel, lovely view overlooking Little Harbor. All private balconies, sliding glass doors. Pool. Walk to ferry. No air conditioning. Dogs permitted, must be accompanied by owner at all times. Open Apr. to Oct.

Shoreway Acres Motel. *Expensive.* Shore Rd. 540-3000. Resort atmosphere with indoor and outdoor pools. Breakfast room, spacious grounds. Near downtown shops, restaurants. Discount on golf, island boats. Special activities. Excellent package plans. Open yr.-round.

Sleepy Hollow. *Expensive.* Woods Hole Rd. 548-1986. Pool, near restaurant, saltwater beach, island boats, bike path. Clean, comfortable rooms. Open May 15 to Columbus Day.

Tides Motel. *Expensive.* Clinton and Grand Aves., Falmouth Heights. 548-3126. Overlooks Nantucket Sound and Falmouth Harbor. Near downtown area. Private beach, some kitchenettes. No air conditioning. No pets. Open May to Oct.; off-season rates.

Carlton Circle Motel. *Moderate.* Sandwich Rd., E. Falmouth, 548-0025. Pool, small cocktail lounge, Picnic grounds and grills. Near golf, theater. Some air conditioning. Efficiencies. Open yr.-round.

Elm Arch Inn. *Moderate.* Elm Arch Way, off Main St. 548-0133. Charming rooms in historic inn. Downtown location with privacy; short walk to shops, restaurants. Quaint sitting rooms, pool, patio room. No pets. Open yr.-round.

Falmouth Heights Motor Lodge. *Moderate.* Falmouth Heights Rd. 548-3623. Large picnic area, pool. Family motel. Across street from harbor, near beach, restaurants, island boats. Free coffee. No pets. Open Apr. to Oct.

Great Bay Motel. *Moderate.* Main St., Teaticket. 548-5410. Good family motel. Near all recreational facilities, shopping, picnic area. 23 units, no pets. Open Apr. to Nov.

Ideal Spot. *Moderate.* Rte. 28A, W. Falmouth. 548-2257. Outside recreational and picnic area. Mostly efficiencies, up to 6 occupants. Close to saltwater beaches; pleasant atmosphere.

John Parker Village. *Moderate.* Off Andrews Rd., E. Falmouth. 548-5933. Family resort area. Wooded area, pool, private beach on freshwater pond, boating. Children's play area, game room, golf. All efficiencies, some studios. Daily maid service. In season, by the week $400. Open May to Oct.

Ox-Bow Inn. *Moderate.* Rte. 28, Teaticket. 548-6677. A centrally located family motel. Clean, award-winning grounds. Set back from road; picnic benches, courtyard around pool. Near shopping, restaurants. Open Apr. to Oct.

Red Horse Inn. *Moderate.* Falmouth Heights Rd., Falmouth Heights. 548-0053. Across street from harbor, island boat, near shopping, restaurants. Pool, 22 units, some guest rooms with common bath. Open Apr. to Nov.

Shore Haven Lodge. *Moderate.* Shore St. 548-1765. Cottages and rooms across street from Falmouth Beach. Family rooms for 5 people. Walk to downtown. Indoor lounge. Pets. Open Memorial Day to late Sept.

Spenser's Town and Beach Motel. *Moderate.* Main St. 548-1380. Central location near restaurants, shops, beaches. Air conditioning. Open May to Oct.

Studio Motel. *Moderate.* Falmouth Heights Rd., Falmouth Heights. 548-1513. On harbor, some waterfront units. Clean, pretty setting. No room phones. Coffee hut, some fridges. Closed Jan.

Sunset Motel. *Moderate.* Rte. 28A, N. Falmouth, 563-3661. Pool, country setting. Near restaurant, golf, theater. Picnic area. Open May to Jan.

MASHPEE

New Seabury Inn. *Deluxe.* Shore Drive West, New Seabury, 477-9111. Oceanfront resort, restaurant, lounge. 2 excellent golf courses, 16 tennis courts, beach and cabana club, marina. Located on 2,700 acres. 1-, 2-, and 3-bedroom suites. Full kitchen or kitchenette in most units. Open yr.-round.

Popponesset Inn. *Deluxe.* Shore Dr., New Seabury, 477-1100. Restaurant, lounge, golf courses, 16 tennis courts, beach and cabana club and marina. Cottages, many with fireplace, kitchen.

SANDWICH

Dan'l Webster Inn. *Deluxe.* Main St. 888-3622. Attractive reproduction of original 1694 Inn at site. Near museums, shops. Includes restaurant, tavern, entertainment, gift shop. Pool, patio. Indoor movies. Near Sandwich marina; pick-up service for boating guests. MAP. Yr.-round; off-season rates.

Country Acres. *Moderate.* Rte. 6A. 888-2878. Pleasant setting, 7 acres. Crib and fridge rental. Near historic village, waterfront, restaurants. No pets. Off-season and special rates.

Earl of Sandwich Motor Manor. *Moderate.* Rte. 6A, E. Sandwich. 888-1415. Well-maintained; pretty picnic area with grills. Continental breakfast. Near golf, shopping.

Old Colony Motel. *Moderate.* Rte. 6A, E. Sandwich. 888-9716. Heated outdoor pool; picnic area. Near beach, restaurant. 10 units. Open Apr. through Sept.

Sandy Neck Motel. *Moderate.* Rte. 6A, E. Sandwich. 362-3992. Near ocean beach, sand dunes. 12 units. No pets. Open yr.-round.

Sandy's Motor Lodge. *Moderate.* Rte. 6A. 888-2275. Pool, restaurant; 26 units, including efficiencies. Near village, marina, shopping, museums. Pets permitted. Yr.-round; off-season rates.

Seven Brothers Motel. *Moderate.* Rte. 6A. 888-0710. Pool, sundecks. Lovely picnic/recreation area overlooking saltwater marsh. Continental breakfast. Near restaurant, shops. Open Apr. to Nov.; off-season rates.

Shady Nook Inn. *Moderate.* Rte. 6A. 888-0409. Heated pool, coffee shop. Near campgrounds, marina, fishing, village. Pets during off-season only. Cottage and efficiencies. Open yr.-round; off-season rates.

Spring Hill Motor Lodge. *Moderate.* Rte. 6A, E. Sandwich. 888-1456. Picnic area, continental breakfast, near golf, beach. Air-conditioning extra. Efficiencies. Open yr.-round.

The Cape Cottages and Motel. *Inexpensive.* Ploughed Neck Rd. 888-0676. Near ocean beach. Recreation/picnic area, play area for children. Open mid-May to Columbus Day; off-season rates.

 DINING OUT. Restaurants in the Upper Cape may offer waterfront dining, fresh seafood, ethnic specialties, nifty brunches. No two places are alike. Reservations are a good idea in the summer, although not all places will take them. With a few exceptions, casual dress is acceptable.

The ratings are based on the average cost for a single dinner without drinks, tip or tax: *Deluxe,* $18 and up; *Expensive,* $15 and up; *Moderate,* $9–$15; and *Inexpensive,* under $9.

BOURNE

The Bridge Restaurant. *Moderate.* Rte. 6A, Sagamore. 888-9708. Unpretentious good food, Italian, fresh seafood.

The Chart Room. *Moderate.* Shore Rd., Cataumet. 563-5350. Waterview, outdoor porch overlooking Red Brook Harbor. Good luncheon menu. Swordfish and bluefish specialities. Dinner served 6–10. Piano bar. Memorial Day to Labor Day.

The Dolphin Inn. *Moderate.* Taylor's Point, Buzzards Bay. 759-7522. 5 specials nightly. Lobster requires 24-hr. notice. Near Mass. Maritime Academy. On the water. Piano entertainment weekends. Open yr.-round; closed Sunday off-season.

Joseph Jefferson Inn. *Moderate.* Off Lincoln Ave. 759-4434. Historic home on Buttermilk Bay. Maryland crab, prime rib, lobster. Serves breakfast, lunch, and dinner. Bar. Open yr.-round; closed Tues. and Wed. off-season.

Bob's Sea Grill. *Inexpensive.* Main St., Buzzards Bay. 759-9943. Clambake, seafood specialty. Piano and guitar entertainment, bar. Open yr.-round.

Captain Barlow House. *Inexpensive.* Rte. 28 Pocasset. 563-5351. Steak, seafood menu. Bar. Open yr.-round.

Grandma's Restaurant/Grandpa's Tavern. *Inexpensive.* On Bourne Rotary, Buzzards Bay. 799-2526. Sandwiches, seafood. Family dining. Take-out pies.

Lobster Trap. *Inexpensive.* Shore Rd., Buzzards Bay. 759-3992. On the water, outside deck. Can bring own liquor, set-ups provided. Informal. Seafood, mostly deep-fried. Lunch, dinner 11:30–8, May to Sept.; closed Monday.

Mezza-Luna Restaurant. *Inexpensive.* Main St., Buzzards Bay. 759-4667. Italian cuisine, prime rib. Open yr.-round.

Quintal's Restaurant. *Inexpensive.* Rte. 6, Buzzards Bay. 362-6062. Well-known seafood spot; family restaurant, huge seafood platter; serves breakfast, lunch and dinner. *Poseidon Lounge.* Open daily, yr.-round.

Ruggiero's. *Inexpensive.* On the Bourne Rotary. 759-3939. Serves breakfast, lunch, dinner. Italian and seafood. Good family spot.

Sagamore Inn. *Inexpensive.* Rte. 6A, Sagamore. 888-9707. Local favorite for Italian and American food. Lunch and dinner. Closed Jan. thru March.

Sandy's Restaurant. *Inexpensive.* Rte. 28, near Bourne Bridge. Fried clams, chowder, fish. Generous portions. Open yr.-round.

FALMOUTH

Cape Codder Hotel. *Expensive.* Cape Codder Rd., N. Falmouth. 540-1900. Oceanview dining room, early 1900's resort atmosphere. French style cuisine, seafood. Also cocktail lounge, brick patio. Open May to Oct.

Regatta Restaurant. *Expensive.* Scranton Ave. 548-5400. Prime harborfront location. Specializes in Cape Cod and Continental cuisine, fresh-caught native fish, Oyster Bienville, Scallops Sebastian. Extensive collection of good wines. Lunch and dinner, Sunday brunch. May to mid-Oct.

Wickertree. *Moderate to Expensive.* At Rte. 151 and 28A, N. Falmouth. 563-6061. Formal, leisurely dining. Continental and French cuisine, veal, Chateaubriand, desserts. Raw bar includes crab, shrimp, lobster. Serves luncheon, except Mon., and dinner daily in season. Open patio, lounge. Valet service evenings, reservations recommended.

Boat House. *Moderate.* Scranton Ave. 548-7800. Small, comfortable, with open porch on harbor. Informal, nightly specialties, lobster bisque. Lunch, dinner, piano and bar. Open May 1 to Columbus Day.

Coonamesset Inn. *Moderate*. Corner Jones and Gifford. 548-2300. Serves lobster, duck. Breakfast, lunch, dinner, daily, yr.-round. Country inn atmosphere, jackets preferred. Lounge.

Dome Restaurant. *Moderate*. State Rd., Woods Hole. 548-0800. A Buckminster Fuller geodesic dome. Serves New England cuisine, native seafood, prime rib. Breakfast 7–10, dinner 5–10. Sunday brunch. Open daily May to Oct.

Dorsie's. *Moderate.* 763 Main St. 540-5710. Steaks, salad bar. Dinner served till midnight, yr.-round.

Executive Restaurant. *Moderate*. Rte. 28, Teaticket at the Admiralty. 548-4240. Extensive Continental menu, domestic and imported wine list. Veal, beef, seafood specialties. Yr.-round; breakfast in-season, weekends dinner.

Flying Bridge. *Moderate*. Scranton Ave. 548-2700. Overlooks Falmouth Harbor, outdoor decks. New England cuisine, baked stuffed lobster, roast beef. Serves lunch and dinner daily, mid-Apr. to mid-Oct. Jacket suggested. Bar, entertainment.

Golden Swan. *Moderate*. 323 Main St. 548-9891. European atmosphere. Continental cuisine, Veal Golden Swan. Imported wines and beer. Dinner in-season, also lunch off-season. Open yr.-round, closed Sun.

Landfall. *Moderate*. 2 Water St., Woods Hole. 548-1758. A Cape Cod classic, on the water, nautical decor. Swordfish, lobster. Serves lunch and dinner daily, mid-June to mid-Sept. Bar, piano music.

Lawrence's Restaurant. *Moderate*. Nantucket Ave., Falmouth Heights. 548-4441. Popular and reliable. Steamed clams, swordfish, homemade bread, pies. Casual; late breakfast, lunch, dinner. Bar, piano. Daily June to Labor Day.

Nimrod. *Moderate*. Dillingham Ave. 548-4370. Charming old inn, small dining rooms, fireplace. Continental cuisine, rack of lamb, fresh seafood. Lunch, dinner daily, yr.-round. Bar, entertainment weekends.

Amigo's. *Inexpensive*. Rte. 28, Teaticket. 548-8510. Small, comfortable; specializes in Mexican foods; 17-oz. Marguerita. Open daily, yr.-round, for lunch and dinner.

Big Fisherman. *Inexpensive*. Rte. 28 E. Falmouth. 548-4266. Good family restaurant, seafood and beef specialties. Early-bird special. Lunch served Labor Day to Memorial Day, dinner yr.-round. Closed Mon. off-season. Family owned and operated.

Captain Kidd Bar and Restaurant. *Inexpensive*. 548-8563. Waterfront, on Eel Pond; open porch. Restaurant open June to Labor Day, dinners only; serves poached veal, steamed mussels, Chicken Penzance. Bar open yr.-round, serves sandwiches. Popular, casual.

Elsie's. *Inexpensive*. 553 Palmer Ave. 548-6263. Family business that made a name in Cambridge. German-style foods, specialties Reuben sandwich and fancy pastries. Serves lunch and dinner, Apr. 1 to Oct. 15.

Golden Sails. *Inexpensive*. Rte. 28, E. Falmouth. 548-3521. Chinese and Polynesian food. Serves lunch and dinner daily, yr.-round. Take-out service.

Grasmere Pub. *Inexpensive.* Gifford St. 548-9861. Nice atmosphere, fireplace. Portuguese specialties, kale soup, linguica, fish chowder. Good salad bar. Open for lunch and dinner yr.-round.

Hearth and Kettle. *Inexpensive.* 874 Main St. 548-6111. American menu, homemade muffins. Good family spot. Early-bird special 12–6. Open 24 hrs. daily June to Labor Day. Open yr.-round; breakfast and lunch menu always available.

Molly's. *Inexpensive.* 29 Depot Ave. 548-9005. Continental menu, scampi, crêpes, seafood, steaks. Dinner only. 2 bars, entertainment. Open yr.-round; closed Mon.

Sheraton Inn. *Inexpensive.* 291 Jones Rd. 540-2000. Continental cuisine, Lobster Savannah, Bouillabaisse. Family-oriented; children's menu. Breakfast, lunch, dinner daily, yr.-round. Lounge.

Silver Lounge. *Inexpensive.* Rte. 28A, N. Falmouth. 564-4355. Pleasant, casual atmosphere. Steaks, seafood, deli sandwiches. Daily specials. Caboose-car dining room, fireplace. Open daily, yr.-round. Full menu from 11:30 P.M.–1 A.M.

Steakery. *Inexpensive.* 704 E. Main St. 540-0053. Beef specialties, seafood. A worthwhile 2-for-1 special. Dinner only; bar. Casual. Open nightly, yr.-round.

Town House. *Inexpensive.* 273 Main St. 548-0285. Good, basic menu; seafoods, swordfish, bluefish in season. Serves full menu from 11:30 A.M.–10 P.M. Daily, May to Columbus weekend.

MASHPEE

New Seabury Restaurant. *Expensive.* Shore Dr. West, New Seabury. 477-2402. Oceanview. Traditional and Continental cuisine with veal and seafood specialties. Lunch, dinner; lounge, entertainment, dancing. Open daily March through Dec.

Popponesset Inn. *Expensive.* Shore Dr. West, New Seabury. 477-1100. Located on Nantucket Sound. Continental breakfast, lunch, dinner. Veal, frogs' legs, and lamb chop specialties. Bar and entertainment dancing. Open June to Sept.

Bobby Byrnes. *Inexpensive.* New Seabury Plaza. 477-0600. Pub atmosphere. Popular spot with all ages. Good soup and sandwich menu. Meals served 11–11. Sunday brunch. Children welcome until 9 P.M.

The Flume. *Inexpensive.* Rte. 130. 477-1456. Serves lunch, dinner; outdoor patio, woods setting. Specialties swordfish with anchovies, scrod, Newburg. Open yr.-round, closed Mon. and Tues. after Labor Day.

Roberto's Quiche and Chowder House. *Inexpensive.* Mashpee Rotary. 477-9741. Breakfast, lunch, dinner; outdoor patio. Light meals, variety of quiches and chowder. No credit cards, travelers checks only. Dinner served in summer only, breakfast and lunch yr.-round.

SANDWICH

Dan'l Webster. *Moderate.* Main St. 888-3622. Classical and American cuisine, with seafood filet and Chicken Joinville specialties. Breakfast, luncheon, dinner, and Sunday brunch, with champagne and harp music. Tavern room, piano, guest singers, dance quartet. Open yr.-round; closed Christmas Day.

Eli's. *Moderate.* Rte. 6A, E. Sandwich. 888-4535 Seafood, Greek specialties. Unusual appetizers. Serves luncheons and dinner, Open yr.-round; closed Mon. Good bar, comfortable atmosphere, popular with locals.

Pilot's Landing. *Moderate.* Gallo Rd. 888-6977. Canal side location near marina; outside tables. Brunch, lunch, dinner; varied menu includes seafood medley, Lounge, 2-piece band, dancing on weekends. Open yr.-round, daily in season, Thu. through Sun. off season

Tupper Tavern. *Moderate.* Rte. 6A, Angelo's Plaza. 888-0289. Family restaurant, booths, breakfast, lunch, dinner. Traditional menu. Bar. Open daily, yr.-round.

Alexander's. *Inexpensive.* Rte. 6A, E. Sandwich, 362-4303. Features native seafood, clam chowder, lobster serendipity, and Cape Cod clambake. Serves lunch, Sunday brunch, dinner, daily in season, Thu. through Sun. off-season. Small cocktail lounge, fireplace. Children welcome.

Horizons Beach Club. *Inexpensive.* Town Neck Rd. 888-6166. Spectacular view of Cape Cod Bay. Sundeck tables. Serves light lunches and dinners, sandwiches, salad, and quiche. Bar Entertainment.

Sandy's Restaurant. *Inexpensive.* Rte. 6A. 888-6480. Family seafood restaurant. Good reputation. Lunch, dinner. Open daily, yr.-round, 11:30–9:30.

Simple Fare. *Inexpensive.* Rt. 6A. 888-5979. Small family restaurant, traditional menu. Homemade ice cream. Popular clam chowder. No personal checks or credit cards. Open daily yr.-round.

Wakeby Junction, *Inexpensive.* Cotuit Rd., S. Sandwich. 477-9761. Breakfast, lunch in log cabin, rustic decor, loft. Open 5:30 A.M –3:00 P.M., 6:30 Sun. Good breakfast spot.

 NIGHT LIFE. Bourne. *Casey's Pub*, Rte. 28, Bourne; darts, live entertainment, sing-along; open year-round, 11–1 *Chart Room*, Shore Rd., Cataumet; bar and restaurant overlooking Red Brook Harbor; piano bar, duo plays requests; summers only; weekends between Labor Day and Columbus Day. *Grandpa's Tavern*, at the Bourne Rotary, Buzzards Bay; live band, dancing; open year-round.

Falmouth. *The Boat House*, Scranton Ave., on Falmouth Harbor; open-air tables, piano nightly, informal, cozy; May 1 to Columbus Day. *Brandy's*, at the Sheraton Falmouth, Jones Rd.; house band, pop and contemporary music, special shows, belly dancers; open year-round, 7 nights. *Captain Kidd*, Water St., Woods Hole; popular waterfront bar, sandwiches, steamers; closed Jan. *Century Irish Pub*, 29 Locust St.; live Irish music nightly, May 1 to Sept.; happy hours. *Coonamessett Inn*, Jones Rd.; swing and contemporary music and dancing, nightly during summer, weekends; bar and restaurant, open year-round. *Dome*, Woods Hole Rd., Woods Hole; lounge, organist; open May–Oct. *Dorsie's*, Main St., Falmouth; piano, guitar, vocal entertainment, 9–1 Mon.–Sat. dixieland on Sun.; dancing. *Executive Lounge* at the Admiralty Inn, Rte. 28, Teaticket; live entertainment nightly, year-round; pop music, dancing, floor shows; happy hour daily, 4–7. *Flying Bridge*, Scranton Ave.; classy bar, wrap-around deck overlooking Falmouth Harbor; live entertainment 9–1; dancing. *Molly's*, Depot Ave.; small, intimate room with loft; piano, vocalist; daily, except Mon. *Nimrod*, Dillingham Ave.; pianist, trio on weekends, popular music, dancing. *Quarterdeck*, Main St.; popular bar and restaurant, stained glass, other interesting details; serves food late. *Silver Lounge*, N. Falmouth, Rte. 28A; family restaurant/lounge; nautical decor, full menu served from 11:30 to 1; open year-round, no credit cards.

Mashpee. *Bobby Byrnes Pub*, New Seabury Plaza; comfortable pub atmosphere, good light menu, jukebox; year-round. *On the Rocks*, Rte. 28, near rotary; live groups, some well-known, rock, top 40, disco; big dance floor, open May Labor Day, 8–2. *The New Farm*, Rte. 151; live entertainment, top 40, blue grass, dancing; open year-round, daily.

Sandwich. *Dan'l Webster Inn*, Main St.; tavern, popular groups, ragtime, piano and vocal, dancing; open year-round. *For the Good Times*, Rte. 130; country/western performers, including owner Bobby Gage; 50's night Wednesday; big dance floor, loft; entertainment 9–1, sandwich menu; year-round, closed Mon. *Horizons Beach Club*, Town Neck Rd.; guitar and vocal entertainment, sing-along, oceanfront deck; open year-round. *Pilot's Landing*, Coast Guard Rd.; piano and vocal entertainment summers; bar, restaurant, near marina and canal.

THE MID-CAPE

by

KEVIN FIELDING

After working as a commercial editor in New York City for 11 years for the CBS Television Network and the National Association of Broadcasters, Mr. Fielding discovered he still had sand in his shoes and returned to Cape Cod, where he had spent his boyhood. Today he is a freelance writer based in Hyannis.

The Mid-Cape is the busiest part of Cape Cod. It covers approximately 100 square miles and includes three towns—**Barnstable, Yarmouth,** and **Dennis.** Each town is in turn divided into villages. Barnstable has seven villages—including Hyannis, the urban center of the Cape, with the bus terminal, the airport, the docks for pleasure boats, fishing vessels, and the ferries to the islands of Martha's Vineyard and Nantucket. The other villages of Barnstable are Cotuit, Marstons Mills, Osterville, Centerville, West Barnstable, and the village of Barnstable, which is also the County seat.

Yarmouth, growing from a rural community to a seaside resort, has areas of quiet charm for year-round residents and sections crowded with motels and restaurants that have grown up to accommodate the influx of summer visitors. West Yarmouth, South Yarmouth, Bass River, and Yarmouth Port are the other villages of the town.

Dennis, centrally located like Yarmouth and with some of the most beautiful beaches on the Cape, includes West Dennis, Dennisport, South Dennis, and East Dennis.

The Mid-Cape extends from Cotuit and West Barnstable on the west to Dennisport and East Dennis on the east. Sandy Neck, an eight-mile-long barrier beach with dunes, beach grasses, and marshlands is off shore on the north, jutting into the cold, dark-blue waters of Cape Cod Bay. This is the quiet side of the Cape. Six miles across on the south are the warm waters of Nantucket Sound with its many busy harbors. This south side of the Mid-Cape, with its excellent sandy beaches, is more crowded, especially during the summer season.

The Mid-Cape is a curious blend of the past and the present, the rural and the urban, the old and the new. Some of the people are proud Cape Codders with family roots here; others came first for a vacation holiday but in retirement returned for what is considered a wonderful way of life. For the most part, residents are here because they want to be. Winters are mild and summers cool. The spring season is short, but forsythia and rhododendron abound. The smell of the salt air is invigorating. In the summer months, ocean beaches and harbors are busy with activity. Autumn brings vibrant colors and migrating birds. The year-round resident reclaims his beaches for long walks in solitude.

The Mid-Cape is a study in contrasts. In some parts there is almost a carnival atmosphere, yet stately homes and weathered Cape Cod cottages line quiet village streets. Busy modern shopping centers are not far from tiny specialized shops. There are no huge factories with billowing smokestacks. There is commercial fishing and limited farming of crops like cranberries. But the biggest and most important industry is tourism.

Brief History of the Mid-Cape

The Cape's history is closely woven with much of today's tourism. The towns of the Mid-Cape are rich in stories and legends of the past. Native Americans, early settlers and daring sea captains seem to come to life in this territory to which they once laid claim.

Before the visits of the Norsemen to what they called "the long land," before Bartholomew Gosnold gave the place the name "Cape Cod," before Captain John Smith made the first map of Cape Cod Bay, and long before the Pilgrims settled at Plymouth, Indians lived on these lands. Three of the 30 small tribes of the Wampanoags—the Cummaquid, the Mattakeese, and the Nobscusset—lived in huts and wigwams along the shores of the Mid-Cape. Fishermen and farmers, they were a peace-loving and self-sufficient people.

In the early days of the Plymouth Colony, before there were any settlements in the Mid-Cape, Myles Standish and ten of his men came across Cape Cod Bay to what is now Barnstable in search of John Billington, a somewhat troublesome and adventurous boy, who had wandered off through the woods. The friendly Indians on the shore had given refuge to the youth. It was their chieftain, the young sachem Iyannough, who reunited the group and gave them fresh water and provisions for the trip back to Plymouth.

Although years later, in 1661, war was waged over much of southern New England by the son of Massasoit, known as King Philip, the local Indians remained friendly. They worked alongside the white man. And since the Indians didn't care if they owned the land, as long as they could hunt all over, they sold large stretches for such low prices as four coats and three axes. All of what is known today as Hyannis, Hyannis Port, Centerville, and Craigville was purchased for "twenty pounds and two small breeches."

The first settlers in the Mid-Cape felt suffocated by the rigid social structure of the Plymouth and Massachusetts Bay settlements. Looking for greener pastures, they settled on the north shore by the great salt marshes. The ministers of the church, leaders in all aspects of Colonial life—religious, political, and social—brought their followers in small groups. The Reverend Joseph Hull, a contentious minister known for his fiery sermons, was attracted to Barnstable by the wet marshlands suitable for the grazing of his herd of cattle. He stayed for only a few years. The Reverend John Lothrop was the first to settle permanently in the Mid-Cape area. He was responsible for making Barnstable a thriving, flourishing community. Imprisoned, persecuted, and finally expelled from England because of religious beliefs, he and 22 followers, members of the Congregational Church, located here in 1639. Almost immediately, the towns of Barnstable and Yarmouth were incorporated. Farming was the principal occupation. Soon other ministers and their flocks arrived in search of a freer life.

Although the towns were engaged primarily in farming, eventually the people looked to the sea. Sandy Neck, off Barnstable, was a prime spot for shore whaling. The large trees that existed at the time were cut down to fire the tryards used in the processing of whale oil. It was a change from farming and very profitable. When the drift whale supplies diminished, the men turned to deep-water, off-shore whaling and fishing. Thus the once farmers became seafaring men; however, it took more than a century for this to happen.

In 1761, James Otis, a lawyer from Barnstable, delivered a fiery address before the Superior Court of Massachusetts and kindled the first sparks of the Revolutionary War. The economy of the Cape in the years ahead became dismal. British blockades prevented Cape vessels from sailing. By the 19th century, the merchant fleet of packets was again sailing up and down the coast carrying salt, a new industry started in Dennis; but this time even the War of 1812 did not stop the skillful Cape skippers from running blockades. Trading, fishing, and whaling prospered.

From 1820 through the 1860s, the American clipper ships put the new republic on the charts. These fast ships carried cargo around the world, and many of their captains were from the Mid-Cape. Records show that over 800 shipmasters came from Barnstable. At any one time there would be 50 clipper ship captains living in each town. The Cape skippers commanded respect at home and abroad, and were considered equal to any situation. They built beautiful homes with treasures from around the world. Many of these homes have been kept up and are open to visitors.

As you tour the Mid-Cape, you'll find evidence of the Indians, the ministers and their followers, the early settlers, and the daring shore-packet and deep-sea clipper captains in the old homes, the cemeteries, the monuments, the churches, courthouses, and street and community names. These early stewards of the Cape are not forgotten.

Hyannis and Hyannis Port

The most appropriate place to begin touring the Mid-Cape is at the largest village on Cape Cod, Hyannis—the hub of the Cape. Although it is a town in size, it is a village of the town of Barnstable. Named after the Indian chieftain who helped the Pilgrims, sachem Iyannough, Hyannis today is the Cape's commercial and transportation center. In the summer it is a busy, hectic place; in the winter, it is a quiet seashore village with many retired year-round residents. Although it does not have the charm of other parts of the Cape, Hyannis does have its own distinctive qualities.

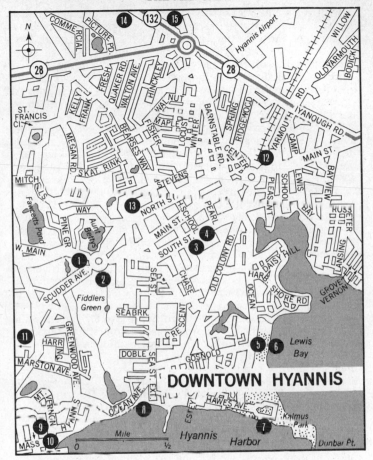

DOWNTOWN HYANNIS

Points of Interest

1) Melody Tent
2) West End Marketplace
3) St. Francis Xavier Church
4) Octagonal House
5) John F. Kennedy Memorial Park
6) Veterans' Beach
7) Kalmus Beach
8) Sea Street Beach
9) St. Andrews' Episcopal Church
10) Sunset Hill
11) Hyannis Port Golf Club
12) Colonial Candle
13) Village Market Place
14) Cape Cod Mall
15) Capetown Mall

In recent years it has been one of the fastest-growing communities in Massachusetts, complete with hotels, motels, condominiums, ethnic restaurants, theaters, night clubs, a hospital, fast-food chains, an airport, bus terminal, business offices, and the large Cape Cod Mall, with 80 department and specialty stores.

Three parallel streets run through the heart of Hyannis. Main Street is one way, from east to west. South Street runs from west to east, and North Street is open to two-way traffic. With these streets in mind, you can easily find your way around.

The famous Melody Tent is at the west end of town. During the summer there are nightly performances of Broadway musicals with leading stars like Carol Channing, Dionne Warwick, and Loretta Lynn. On Wednesday mornings there is children's theater.

Close by the tent on the west end rotary is Dunfey's, a large resort hotel with a par-three golf course, open to the public. In the hotel is a popular discotheque, Tingles.

Within walking distance are a number of fine restaurants, and at the West End Marketplace, a mini-mall, is a carousel and interesting shops. Nearby on South Street is St. Francis Xavier Church, where President John F. Kennedy worshiped in the summer. The pew that he used regularly is marked with a plaque. A few doors down on South Street is the Octagonal House (a private home), designed and built in 1850 by Captain Rodney Baxter, a prominent clipper ship master.

Pleasant and Ocean Streets run off South Street. Here are the docks and boats for deep-sea fishing, harbor tours, and ferries to Martha's Vineyard and Nantucket. At this location in 1666, Nicholas Davis, considered the first businessman of Hyannis, built a warehouse and packed barrels of oysters in brine for shipment to Connecticut, Rhode Island, and New York.

The *Hy-Line* boats run regularly scheduled trips from the Ocean Street docks to the Islands. Tuesday and Thursday evenings one of the Hy-Line boats sails on Lewis Bay for several hours of Jazz music and dancing. The Hy-Line Hyannis Port Harbor Cruise leaves every 30 minutes daily and is the best way to catch a glimpse of the Kennedy Compound. At the Pleasant Street docks you'll find the Steamship Authority's large craft that can accommodate cars.

Overlooking the water on Ocean Street is the John F. Kennedy Memorial Park. Veterans' Beach is next to the park. Hyannis's other two beaches, Kalmus and Sea Street, are close by. All have picnic tables and bathing facilities.

Nearby is Hyannis Port, a posh residential community and the site of the Kennedy Compound. Since the fences and shrubbery are quite high, there is very little to see. However, the beautiful St. Andrew's Episcopal Church, the Hyannis Port Golf Club, and Sunset Hill with its view of the harbor, are worth a visit. The sachem Iyannough, the Indian chieftain who died in 1623, is said to have been the first summer resident of the village.

Back at the east end of Hyannis you'll find the Colonial Candle of Cape Cod. This is the largest candle outlet in the world. The free factory tour brings alive the early art of candlemaking. Next door is the depot for a turn-of-the-century train, which leaves several times daily for a 40-minute, countryside ride to the village of Sandwich. After spending a few hours in that historic town, you will be taken back to Hyannis.

At the west end of town at the corner of North Street and Stevens is the Village Market Place. Open seven days a week, this brick-paved marketplace with fine specialty shops and two restaurants provides a pleasant shopping experience, with fountains, flowers, and comfortable benches.

Within a short drive of the center of Hyannis there are ice and roller skating rinks, shopping malls—Cape Cod and Capetown Mall—cinemas, tennis courts, golf courses, and arcades. There are *Gray Line* bus tours, airplane tours at the nearby airport, and bicycle, moped, and canoe rentals. The possibilities for enjoyment are seemingly endless in this tourist-oriented community.

West Barnstable and Barnstable Village

On the north shore of the Mid-Cape, along Route 6A, are the old villages of West Barnstable and Barnstable Village. This part of the town of Barnstable settled first and it is rich in history. Both villages have somehow avoided the development that has taken place elsewhere. West Barnstable is pastoral and still has good farmland. Barnstable Village is the County seat and the political center of the area. Off-shore is the barrier beach, Sandy Neck, and the great salt marshes that served for cattle grazing in Colonial times.

For a complete historical driving tour of the villages, start at the intersection of Route 149 and 6A. The cemetery at the corner is the resting place of many early settlers. The most prominent marker can be seen from the road, that of "Mad Jack" Percival, a famous naval captain. His last command was of *Old Ironsides* on her voyage around the world in the mid-1840s. This capable but eccentric skipper served with Admiral Nelson in the Battle of Trafalgar in 1805.

A half mile down Route 149 is the West Parish Meeting House, a church built by the early Congregationalists, who were led by the Reverend John Lothrop, a dominant force in the rise of the settlement. His second home is standing today and is part of the Sturgis Library on Route 6A in Barnstable Village, just to the east.

About a third of a mile east on Route 6A from the Route 149 junction is a boulder and plaque marking the home of James Otis of Revolutionary War fame. Known as the Patrick Henry of the North, he helped kindle the first sparks of war in a famous speech in Boston. The bell atop the West Parish Church was made by Paul Revere, and donated by James Otis.

Near Route 6A on Route 132 is the Cape Cod Community College, situated on 120 acres of land. Since its beginnings in 1961, its presence has been a cohesive force in the intellectual community of Cape Cod. In the college library, the William Brewster Nickerson Memorial Room contains the world's largest collection of books and material about Cape Cod—over 15,000 books, manuscripts, records, and ship's logs. Opposite the College, on Route 132, is the Cape Cod Conservatory, which offers study in music, art, and dance.

As you drive east on winding Route 6A, you'll pass Sacrament Rock, where Reverend Lothrop and his followers celebrated their first church service. Lothrop Hill, where the minister is buried, is just east of Governors Way.

Before entering Barnstable Village on Route 6A, you will pass by the Sturgis Library, the oldest library building in the United States. The Olde Court House is just beyond, and on the right is the Barnstable Village Hall—home today of the Barnstable Comedy Club and in the summer of the Atlantic Theatre Company. Diagonally across the street is the Barnstable Inn. Now a restaurant, this old home is said to be haunted by five ghosts.

In the center of Barnstable Village is the Crocker Tavern, built in 1754. Here during stagecoach days travelers were fed and housed on the long, three-day trip to Boston. One fall night in 1827, men left their card game in this tavern and rushed to save town records when the Court House caught fire. Unfortunately, few records were saved and it took years to straighten out land titles. This old hostelry is now owned by the New England Society for the Preservation of Antiquities and is open to the public.

Close to the village is Barnstable Harbor, with its fleet of fishing and charter boats. This is the site of the annual Mid-Cape tuna fishing tournament. The only beach in the area is near the Mattakeese Restaurant, where diners can look out over the harbor. Whale-watching trips leave daily from the pier on a large boat holding about 75 people.

Antique and gift shops abound on Route 6A in West Barnstable and Barnstable Village. If you are interested in handwoven fabrics, the Blacks, tweed weavers for 20 years, have their shop on Route 6A in West Barnstable and give loom demonstrations.

Just east of the traffic lights on Route 6A, and on top of Cobb's Hill, is the old Custom House. Beginning in 1789, the village served as headquarters of a custom district. For over a century foreign ships were cleared at this port of entry. The present building was built in 1856 and served this purpose until 1913, when it became a Post Office. Today it is the Trayser Memorial Museum and is filled with Colonial and Indian treasures.

A little farther on Route 6A, about opposite the Cummaquid Post Office, is a marker commemorating the grave of sachem Iyannough, friend of the early settlers who died at the age of 26. Hyannis and Wianno are named after this early chieftain.

Also on Route 6A at this point is the Cape Cod Art Association in a modern structure close to the road. Open year-round, the Association holds exhibits and sales of Cape artists from April through December and offers free outdoor art lessons during the summer.

All along the beautiful Old King's Highway (Route 6A) are the magnificent homes of early sea captains. This stretch of road is one of the most beautiful drives on the Cape.

Cotuit, Osterville, Marstons Mills, Centerville

On the southwestern corner of the Mid-Cape is the residential village of Cotuit. Spared the commercial development that has affected other Cape communities, Cotuit has remained a quiet summer residence for the affluent. There is one variety store, a gas station, and beautiful homes on the bluff. The winter residents who are not writers or retired professionals find employment in other villages of the Cape, some even commute to Boston.

In 1658, the land that now makes up the village was purchased from the Indian Paupmumuck, sachem of the South Sea. Until 1800, Cotuit was sparsely settled farming country. In the Indian language the name means "Long Fields."

In the 1820s, Cotuit began to grow and prosper and did so until the decline of the shipping trade at the end of the 19th century. Captain William Childs started the Cotuit oyster business. The shellfish were packed in barrels and shipped by wagon and train to Boston and New York. The Cotuit Oyster Company is still operating. During its growth period Cotuit had a fleet of 25 coasting vessels averaging 300 tons. Besides the now-famous Cotuit oysters, the village was also involved in shipbuilding, saltmaking, fishing, and cranberry growing.

Among the more interesting tourist attractions in Cotuit on Main Street is the Samuel Dottridge Homestead, built in the 1700s. Operated by the Historical Society, the old home has many early American articles on exhibit. Nearby on Main Street is the old Cotuit Post Office, the first building in the United States built (in 1821) specifically as a Post Office.

At the town beach, back in 1916, the Cotuit Mosquito Yacht Club, a sailing club for young people, was founded. There is no clubhouse and the dues are small. However, you must be under 25 and unmarried to hold office.

Out at the corner of Route 28 and Route 130 is that part of Cotuit known as Santuit. At this intersection is the 1739 home of Ebenezer Crocker. One of the first residents of the village, he pulled the house from West Barnstable with 17 oxen. It has since been enlarged.

Heading east on Route 28 you will see signs directing you to the village of Osterville. Although Osterville was purchased from the Indians in 1648, there were few settlers here until after 1700. The people of the village changed the name from Oyster Island to Osterville in 1815.

Today, Osterville is a charming village with designer shops on its main street. Many retired and semi-retired people have built or bought houses in the village in recent years.

At the corner of West Bay and Parker roads is the Captain Jonathan Parker House, home of the Osterville Historical Society and Museum. Built in 1798, the house is open to the public and exhibits antique china, glass, dolls, and other artifacts. The Boat Shop Museum is also on the property.

Close by there are two sections of Osterville, Wianno and Oyster Harbors. Both are exclusive summer resorts with yacht clubs, golf courses, and beautiful homes. Oyster Harbors was once called Grand Island and Screecher's Island. Hannah Screecher was a legendary village maiden who, while wandering on the island one day, say some pirates led by Captain Kidd burying a treasure chest. They disposed of her cruelly and tossed her into the treasure pit. Some say that her spirit has since hovered over the treasure as she, with blood-curdling screeches, warns others away from the tainted gold.

Just off West Bay Road is the Crosby Boat Yard. Over a century ago the now-famous Cat Boat was designed and built here. Once seen everywhere along the shore, this sailboat, with its retractable centerboard allowing it to cross shallow water, was said to "come about quick as a cat."

On the other side of Route 28, continuing east, is the village of Marstons Mills, one of the few untouched, quiet villages on the Cape. This is an inland village with no ocean front. It does, however, have three beautiful clear ponds—Mystic Lake, Middle Pond, and Hamblin's Pond. Settled in the first migration from the north to the south shore, the village became a center for milling. The stream, Goodspeed's River, provided power for many grist mills and fulling mills. The first Marston arrived in 1738 and ran a mill for many years at a location that is now at the corner of Route 28 and 149—today just a herring run. In the center of the village is a general store and a gas station. There is very little else here except scattered homes and the Race Lane Stables, where an annual horse show takes place in August.

The village of Centerville is on both sides of Route 28 just before you reach Hyannis heading east. Part of the village is quiet and residential and the other section, known as Craigville, is tourist-oriented. Craigville Beach is one of the best on the south shore. Next to the beach is the Craigville Conference Center, where many church-related activities take place throughout the year. In the summer, Craigville hosts the annual Writers' Conference.

On Main Street in Centerville, you'll find the Historical Society in the Mary Lincoln House, which has antique furniture, old costumes, bird carvings, dolls, and Sandwich glass. Many old sea captains' houses are in this area. One was occupied for years by Dr. Herbert T. Kalmus, co-inventor of Technicolor. He donated 40 acres in Hyannis at Dunbar's Point, which is now called Kalmus Beach. In the center of the village is the Old Centerville Country Store, where you can still buy penny candy.

On the other side of Route 28 is a quiet residential part of Centerville by the Wequaquet Lake—the second largest lake on the Cape. In the summer there are sailfish races at the Wequaquet Yacht Club, and in the winter, wind sailing on the ice.

Close by the lake is Phinney's Lane, where most of the early history of this village took place. Here stood Solomon Phinney's Tavern, the schoolhouse, the village church where day-long sermons were held, and the training grounds for the town's military companies. Above the lake, on Route 6, is an overview known as Shoot Flying Hill. Here the Indians would position themselves to shoot the geese flying from the ocean to the lake.

West Yarmouth, South Yarmouth, Bass River

The village of West Yarmouth begins just outside of Hyannis center to the east on Route 28. This stretch of road through West and South Yarmouth on the south shore is one of the busiest sections of the Cape because of the number of summer cottages, motels, and beaches in the area. In the summer it is often so congested that the driving becomes stop-and-go.

Yarmouth, like Barnstable, is one of the fastest-growing towns in the state. In recent years, there has been a great deal of construction of year-round homes.

A major summer attraction in West Yarmouth on Route 28 is the Aqua Circus, with dolphins and performing sea lions. There is also a petting zoo. Close by on Mill Pond is the Baxter Grist Mill, built in 1710. For several generations, this mill ground corn with water-wheel power. It is now owned by the Town of Yarmouth; visitors are welcome.

That part of South Yarmouth that is close to Bass River was at one period heavily populated by Indians. During Colonial times, and even as late as 1779, there were many wigwams in this area. Wars and smallpox took their toll on the Indians and by the time of the War of 1812, they were disappearing quickly. At the Indian Burying Ground, on Indian Memorial Drive off Station Avenue and overlooking Long Pond, there is a stone marker that reads: "On this slope lie buried the last native Indians of Yarmouth."

Many of the white settlers in South Yarmouth were Quakers. The area was even called Friends Village. In 1809 they built the Friends Meeting House on North Main Street, which is open to the public today. You will note there is a partition down the center of the room to divide the sexes for separate business meetings. The nearby cemetery has uniform markers with no epitaphs—the Quakers felt all were equal in God's eyes.

There is an ancient windmill in South Yarmouth. The Judah Baker Mill is located on Willow Street. Built in 1791 in South Dennis, the mill was moved to West Dennis, and finally, in 1863, to its present site. For those interested in unusual architecture, nearby is the Davis House of Seven Chimneys. Four old houses were moved together and connected with passageways.

If you drive up Station Avenue toward Route 6, you will come to White's Path and the Cape Cod Coliseum. Many functions are held here during the summer, from wrestling to rock concerts. In the winter, it is used primarily for ice skating. Also in South Yarmouth there is a fitness center, bikes rentals, the Mid-Cape Racquet Club, and two good golf courses. At Bass River, which is actually part of South Yarmouth, there are boat rentals. Charter boats leave from Merry Mill. The *Champion Line* offers scenic cruises on the Bass River past riverfront estates, old captains' houses, and other historic landmarks of Yarmouth's Gold Coast.

Smuggler's Beach, at the mouth of the Bass River, has an

interesting history. When the British Parliament imposed the Sugar Act of 1764, levying taxes on lumber, food, rum, and molasses, the Colonists used this beach for smuggling goods ashore. Because of the shallow water it was perfect for small boats wishing to avoid pursuit. During Prohibition, rum runners used the beach for the same reason.

Yarmouth Port, Yarmouth, Dennis, East Dennis

The villages of Yarmouth Port and Yarmouth are on the north shore of the Mid-Cape on Route 6A, as are the villages of Dennis and East Dennis.

The first elderly resident of the area was the Reverend Stephen Bachiler who, at the age of 75, walked here in the dead of winter from the Plymouth Colony with some of his followers to start a new settlement and church. They survived the walk and the winter, but stayed only a year before moving on—the minister died back in England at the age of 100.

Just after the Reverend Bachiler left, three permanent settlers moved in—Anthony Thacher, John Crowe, and Thomas Howes. These were hard-working men, more interested in developing the land than in religious quarrels. Anthony Thacher had just survived, along with his second wife, a shipwreck in a hurricane. The last of his nine children from an earlier marriage went down with the ship and the rest of the passengers, but within four years Thacher was a man of property and position. He had a son, John, who grew up, married, and had 21 children. The house he built in 1664, the Colonel John Thacher House, is open to the public today and is located at Thacher Road and Route 6A in Yarmouth Port.

Next door is the Winslow Crocker House, built in 1780 and owned today by the Society for the Preservation of New England Antiquities. This house is also open to the public. There is an interesting gun room hidden behind the fireplace.

At one time 50 sea captains lived along this one-mile stretch of Route 6A, which was dubbed Captains' Row. One of the houses, the Captain Bangs Hallet House, is the home of the Historical Society of Old Yarmouth. Built in 1740, the house has been restored and filled with antique furnishings and china. The Society provides visitors with a helpful booklet about the old houses of the area. Next to the Hallet House are the Botanic Trails, winding for two miles through fields, forests, and pond areas. The hike gives you a feeling for the area as it must have been for the early settlers. These marked trails are here today thanks to a grant from a descendant of that early settler, Anthony Thacher.

At the end of Center Street in Yarmouth Port is a little cove called Bass Hole. A nearby boardwalk goes out over the marshes. Long before the Pilgrims, it is said that the Vikings landed on Cape Cod at Yarmouth around A.D. 1003. Legend has it that Leif Ericksson's brother, Thorvald, landed to repair his ship at Bass Hole and was killed by the natives.

In the center of the village of Yarmouth Port are several other points of interest. The New Church, near the village green, is actually a very old church and was the most influential in Yarmouth in the late 1800s. The Village Pump, where household water was drawn and horses watered, is located at the corner of Summer Street and Route 6A. Built in 1886, it was the main source of water for the town for many years. The Summer Street Cemetery has some of the oldest grave markers on the Cape. The Old Yarmouth Inn is the Cape's oldest, dating back to 1696. It is said that from this inn, which is a restaurant today, Sam (Black) Bellamy, who ran a profitable packet line along the coast, was shanghaied with a half dozen other Cape Codders. Recovering from the effects of their drugged drinks consumed at the tavern, they found themselves aboard a British man-of-war at sea. Organizing the other captives, Bellamy slew the officers and took over the ship. Raising the Jolly Roger, he began a long career as a pirate roaming the Atlantic and has since been the subject of many bloody naval stories.

The villages of Yarmouth Port and Yarmouth, along the Olde King's Highway, are part of one of the most attractive areas on Cape Cod. There are few places to stay on this side of the Mid-Cape, but there are some fine restaurants and many shops for browsing. The residents of the area have long been concerned with preserving its character and charm.

Continuing east on Route 6A, you will pass into Dennis and East Dennis. When the east precinct of Yarmouth separated to become a town in 1793, it was named after the popular Reverend Josiah Dennis, pastor of the First Meeting House of Yarmouth. The Josiah Dennis Manse, the minister's home, has been restored and is open to the public. On the corner of Nobscusset and Whig streets, the house is a two-story saltbox on three acres of land bounded by a creek and a stone wall. As in Yarmouth, Dennis and East Dennis contain some very exceptional old Colonial houses and sea captains' homes; most have date markings.

The Shiverick Shipyards, where many clipper ships were built from 1820 to 1850, were located in East Dennis. The first of these beautiful, fast ships was the *Revenue*. Other Dennis clippers famous in their day include the *Wild Hunter*, the *Belle of the West*, and the *Hippogriffe*.

Cranberry growing has been, and still is, an important part of the Cape's economy. Henry Hall of Dennis is said to be the originator of the cranberry bog as we know it today. About 1816, he discovered that the vines grew more rapidly with proper irrigation and the addition of sand to the soil.

For those interested in good summer theater, the Cape Playhouse at Dennis, just off Route 6A, is one of the oldest and finest summer playhouses in the country. Started in 1926, the theater has featured such players as Bette Davis, Gregory Peck, and Henry Fonda. For many of the stars, it was their first professional appearance. The Playhouse's summer season begins in July and runs to Labor Day. On the property is the Cape Cinema, which has the largest ceiling mural in the world. Painted by Rockwell Kent, the mural is currently undergoing restoration.

A popular geographical point of interest in Dennis is the Scargo Lake and Tower. The lake is named after Princess Scargo, the daughter of the chief of the Nobscusset Indians. Legend has it that the lake was dug by squaws of the tribe for the pet fish of the Princess, and the nearby Scargo Hill was built with sand from the lake. There is a stone tower on the hill, which visitors can climb for the highest vantage point in the Mid-Cape area—you can see 80 miles on a clear day. Close by, just off Route 6A, is the Indian Cemetery, with a single granite slab inscribed: "Burial ground of the Nobscusset Tribe of Indians of which Tribe Mashantampaine was Chief."

One of the members of the tribe was a hermit who lived alone in a cave now known as Hokum Rocks. Legend says that when anyone approached the cave he would say, "Ho kum?," meaning "Who comes?" The Hokum Rocks can be reached by the Old Bass River Road. This is a good picnic spot for the children.

As you continue driving east on Route 6A, you will pass into the village of East Dennis. One of the first residents of this village was Richard Sears, known as "Sleepy John." In 1776, when the British blockades prevented coastal trading, he set out to develop a method of extracting salt from sea water through evaporation. Known as Sears Folly, his saltmaking process was soon taken seriously and became a major industry. Saltworks soon sprang up all over the Cape. Captain Sears' old home is located on North Street off Cold Storage Road in East Dennis.

If you wish to get away from the crowds, you might consider a walk in the beautiful Fresh Pond Conservation Area. For bicycle enthusiasts, the special bike trail that leads down to the Lower-Cape begins at Dennis on Route 6A.

Quiet country inns, good restaurants, historic sites, fresh and saltwater swimming, and fine shops mark this part of the Mid-Cape.

West Dennis, South Dennis, Dennisport

There are a number of confusing names on Cape Cod. One of them is "West Dennis," which is actually south of both Dennis and South Dennis. On the south shore, West Dennis begins at the Bass River Bridge. As you head east on Route 28, you will pass many motels, cottages, restaurants, and gift shops. The West Dennis beach is one of the best on the south shore; turn right on School Street. The original lighthouse has been converted and is now part of the Lighthouse Inn, a summer resort with a fine restaurant.

West Dennis was originally called "Crow Village," named after John Crow, the first settler. One of his descendants, Captain Levi Crowell, built a home on Church Street in 1827. The house, which is standing today, was once used by a family member as a publishing house. The firm relocated to New York City and became the Thomas Y. Crowell Publishing Company, which is now part of Harper & Row.

The village of South Dennis is just north off Route 28. It has no ocean shoreline, although the Bass River weaves throughout the area. Taking Old Main Street, you will immediately encounter the South Parish Congregational Church, which boasts the oldest working organ in the United States. Built in 1835 on the site of the original meeting house, this church was the worship place for many early sea captains. There is a plaque on the wall listing 102 captains who lived in or near the village. The cemetery beside the church has markers dating from 1795. Many of them are for sea captains; and as is often true of the graves of early seafaring men, they simply say, "Lost at sea."

Within walking distance on Main Street is the Jericho House—so named because, before restoration, the walls were almost falling down. Open to the public, this 1801 full-Cape house has floor and roof boards up to two feet wide. It is difficult to imagine today but, 200 years ago, there were forests of large trees on the Cape. Behind the house is the Barn Museum, with exhibits of the early saltmaking and cranberry industries. A driftwood collection is located in the basement.

For jogging enthusiasts, at the corner of Access and Old Bass

River roads, is a one-and-a-half-mile trail called the "Lifecourse." With 20 exercise stations, the winding path through the woods is open to the public free of charge. Close by on Access Road, in front of the police station, is an exhibit of early Colonial forms of punishment. One Route 134, just off Route 6, is the Melpet Riding Stable, with plenty of wooded trails and horses.

Heading east, the last village of the Mid-Cape is Dennisport. Using Shad Hole Road off Route 28, you arrive at the ocean. The Union Wharf Packing Company was located here in the 1850s. All along this shore there were grocery stores, sailmakers, and ships chandlers. Sea clams were packed and shipped from this spot, but today it is a prime summer resort area, with cottages, summer homes, and condominiums. On Lower County Road is Seaview Playland, an amusement center offering everything from pedal boats to miniature golf.

The village of Dennisport is typical of many of the villages of the Mid-Cape. There is the busy main street shopping area, history, beautiful beaches, and the ever-present cedar-shingled houses left to weather and turn gray in the salt air, with white picket fences covered with rambling roses.

There are many things to enjoy on Cape Cod, chief among them the natural beauty of this gentle, narrow strip of land. As tourists are welcomed to the area, the unspoken credo of the Cape Cod Chamber of Commerce could almost be the words of an old Indian prayer: "The Creator made the world—come and see it."

PRACTICAL INFORMATION FOR THE MID-CAPE

HOW TO GET AROUND. While distances are not great, the automobile is essential on Cape Cod. There are three main roads passing through the Mid-Cape from west to east. Rte. 6A—the Olde King's Highway—is a tree-shaded, winding-road through the older villages on the north shore by Cape Cod Bay. Rte. 6 is a double highway in the middle of the Cape, the quickest route between towns. Rte. 28 is the major road on the south side of the Cape and it is busy with commerce. Rtes. 130, 132, 134, and 149 are the major connecting roads between the north and south shore of the Mid-Cape. Hyannis is the transportation center of the Cape. Here all connections can be made,

Car rental: *Avis* and *Hertz* operate car rentals at the airport. *Mr. Rent-A-Car* is located at the airport rotary. Taxis are in every town.

By air: The airport, located near the center of Hyannis, has three airlines. *PBA* flies regular passenger service to Boston and New York and other cities as well as the islands of Martha's Vineyard and Nantucket. *Will's Air* and *Gull Air* handle air freight and charters to the Islands.

By bus: The bus terminal is located at Center St. in Hyannis. The *Cape Cod Bus Lines* operate daily between Hyannis and Provincetown. Schedules are available at the ticket office. *Bonanza, Greyhound, Plymouth,* and *Brockton* bus companies all have regularly scheduled buses to Boston and Providence and other off-Cape cities with connections to all points.

By ferry: The *Steamship Authority,* the large ferry service, leaves the Mid-Cape at the Pleasant Street Dock in Hyannis for the islands of Martha's Vineyard and Nantucket. Car reservations must be made ahead. Check schedule for rates and times. From spring to mid-September, the *Hy-Line* boats leave the Ocean Street Docks.

By moped and bicycle: For rent by the hour, day, or week. The Mid-Cape has few official bike trails. One begins in Dennis heading to the outer Cape. The service road running parallel to Rte. 6 is often used between Hyannis and Sandwich. Maps are offered at the Dennis Chamber of Commerce for historical bike tours.

All Cape Rental Center—255 Lower County Rd., Dennisport.
Dennis Cycle—1594 Rte. 6A, East Dennis.
Cape Cod Bicycle and Sport Co.—Dunfey's Hotel, Hyannis.
Shwinn Bikes—North St., Hyannis.
Osterville Bicycle Service—1356 Main St., Osterville.
Hall Oil Co.—Rte. 132, South Dennis.
The Outdoor Shop—928 Rte. 28, South Yarmouth.
Jason's Bike Shop—606 Rte. 28, West Yarmouth.

MEDICAL EMERGENCIES. Cape Cod Hospital, 27 Park St., Hyannis. Phone: 771-1800
    Hyannis Medical Center, Rte. 132, Hyannis. Phone: 771-7520
    Mid-Cape Medical Center, Rte. 28 at Bearse's Way, Hyannis. Phone: 771-4092

TOURIST INFORMATION SERVICES. *Cape Cod Chamber of Commerce* (open year-round). Junction of Rte. 6 and Rte. 132, Hyannis, Massachusetts 02601. Phone: 362-3225. *Dennis Chamber of Commerce* (open Memorial Day until Labor Day). Intersection of Rtes. 28 and 134, South Dennis, Massachusetts 02660. Phone: 398-3573. *Yarmouth Chamber of Commerce* (open Memorial Day until Labor Day). Rte. 28, West Yarmouth, Massachusetts 02673. Phone: 775-4133.

RECOMMENDED READING. *Barnstable—Three Centuries of a Cape Cod Town.* Trayser, Donald; Parnassus Imports, Yarmouth Port, Massachusetts, 1939 (reprinted 1971). *Cape Cod.* Berchen, William, and Dickens, Monica; Penguin Press, New York, 1975. *Cape Cod's Way.* Corbett, Scott; Thomas Crowell Co., New York, 1955. *Cape Cod in Color.* Vuilleumier, Marion, and Lazarus, Julius; Hastings House, New York, 1977. *Cape Cod—Its People and Their History.* Kittredge, Henry C.; Houghton Mifflin, Boston, 1930 (reprinted 1968). *Hiking Cape Cod.* Mitchell, J. H., and Griswald, Whit; Fast and McMillan, Charlotte, North Carolina, 1978. *The Seven Villages of Barnstable.* Written by its people on the occasion of the 200th birthday of the United States; published by the Town of Barnstable, Barnstable, Massachusetts, 1976. *Short Bike Rides on Cape Cod.* Griffith, Jane, and Mullen, Edwin; Penguin Press, New York, 1977. *We Chose Cape Cod.* Corbett, Scott; Chatham Press, Chatham, Massachusetts, 1970. *Yesterday's Cape Cod.* Lawson, Evelyn; Seemann Publishing Co., Inc., Miami, Florida, 1975.

SEASONAL EVENTS. During the off-season on the Cape, events for the most part are sponsored by churches, schools, and special interest clubs. There are arts and crafts exhibits, flower shows, and musical affairs. There are athletic competitions, literary meetings, and a dog show at the Cape Cod Mall.

Memorial Day (May 31st) ushers in the busy summer season with the *Figawi Race;* boats of all sizes race from Hyannis to the island of Nantucket. During the summer, dates and locations vary. There are weekly band concerts in every town; there are street festivals in Hyannis and Dennis (the one in Dennis lasts for a week; the Hyannis festival, for two days). There are auctions, flea markets, and yard sales. Numerous athletic events include golf tournaments, swimming competitions, softball, tennis, baseball, and a women's road race. There are art shows, musical celebrations, bridge tournaments, a horse show at Marstons Mills, sailing regattas at all the harbor yacht clubs and at Lake Wequaquet, as well as tuna- and shark-fishing competitions at Barnstable Harbor and Lewis Bay. Residents and visitors alike should check weekly listings in the newspapers: the *Cape Cod Times,* the *Barnstable Patriot,* and the *Register.*

HISTORIC SITES. Much of the history of the Mid Cape is hidden in old churches, old houses, and old cemeteries. Throughout the towns are plaques commemorating noteworthy citizens and events. In many of the villages the historical societies provide lists of the dozens of old homes in the area open free of charge or for a nominal fee.

Barnstable. *Crocker Tavern,* Rte. 6A, Barnstable Village. Open summer only, Tues. and Sat., 1–5 P.M. Built in 1754 as a tavern. Eighteenth-century furniture and historical exhibits.

Lothrop Hill Cemetery, Rte. 6A, Barnstable. Earliest marked cemetery in Barnstable. Rev. John Lothrop, a driving force in the early settlement, is buried here.

The Olde Colonial Court House, Rendezvous Lane and Main St., Barnstable Village. Open Mon. through Fri., 1:30–4 P.M. Erected in 1772, the old building, filled with artifacts of the past, is operated by Tales of Cape Cod, the Cape Cod Historical Society.

Old Customs House, Main St., Barnstable Village. Now the Donald Trayser Memorial. (See listing under Museums.)

Plaques include memorials to: James Otis on Rte. 6A near Rte. 149, West Barnstable. Called the "Patrick Henry of the North," he was a fiery leader in the Revolution. Also "Mad Jack Percival" at Old West Cemetery, corner of Rte. 6A and Rte. 149, West Barnstable. Grave of eccentric skipper who commanded *Old Ironsides* on her 459-day voyage around the world.

Sacrament Rock, just east of Rte. 6A and Rte. 132, West Barnstable. A fragmented boulder with a bronze marker to indicate the place where Rev. John Lothrop and his congregation held their first religious service in 1639.

Sturgis Library, Main St., Barnstable Village. Oldest library building in United States. (See listing under Libraries.)

West Parish Meeting House, Rte. 6A and Old Meeting House Way, West Barnstable. Open daily 9–5 P.M. Sunday service at 10 A.M. Oldest Congregational Church still in existence. Built in 1717, now completely restored. Gilded cock was brought from England; bell was made by Paul Revere.

Centerville. *The Mary Lincoln House,* 513 Main St., Centerville. Open June to mid-Sept., Wed. thru Sun., 2–3:30 P.M. Headquarters for the Centerville Historical Society. In the Centerville Square is a monument to the Civil War dead. Chiseled in the granite are the names of the 30 villagers who died in the conflict.

Cotuit. *Samuel Dottridge Homestead,* 1148 South Main St., Cotuit. Open July and Aug., Thu. 3–5 P.M., Sun. 4–6 P.M. House was moved by oxen to Cotuit from Harwich in early 1800s. Now maintained by Historical Society of Cotuit-Santuit. Hostess will direct visitors to other old houses in the neighborhood, some brought over from Nantucket by the old sea captains.

Cummaquid. *Grave of Sachem Iyannough,* Rte. 6A across from Post Office. Slate marker reads: "On this spot was buried Sachem Iyannough, friend and entertainer of the Pilgrims July 1621."

Dennis. *Jericho House,* Old Main St. and Trotting Park Rd., West Dennis. Open July and Aug., Wed., Fri., and Sat., 2–5 P.M. Town maintains this old house as headquarters for the Dennis Historical Society.

Curious Forms of Colonial Punishment. Outdoor exhibit in front of Police Station, Dennis. Open during daylight hours. Includes authentic pillories, stocks, and whipping post.

Siverick Shipyard Marker, Sesuit Neck Rd., East Dennis. Bronze plaque depicting famous shipyard as it looked in the days of the clipper ships.

South Parish Congregational Church, Main St., South Dennis. Visitors welcome at all services. Church commemorates the 102 sea captains that lived in area. Organ is oldest pipe organ in actual use in America.

Hyannis. *First Baptist Church,* 486 Main St., Hyannis. Open year-round every morning Sun. thru Fri. Dates back to 1772. In the old days each member built his own pew.

John F. Kennedy Memorial, Ocean St., Hyannis. Circular fieldstone memorial with presidential seal, fountain, and small pool.

St. Francis Xavier Church, South St., Hyannis. Open every day. Church where John F. Kennedy and his family worshipped during the summer. Plaque on second bench in the chapel indicates his pew.

Hyannis Port. *The Kennedy Compound,* Irving and Scudder Aves. Four houses practically hidden by bushes and fences. Scene of activity during President Kennedy's years in the White House. Best viewed from the harbor. (See Tours.)

Osterville. *Captain Jonathon Parker House,* Parker Rd., Osterville. Open July thru Sept., Thu. and Sun. 3–5 P.M. Maintained by Osterville Historical Society.

Yarmouth. *Captain Bangs Hallet House,* Rte. 6A at Strawberry Lane, Yarmouth. Open during the summer, Mon. through Sat., 10–12 noon and 2–4 P.M. Home of Yarmouth Historical Association.

Baxter Grist Mill, Rte. 28, West Yarmouth. Open daily. Built in 1710. Restored to working condition.

Indian Monument, off Station Ave., South Yarmouth. Boulder engraved: "On this slope lie buried the last native Indians of Yarmouth."

MUSEUMS. Barnstable. *The Donald Trayser Memorial Museum,* on Rte. 6A at the corner of Phinney's Lane, is called Barnstable's "memory bank." Relics of Colonial times, Indian tools, marine paintings, ships in bottles. Open during the summer Tues. through Sat., 1:30–4:30 P.M.

Centerville. *The Centerville Historical Society Museum* is in the Mary Lincoln House at 519 Main St. Costume collection, dolls, antique furnishings, bird carvings, and quilts.

Cotuit. *The Santuit and Cotuit Historical Society* is located in the Samuel Dottridge House on Main St. in Cotuit Village. This old home is authentic early American and includes furnishings that date from 1800 to 1850. The barn behind the house is a museum of early American memorabilia. Open during the summer Thu. and Sun. afternoons, 3–5 P.M.

East Dennis. *The Old Sound Museum,* near Rte. 6A and Rte. 134. Antique phonographs, radios, recordings. Open Tues. through Sun., 10 A.M.–6 P.M., from mid-May through Oct.

Osterville. *Osterville Historical Society and Museum,* corner of Parker Rd. and West Bay Rd. Examples of Sandwich glass, Lowestoft porcelain, period furniture, early American pottery and pewter. Primitive and document rooms. Open during the summer Thu. and Sun., 3–5 P.M.

South Dennis. *Jericho Historical Center,* corner of Old Main and Trotting Park Rd. Old farm equipment and a driftwood zoo. Open during the summer Wed., Fri., and Sat., 2–5 P.M.

Yarmouth. *Captain Bangs Hallet House,* Rte. 6A at Strawberry Lane, Yarmouth. Operated by the Historical Society of Yarmouth. Early American exhibits. Open weekdays July through Sept., 1–4 P.M.

From all of the historical societies, lists may be obtained of old houses open to the public. Admission to the museums and houses is either free or requires a very small charge.

LIBRARIES. *Albert Einstein Library.* A new library on the Cape in temporary quarters at the Olde Colonial Courthouse on Rte. 6A in Barnstable Village. The library will eventually be located in a new structure on Rte. 6A in Yarmouth Port. The collection of literature and film is the largest of Einstein materials outside of the Institute for Advanced Study in Princeton, New Jersey.

Cape Cod Community College Library. The William Brewster Nickerson Memorial Room contains the largest collection of books and material about Cape Cod. Over 15,000 books, manuscripts, records, ship's logs, and much more have been gathered and catalogued. Open for research to the public daily. Off Rte. 132 in West Barnstable.

Centerville Library. Located at 585 Main St. in Centerville. Many of the village libraries contain special collections. The Centerville Library houses a 42-volume collection of the transcripts of the Nuremberg Trials.

Cotuit Library. On Main St., Cotuit. With a collection of ship models, this library houses the Kirkman collection of beautifully bound volumes of the classics considered a gentleman's library.

Hyannis Public Library. On Main Street, Hyannis. The largest public library in the mid-Cape area houses considerable material on the late President John F. Kennedy. Part of the building consists of the old cottage library with its original fireplaces dating back to 1800. Home of an early Cape skipper, Captain Hallet.

Osterville Library. Wianno Ave., Osterville. Open for reading, as well as free movies, book talks, and special exhibits.

Sturgis Library. Rte. 6A in Barnstable Village. The home of John Lothrop, a Colonial minister, who built the house in 1644, making Sturgis the oldest library building in the United States. It was later the ancestral home of William Sturgis who became a sea captain at the age of 19. The library has the best Cape Cod genealogical collection in New England. Excellent maritime history collection. More than 1500 charts and maps.

Public libraries in the Mid-Cape are all open year-round, but the hours vary and schedules should be checked. Massachusetts residents may obtain free library cards; non-residents must pay $10 in order to take out books. Browsers are always welcome.

TOURS. Railroad. *Cape Cod and Hyannis Railroad.* Center St., Hyannis. 771-1145. Scenic train ride from Hyannis to Sandwich. 55 minutes one way. Three types of tours offered.

Bus. *Cape Cod Adventures.* P.O. Box 433, Cummaquid. 362-8001. Packaged group tours around Cape and Islands. Guides will also serve out-of-town buses.

Cape Cod Tour and Conference Associates (Cape Cod Bus Lines). 712 Main St., Hyannis. 771-5165. Day-long tour from Hyannis to Provincetown. June to Sept. Leaves from different locations and at different times.

Gray Line of Cape Cod. Leave from Melody Tent, West Main St., Hyannis. 778-0182. Bus tours to Lower-Cape and around Martha's Vineyard.

Oceanside Tours. 299 Main St., West Yarmouth. 771-8864. Bus tour to historic places in Barnstable, Yarmouth, and Dennis. Passes through 13 villages.

Boat. *Hy-Line—Hyannis Harbor Tours.* Ocean Street Dock, Hyannis. 775-7185. From late March until late Nov. Every 30 minutes a boat departs. Best way to see the Kennedy Compound.

Hy Line Nantucket/Martha's Vineyard Hyannis Boats. Ocean St. Dock, Hyannis. 775-7185. 1 hr. and 45 mins. to Martha's Vineyard, 2 hrs to Nantucket. From early spring to mid-Sept. Check schedules.

Island Voyages. 125 Pleasant St., Hyannis. 771-7211. Day tours from hotel to Islands.

Scenic Cruises of Bass River (*Champion Line*). Rte. 28, Merry Mill Complex, Bass River, South Yarmouth. 394-1977. Four one-hour trips daily, spring through fall. Free parking.

Steamship Authority. 540-2022. Large ferry service to Martha's Vineyard and Nantucket. Leaves Mid-Cape daily at Hyannis Pleasant St. Dock, April–January. Car reservations must be made in advance. Rates and schedule vary, so should be checked.

Whale Watching. Off Mill Way, Barnstable Harbor, Barnstable Village. 771-3076. Five-hour trip daily through the summer on a 60-foot boat holding 75 people.

Brochures with schedules available at information booths, motels, and restaurants. (See listing for Craftsmen.)

 SHOPPING. Shopping on the Cape is an adventure, with malls and mini-malls, main street stores, and out of the way places like Common West in Hyannis and Captain's Row in Yarmouth Port. Antique shops, arts and crafts centers, and art galleries are listed under separate headings. There are many noteworthy shops in the Mid-Cape area. Here are a few:

Barnstable. *The Basket Shoppe,* Rte. 6A and 132, West Barnstable; more than 3,000 items available in this complete straw market. *Packet Landing Iron,* Rte. 6A, West Barnstable; wrought-iron plant stands, hangers, and railings. *Salt and Chestnut,* Rte. 6A at Maple St., West Barnstable; weather vanes—new, antique, or design your own.

Centerville. *The 1856 General Store,* Main St., Centerville; penny candy still available.

Cotuit. *Gyda Gundersen Scandinavian Imports,* Rte. 28 and Main St., Cotuit; a distinctive collection of imported brass, crystal, and china.

Dennis. *Garden Accents,* Rte. 6A, Dennis; unusual antiques and hand-crafted garden accessories. *The Country Peddler,* Rte. 28 at Center St., Dennisport; specializing in antique clocks. *Hazelton's,* Main St., Dennisport; the most complete gift shop in the area. *Christmas Commons,* Rte. 28, West Dennis; a variety of items at reasonable prices; the store has other locations in Hyannis and Yarmouth.

Hyannis. *The Brass Shop,* 111 Airport Rd., Hyannis. *Cardoos,* The Village Marketplace, Hyannis; breads, spices, teas, cheeses—gastronomically ethnic. *The Irish Cottage,* Main St., Hyannis; imports of knits, Belleek crystal. *Lorania's Book Shop,* Main St., Hyannis; a wide variety of books, especially those on Cape Cod.

Osterville. *Abigail's Children's Boutique,* 27 Wianno Ave., Osterville; special toggery for children. *Bottega,* 40 Wianno Ave., Osterville; fine Italian leather. *Eldred Wheeler,* 857 Main St., Osterville; cabinetmakers; fine reproductions of 18th-century American furniture. *House and Garden,* Main St., Osterville; for those who enjoy wandering in a deluxe hardware store. *Lily Pulitzer,* Main St., Osterville; resort wear. *The Wool Shop,* Main St., Osterville; famous for yarns and distinctive apparel for men and women.

Yarmouth. *Country Design,* Main St., Yarmouth Port; plantation furniture and country items. *The White Dove,* 311 Main St., West Yarmouth; authorized Hummel and Norman Rockwell representative in the Cape Cod area.

ANTIQUES

Antique shops are seemingly everywhere on the Cape. Collecting old treasures has become a popular pastime. Most dealers have at least one specialty. By driving on Rte. 6A and Rte. 28, you will come upon the following fine antique shops.

Barnstable Village. *The Whale's Tooth,* Rte. 6A; seven dealers under one roof.

Cummaquid. *Cummaquid Antiques,* Rte. 6A; porcelain furniture.

Dennis. *Chalke Garden,* 848 Rte. 6A; country antiques, dolls, toys. *Dorymen,* 632 Rte. 6A; cupboards, paintings, decoys. *The Pack Rat,* 776 Main St.; just as you would imagine. *Poor Me Antiques and Collectibles,* 841 Main St.; toys of the past.

Hyannis. *Carrousel Antiques,* Main St. *Stone Antiques,* Sherman Square. *Vagen Antiques,* Sherman Square.

Osterville. *Rosemary's Antiques,* 870 Main St.

South Yarmouth. *Bass River Antiques,* 1268 Bridge St.; big variety.

West Barnstable. *Kenneth Moore,* Rte. 6A; at Lamb and Lion. *Ludwig's Antiques,* 1595 Main St. *Ted Harmon Antiques,* Main St.; decoys. *The Whipple Tree,* Rte. 6A; butter churns; items for country kitchen.

West Dennis. *Bog Antiques,* 304 Main St.; furniture, decoys, wicker, brass.

Yarmouth Port. *Gilpin,* 431 Main St. *Lil-Bud Antiques,* 141 Main St.; early American pattern glass. *Nickerson Antiques,* 162 Main St.; Oriental rugs.

There are three auction houses in the Mid-Cape area that have regular auctions but you must check newspapers for dates: *Airport Auctions,* 127 Airport Rd., Hyannis; *Richard A. Bourne,* Corporation Rd., Hyannis; and *Robert C. Eldred Co.,* Rte. 6A, Dennis

CRAFTSMEN

Barnstable Village. *Crewel, needlepoint, hooked rugs,* Madame Le Farge, Main St.; 362-9511. *Redwood Clocks,* Richard White, clockmaker. 20 Granite Lane; 362-4822.

Centerville. *Decorative painting on wood* Audrey Anderson, 23 Elliott St.; 775-8087. *Decorative painting on wood, slate, and tin,* Audrey Ward, 150 Buckskin Path; 771-2846. *Needlepoint Portraits,* by appointment; 70 Main St.; 771-4312. *Ship carving—Woodcarving,* Roy Dupay, 1301 Bumps River Rd.; weathervanes, eagles, signs; 775-2215. *Woodburning,* Carolyn La Fleur, 192 Great Marsh Rd.; carving on sugar pine; wooden purses and key chain plaques; 771-5160.

Cotuit. *Original native sheepwear and buckle works* (The Hirsel), Anne and Joe Barrett, Box 44; 428-5374.

Cummaquid. *Copper lanterns, lamps, weathervanes, mountings,* John Kopas (Mail: Commaquid Post Office); 775-7704. *Pottery* (New England Art Gallery), Louis Vuilleumier, Rte. 6A; demonstrations daily during summer; 362-2686.

Dennis. *Leathercraft,* Pauline Haskell, 5 Gates Path; handbags, belts, and wallets; 385-5056. *Pottery* (Hesperus), Nobscusset Settlement, Rte. 6A; open daily during the summer, weekends Sept. to Christmas; 432-3704. *Pottery,* Harry Holl (Scargo Stoneware), 30 Potter's Way; frequent demonstrations of potter's wheel; 385-3894. *Wood engraving—Silk screening,* David Grose (Grose Gallery) 528 Rte. 6A; 385-3434

Dennisport. *Scrimshaw,* Main St.; 398-2321.

East Dennis. *Functional pottery and Egyptian paste jewelry,* Gail Turner, corner of Sea and South, (Millstone Pottery); 385-4214.

Hyannis. *Colonial Candle of Cape Cod,* 238 Main St.; free factory tour brings alive time-honored art of candlemaking; Mon. through Fri. 9-3; no call necessary. *Old Harbor Candle Factory,* Scudder Ave., Hyannis Port; free tour of the factory with the fragrance of bayberries. *Dolls,* Helen Flett, 31 Newton St.; repairing and costuming of antique dolls; by appointment; 775-9401. *Dolls,* Caroline La Fauci, 37 King's Way; applehead dolls and stuffed dolls; 775-8567. *Musical Instruments,* Thomas Bednark, Pine St.; makes dulcimers, guitars; 775-9099. *Shellcraft,* Snow Creek Dr.; items made with seashells; 775-3671. *Silversmith Jeweler,* Brian Faunce, Main and Winter St.; 775-1373.

Marstons Mills. *Leather products* (Sundance), Rte. 28; open year-round; visitors can watch the cutting, staining, tooling, and stitching.

Osterville. *Needlepoint,* Madeline Horn, 851 Main St.; fine original handpainted needlepoint canvases; 428-6196.

Santuit. *Gold and silver jewelry,* Bernard Kelly, Rte. 28; custom work by silversmith; 428-5898. *Needlery, painting, wall hangings* (Sparre Studios), Rte. 28 at Rte. 30 junction; weaving demonstrations; 428-9757.

South Dennis. *Fiber Works,* Jane Fleming, 6 Holly St.; macrame curtains, lamps, wall hangings; 394-2460. *Handbags,* 14 Uncle Bill's Way; fabric bags with hand-crafted wooden handles; 394-2555. *Polish Paper Cutting,* Mira-Slava Pissarenko, Old Main St.; this unusual art demonstrated by appointment; 394-4204. *Wooden Toys,* Marion R. Phelps, 11 Sycamore Lane; children's wooden toys; 394-7118.

South Yarmouth. *Quilts, tote bags, toys* (Vinland Patchworks), Amanda Barabe, 94 Blue Rock Rd.; 398-0261. *Wooden animals,* Carleton L. Staples, 9 River Dr.; hand-carved animals; by appointment; 398-9355. *Wampum jewelry, pewter, scrimshaw* (Yankee Crafters), 48 North Main; 394-0557.

West Barnstable. *Textile weaving* (The Blacks), 625 Main St.; three generations of a family, weaving fine textiles; daily 9:30–5 P.M.; 362-3588. *Decoys and bird carvings,* Ted Harmon, Main St.; 362-2766. *Dolls,* Nan Haydon, Rte. 6A; handmade dolls; costuming of antique dolls; 362-6003. *Decorative iron, blacksmithing, custom work* (Packet Landing Iron), Chester Ciborowski, Rte. 6A; 362-2697. *Weathervane replicas and miniatures* (Salt and Chestnut), Marilyn Strauss, Rte. 6A; 362-3012. *Wood and stained-glass tables and mirrors* (Wood 'n' Glass), Rick and Ellen Moran, Box 204; 362-9589.

West Dennis. *Bird carvings,* Randy and Elaine Fisher, 5 Walden Place; hand-carved and painted birds; 385-2880. *Cranberry scoops,* Sabra Stockdale, 34 Church St.; primitive Cape Cod scenes; custom work; 394-7625. *Needlecraft* (Gull House Needlecraft), 85 School St.; needlepoint and crewel supplies and instructions; 394-8407.

West Yarmouth. *Jewelry and bowls of copper and silver,* Mary and Bob Davies, 34 Jay Bird Lane; 775-1821. *Scrimshaw,* Andrew G. Osterberg, 61 Meadow Brook Rd.; scrimshaw jewelry; by appointment; 771-1492.

Yarmouth Port. *Jewelry making,* Ross Coppelman, 364 Main St.; open daily; 362-6108. *Patchwork,* Mary Salvaggio Arnold, Box 107; gifts and wall hangings; 771-8237. *Pewter Crafters of Cape Cod,* Barrie Cliff, 927 Main St.; complete line of contemporary and traditional hollowware and jewelry; 362-3407. *Scrimshaw* (Whale's Tooth Antiques), Rte. 6A; items made to order; 362-6808.

 ARTISTS AND GALLERIES. The Cape and Islands have long been recognized for their art colonies. In the Mid-Cape area are many artists and galleries. There are two principal centers in Barnstable for nurturing fine art talent: *The Cape Cod Art Association*, Rte. 6A, Barnstable, and *The Cape Cod Conservatory*, Rte. 132, West Barnstable. Both have art courses as well as exhibitions of the works of established artists.

Cotuit. *The Gallery of Art Waves*, 3778 Rte. 28; 19th-century American oils and watercolors; Mon. through Sat., 9–5:30.

Cummaquid. *Barber Gallery*, Main St.; contemporary impressionist paintings; oils and pastels by Samir Barber; open daily June through Oct.

Dennis. *Grose Gallery*, 524 Rte. 6A; silkscreens; tours available; open daily 10–5. *Murtha Berrien Studio*, 123 New Boston Rd.; open daily. *Ruth Waite Studio Gallery*, 239 Main St. (Dennisport); open daily.

Hyannis. *David Lee Galleries*, Chart Village; lithographs, etchings, oils, watercolors; open daily, 9:30–9:30. *Robert Brooks Art Gallery*, 762 Falmouth Rd.; oil paintings, watercolors, ships; open daily year-round; visitors welcome. *Signature Gallery*, Chart Village; representing more than 200 American artists; open daily, including Sun. *Visual Arts Center of Barnstable*, 239 Main St.; William Regan holds classes and has frequent exhibitions. *Vagen Gallery*, 5 Sherman Square; American primitives; Mon. through Sat., 9–5.

Osterville. *"Birdsey" on the Cape*, 12 Wianno Ave.; watercolors and oils by Bermuda's Alfred Birdsey; paintings and prints of Cape Cod; Mon. through Sat., 9:30–5. *Robert E. Driscoll Gallery*, West Bay Rd.; marine paintings; watercolors of flowers and birds; June through Nov., 10–6.

Yarmouth Port. *Yarmouth Port Galleries*, Rte. 6A; primitive paintings by Davis.

SPORTS. See separate headings for Golf, Tennis, Boating, and Beaches. See Roller Skating and Ice Skating under children's events.

Bowling. *Cape Bowl*, 441 Main St., Hyannis (tenpin). *Cape Bowl Yarmouth*, 1067 Main St. *South Yarmouth* (candlepin and tenpin).

Cape Cod Baseball League. 42-game season, admission free, schedule available with locations and times of games.

Diving. *Ship Mate Dive Shop*, Sesuit Harbor, East Dennis; boats, instruction in SCUBA diving, and all equipment provided; daily.

Horseback Riding. *Holly Hill Farm*, Marstons Mills. *Melpet Riding Stable*, Rte. 134, East Dennis. *Race Lane Farm*, Osterville Rd., West Barnstable; rentals and lessons—rates vary.

Life Course. *Access Road* (near Rte. 134), Dennis; a walking/jogging course with exercise stations and handball court.

Nautilus Programs. *Mid-Cape Fitness Center*, Station Ave., South Yarmouth. The *Dunfey Hotel*, West End Circle, Hyannis.

Racquetball. *Hyannis Racquetball Club*, Centerville. *Mid-Cape Racquet Club*, White's Path, South Yarmouth. *Racquetball Club*, Rte. 28, South Yarmouth.

GOLF COURSES

Golf is very popular from spring through fall. Of the 33 courses on the Cape and Islands, ten are in the Mid-Cape area.

Bass River Golf Course, High Bank Rd., South Yarmouth; public, 18 holes, 6,200 yards, par 72.

Blue Rock Golf Course, off High Bank Rd., South Yarmouth; public, 18 holes, 2,770 yards, par 54.

Cotuit Highround Golf Course, Crocker Neck Rd., Cotuit; public, 9 holes, 1,121 yards, par 28.

Cummaquid Golf Course, off Main St., Cummaquid; private, 18 holes, 6,273 yards, par 71.

Dennis Pines Golf Course, Rte. 134, East Dennis; public, 18 holes, 7,029 yards, par 72.

Dunfey's (Fiddler's Green), West End Circle, Hyannis; public, 18 holes, 2,767 yards, par 54.

Hyannis Port Club, Hyannis Port; private, 18 holes, 6,203 yards, par 71.

Iyannough Hills Golf Course, Rte. 132, Hyannis; public, 18 holes, 6,249 yards, par 72.

Oyster Harbors, Oyster Harbors, Osterville; private, 18 holes, 6,687 yards, par 72.

Wianno Golf Course, Parker Rd., Osterville; private, 18 holes, 6,049 yards, par 71.

TENNIS COURTS

Centerville. Off Bumps River Rd., near Elementary School; no charge.

Cotuit. *Kings Grant Racquet Club,* Main St.; 7 courts for rent.

Dennis. *Dennis Racquet and Swim Club,* off Oxbow Way; lessons and courts for rent. *Marine Lodge,* North St., Dennisport. *Dennis Tennis Club,* 608 Main St., South Dennis. (Roughly $4. per hour in summer.)

Hyannis. *Tennis of Cape Cod,* Rte. 132; indoor courts, 7 P.M.–11 P.M. daily; at the Old Barnstable Junior High School, off South St., Barnstable High School, off West Main St., and Barnstable Middle School, off Rte. 28; there is no charge.

Osterville. Off West Bay Road; 2 courts, no charge.

West Barnstable. *Cape Cod Community College,* Rte. 132; open 7–7 during the week, and 9–7 weekends; $2. per hour. Rte. 6A; no charge.

Yarmouth. *Blue Rock Tennis Courts,* South Yarmouth. *Johanson Tennis,* West Yarmouth Rd., West Yarmouth. *Mid-Cape Racquet Club,* White's Path, South Yarmouth; indoor and outdoor courts, family rates. *Dennis-Yarmouth Regional School,* Station Ave., South Yarmouth; hard-top courts, no charge.

FISHING AND SHELLFISHING. Saltwater: Bluefish, tuna, and striped bass abound in Cape waters. Bottom fishing for cod, tautog, flounder, and pollack is always good (see boating listing). No license required for saltwater fishing.

Freshwater: Rainbow, brook, and brown trout, black bass, pickerel, pout, and perch are all plentiful in the ponds, lakes, and streams. A Massachusetts license is required for freshwater fishing and may be purchased at each town hall Residents: $11.25 for a 7-day license. Nonresidents: $17.25 for a 7-day license.

Shellfishing: Clams, quahogs, bay scallops, and other shellfish, plus seaworms, are controlled by local regulations, and permits are required by each town for a nominal fee. Edible crabs, up to 50 per day, may be taken for family use by means other than pots or traps.

A free pamphlet is available from the *Cape Cod Chamber of Commerce,* "The Sportsman's Guide to Cape Cod," published annually. This invaluable booklet includes a map and directions to all the best spots for fishing, launching boats, and access locations. It is also available at the many bait and tackle stores throughout the communities. (See RECOMMENDED READING, above.)

BOAT RENTALS AND CHARTERS. Sportsfishing Charter Boats: At the Barnstable Harbor off Rte. 6A in Barnstable Village there are ten boats from 32- to 52-feet long. Full-day and half-day trips are available on these fully equipped and licensed boats for bass, blues, and tuna. Regular charter—maximum six people. Split charter—maximum four people. Rates: $200, six-hr. trip; $260, eight-hr. trip; $320, all day; and $345, tuna. Phone: 362-3908. Charters are also available at comparable rates at the Lewis Bay Marina off South St. in Hyannis, at the Ocean Street Docks in Hyannis, at the Champion Lines on Rte. 28 in West Dennis (at the Bass River Bridge), and at the Crosby Boat Yard in Osterville.

Party Boats: The *Champion Lines* at Bass River on Rte. 28 has deep-sea fishing parties, scenic river cruises, and evening cocktail cruises. In East Dennis at Sesuit Harbor, the *Albatross* leaves daily as does the *Hy-Line* fleet at the Ocean Street Docks in Hyannis. These party boats bottom-fish, taking ten to 60 fishermen at a time for roughly $10–$13 per person, children slightly less.

Small Boat Rentals: Sunfish, canoes, windsurfers, motorboats, daysailors, and sailing dinghies can be rented at *Merry Mill Boat Rentals* in West Dennis (Bass River Bridge). With a driver's license and a $40 deposit, the rates range from $7–$11 per hour—adjustments are made for longer rentals.

Daysailing: In Centerville, the 40-foot sloop *Shoe Horn* makes daily 8:30 A.M.–4:30 P.M. trips to Martha's Vineyard for up to six passengers. Phone: 775-0371. At the Ocean Street Docks in Hyannis, the Hyannis Harborview

Marine offers a choice of a 39-foot ketch, a 40-foot sloop, or a 44-foot yawl for a seven-hour day on Nantucket Sound, at $200 for six people. Phone: 775-4420.

 PUBLIC BEACHES. Cape Cod is widely known for its beautiful beaches. Most saltwater beaches offer bath houses, sanitary facilities, and in many cases, a snack bar. Dogs are not allowed on the beaches during the summer season between 9 A.M. and 5 P.M. Other small restrictions are posted at each beach. Most of the beaches require either a town beach sticker (available at the town halls) or a parking fee. Water on the south side of the Cape is warmer than on Cape Cod Bay.

Barnstable. Resident stickers: $3 for season. Non-resident: $10 per week or $60 for season. Otherwise parking is $3 per day. *Craigville Beach,* Craigville Beach Rd., Centerville. *Dowses Point,* Wianno Ave., Osterville (limited to Barnstable residents). *Hathaway's Pond,* Phinney's Lane, Barnstable (freshwater). *Kalmus Park,* Ocean St., Hyannis. *Sandy Neck Beach,* off Rte. 6A, West Barnstable (on Cape Cod Bay and offering dune buggy trails for an additional fee). *Sea Street Beach,* Sea St., Hyannis. *Veterans' Memorial Park,* Ocean St., Hyannis.

Dennis. Resident stickers: $5 for season. Non-resident: $7 per week or $35 for season (staying in Dennis); $50 per season for non-Dennis Cape residents. Otherwise, parking is $3 per day. *Chopin Beach,* off Rte. 6A, Dennis (much of area only by foot). *Cold Storage Beach,* Cold Storage Rd., East Dennis (north shore). *Corporation Beach,* off Corporation Rd., Dennis. *Glendon Road Beach,* Glendon Rd., Dennisport. *Haigis Street Beach,* Old Wharf and Lower County Rd., Dennisport. *Horsefoot Path Beach,* off Rte. 6A, Dennis (no parking). *Howes Street Beach,* off Rte. 6A to Seaside Ave. to Howes St., Dennis. *Inman Road Beach,* off Chase Rd., Dennisport. *Mayflower Beach,* off Dunes View Rd., Dennis. *Princess Beach,* Rte. 6A, Dennis (freshwater). *Raycraft Beach,* off Chase Rd., Dennisport. *Scargo Lake Beach,* Rte. 6A, Dennis (freshwater). *Sea Street Beach,* off Rte. 28, Dennisport. *Sea Street Beach,* off Rte. 6A, East Dennis. *South Village Road Beach,* West Dennis side of Swan River Bridge. *West Dennis Beach,* Lighthouse Rd., off Lower County Rd., West Dennis (parking here for 1500).

Yarmouth. Resident stickers: $3 for season. Non-resident: $14 per week, $30 for season. Otherwise, parking is $3 a day. *Bass Hole Beach,* Center St., off Rte. 6A (north side). *Bass River Beach,* Shore Drive, off Rte. 28 in Bass River. *Bay View Street Beach,* Rte. 28, Hyannis Park, West Yarmouth. *Colonial Acres Beach,* Rte. 28, West Yarmouth. *Englewood Beach,* Berry Ave., West Yarmouth. *Parker River Beach,* Shore Dr., Bass River. *Sea View Beach,* Rte. 28, Bass River. *Thatcher Town Beach,* Rte. 28, Bass River. *Wind Mill Park,* Willow St., Bass River. *Sea Gull Beach,* off South Sea, West Yarmouth.

PARKS AND PICNIC AREAS. Although there are no major parks or forests in the Mid-Cape region, there are many roadside picnic areas with a pleasant view. Many of the public beaches also have picnic tables. Some of the following provide grills and comfort stations:

Centre Street Park, Yarmouth. *Hokum Rocks*, off Rte. 6A, Dennis. *Kennedy Memorial Park*, Ocean St., Hyannis. *Long Pond*, South Yarmouth. *Scargo Pond*, off Rte. 6A, Dennis. *Wilbur Park*, South Yarmouth. *Wind Mill Park*, off Rte. 28, Bass River. *Wings Grove*, South Yarmouth.

TRAILER FACILITIES AND CAMPING. The Mid-Cape has limited trailer and tent camping facilities. The trailer park sites listed should be called a year in advance.

Dennis. *Airline Mobile Home Park*, Old Chatham Rd., South Dennis; 385-3616: complete hook-ups, 75 sites; baths and showers, swimming pool, ice, groceries, some tent sites, no dogs; open Apr. 15 to Oct. 15. *Camper's Haven*, Old Wharf Rd., Dennisport; 398-2811: 230 sites, private beach, electricity and water hook-ups, some sewerage, trailer storage in winter, no dogs; open Apr. 15 to mid-Oct.; $56 per week. *Grindell's Ocean View Park*, Old Wharf Rd., Dennisport; 398-2671: 3 sites for motorhomes, 6 for trailers; electric and water hook-ups, sewerage, no dogs; open Memorial Day to Oct.; $650 for season, $100 per week.

Yarmouth. *Bass River Mobile Homepark*, 88 Willow St., Bass River, South Yarmouth; 398-2011: 25 transient sites; water and electric hook-ups, no sewerage, no tents, no open fires; $9 per night, $60 per week.

 WHAT TO DO WITH THE CHILDREN. There are always activities for the children and the whole family to enjoy regardless of the weather. There are numerous movie theaters and drive-ins throughout the region. (See Stage listing for children's theater.)

Amusement Park: *Seaview Playland*, Lower County Rd., Dennisport. Eighty-five amusement devices from miniature golf to pedal boats.

Aquarium: *Aqua Circus*, Rte. 28, South Yarmouth. A marine aquarium and zoological park. Open daily during the summer, 9:30 A.M.–9 P.M. and in the off-season, 10 A.M.–5 P.M. There are five shows each day featuring dolphins, sea lions, and seals. There is a petting zoo, a picnic area, and the largest seashell collection on the East Coast.

Arcade: *School's Out Arcade*, Capetown Plaza, Hyannis. Electronic games to sharpen reflexes and entertain the whole family. Open seven days a week.

Carousel: A merry-go-round is on the second floor of the West End Marketplace, Main St., Hyannis.

Ice Skating: *Kennedy Memorial Skating Rink*, Bearses Way, Hyannis, and the *Cape Cod Coliseum*, White's Path, South Yarmouth. Both are open for skating during the winter months. Check yearly schedules.

Roller Skating: *Cape Skate,* Plant Rd. (behind Capetown Mall), Hyannis; and *Pro-Skate,* High School Rd. Ext., Hyannis. Skate rentals. Special sessions on rainy days. Open year-round.

Taffy Pulling: *The Cape Cod Salt Water Taffy Company,* Rte. 28, South Yarmouth, makes three million of the sodium-free confections each year and ships them all over the world. Taffy-pulling demonstrations out front every afternoon during the summer.

 STAGE. Cape Cod has long been recognized for its summer theaters. A wide range of plays and musicals are presented in July and August. Tickets are available at moderate prices at the box offices.

Atlantic Theatre Company, Barnstable Village Hall, Rte. 6A, Barnstable Village. This academic theater company from the Yale School of Drama performs three plays each summer season at the winter home of the *Barnstable Comedy Club.* In addition to mainstage productions, the company presents cabaret entertainment Thu. through Sun. at the close of the major show. Children's theater of fairy tales and fables is presented in July.

Barnstable Comedy Club, Rte. 6A, Barnstable Village. Three major productions are staged during the winter months. The BCC is the oldest amateur theater group in New England.

Cape Playhouse, Off Rte. 6A, Dennis. In 1981, the Playhouse celebrated its 55th season. Stars such as Bette Davis, Gregory Peck, Sandy Dennis, and many more have performed on this stage. Each year top Hollywood and Broadway stars appear in well-produced plays and musicals during the summer months. Friday mornings, there are two performances of children's theater.

Melody Tent, West Main St., Hyannis. Started in 1950, this theater-in-the-round tent is now a summer landmark. Headliners such as Carol Channing, Crystal Gayle, and Sergio Franchi perform either in a musical or in concert. On Wednesday mornings the Melody Tent features professional children's theater. Plays such as *Cinderella, Pied Piper,* and *Hansel and Gretel,* as well as workshops and displays, are presented by several national companies.

 MUSIC. *Cape Cod Coliseum,* White's Path, South Yarmouth. Features rock concerts throughout the summer months. Prices vary.

Cape Cod Conservatory of Music and Art, Rte. 132, West Barnstable. A variety of year-round musical events.

Cape Cod Melody Tent, West Main St., Hyannis. 775-9100. Summer season only. Musicals and singing stars in concert.

Cape Cod Performing Arts Association, annual summer concert series. Different groups provide a varied program of music in different locations. Write Box 205, Yarmouth Post, Massachusetts 02675 for details.

Cape Cod Symphony Orchestra, Mattacheese School, West Yarmouth.

362-3258. Royston Nash, Musical Director. The orchestra observed its 20th anniversary season in 1981. Featured are outstanding visiting soloists. Season ticket is $24 for four events—Oct., Dec., Mar., and May.

Paul Jones' All Star Jazz Band, evening cruise on Lewis Bay. Tues. and Thurs., 9 P.M. from Scudder Ocean St. Dock in Hyannis. Returns at midnight. Passage is $7.50 per person. Refreshments on board.

HOTELS AND MOTELS. It will be noted that most of the accommodations in the Mid-Cape area are on the south side. Our price rating is based on double occupancy, European plan, in season (all have off-season rates). *Deluxe,* $60 and up; *Expensive,* $42–$60; *Moderate,* $30–$42; and *Inexpensive,* $18–$30.

BARNSTABLE VILLAGE

The Lamb and the Lion. *Expensive.* 2504 Main St. (Rte. 6A). 362-6823. In historic, noncommercial area. Swimming pool. Open year-round.

CENTERVILLE (CRAIGVILLE)

Centerville Corners Motor Lodge. *Expensive.* South Main St. 775-7223. Restaurant, bar. Pool, saunas, game room. Walking distance to beach. Open year-round.

Craig-Tide Cottages. *Expensive.* Craigville Beach Rd. 775-2021. 3-bedroom cottages with fireplace, porch, picnic tables. Across street from beach. Open May–Oct.

Ocean View Motel. *Expensive.* Craigville Beach Rd. 775-1962. Directly on beach. Clean, spacious, modern rooms. Sundecks, balconies. Open May–Oct.

Trade Winds Inn. *Expensive.* Craigville Beach Rd. 775-0365. Charming inn. Dining room. Cocktail lounge. Entertainment. Private beach. MAP. Open year-round.

Coral Village on Craigville Beach. *Moderate.* Craigville Beach Rd. 775-2971. Oceanfront 1-, 2-, and 3-bedroom cottages. Motel rooms also. Open May–Oct.

Craig Village by the Sea. *Moderate.* Craigville Beach Rd. 428-2420. Cottages and efficiencies. Beach privileges. Open May–Nov.

Craigville Manor Lodge and Cottages. *Moderate.* Lake Elizabeth Dr. (off Craigville Beach Rd.). 775-1265. Operated by United Church of Christ for church groups and others. Pleasant surroundings. Restaurant. MAP. Open year-round.

Craigville Motel. *Moderate.* Shoot Flying Hill Rd. (just off Rte. 6). 362-3401. Not near beach. Restaurant. Pool. Open year-round.

Long Beach Studio Apartments. *Moderate.* Long Beach Rd. 775-2021. Knotty pine efficiency apartments. Facing Centerville River. Across street from Craigville Beach. Open May–Nov.

Ranch Rail Motor Court. *Moderate*. Rte. 28. 775-1319. Cottages and units with kitchens. Pool. Picnic tables. One mile to Craigville Beach. Open year-round.

Suni-Sands Motel and Cottages. *Moderate*. Craigville Beach Rd. 775-0088. Cottages for 2–6 persons. Free beach privileges. Motel rooms for 2–4 persons. Pool. Open May–Oct.

COTUIT

Cotuit Inn. *Moderate*. Cotuit Village Center. 428-5000. View of Cotuit Bay. Some housekeeping units. Handy to beaches, golf, tennis. Open year-round.

DENNIS

Bayview Cottages. *Moderate*. Bay View Rd. 385-2060. Duplex waterfront cottages. 2 and 3 bedrooms. Safe, sandy beach. Open May–Oct.

Dennis Bayside Motel. *Moderate*. Rte. 6A. 385-9770. Small and quiet. Pool. Morning coffee. Near beach and restaurants. Open Apr.–Labor Day.

Flax Pond Motel of Dennis. *Moderate*. Rte. 6A. 385-3464. Pool. Children's playground. Full breakfast available. Conveniently located. Open summer months.

Ocean Vista. *Moderate*. Mandico Rd. 385-3029. On the ocean. Modern housekeeping units. Picnic tables. Sundecks. Open May–Nov.

Silver Sands. *Moderate*. Dr. Bottero Rd. 385-5020. Ocean front apartments and cottages. Fully equipped. Private beach and playground. No pets. Open during the summer.

The Willows. *Moderate*. 79 Seaside Ave. 385-3232. Country inn. Apartments and efficiencies. Conveniently located. Open year-round.

DENNISPORT

The Soundings Resort Motel. *Deluxe*. 78 Chase Ave. 394-6561. Waterfront. Private Beach, pools, putting green. Coffee shop on premises. Restaurant nearby. Open April–Nov.

The Breakers Motel. *Expensive*. Chase Ave. 398-6905. Oceanfront, balconies, pool. Children welcome. Open April–Oct.

The Colony Beach Motel. *Expensive*. Old Wharf Rd. 398-2217. Oceanfront, pool. Near restaurants and activities. Open May–Sept.

Cross Rip Resort Motel. *Expensive*. Chase Ave. 398-6600. Oceanfront, pool. Near restaurant. Open May–Oct.

Edgewater Motor Lodge. *Expensive*. Chase Ave. 398-6922. Overlooking ocean. Some efficiencies. Restaurant nearby. Apr.–Nov.

Shifting Sands. *Expensive*. Chase Ave. 398-9145. Private beach, oceanfront. 1-minute walk to restaurant. Open June–Oct.

Spouter Whale Motor Inn. *Expensive*. 405 Old Wharf Rd. 398-8010.

Private beach. Continental breakfast. Terrace overlooking ocean. Open May–Oct.

Three Seasons Motor Lodge. *Expensive.* Old Wharf Rd. 398-6091. On beach. 60 units. Coffee shop, cocktail lounge. Open April–Oct.

Acorn Cottage. *Moderate.* 35 Longell Rd. 394-6352. 3- and 4-bedroom cottages. Porches, fireplaces, kitchens. Walk to beach and stores. Ideal for families. Open through summer.

Ahern Cottages. *Moderate.* Old Wharf Rd. 398-9438. 2- and 3-bedroom cottages. 1-minute walk to beach. Open during summer.

Beachwalk Motel. *Moderate.* 120 Lower County Rd. 394-3589. In quiet grove. Some efficiencies. Short walk to beach and restaurants. Open May–Oct.

Blue Ocean Cottages. *Moderate.* 35 Old Wharf Rd. 398-8278. On sandy beach, 25 feet from water. Well-equipped cottages. Open June–Oct.

By the Sea. *Moderate.* Chase Ave. 398-8685. Oceanfront lodge. Free continental breakfast. Restaurant on premises. Open May–Oct.

Cape Pine Motel. *Moderate.* 177 Lower County Rd. 394-8820. 1 block to beach. Restaurant nearby. Bar. Some efficiencies. Open year-round.

Captain's Row. *Moderate.* Old Wharf Rd. 398-3117. Oceanfront cottages. 1 and 2 bedrooms. Private beach. Friendly atmosphere.

Colonial Village Motel and Cottages. *Moderate.* Lower County Rd. 398-2071. 4-room cottages. In pine grove. Fireplaces, pool. Short walk to beach and town. Open Apr.–Oct.

Cornell Villages. *Moderate.* Lower County Rd. 394-4091. 1-, 2-, and 3-bedroom cottages. Pool. Walk to beach. Open May–Oct.

Corsair Resort Motel. *Moderate.* 41 Chase Ave. 398-2279. Private beach, pool, balconies. Free coffee. Restaurant nearby. Open Apr.–Oct.

Cutty Sark Motor Lodge and Inn. *Moderate.* 396 Old Wharf Rd. 398-9116. Across street from beach. Restaurant nearby. Open May–Sept.

Delray—Lauderdale Resort Motel. *Moderate.* Captain Chase Rd. 398-3441. 100 yards from beach. Quiet, relaxing. Motel and efficiencies. Open Apr.–Nov.

Dennisport Motel. *Moderate.* Rte. 28. 394-8531. 23 units, 2 restaurants. Walk to cinema, shopping. 1½ miles to ocean. Open Apr.–Oct.

Dino's By The Sea. *Moderate.* Chase Ave. and Inman Rd. 398-8685. Private beach. Large porch. Guest house with 14 rooms. Free continental breakfast. Restaurant. Open May–Sept.

Fisherman's Village. *Moderate.* 10 Lower County Rd. 398-8561. Well-equipped cottages. On Swan River. Boats. Walk, drive, or row to beaches. Open Apr.–Oct.

Four Seasons. *Moderate.* Northern Ave. (off Lower County Rd.) 398-0553. 1- and 2-bedroom cottages. Fully equipped. Near beach. Open year-round.

Gaslight Resort Motel. *Moderate.* Chase Ave. 398-8831. Overlooking ocean. Morning coffee. Near restaurant. Open May–Oct.

Holiday Hill Motor Inn. *Moderate.* 352 Main St. 394-5577. Snack bar, game room. 56 units. Pool. Near sandy beaches. Open May–Oct.

Innisfree of Dennisport. *Moderate*. 32 Inman Rd. 394-6041. Breakfast. An old Cape Cod inn within 100 yards of Nantucket Sound. Excellent location. Warm, hospitable atmosphere. Open Memorial Day to Labor Day.

Jonathon Edwards Motel. *Moderate*. Rte. 28. 398-2953. Continental breakfast. Game room. Shuffleboard. Pool. Near beaches and restaurants. Open year-round.

The Lamplighter Motor Inn. *Moderate*. Rte. 28. 398-8469. Family oriented. Picnic tables. Free coffee. Minutes to restaurants. Open Apr.–Oct.

Larry Leone Cottages. *Moderate*. 55 Lower County Rd. 394-0059. 1-, 2-, and 3-bedroom cottages. Children welcome. Babysitter available. Some waterfront units. Open May–Oct.

Marine Lodge Cottages. *Moderate*. 11 North St. 398-2963. In pine grove. Well-equipped cottages. Pool. Tennis. Picnic tables. Open Apr.–Nov.

Oceanside Motel. *Moderate*. Old Wharf Rd. 394-5359. Cottages overlooking ocean. Pool. Children welcome. Open May–Oct.

The Old Landing. *Moderate*. Old Wharf Rd. 398-3703. Cottage colony by the beach. 1-, 2-, and 3-bedrooms. Pool. Snackbar. Open Apr.–Oct.

Santucket Motel. *Moderate*. Chase Ave. 398-2981. Ocean view. Private beach. Restaurant adjacent. Open May–Oct.

Sea Lord Resort Motel. *Moderate*. Chase Ave. 398-6900. Beach across street. Pool. Free continental breakfast. Near restaurants. Open May–Oct.

Sea 'n Sand Resort Motel. *Moderate*. Captain Chase Rd. 398-8521. Efficiency units. 3-minute walk to beach. Open Apr.–Nov.

Sea Shell Motel. *Moderate*. 45 Chase Ave. 398-8965. Private beach. Refrigerators in every room. Free continental breakfast. Open year-round.

Sea View Village. *Moderate*. Lower County Rd. 398-9084. Modern cottages, 1 to 5 bedrooms. Private beach. Recreation on premises. Open May–Oct.

Skipper Cottages. *Moderate*. Captain Chase Rd. 398-3952. 1- and 2-bedroom housekeeping units. Completely equipped. 500 feet to beach. Open May–Oct.

Sun Deck Village. *Moderate*. 128 Sea St. 398-3164. 1- and 2-bedroom efficiency units. Short walk to Sea St. Beach. Picnic area. Open year-round.

Surf Motel. *Moderate*. Captain Chase Rd. 398-8621. 500 feet to beach. Quiet adult community. Open year-round.

William and Mary Motel. *Moderate*. 398-2931. 433 Lower County Rd. 1 block to beach. Restaurant adjacent. Kitchenettes. Pool. Open May–Oct.

Bambi Cottages. *Inexpensive*. 235 Division St. 394-2659. Quiet, safe street. Good for children. Walk to center of village. Open May–Oct.

Cape Haven Motel. *Inexpensive*. Lower County Rd. 394-1065. Efficiency units. Well-equipped. Short walk to beach. Picnic tables. Open year-round.

Connie's Cozy Cabins. *Inexpensive*. Rte. 28. 394-5145. Housekeeping units. 3-minute drive to beach. Open summer months.

Cricket Court. *Inexpensive.* 130 Rte. 28. 398-8400. Rent by week. 10 cottages. Near beach, shops, golf. Pets accepted. Open Apr.–Oct.

Dolphin Cottages. *Inexpensive.* 291 Lower County Rd. 394-8519. 5-minute walk to beach. Well-equipped cottages. Rentals by week. Open June–Sept.

Ocean View Lodge and Cottages. *Inexpensive.* Depot St. 398–3412. 100 yards to fine beach. 2-bedroom cottages. Efficiencies. Open through summer.

Old Wharf Inn. *Inexpensive.* 402 Old Wharf Rd. 398-2804. Across street from beach. Rooms and some efficiencies. Free morning coffee. Open May–Oct.

Pier 28 Motor Lodge. *Inexpensive.* 16 Main St. 394-2377. On Swan River. Close to everything. Rooms and efficiencies. Open year-round.

EAST DENNIS

Sesuit Harbor Motel. *Moderate.* Rte. 6A. 385-3326. Historic district. Rural setting. Pool, tennis. Near restaurants and beaches. Open year-round.

Stage Coach Motel. *Moderate.* 1706 Main St. (Rte. 6A). 385-3626. Cottages and efficiencies. Near Sesuit Harbor. Morning coffee. Space for boats. Open May–Oct.

HYANNIS

Dunfey Hyannis Hotel. *Deluxe.* West End Circle. 775-7775. Beautiful resort. Golf, tennis, indoor and outdoor pools, health spas, restaurants, bars, and nightclub. Private balconies. Supervised activities for children, car rentals, conference facilities. Open year-round.

Sheraton Regal of Hyannis. *Deluxe.* Rte. 132. 771-3000. Putting green, indoor and outdoor pools, game room, whirlpool, 2 restaurants, bar and nightclub. Open year-round.

Heritage House. *Expensive.* 259 Main St. 775-7000. Pool, saunas. Restaurants, bar. Convenient location. Open year-round.

Holiday Inn. *Expensive.* Rte. 132. 775-6600. Near airport and shopping mall. Indoor pool. Dining room. Lounge with dancing. Open year-round.

Howard Johnson's. *Expensive.* Main and Winter St. 775-8600. Center of downtown. Pool, saunas. Restaurants, cocktail lounge. Open year-round.

Hyannis Holiday Motel. *Expensive.* 131 Ocean St. 775-1639. Overlooking Lewis Bay. Pools, sundeck. Near restaurants. Open Apr.–Oct.

Hyannis Inn Motel. *Expensive.* 473 Main St. 775-0255. Restaurant, pool, bar, health spa, game room. In center of town, near excursion boats and shops. Open year-round.

Hyannis Regency. *Expensive.* Rte. 132. 775-1153. Restaurant, pool, bar, game room, whirlpool, exercise room, saunas. Nearby golf and tennis at reduced rates. Constructed in 1981. Open year-round.

Hyannis Travel Inn. *Expensive.* 16 North St. 775-6633. Saunas. Free continental breakfast. Near restaurants and center of town. Heated indoor pool and outdoor pool. Open year-round.

Lewis Bay Lodge. *Expensive.* 53 South St. 775-6633. Pool, restaurant, bar. Overlooks harbor. Marina on premises. Open Apr.–Dec.

Quality Inn Charles. *Expensive.* 662 Main St. 775-5600. Pools, tennis, movies. Restaurant, cocktail lounge. In center of town. Open year-round.

The Angel Motel. *Moderate.* Rte. 132. 775-2440. 2 miles from town. Pool, picnic area. Restaurant nearby. Open May–Oct.

Anric Oceanside Motel. *Moderate.* 549 Ocean St. 771-5577. Across street from beach. Picnic area. Quarter mile to island boats. Open May–Labor Day.

Bouchard's Tourist Home and Cottages. *Moderate.* 83 School St. 775-0912. 100 yards to Hyannis waterfront and docks. Restaurants nearby. Cottages and apartments. Open year-round.

Breakwater Cottages. *Moderate.* 432 Sea St. 775-6381. All housekeeping units. 1, 2, and 3 bedrooms. On the beach. Pool. Good location. Open year-round.

Candlelight Motor Lodge. *Moderate.* 447 Main St. 775-3000. Downtown Hyannis. Near restaurants. Bar. Convenient. Open year-round.

Captain Gosnold Village. *Moderate.* 230 Gosnold St. 775-9111. Motel and 1-, 2-, and 3-bedroom cottages. Pool, picnic tables, playground for tots. No air-conditioning. Walk to beach. Open May–Nov.

Cascade Motor Lodge. *Moderate.* 201 Main St. 775-9717. Pool, waterbeds. Near restaurants, shops. Open year-round.

Country Lake Lodge. *Moderate.* Rte. 132. 362-6455. On lake; rowboats are available. Pool, shuffleboard, picnic tables. Some efficiencies. Open Apr.–Oct.

Harbor Village. *Moderate.* Marstons Ave. 775-9744. Cottages off highway. Pine grove. 1, 2, and 3 bedrooms; all have fireplaces and sundecks. Fully-equipped kitchens. Open Apr.–Oct.

Hill's Dining Room and Inn. *Moderate.* 530 West Main St. 775-0344. A few modern motel rooms. Free continental breakfast. 1 mile from center of town. Restaurant and lounge. Open Apr.–Jan.

Hyannis Harborview Motel. *Moderate.* 213 Ocean St. 775-4420. Pools, saunas, lounge. Near restaurants. Across street from docks. Open Apr.–Oct.

Hyannis Motel. *Moderate.* Rte. 132. 775-8910. Pool. Restaurant nearby. 1 mile from center of town. Open year-round.

Hyannis Star Motor Inn. *Moderate.* Rte. 132. 775-2835. Pool, play area. Pets welcome. Restaurant nearby. Open year-round.

Hyannis Town House Motor Inn. *Moderate.* 33 Ocean St. 775-3828. In center of Hyannis. Short walk to boats to islands. Open Apr.–Oct.

Iyannough Hills Motor Lodge. *Moderate.* 1470 Iyannough Rd. 771-4804. Pool, saunas, game room, golf course, 6 indoor tennis courts, children's playground. Accommodations for handicapped. Open year-round.

Koala Inn. *Moderate.* 867 Iyannough Rd. 771-6100. Pool. Pets welcome. Morning coffee. Adjacent to Cape Cod Mall. Open year-round.

Newtowne Motor Lodge. *Moderate.* 119 Ocean St. 775-7862. Opposite town dock. In room coffee. Near restaurants. Open year-round.

Park Square Village Apartments. *Moderate.* 156 Main St. 775-5611. Main building was home of 19th-century shipmaster. Restaurant nearby. Laundry, play barn, shuffleboard, picnic tables. Open year-round.

Presidential Motor Lodge. *Moderate.* Rte. 132. 362-3957. On lake. Fishing, boating, miniature golf. Continental breakfast. Open May–Oct.

Rainbow Resort Motel. *Moderate.* Rte. 132. 362-3217. Lakefront location. Play area, children's pool. Restaurant. Open year-round.

Sands Motor Lodge. *Moderate.* Rte. 132. 775-9000. Walking distance to Mall and restaurants. Play area. Free coffee. Open year-round.

Sea Breeze Motel. *Moderate.* 397 Sea St. 775-4269. Close to the ocean. 1 mile from center. Private setting, but near activities. Open year-round.

The Warburtons by the Beach. *Moderate.* 388 Sea St. 775-4612. Old captain's house. Near scenic harbor. Sea breeze for air conditioning. Complimentary morning coffee. Family business for 22 years. No pets. Some motel units. Open May–Sept.

Windrift Motel. *Moderate.* Rte. 28. 775-4697. Half mile from town. Pools, play area. Convenient to restaurants and activities. Open Apr.–Oct.

Glo Min Cottages and Motel. *Inexpensive.* 182 Sea St. 775-1423. Motel rooms, efficiencies, and cottages. In residential area. Near restaurants. No air conditioning. Open year-round.

Greenbrier Motor Lodge. *Inexpensive.* Rte. 132. 775-2181. Pool. Walk to Cape Cod Mall. Open year-round.

The Mains'l Motel. *Inexpensive.* 535 Ocean St. 775-5725. Cross ventilation. Across street from beaches. Walk to restaurants and town. Open year-round.

Salt Winds Guest House. *Inexpensive.* 319 Sea St. 775-2038. 3-minute walk to beach. Cross ventilation, no air conditioning. Rooms with a good yard. Open Apr.–Labor Day.

Sea Side Pines. *Inexpensive.* Craigville Beach Rd. West Hyannis Port. Motel rooms and cottages. Convenient location. Private beach. Open May–Oct.

Terry's Inn and Cottages. *Inexpensive.* Corner of Park Ave. and Glenwood. 1 minute from Lewis Bay and beach. 5-minute drive to Hyannis center. Open May–Oct.

OSTERVILLE

East Bay Lodge. *Deluxe.* East Bay Rd. 428-6961. Comfortable accommodations. Good restaurant and lounge. 3 tennis courts. Near the water. Open year-round.

Micha's Pond Summer Rentals. *Moderate.* Oakville Ave. 428-8784. 1- to

5-bedroom light-housekeeping cottages. Swimming pool. Barbecue. Open summer months.

Osterville Fairways Motor Inn. *Moderate.* 105 Parker Rd. 428-2747. Quiet surroundings. Overlooks Wianno Golf Course. Convenient to shopping. Open year-round.

SOUTH DENNIS

White Pond Cottages. *Moderate.* Old Chatham Rd. 385-3930. 2-bedroom cottages on lake. Private beach, picnic area, rowboats. Open June–Oct.

SOUTH YARMOUTH (BASS RIVER)

Red Jacket Beach Motor Inn. *Deluxe.* South Shore Dr. 398-6941. 1,000-foot private beach, indoor and outdoor pools. Restaurant, lounge. 150 very nice rooms. Saunas and exercise rooms. Open Apr.–Nov.

Beach House Motor Lodge. *Expensive.* 73 South Shore Dr. 394-6501. On ocean. Private balconies. Private beach. Free continental breakfast. Open Apr.–Nov.

Blue Water Resort. *Expensive.* South Shore Dr. 398-2288. Indoor and outdoor pools, private oceanfront beach. Restaurant, coffee shop. Putting green, shuffleboard. Open Apr.–Nov.

Ocean Mist Motor Lodge. *Expensive.* 97 South Shore Dr. 398-2633. Directly on ocean. Motel rooms and efficiencies. Quiet pine grove with chaise lounges. Open Apr.–Oct.

Riviera Beach Motor Inn. *Expensive.* South Shore Dr. 398-2273. Private beach. Very nice accommodations. Balconies. Restaurant, lounge. 110 units, looking out over Parker's River. Open year-round.

Smugglers' Beach Motor Lodge. *Expensive.* South Shore Dr. 398-6955. On the ocean. Private beach. Pool. Near everything. Sundeck. Children over 15. Open year-round.

Surf and Sand Beach Motel. *Expensive.* South Shore Dr. 398-2341. Oceanfront, private beach. Balconies. Comfortable. Open year-round.

Surfcomber on the Ocean. *Expensive.* South Shore Dr. 398-9228. Oceanfront, private beach. Efficiencies. Pool. Restaurant nearby. Open May–Oct.

Yarmouth Seaside Village. *Expensive.* 135 South Shore Dr. 398-2533. Cape Cod architecture. 52 cottages with kitchens and heat. 400 feet from beach. 20 units have fireplaces. Maid service. Open May–Oct.

American Motel. *Moderate.* 203 Main St. 398-9503. In-room coffee. Refrigerators in rooms. Open year-round.

Bass River Motel. *Moderate.* Rte. 28. 398-2488. Spacious grounds. Some efficiencies. Open year-round.

Beach 'n Town Resort Motel. *Moderate.* Rte. 28. 398-2311. Refrigerators in rooms. Cook-out area. Pool. Free coffee. Open March–Dec.

Blue Rock Motor Inn and Golf Course. *Moderate*. Todd St. 398-6962. Overlooking pool and golf course. Balconies. Restaurant. Open Apr.–Nov.

Brentwood Motor Inn. *Moderate*. Rte. 28. 398-8812. Pools, whirlpool. Free coffee. Short walk to restaurants. Open year-round.

Cap'n Gladcliff Motel. *Moderate*. Rte. 28. 394-9828. Central. Near beaches, restaurants. Pool. Free coffee. Family suites and apartments. Open year-round.

Captain Jonathon Motel. *Moderate*. 1237 Rte. 28. 398-3480. 3-minute drive to beach. Free continental breakfast. Owner operated. Open year-round.

The Dunes Motel. *Moderate*. 170 Sea View Ave. 398-3062. Short walk to beach. Pool, play area. Children welcome. Open May–Oct.

Even Tide Motel. *Moderate*. 117 Sea View Ave. 398-3385. 1 mile to beaches. Quiet. Pets allowed. Free coffee. Open Apr.–Oct.

Harbeth Cottages. *Moderate*. 253 South Shore Dr. 398-9134. 2-bedroom cottages. Private beach, tables and outdoor grills. Convenient. Open during the summer.

The Jolly Captain Motor Lodge. *Moderate*. 1376 Bridge St. 398-2253. A motel-boatel. Fishing dockside, sea-plane landing. Refrigerator in room. Open Apr.–Nov.

Riverview Motor Lodge. *Moderate*. 37 Neptune Lane. 394-9801. Lodge has rooms, separate building has efficiencies overlooking Parker's River. Pool. Free continental breakfast. Near restaurants. Open year-round.

Village Green Motel. *Moderate*. South Shore Dr. 398-2167. Studios and efficiencies. Pool. Coffee shop. Open year-round.

The Windjammer. *Moderate*. South Shore Dr. 398-2370. Across street from beach. Pool. Special golf package. Near restaurants. Open Apr.–late Oct.

Yarmouth Motel. *Moderate*. 759 Rte. 28. 398-3122. Attractive units. Pool. Near beaches and resort activities. Open May–Oct.

The Anchorage. *Inexpensive*. South Shore Dr. 398-8265. Small motel lodge. Opposite Sea View Beach. Free continental breakfast. Open year-round.

Pine Knot Motel. *Inexpensive*. Rte. 28. 398-3315. Family units. Some kitchens. 2 minutes to beach and restaurants. Open year-round.

Yarmouth Anchorage. *Inexpensive*. 31 Pond St. 398-2751. Housekeeping cottages. Convenient location. Open year-round.

WEST BARNSTABLE

Buttonwood Acres. *Moderate*. On Garrett's Pond. 362-3758. Quiet cottages. Sandy lake. Secluded. Cottages well-equipped. Open May–Oct.

Holiday Farm Cottages. *Moderate*. Rte. 6A. 362-6185. Ideal for children. Safe sandy beach. Well-equipped cottages. Open May–Oct.

WEST DENNIS

Lighthouse Inn. *Deluxe*. Lighthouse Rd. 398-2244. Directly on the ocean beside the West Dennis Beach. Resort hotel with pool, private beach, tennis, play area. Supervised program for children. Game room. Part of the inn was the original Dennis Lighthouse. Restaurant on the water. MAP. Open Apr.–Sept.

Ballast Motel. *Moderate*. Rte. 28. 394-2101. 42 units. 2 minutes to West Dennis Beach. Pool. Free continental breakfast. Open Apr.–Oct.

Barnacle Motel. *Moderate*. Rte. 28. 394-8472. 35 units. Pool. Continental breakfast. Short walk to beach. Open May–Oct.

Bay Leaf Cottages. *Moderate*. Bay Leaf Way. 394-4113. 2- and 3-bedroom cottages. Convenient to village and restaurants. 2-minute drive to beach. Open June–Oct.

Cape Circle Cottages. *Moderate*. School St. 398-8530. Walk to beaches, restaurants, and bike rentals. Picnic areas, children's playground. Open May–Oct.

Crosswinds Cottages. *Moderate*. Loring Ave. 398-8862. Ocean view and marsh view. 2-bedroom housekeeping cottages. Open May–Oct.

Grand Cove Cottages and Apartments. *Moderate*. Rte. 28. 398-2564. 2–6 persons per cottage. Well-equipped. Convenient. Open June–Sept.

Kelly's Cottages. *Moderate*. Off Rte. 28. 398-3076. On Bass River. Safe beach for children. 2- and 3-bedroom, well-equipped cottages. Open June–Oct.

Marina Motor Lodge. *Moderate*. Rte. 28. 394-4764. Overlooking Bass River. Convenient to everything. Short walk to marina. Play area, putting green. Continental breakfast. Open May–Oct.

Pine Cove Inn and Cottages. *Moderate*. Rte. 28. 398-8511. Waterfront cottage colony. Guest house has rooms. Sundeck overlooking water. Open summer months.

Plantation Motel. *Moderate*. Rte. 28. 398-3868. 26 units. Near everything. Free continental breakfast. Open Apr.–Oct.

Toy Village. *Moderate*. Off Rte. 28. 771-7982. On Bass River's Grand Cove. Waterfront. Private. Housekeeping cottages. Open year-round.

Dennis West Motor Lodge. *Inexpensive*. Main St. (Rte. 28). 394-7434. 22 units. Walk to restaurants. Pool. 2 minutes to beach. Marina nearby. Picnic area. Free morning coffee. Open Apr.–Oct.

Elmwood Inn. *Inexpensive*. 57 Old Main St. No telephone. On Bass River. Private beach. Beautifully restored inn. Open Apr.–Nov.

Halfway Guest House. *Inexpensive*. Rte. 28. 398-6758. Overlooking Bass River. Walking distance to restaurants and churches. Continental breakfast. Open June–Oct.

The Pines on Kelley's Pond. *Inexpensive*. Pond St. 398-8422. 4-room cottages. 1 mile to West Dennis Beach. Fully equipped. Families welcome. Open May–Oct.

Rainbow Pine Cottages. *Inexpensive.* School St. 398-3904. Well-equipped cottages. In pine grove. Play area. Near beach. Open year-round.

WEST YARMOUTH

American Host Motel. *Moderate.* Rte. 28. 775-2332. Whirlpool. Miniature golf, kiddies pool, cook outs. Near restaurants. Open Apr.–Nov.

Americana Holiday Motel. *Moderate.* Rte. 28. 775-5511. Pools. Play area. Near restaurants. Free morning coffee. Shuffleboard, putting green. Open year-round.

Beachway Motel. *Moderate.* 498 Main St. 775-0399. Pool, picnic area. Free coffee. Cozy rooms with some efficiencies. Owner managed. Open March–Nov.

Cape Sojourn Motel. *Moderate.* 149 Main St. 775-3825. Whirlpool, putting green, game room, play area. 60 units. Morning coffee. Open Apr.–Nov.

Cape Traveler Motor Inn. *Moderate.* Rte. 28. 775-1225. 29 units. Pool, playground, sundeck, shuffleboard. Coffee shop. Quiet, off highway. Near restaurants. Open Apr.–Oct.

Colonial Acres Resort Motel. *Moderate.* 114 Standish Way. 775-0935. Ocean view. Private beach on Lewis Bay. Cross ventilation. Balconies. Coffee shop. Open May–Oct.

Green Harbor on the Ocean. *Moderate.* Baxter Ave. 771-1126. Shorefront cottages. Pool, private beach. Well-equipped kitchens, sundecks. Open long season.

Holiday Hearth Motel. *Moderate.* 488 Main St. 775-0414. Indoor and outdoor pools, shuffleboard, playground. Short walk to restaurants. Open year-round.

Hunter's Green Motel. *Moderate.* Rte. 28. 771-1169. Colonial-style motel with 74 units. Indoor and outdoor pools. Restaurants nearby. Open Apr.–Oct.

Irish Village Motel and Cottages. *Moderate.* Rte. 28. 771-0100. 70 units, some efficiencies. Restaurant, gift shop, lounge. Pools, sauna. Open except for Dec. and Jan.

Mayflower Motel. *Moderate.* Rte. 28. 775-2758. Near restaurants and shops. Pool, play area. 2-bedroom kitchen apartment available. Open year-round.

Snug Harbor Motor Lodge. *Moderate.* Rte. 28. 775-4085. 50 units. Indoor and outdoor pools, whirlpool, game room. Free coffee. Within walking distance of restaurants. Children in same room free. Open year-round.

Thunderbird Motor Lodge. *Moderate.* Rte. 28. 775-2692. 140 units. Modern. Back from highway. Pools, tennis courts, saunas, playground, whirlpools. Package plans. Open year-round.

Tidewater Motor Lodge. *Moderate.* 135 Main St. 775-6322. 42 units. Convenient location. Pools, sauna. Open year-round.

Town 'n Country Motel. *Moderate.* Rte. 28. 771-0212. Pools, play area, saunas and whirlpool. Pets allowed. Restaurant nearby. Open Apr.–Nov.

Yarmouth Gardens Motor Lodge. *Moderate.* 497 Main St. 771-1998. Beautiful grounds. Pool, playground, game room. Convenient to restaurants. Owner operated. Open year-round.

Yarmouth Shores. *Moderate.* 29 Lewis Bay Blvd. 775-1944. Housekeeping cottages. Private beach. Open May–Oct.

Squire John Motel. *Inexpensive.* Rte. 28. 775-2238. Close to Hyannis, beaches, and restaurants. Free coffee. Open year-round.

YARMOUTH PORT

Old Yarmouth Inn. *Moderate.* Main St. (Rte. 6A). 362-3191. 10 rooms and 2 suites. Historic district. Complimentary breakfast. Restaurant. Open year-round.

The Village Inn. *Moderate.* Main St. (Rte. 6A). 362-3181. Historic district. Home of sea captain in clipper ship era. Free continental breakfast. Open year-round.

HOSTELS. *Hy-Land Youth Hostel,* 465 Falmouth Rd., Hyannis, Massachusetts 02601. 775-2970 or 771-1585. Accommodations and recreational opportunities. Advance reservations recommended. Open year-round. Membership in American Youth Hostels, Inc. is required.

 DINING OUT. The Mid-Cape has many fine restaurants. Not listed, but scattered throughout the three towns, are all of the fast-food chains. Our ratings are based on the average cost for a full meal, exclusive of alcoholic beverages, tax, and tip. *Deluxe,* $18 and up; *Expensive,* $15 and up; *Moderate,* $9–$15; and *Inexpensive,* under $9.

BARNSTABLE VILLAGE

Anthony's Cummaquid Inn. *Moderate.* Rte. 6A. 362-4501. Colonial mansion. A distant view of the ocean and salt marshes. Open for dinner. Fish and meat specialties. Lounge with fireplace. Spacious. MC and Anthony's credit cards only. Open year-round.

Barnstable House Restaurant. *Moderate.* 3010 Main St. 362-4911. Relaxed dining in a restored 18th-century colonial home. Gracious service. Roast prime of beef a specialty. Reservations suggested. Open year-round.

The Dolphin. *Moderate.* Rte. 6A. 362-6610. Overlooking salt marshes. Cozy atmosphere, pine panelling, paintings by local artists, nautical decor. Variety of seafood specials, plus full menu. Family operated for 25 years. Music. Casual dress. Open year-round; closed Sun.

Harbor Point Restaurant. *Moderate.* Harbor Point Rd. 362-2231. Overlooking Sandy Neck and Barnstable Harbor. Open for dinner. Seafood, beef, and homemade desserts. Dress casual. Reservations suggested. Open May–Nov.

Mattakeese Wharf. *Moderate.* Barnstable Harbor. 362-4511. Waterfront. Built on pilings extending out into water. Seafood a specialty, but a full menu. Informal atmosphere but proper dress (no shorts, bare feet, or bathing suits) required. Organ music at dinner. Open daily, May–Oct.

CENTERVILLE

Craigville Inn Restaurant. *Moderate.* Lake Elizabeth Dr. 775-1265. Full-course dinners, salad bar, home-baked desserts. No liquor. Children's menu. Casual dress. By reservation only. No credit cards. Open year-round.

Village Corners Restaurant. *Moderate.* South Main St. 775-4234. Pleasing atmosphere. Patio dining in garden setting or in the intimate candle-lit dining room. Continental cuisine. Innovative dishes. Reservations suggested. Open year-round.

Four Seas. *Inexpensive.* 360 Main St. 775-1394. Luncheon only. Special sandwiches and famous homemade ice cream. Open May–Sept.

Lock 'n Oar. *Inexpensive.* Rte. 28. 775-6730. Relaxed, informal, family atmosphere. Chef owned. Stuffed sole Newburgh a specialty. Italian specialties. Open year-round (closed Sun., Sept.–May).

DENNIS

Dennis Inn Restaurant. *Moderate.* Hope Lane. 385-3650. A restaurant worth finding. Relaxing atmosphere. Fresh seafood and the specialty, Veal Oscar. Open all summer, weekends Apr.–May and Oct.–Nov. Piano and vocal in lounge. Reservations necessary.

Playhouse Restaurant. *Moderate.* 30 Hope Lane. 385-8000. On grounds of famous Cape Playhouse. Quiet atmosphere with fresh flowers, white tablecloths, and candles. House specialty of owner-chef is native seafood medley. Piano in lounge. Reservations requested. Sometimes closed for short period during winter.

Red Pheasant Inn. *Moderate.* 902 Rte. 6A. 385-2133. Restored 200-year-old barn with wide floor boards. Specialties include Veal Vernaise, Filet of Sole Meunière, and Shrimp Dijon. Garden room café has hanging plants for intimate dining. Piano. Open year-round except Christmas and New Year's. Reservations appreciated.

Capt'n Frosty's Fish and Chips. *Inexpensive.* Rte. 6A. 385-8548. Luncheon-dinner menu available all day. Children's menu. Informal. Casual indoor dining and outdoor on brick terraces. Open May–Sept.

Gina's. *Inexpensive.* Taunton Ave. 385-3213. On the waterfront. Friendly atmosphere. Full-course dinners. Casual. Open during the summer.

Joe Mac's Bar and Grill. *Inexpensive.* 85 Taunton Ave. 385-3569. Casual. Fried seafood and Italian specialties. Open year-round.

DENNISPORT

Café Italia. *Moderate*. 327 Main St. (Rte. 28). 398-9221. Dinner only. Family restaurant with children's menu. Italian and American specialties. Organ and piano music. Open year-round.

Captain's Clambake Emporium. *Moderate*. 410 Lower County Rd. 398-0331. The traditional clambake—lobsters, steamers, corn on the cob—cooked before your eyes. Player piano, casual atmosphere. Children's menu. Reservations are suggested. Open Apr.–Oct.

Captain Williams House. *Moderate*. 106 Depot St. 398-3910. Open for dinner. Authentic Colonial surroundings enhanced by candlelight. Specializing in prime rib and delicacies from the sea. Lounge. Open Apr.–Oct.

Ebb Tide. *Moderate*. 94 Chase Ave. 398-8733. Rustic restaurant in old Cape Cod home. Four candle-lit dining rooms and canopied outdoor terrace. Lobster Pie and Shrimp Ebb Tide specialties. Children's menu. Open May–Oct.

Jake Cassidy's. *Moderate*. 76 Chase Ave. 398-0228. A renovated private estate. One room with ceiling to floor fireplace. Food is "American with style." Specialties include Chicken Cassidy and Cassidy's Cape Salad Bowl. Piano. Open 7 days a week, May–Sept.

Bob Brigg's Wee Packet. *Inexpensive*. Lower County Rd. 396-8680. Family run for over 30 years. Children's menu. Large selection of seafood dishes. Everything cooked to order. Wine and beer only. Open May–Oct.

Brass Kettle. *Inexpensive*. 640 Rte. 28. 398-2888. Family restaurant. Children's menu. American with a homemade touch. Specializing in desserts. Open year-round.

Clancy's. *Inexpensive*. Upper County Rd. 394-6661. Irish pub atmosphere. On Swan River with deck overlooking water. Luncheon specials. Irish entertainment nightly. Open year-round.

Dino's By the Sea. *Inexpensive*. 57 Chase Ave. 398-8685. Casual atmosphere. Fried seafood. Greek salad. Fast service. No credit cards. Open May–Sept.

Paolo's Italian Garden. *Inexpensive*. 394 Lower County Rd. 398-9291. Casual atmosphere. Italian specialties. A family-run operation. Children's menu. Guitar music during summer dinners. Open year-round.

Seven Seas Fish Market. *Inexpensive*. 435 Main St. 394-4816. Rustic casual atmosphere. Menu mainly seafood. Open year-round.

Swan River Seafood Restaurant. *Inexpensive*. 5 Lower County Rd. 394-4466. Family-style restaurant with views of Swan River, marshes, and a windmill. Complete range of fresh seafood dishes. Children's menu. Open May–Oct.

Three Seasons Restaurant. *Inexpensive*. 421 Old Wharf Rd. 398-6091. Open for breakfast and lunch only. Salads and sandwiches. Patio available for luncheon on pleasant days. Open May–Oct.

Unicorn Publick House. *Inexpensive.* 63 Lower County Rd. 394-7140. Simple surroundings. Specials include Steak Teriyaki and crocks of Cape Cod clam chowder. Children's menu. Open May–Oct.

EAST DENNIS

The Galley. *Inexpensive.* Rte. 134. 385-9777. Muffins and coffee in morning. Luncheon and dinner menu of seafood, chicken, and burgers. Spacious dining room. Casual. Open during summer.

Lower Deck Lounge. *Inexpensive.* Rte. 134 and 6A. 385-3939. Nautical setting. Casual relaxing atmosphere. Simple menu featuring charcoal grill specialties. Guitar music in evening. Open in summer.

Marshside Restaurant. *Inexpensive.* 26 Bridge St. 385-3555. Seafood. Simple but good. Casual atmosphere. Summer months.

HYANNIS

Toni Lee's. *Deluxe.* 645 Main St. 771-7340. A single-menu restaurant with one sitting at 7:30 P.M. for 23. Different menu each day, with all ethnic and regional patterns explored. Reservations required by 1 P.M. Open year-round.

Dom's. *Expensive.* 337 Main St. 771-6213. Gourmet, regional Italian dishes. Pasta made on the premises. Superb veal dishes. Small, intimate dining room. Reservations required. Open year-round.

Dunfey's Silver Shell Restaurant. *Expensive.* West End Rotary. 775-7775. Specializing in seafood. Elegant atmosphere. Salad bar and dessert cart, good clam chowder. Reservations suggested. Open year-round.

Three Thirty One. *Expensive.* 331 Main St. 775-2023. Continental cuisine in contemporary setting. Evening meal only. Completely remodeled and tastefully decorated. European flair, from appetizers to dessert. Open year-round.

The Asa Bearse House. *Moderate.* 415 Main St. 771-4131. In heart of Hyannis. An authentically restored 1840 sea captain's home. Victorian decor in 2 dining rooms. Outdoor patio during summer. Piano music in intimate lounge. Variety in menu. Reservations suggested. Open year-round.

The Captain's Chair. *Moderate.* 166 Bay View St. 775-5000. On waterfront overlooking Lewis Bay. Warm, inviting nautical atmosphere. Seafood specialties—lobster and clams from local fleets. Organ music. Reservations suggested. Open year-round.

Flounders. *Moderate.* Village Market Place. 771-7231. Greenhouse atmosphere with brick, brass, mirrors, and greenery. Varied menu. Open year-round.

The Gazebo. *Moderate.* At the Airport. 771-8480. Cheerful interior with wicker, plants, and mirrors. Continental cuisine. Reservations suggested. Open year-round.

Heritage House Dining Room. *Moderate.* 259 Main St. 775-7000. Prime ribs of beef featured in candle-lit dining room. Children's menu available. Reservations requested. Open year-round.

Hill's. *Moderate.* 530 West Main St. 775-0344. Family operated for 40 years. A tradition of fine New England style food. Warm, cozy atmosphere in a colonial setting, flower and vegetable gardens outside the window. Open for dinner only from Apr.–Dec.; closed Tuesdays.

Holiday Inn—The Yardarm Restaurant. *Moderate.* Rte. 132. 775-6600. Open for lunch and dinner. Daily specials served in pleasant surroundings. Open year-round.

Hyannis Regency. *Moderate.* Rte. 132. 775-1153. Luxurious surroundings in the newest hotel in Hyannis. Daily specials. Open year-round.

John's Loft. *Moderate.* 8 Barnstable Rd. 775-1111. Rustic atmosphere. Brick fireplace with old tools. Crabmeat casserole the specialty. Salad wagon. Reservations suggested. Open every day except Christmas.

Lewis Bay Restaurant. *Moderate.* 53 South St. 775-6633. Veal dishes, seafood, prime rib of beef served in a dining room overlooking the water. Open year-round. Reservations recommended.

Luigi's. *Moderate.* Old Colony Rd. 771-4131. For dinner only. Italian specialties. Family business for over 40 years, now in a quiet location. Small bar. Informal, country-style. Open year-round.

Mari-Jean's. *Moderate.* 680 Main St. 771-2245. Low, beamed ceilings. European and American cuisine. Paella a specialty. Generous portions. Very cozy. Open year-round.

The Marlin. *Moderate.* Iyannough Rd. 775-3840. For dinner only. Seafood from fish market on premises. Spacious. Children's menu. Open year-round.

Mayflower Restaurant. *Moderate.* 334 Main St. 775-1100. New England specialties, served in pleasant surroundings. Open year-round.

Mildred's Chowder House. *Moderate.* 290 Iyannough Rd. 775-1045. Large, roomy, comfortable and relaxing. Famous for clam chowder. Casual family-style atmosphere. Open year-round.

Mitchell's Steak and Rib House. *Moderate.* 451 Iyannough Rd. 775-6700. Steak and prime ribs the specialty. The clam chowder won contest as Mid-Cape's best. Casual and intimate atmosphere. Open year-round.

The Paddock. *Moderate.* West Main Rotary. 775-7677. Candlelight, fresh flowers, linen-covered tables in Victorian atmosphere. Duckling, beef, and lobster among specialties. In summer, luncheon in the "backyard" in a garden café atmosphere. Open for dinner year-round.

Quality Inn Charles. *Moderate.* 662 Main St. 775-1918. Open for all meals, but the dinner is special. Served "in the round" overlooking Main Street, with singing waiters and waitresses. Salad bar has 21 items. Open year-round.

Red Coach Grill. *Moderate.* Airport Rotary Circle. 775-0135. Specializing in prime rib of beef. Salad bar. Comfortable surroundings. Open year-round.

Sheraton Regal. *Moderate.* Rte. 132. 771-3000. French tableside service. Specializing in seafood and gourmet cuisine. Open year-round.

Tiki Port. *Moderate.* Capetown Mall. 771-5220. Chinese and Polynesian cuisine. Cantonese and Mandarin dishes. Oriental atmosphere. Reservations suggested. Open year-round.

Back Side Saloon. *Inexpensive.* 209 Main St. (rear). 771-0727. Turn-of-the-century atmosphere. Chowders, seafood, steak. Informal. Open year-round.

Baxter's Fish and Chips. *Inexpensive.* 177 Pleasant St. 775-4490. Overlooking harbor on a dock. Nautical atmosphere. Seafood specialties. The restaurant, along with the lounge, is very popular. No credit cards. Open during summer months; closed Mondays.

Bobby Byrne's Hyannis Pub. *Inexpensive.* 345 Rte. 28. 775-1425. Casual, friendly pub atmosphere. All-day sandwich menu. Bar with jazz during the summer. Dinner specials. Open year-round.

Charlie's Place. *Inexpensive.* 751 West Main St. 771-6506. Family restaurant. Widely varied choices. 2 dining rooms. Children's menu. Daily, year-round.

Claws. *Inexpensive.* 700 Main St. 775-2936. Warm, unpretentious atmosphere. Hanging plants. Homemade chowder. Native seafood. Children's menu. Open year-round.

Dockside Inn. *Inexpensive.* 53 South St. 775-6633. Small dining room and porch with bar overlooking Lewis Bay Marina. Fish plates and chowders the specialty. Open year-round

Dragon-Lite. *Inexpensive.* 620 Main St. 775-9494. Chinese and Polynesian food. Small and comfortable. Reservations preferred. Open year-round.

East End Pub. *Inexpensive.* 247 Main St. 775-7488. Daily specials and deli sandwiches. English pub atmosphere with stained glass. No credit cards. Open year-round.

Fiddlebee's. *Inexpensive.* 72 North St. 771-6032. One of the oldest houses in Hyannis, recently remodelled allowing dining on a loft above the bar. Plants, brick wall, and copper artifacts throughout. Varied menu. Open year-round.

Hearth 'n Kettle. *Inexpensive.* Main St. 771-3737. Friendly family-type restaurant. A colonial atmosphere. Varied menu. Open every day except Christmas, 24 hours a day during summer.

M.D. Armstrong's. *Inexpensive.* 720 Main St. 771-3222. Good food and service. Very popular. Spacious and comfortable. Bar. Open year-round.

My Place. *Inexpensive.* 586 Main St. 771-7445. Small, homey, congenial restaurant. Greek and mid-eastern dishes. Open year-round.

Shirdan's. *Inexpensive.* Airport Rotary. 775-5810. A cozy, family-oriented restaurant for breakfast, lunch, and dinner. Menu extensive, from chicken pot-pie to roast beef. Open year-round.

Urano's. *Inexpensive.* 50 Sea St. 771-7371. For dinner only. Small but comfortable. Owned and operated by Chef Urano, who is a frequent guest on Boston TV programs. Italian specialties. Open year-round; closed Mondays during off-season.

Villa Vecchione. *Inexpensive.* 3 Sherman Square. 775-0682. Small Italian restaurant with sidewalk café. Specialties include vegetarian-style dishes. Informal and popular. Open Apr.–Nov.

Wursthaus. *Inexpensive.* Cape Cod Mall. 771-5000. German-American food served in a friendly old-world Bavarian atmosphere. Düsseldorf steak and potato dumplings a specialty. Children's menu. Open year-round.

OSTERVILLE

East Bay Lodge. *Expensive.* East Bay Rd. 428-6961. One of New England's fine restaurants. The elegance of the past with an award-winning menu. An outstanding buffet, salad bar, and special dessert table. Open for dinner year-round, for lunch and dinner during the summer.

Wimpy's. *Moderate.* Main St. 428-6300. Seafood is the main item on menu. A formal dining room, a family-style dining room, and a snack bar. Reservations appreciated. Open year-round.

SOUTH DENNIS

Jim's Pier 134. *Inexpensive.* Rte. 134. 385-3367. Relaxing surroundings. You can see your lobster swimming before dinner. Seafood specialties. Open Apr.–Nov.; closed Tues. and Wed. in the spring and fall.

Joe Mac's Bar and Grill. *Inexpensive.* 85 Taunton Ave. 385-3569. Casual family-style atmosphere. Specializing in fried seafood and Italian dishes. Open year-round.

SOUTH YARMOUTH (BASS RIVER)

The Camelot Room. *Moderate.* 742 Rte. 28. 398-8775. For dinner only. Fresh seafood. Blue-ribbon beef. 26 entrees. Pleasant surroundings. Open April–Jan.; closed Mondays in off-season.

Red Jacket Beach Motor Inn. *Moderate.* 5 Shore Dr. 398-6941. Seafood Newburg a specialty. Quiet casual atmosphere. Tables at window look out over Nantucket Sound. No credit cards. Open Apr.–Nov.

The Riverway Lobster House. *Moderate.* Rte. 28. 398-2172. Open for dinner. Casual elegance and friendly service. Restaurant has been a Cape tradition for almost 40 years. Fresh seafood and prime ribs. Children's menu. Reservations suggested. Open year-round.

Skipper. *Moderate.* 152 South Shore Dr. 394-7406. Overlooking Nantucket Sound. From the "catch of the day" to Chateaubriand. Open May–Oct.

Bass River Fish Market Seafood Restaurant. *Inexpensive.* 15 Mill Lane. 398-6434. Nautical setting. Fresh fish from the market on premises. Open year-round.

J. F. Murphy's Restaurant. *Inexpensive*. 1329 Rte. 28. 398-9720. Irish charm and hospitality in an informal relaxed setting. A family operated restaurant serving roast beef, fresh seafood, and corned beef and cabbage on Thu. Children's menu. Open Apr.–Nov.; closed Mondays in off-season.

Russell's Landing. *Inexpensive*. At Parker's Way, Rte. 28. 394-7652. Casual, cozy atmosphere. Specialty is a "bucket of seafood" and home-made bread. Open year-round.

Sportsmen's Pub. *Inexpensive*. 731 Main St. 394-4048. Casual Cape Cod atmosphere. Steak, lobster, haddock at reasonable prices. No credit cards. Open year-round.

200 Mile Limit. *Inexpensive*. Rte. 28. 394-4593. Casual, nautical atmosphere. Seafood specials. Open year-round; closed Sun.

WEST BARNSTABLE

Ojala Farm. *Inexpensive*. Rte. 6A, 362-6924. Luncheon only. A small family-operated restaurant specializing in Finnish foods. Same location for 27 years. Home-baked bread and pies. Well worth finding. Open June–Sept.; closed Sat., Sun., and Mon.

WEST DENNIS

The Columns. *Moderate*. Rte. 28. 398-8033. For dinner only. Candle-lit dining in a restored mansion of a sea captain of the 1860s. Steak Diane and Veal Cordon Bleu are specialties, along with flaming desserts. Piano. Open year-round.

Golden Anchor. *Moderate*. Rte. 28. 394-5225. For dinner only. Singing waiters and waitresses. Native seafood and beef dishes. Open June–Sept.

The Lighthouse Inn. *Moderate*. Lighthouse Rd. 398-2244. 3 meals a day in a dining room overlooking the ocean. Homemade bread and full-course dinners. Menu varies. Children's menu. Open June–Sept.

Celebrities. *Inexpensive*. 581 School St. 394-7333. Contemporary casual atmosphere. Specializes in charbroiled steaks. No credit cards. Open year-round.

Punchy's Pizza Shack. *Inexpensive*. 74 School St. 394-9177. A very good gourmet pizza served in a friendly atmosphere. Open year-round.

Snowden's Horsefoot Cove. *Inexpensive*. 116 Rte. 28. 394-1600. For lunch and dinner. The open deck overlooks Bass River. Native seafood the specialty. Open May–Oct.

WEST YARMOUTH

Bloom's Prime Rib House. *Moderate*. 633 Rte. 28. 775-0524. Dinner only, in a cozy, candle-lit dining room. Homemade bread, a good salad bar, and the specialty, prime ribs of beef. Open year-round.

Casa Mia. *Moderate.* Rte. 28. 771-6251. Authentic Italian cuisine. Casual atmosphere. Reservations preferred. Open daily at 4:00 P.M. year-round.

Dorsie's Steak House. *Moderate.* 325 Rte. 28. 771-5898. Open for dinner only. Dark paneling, stained glass, brass artifacts in a comfortable atmosphere. A popular restaurant with a full salad bar, piano music, and daily specials. Open year-round.

Yarmouth House and Restaurant. *Moderate.* 335 Main St. 775-0524. For lunch and dinner. Gay 90s setting. Open charcoal pit. Prime ribs, fresh seafood, steak. Casual. Open year-round.

Fred's Turkey House. *Inexpensive.* 518 Main St. 775-6783. A family restaurant dedicated to home cooking and reasonable rates. Every day is Thanksgiving. Open Apr.–Thanksgiving.

Johnny's Yee's. *Inexpensive.* 228 Main St. 775-1090. Chinese food in a Chinese atmosphere. Spacious with bar and music. Open year-round.

Mama Angie's. *Inexpensive.* 416 Main St. 771-6531. Italian dishes from different regions of Italy. European atmosphere. Outside patio during the summer. Open year-round. Reservations recommended. No credit cards.

YARMOUTH PORT

La Cipollina. *Expensive.* Rte. 6A. 362-4341. Candlelight, chamber music, and classic Italian cuisine. Small and comfortable with good service. Gourmet and good. Reservations suggested. Open year-round.

Chanterelle. *Moderate.* Rte. 6A. 362-8195. Veal Chanterelle and other specialties served in dining room overlooking flowered courtyard of potted plants. Open year-round.

Colonial House Inn. *Moderate.* Rte. 6A. 362-4348. Traditional New England dining in a restored old colonial inn overlooking the village green. Steaks served with continental flare. Children's menu available. For lunch and dinner. Open year-round.

Cranberry Moose. *Moderate.* 43 Main St. 362-3501. For dinner only. A rambling old country inn recently restored. Continental cuisine. Veal, steak, lamb, poultry, and seafood dishes. Children's menu. Reservations requested. Open year-round.

The Gingerbread House. *Moderate.* Rte. 6A. 362-3775. For lunch and dinner. American food served in a traditional New England home built in 1840. Reservations suggested. Open year-round.

Mycono's. *Moderate.* Rte. 6A. 362-3775. Family operated, in an old restored Colonial home. Small quiet dining rooms. Menu features Continental cuisine and Greek specialties. Open year-round.

Old Yarmouth Inn. *Moderate.* 233 Main St. 362-3191. Traditional dishes prepared with style in the atmosphere of a genuine 17th-century stagecoach inn on the historic Olde King's Highway. Reservations suggested. Open year-round.

ICE CREAM PARLORS

Ice cream parlors are ever-popular places, especially during the summer months. The following are some of the best: *Baskin-Robbins*, Village Marketplace, Hyannis. *Brighams*, Rte. 28, South Yarmouth. *Carvel's*, Capetown Plaza, Hyannis. *Four Seas*, South Main St., Centerville (famous for 46 years). *Ice Cream Smuggler*, Rte. 6A, Dennis. *Ice Cream Store*, Rte. 28, Dennisport. *Sundae School Ice Cream Parlor*, Lower County Rd., Dennisport. *Turner's*, West Main St., Hyannis (family operated for two generations). *Vanilla and Chocolate*, Main St., Hyannis (they have 23 other flavors). The large chains, *Friendly's* and *Howard Johnson's*, have stores in many locations throughout the three towns.

 NIGHT LIFE. The Mid-Cape has an abundance of bars, lounges, discos, and nightclubs. During the summer, there is music every night, in the winter, either there is none or just on weekends.

Barnstable. *Asa Bearse House*, 415 Main St., Hyannis; grand piano, jazz trio on weekends. *The Barnstable House*, Rte. 6A, Barnstable Village; weekends, piano and vocals. *Beef'n Bottle*, North St., Hyannis; piano bar. *Blazing Saddles*, Rte. 132, Hyannis; country western. *Captain's Chair*, 166 Bay View, Hyannis; piano, vocals. *Crystal Palace*, 310 Barnstable Rd., Hyannis; band playing contemporary and rock and roll. *Dolphin Restaurant*, Main St., Barnstable Village; duo on piano and trumpet. *East Bay Lodge*, East Bay Rd., Osterville; trio for dancing. *East End Pub*, 247 Main St., Hyannis; contemporary guitar, piano, vocals. *The Gazebo*, at Barnstable Airport, Hyannis; nightly music for dancing. *Harbor Point Restaurant*, Harbor Point Rd., Cummaquid; guitar and vocals. *Heritage House*, Main St., Hyannis; guitar, vocals. *Hill's*, 530 West Main St., Hyannis; piano or guitar, contemporary, vocals. *Holiday Inn Man O'War Lounge*, Rte. 132, Hyannis; top-40 group, dancing. *John's Loft*, 8 Barnstable Rd., Hyannis; sing-along, piano and organ. *The Landing*, 270 Ocean St., Hyannis; rock-and-roll group. *Lewis Bay Nautical Lounge*, 53 South St., Hyannis; piano, vocals. *London Dock Saloon*, 3 Bearse's Way, Hyannis; country western. *Mattakeese Wharf*, off Rte. 6A at Millway, Barnstable Harbor; piano, organ, vocals. *M. D. Armstrong's*, 720 Main St., Hyannis; live entertainment nightly. *Mitchell's Steak House*, Rte. 28, Hyannis; Irish music. *The Mooring*, 230 Ocean St., Hyannis; piano, vocals. *Mother Farrington's*, Main St., Hyannis; piano, vocals, contemporary, duo. *Outrigger Inn*, Rte. 28, Hyannis; dixieland jazz. *Parlor Lounge at the Paddock*, West End Rotary, Hyannis; piano, vocals. *Players*, Capetown Mall, Hyannis; contemporary and rock-and-roll bands, dancing. *Pufferbellies*, Ridgewood Ave., Hyannis; rock-and-roll bands. *Quality Inn at the Charles*, 662 Main St., Hyannis; singing waiters and waitresses. *Sheraton Regal Lion's Den Lounge*, Rte. 132, Hyannis; top-40 group, dancing.

Snuggery at bobby Byrne's Pub, Rte. 28 and Bearse's Way, Hyannis; piano, brass, vocals. *Tingles at Dunfey's Resort,* West End Circle, Hyannis; disco dancing. *Velvet Hammer,* 209 East Main St., Hyannis; rock-and-roll groups, dancing. *Wianno Club,* Seaview Ave., Osterville; trio. *Wimpy's Friars Pub,* Main St., Osterville; vocals, piano, comedy. *Windjammer Lounge,* Airport Shopping Plaza, Hyannis; guitar, vocals, contemporary.

Dennis. *Café Italia,* Rte. 28, Dennisport; piano, organ, vocals. *Celebrities,* 581 School St., West Dennis; rock-and-roll band. *Clancy's,* 8 Upper County Rd., Dennisport; traditional Irish entertainment. *Columns,* 401 Main St., West Dennis; jazz groups. *Heidi's Hideaway at the Dennis Inn,* Scarsdale Rd., Dennis; piano, vocals. *Geoffrey's,* 581 Main St., West Dennis; guitar, vocals. *Improper Bostonian,* Rte. 28, Dennisport; entertainment nightly. *Jake Cassidy's,* 76 Chase Ave., Dennisport; entertainment, mellow music. *Jason's,* 228 Lower County Rd., Dennisport; show band. *Golden Anchor,* Rte. 28, West Dennis; singing waiters and waitresses, Broadway show tunes. *Lower Deck,* 1374 Rte. 134, East Dennis; guitar, vocals. *Paolo's Italian Garden,* 374 Lower County Rd., Dennisport; guitar, vocals. *Red Pheasant Inn,* Rte. 6A, Dennis; piano, vocals, show tunes. *Sandbar,* Lighthouse Rd., West Dennis; piano, vocals, comedy routine. *Snowden's,* 116 Main St., West Dennis; rock-and-roll band. *Twenty-Eight Club,* Main St., Dennisport; group, contemporary.

Yarmouth. *Bloom's Prime Rib House,* 633 Rte. 28, West Yarmouth; nightly entertainment. *Camelot Room,* 742 Rte. 28, South Yarmouth; floor show act. *Cape Cod Irish Village,* Rte. 28, West Yarmouth; Irish show band. *Compass Lounge,* Rte. 28, South Yarmouth; rock-and-roll band. *Deacon's Perch,* Rte. 6A, Yarmouth Port; classical piano. *Dorsie's,* 325 Main St., West Yarmouth; piano, vocals, contemporary. *Johnny Yee's,* Rte. 28, West Yarmouth; cowboy music. *Jonah's Pub at The Blue Water Resort,* 5 Shore Dr., South Yarmouth; contemporary, duo. *Marina Bay Restaurant,* 17 Neptune Lane, South Yarmouth; live music for dancing. *Mill Hill Club,* 164 Main St., West Yarmouth; rock and roll.

THE LOWER CAPE

by

WILSON TURELL JONES

Wilson Turell Jones is a freelance writer-photographer from Barnstable, and a frequent contributor in both fields to Cape Cod Life *magazine and other area publications.*

Split by the 70-degree longitude, the Lower Cape (also known as the Outer Cape) is eclipsed only by the headlands of upstate Maine as the most easterly point in the continental United States. The Cape is often referred to as the "forearm" of Massachusetts—the town of Chatham on the southeast corner lies at the elbow and Provincetown at the fist, a short one-hour drive from the villages of the Mid-Cape. Despite the Cape's reputation for being crowded in the summer, solitude and relaxation are generally a five-minute ride or a 20-minute walk from the main roads. In fact, the narrow peninsula is a walker's dream come true, easily traversed from

East to West or the Bay to the Atlantic in less than a couple of hours without effort. It's easy to take in the sunrise from any of the outer beaches and catch the sunset over Cape Cod Bay in the evening.

Contrasts are part of the nature of the Lower Cape; the expansive clam flats and the great sand dunes, sea captains' homes built during the reign of the majestic ships, and trim postcard cottages of traditional design, long piers serving the fleets, and the small shanties of the oystermen. But that's only the beginning. Towering cliffs glare down at the Atlantic like the face of some storybook giant surveying his quiet domain. Backwater grasses move in whispers as the wind pushes across the wide marshes. Warm water and cool water, freshwater and saltwater, sand beaches and pebble beaches are major enticements. The Lower Cape has something for everyone, even though the seasonal population quadruples when the sun burns hot on the barrier region.

The area draws people of every recreational persuasion and in every season. For those who would forsake the traditional dip in the ocean, the off-season offers the same opportunities as summer. Besides, there's always the local hotel pool. Spring and fall are now recognized as desirable times to visit the Lower Cape. Although generally cooler than inland, spring on the Cape brings with it the fresh scent of blossoming flowers carried on the moist south winds. The nature trails, small businesses, cottage colonies, farms, rivers, and estuaries begin to come to life. There is a slow, but steady pace, geared to reestablish familiarity with the subtleties of the land and sea.

The same pace is evident in autumn, when the tides of vacationers retreat after Labor Day. In recent years, the warm Indian summers have persuaded increasing numbers to enjoy the natural beauty, secluded beaches, and uncrowded shops. The local waters tend to remain relatively warm until the cooling winds of October take effect.

Ice-fishing, ice-boating, hang-gliding, hunting, fishing, golf, and birdwatching are just a few of the diverse winter activities. More hearty souls will still grab their surf boards, even if the temperature is down. Cross-country skiing is becoming more popular every year. And, as always, there is bicycling and hiking on some of the best trails in the nation.

A bonus to the off-season visitor is the reduced rate structure available from hotels, motels, and other accommodations. Inquiries are advisable.

In the Beginning

Historians generally agree that Norsemen, Spanish explorers, and French seamen came to the outer shores of the Cape. Accounts show that in 1602 Captain Bartholomew Gosnold named the land after the abundance of codfish in the coastal waters. Samuel de Champlain anchored at what is now Stage Harbor in Chatham, possibly as early as 1606, to repair a broken rudder. The short visit cost the lives of four men from the Champlain party in skirmishes with the local Indians, the first casualties on the peninsula. Surprisingly, the 2,000 Native Americans of the 1600s were quite benevolent toward the majority of explorers and settlers who came to these shores. Early stories vary. One fact that is undisputed is the arrival of Myles Standish and the *Mayflower* in the harbor off Provincetown on November 21, 1620. While Plymouth eventually offered better farmland and a mainland site for a colony, the tip of the Cape was the first landing site of the 121 Pilgrims from England. The cornerstone of democratic government, The Mayflower Compact, was authored in the tiny cabin of the vessel almost immediately after arrival in the Americas. The document exemplifies the desire of the Pilgrims to honor the ideal that men should be able to live under the rule of the majority through self-government with freedom from persecution. So strong was their commitment to a new ideal that, even though half of the settlers had died during the first winter, when the ship left for Europe, no one returned.

And more settlers would come to Provincetown, to Eastham, to Harwich. The first generation of Cape Codders scattered through eight villages down-Cape: **Brewster, Harwich, Chatham, Orleans, Eastham, Wellfleet, Truro, and Provincetown.**

Cape Cod National Seashore

During the 1930s, a small group of foresighted individuals recognized the perils facing the future of the Lower Cape. Long ago stripped of the great oak and pine forests, overworked farmland and overgrazed meadows succumbed to the elements. Resources were diminished and the relentless pursuit of wind and sand finally won out. Only the coastline had escaped the one inevitable curse of modern man—overdevelopment.

The post-war years of prosperity brought a new influx of residents and tourists, not in large numbers at first, but increasing from year to year. Conservationists saw themselves as protectors of the fragile peninsula, and in the late 1950s the National Park Service focused its attention on the Great Beach running the length of the eastern side of the Cape. A five-man survey crew was given the green light for a one-year project designed to assess the possibility of preserving the dramatic beachfront, companion dunes,

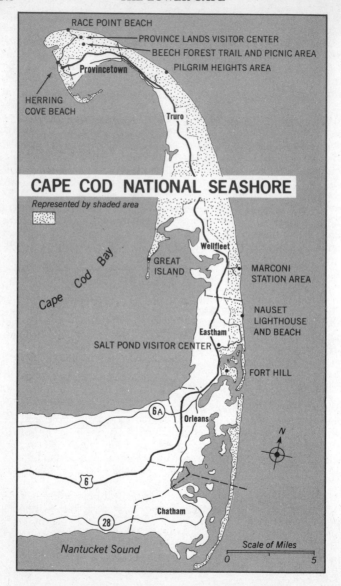

RACE POINT BEACH
PROVINCE LANDS VISITOR CENTER
BEECH FOREST TRAIL AND PICNIC AREA
PILGRIM HEIGHTS AREA

Provincetown

HERRING
COVE BEACH

Truro

CAPE COD NATIONAL SEASHORE

Represented by shaded area

Cape Cod Bay

Wellfleet

GREAT
ISLAND

MARCONI
STATION AREA

NAUSET
LIGHTHOUSE
AND BEACH

Eastham

SALT POND VISITOR CENTER

FORT HILL

6A   Orleans

N

6

28   Chatham

Nantucket Sound

Scale of Miles

0   5

and marshes as public recreation land. Finally, in 1961, the Cape Cod National Seashore was established.

Although some of the land is still privately owned, the National Seashore will eventually include 27,000 acres, with land in six towns: Chatham, Orleans, Eastham, Wellfleet, Truro, and Provincetown. There are four major areas of the park that have been developed for visitors: the Nauset Area in Eastham (with the Salt Pond Visitor's Center), Marconi Station Area in South Wellfleet, Pilgrim Heights Area in Truro, and Province Lands Area in Provincetown (with the Province Lands Visitor's Center). Each of these areas is discussed in detail under the heading for the town in which it is located.

Along the Bay

On the north shore of the Cape, Rte. 6A winds its way into the legacy of the Brewster sea captains. Once a part of Harwich, the north parish was settled in 1656, prospered during the early years of the great trading ships, and with legislative approval, became the Town of Brewster in 1803. "Ninety and nine shipmasters" from the township set out from the waters of Cape Cod Bay on winds both fair and foul to reach the foreign ports of the Orient and Europe. Foreign trade on the seas of the world was their source of prosperity throughout the 1800s.

Georgian, classic Greek revival, and Victorian houses give testimony to an elegant architectural heritage along Brewster's main road and side streets leading to the sea.

As you travel down-Cape (traveling "down-Cape" means that you are heading out toward the tip) on Rte. 6A, you may want to stop at Sealand of Cape Cod, a marine aquarium and park. Open year-round, Sealand lets you get a close look at performing dolphins, sea lions, seals, turtles, and otters. Educational and entertaining, the attraction is a favorite with children.

One mile from Sealand, the Drummer Boy Museum complex is set back on the left against the Bay. Highlights are the ten-foot-high oil paintings depicting America's Revolutionary history. Entitled the American Epic, the artistic drama spans the years 1770–1781. The museum's 30-acre grounds can be identified by the windmill just before the entrance.

A short distance away, the Cape Cod Museum of Natural History, a rapidly growing facility of natural history and marine exhibits, as well as nature trails, rests on 50 acres of land, including pine and oak forests, tidal inlets, and salt marshes. The museum staff provides children's classes, field trips, and birdwatching excursions throughout the year.

East on 6A, a more idyllic park is nestled among the trees of Mill Pond. Turn right on Paine's Creek Road and, after a short distance, turn right on Stony Brook Road. Over the hill you will find Stony Brook Mill. The mill itself, circa 1873, is on the site of the Cape's first grist mill, built in 1663. Two ponds and a fish ladder for migratory alewives (April–May) complement the setting, a favorite with artists, photographers, and nature lovers. The area was once called Factory Village, the hub of Brewster "industry," consisting of four mills and a general store in the early 1700s.

Turn back on Stony Brook Road to Rte. 6A and proceed one mile to the New England Fire and History Museum, a re-created 18th-century Common, featuring a village smith, an apothecary shop, early firefighting equipment, and the Union Firehouse.

History buffs will want to stop at the Town Hall, where the Brewster Historical Society houses artifacts, exhibits, and documents of the town's early history. Behind the Unitarian Church in the center of town, a small cemetery indicates the names of the many men who followed the lure of the sea. Of particular interest is the stone of Captain David Nickerson. It is said that while in Paris during the French Revolution, a young baby was forced on the captain with a plea to deliver the child safely to America. Local legend assumes the child to be the Lost Dauphin of France, son of Louis XVI and Marie Antoinette. On the backside of Nickerson's gravestone is the inscribed name: René Rousseau.

In Brewster center on the left is Lower Road. The second house on the right (a private home) holds a classic widow's walk at the peak of the roof. Built by the famous sea captain Elijah Cobb, the home is a fine example of the Georgian manors on Cape Cod. While in the town center, stop at the Brewster Store, a version of Americana where the popular pastime is sitting on the front stoop to see who drops in to buy the Sunday paper.

On Tubman Road between Rte. 6A and 137, the children will be delighted with Bassett's Wild Animal Farm. A picnic area, swings, a petting zoo, and a host of exotic animals await your amusement and delight. Route 124 to Harwich and Rte. 137 to Chatham connect with Rte. 6A here at Brewster center.

Nickerson State Park

While the sea was the main provider for most, one young man saw the railroad as a path to prominence. The desire of Rowland C. Nickerson to be a country gentleman led first to financial security and eventually to the acquisition of 1,750 acres of land in East Brewster, the largest tract of private land on the Cape. Nickerson's land was abundant with game and fish, and sportsmen and neighbors alike were upset at being denied land privileges.

Ironically, his widow, Addie, relinquished control of the entire acreage to the state with the agreement that it would be a memorial park to her husband and deceased son of the same name. Rowland C. Nickerson State Park became the first state-owned park in the country in 1937.

Today, the park charges nominal day and overnight fees. Services include campsites, fishing ramps, trout-stocked ponds, swimming, bike paths, and sanitary and picnic facilities. There are no commercial amenities within the park, and reservations are not accepted.

The Harwiches

On the South Shore of the Cape along Nantucket Sound, traveling "down-Cape" on Rte. 28, the last buffer towns before the compass points north are collectively called The Harwiches, seven small villages with the town center at the hub. In April and May, you should check the Herring River in West Harwich for the thousands of migratory fish making their way upstream to spawn. Pickled herring lovers are frequent visitors to this area in the spring. Take a look down river toward the south for a classic blend of scenery and Cape-style architecture: a windmill silhouetted against the horizon, one of the many private homes to gain landmark status. A launching ramp is located at the mouth of the river, and the inland waterway winds through the marshes here.

One of the founding towns of the fishing industry on Cape Cod, Harwich boasts five protected harbors, all accessible from the warm waters of Nantucket Sound or Rte. 28 by land.

A year-round population of 9,700 makes this south-coastal town one of the largest on the outer reach. Like most of the townships on the Cape, Harwich was incorporated in 1694 when there were enough residents to support a local ministry. The town boundaries stretched from the southern shore on Nantucket Sound to the Bay on the North. Productive farmland brought the first settlers south from Plymouth Colony. Most of the town's early charm, tradition, and rural quality remain.

Tourism, fishing, and cranberries are the prevalent business ventures in this area. There are many bogs along the back roads, still productive as they have been since the first commercial cranberries were harvested in the 1840s. In September, the Cranberry Harvest Festival marks a week-long celebration, with fireworks, arts and crafts displays, golf tournaments, canoe races, sporting events, and tours of cranberry bogs.

As you pass through Harwich Port, you may want to stop at one of the many fine shops or eateries. If not, take a left at Rte. 39 for town center. Beyond the hustle and bustle of Rte. 28, Harwich is the proverbial "sleepy New England town." A short walk on Main Street will allow you to enjoy Brooks Park (free band concerts in July and August), view the Colonial architecture, have a picnic, or stroll the grounds of Brooks Academy, the first school of navigation. The Academy building is now the home of the Harwich Historical Society, guardian of a significant collection of old documents, maps, and photos of early life on Cape Cod. Freeman Street will return you to Rte. 28 and east to Wychmere Harbor.

Above the harbor, you can stop at a small turnout on the overlook, where you can gaze at pleasure craft and try to visualize the racetrack that once surrounded the cove below the grand Victorian inn.

Saquatucket Harbor lies just ahead, the newest addition to a wide range of marine facilities. You might want to stop for a soda on the dock, dinner on the deck, or let the children feed the wild ducks at harbor's edge. The small port was named after the Indians who once populated the area. Today, it is a mix of commercial fishers and the fair-weather sloops of summer sailors.

Chatham by the Sea

Continuing east on Rte. 28, the road leads to the bent elbow of the Cape and colonial Chatham. Small in size, only 25 square miles, the peninsula village is held by the sea in a cradle of water. Pleasant Bay borders to the North, the Atlantic to the East, Nantucket Sound to the South—65 miles of waterfront.

Chatham was settled as a farm community in 1656, but inevitably the townsfolk found their greatest opportunities in the offshore waters. To fully appreciate the bond between the people of Chatham and King Neptune, take a short loop drive around The Neck to the East end of the village.

From Rte. 28, Queen Anne Road approaches Oyster Pond. Skirt the edge of the pond and, as Robert Frost said, take "the path least travelled," Cedar Street, on the right. Turn left on Battlefield Road to Champlain Road. The Colonial and farming background of the community is evidenced along these roads. Cape half-houses, large fields, and rolling pastures lead to Stage Harbor, where Samuel de Champlain anchored in 1606. Today, sailing races are organized here each Tuesday, Thursday, and Sunday.

Morris Island, a naturalist's haven, lies on the southeast side of the harbor. The island is a link between the mainland and Monomoy Refuge, and many hikers take the 4-mile walk around the east side of the private dwellings across the dike. The Department of the Interior staffs its headquarters building here during the summer.

The Island of Monomoy, a nine-mile-long sand spit, is under

federal protection. It is one of the most vital spots in the Northeast flyway for migratory birds. Nesting and resting fowl of almost every kind frequent the refuge—more than 250 species have been sighted at the sanctuary; 29 are resident colonies. An island of desolate beauty, Monomoy can only be reached by boat (ferry service available).

At 347 Stage Harbor Road, the Chatham Historical Society's exhibits are displayed in, and on the grounds of, the Atwood House, circa 1752. Included are: memorabilia of Cape author Joseph C. Lincoln; the reknowned murals of Alice Stallknecht; the century-old reflector and housing of Chatham Light; memorial stone to Squanto; antiques; glass; artifacts; and herb gardens.

From the Atwood House, return to Bridge Street. As you cross the bridge, you will most likely see people bottom-fishing from the rail. In Mill Pond on the left, "bullrakers" ply the muddy bottom with long rakes in search of shellfish—backbreaking work by any standard. The 20-foot poles and a wire bucket are tools of the trade for these shellfishers.

At the end of Bridge Street, vistas of Nauset Spit, Chatham Light, and Chatham Harbor await. On the bluff, one of the finest views of the Atlantic can be surveyed through public telescopes. Fog shrouds often give the area a dream-like quality.

Along the crest of Shore Road, elegant Victorian hotels and summer cottages share the view with stately houses of purebred Yankee architecture. Some of the finest "bow-roof" homes in the nation are in Chatham. (Bow roofs are curved, resembling the inverted bow of a ship.) Watch for them.

One of the most frequented docks on the Lower Cape, the Chatham Fish Pier at Lydia's Cove, is magnetic to everyone. This is where fishing boats off-load daily catches for the trip to market. The hard-working boats and their crews are the inheritors of the Cape tradition. Visitors are welcome to view the pier activity.

To return to town center, turn left at the traffic light onto Old Harbor Road. If it's a Friday evening in summer, stroll up to Kate Gould Park on Main Street for the Chatham Band Concert, the town's weekly party. A walk around town should include the Railroad Museum and the windmill in Chase Park.

Rejoining Rte. 28 is best-accomplished by turning east on Main Street and north on Shore Road. You will be retracing part of the loop to Rte. 28.

Along the three miles to Chatham Port, the rural highway passes through wooded upland and curls toward Pleasant Bay. At Ryder's Cove, there is a town landing for public access to the bay waters. Marine services are nearby in case you would like to partake in the sailing races on Tuesday, Thursday, and Saturday.

The shore of Pleasant Bay reaches across a small section by

Harwich around the scenic Round Cove area. Less than two miles down the road is Orleans.

The Defiant One

Following the original Indian trail east, Rte. 6A leads to Orleans, the only town on the Cape with a French name. Economics have made it the business center of the Lower Cape, but don't expect Wall Street. You may rejoin the main highway, Rte. 6, to Provincetown, or continue into the center of town on Rte. 6A. Rte. 28 from the south side, Rte. 6 and Rte. 6A all converge one mile to the east of town center at a highway rotary. Here they become Rte. 6, the only highway to the outer villages.

If Orleans is your destination, you may want to pause for a worthwhile side trip. Take a left at the Main Street traffic lights to connect with Rock Harbor Road. A short drive down a winding street lined with gray-shingled Cape houses, white picket fences, and trim gardens will bring you to the harbor. Rock Harbor is where the early packet ships landed, bringing goods, mail, and passengers across the bay from Boston. Upon arrival, a flag was raised on the high ground as a signal to villagers, who would trek down to the dockside to meet the vessel.

Here, during the War of 1812, the Orleans militia turned back British invaders in defiance of an ultimatum to pay ransom for sparing the town from attack. The British frigate *Newcastle,* in her zeal to teach the upstarts a lesson, ran aground in the shallows outside the harbor. Having seized a number of smaller boats, the English impressed a Yankee captain to sail them out of danger. The skirmish ended when the boat was run aground purposely and the British were captured. Victory went to the militiamen of Orleans.

Today, the harbor channel is navigable only during the two hours before and after high tide, but its accessibility to excellent fishing grounds has made it a favorite place for sport-fishing boats and a small fleet of commercial fishers. Charter and party boats put to sea regularly here during the summer season, despite tidal inconvenience. Sunsets over Rock Harbor are worthy of the best artistic and photographic inspirations.

Perhaps you are entering South Orleans from Chatham on Rte. 28. In this case, you will pass a number of country roads to the right of the highway, any one of which will carry you to the shore of Pleasant Bay and public access to water. Looking due east, you will note two islands facing the Nauset sand spit. The smaller of the two, Hog Island, is one of the many in the waters of Southeastern New England where the infamous Captain Kidd stashed part of his treasure, or so the story goes.

As you journey east along the shore of the bay in Orleans, roughly seven miles inside the town line stands the home of Captain John Kendrick, the oldest house in Orleans, a classic full-Cape, circa 1760. Captain Kendrick's beautiful ship, the *Columbia,* earned the distinction of being the first under the American flag to circle the globe.

A five-minute ride from the Kendrick house will bring you to the intersection of Main Street. Take a right turn to Beach Road, where you'll have access to the rolling surf and windswept dunes of Nauset Beach. The long, narrow stretch of sand provides ample opportunity for picnicking, swimming, sunbathing, or quiet walks. From this beach nestled against the Atlantic you may look out to the open ocean and contemplate some of Nauset's early history. The waters off the coast claimed the first recorded shipwreck in 1626, the *Sparrowhawk,* one of 3,000 to have run afoul on the treacherous outer coast.

In 1717, Orleans earned another historical first when the sea created an original Cape Cod canal by powering its way through the northern marshes. The townspeople later widened the swath cut by the sea. Nicknamed "Jeremiah's Gutter," the so-called canal was never really functional as such.

Another distinctive historical note: Orleans is the only spot in the continental United States to receive enemy fire during either of the modern World Wars—during World War I a German submarine fired on commercial barges off the Orleans coast. Four barges were sunk, and one shell is reported to have fallen on American soil during the foray.

Having absorbed some off-shore history, return to the village center and peruse the fine antique shops, stop to eat at one of the many restaurants, or simply browse the stores for gifts and necessities. If you are a summer guest, check with the Board of Trade for time and place of a number of annual events: Fourth of July activities, antique sales, arts and crafts fair, and the Anheuser-Busch half-marathon, a 13-mile road race that draws world-class runners. It is usually held in July. The Orleans Historical Society is also in town, at River Road and School Road. Of particular interest here is the $1,000 ransom demand note of British Captain Richard Raggot, who is known as the catalyst of the Battle of Rock Harbor. One last point of interest in the village is the French Cable Station Museum at Rte. 28 and Cove Road. Built as a terminal for the on-land extension of the transatlantic cable from France, the museum is the forerunner of the communications era.

Now that you've had a rest, you can head for the tip of the Cape by picking up Rte. 6 at the Orleans rotary north of town. As you head for Eastham, be absolutely sure to watch for the "Fort Hill" sign on the right hand side of the highway. On the approach road you will see the Captain Edward Penniman House, a large yellow Victorian home of European design, built in 1867 by the most famous whaling pilot of the outer Cape. Just beyond the home the road curves up over a rise and gives clear view to one of the most pastoral scenes in the National Seashore. Rolling gently to the shores of Nauset, flanked on the north by the Red Maple Swamp, the once-productive farmland lined with stone fences commands an unparalleled view of Nauset Spit, the marshes, and the moors, explored as early as 1605 by Samuel de Champlain. The French adventurer named the area after the Indians living on the surrounding hills. Don't miss it!

Eastham

Eastham, one of the four original Cape towns, was not settled until 1646. The district at one time included Orleans in the south and Wellfleet in the north. Like most of the Cape townships, Eastham has a varied and significant history. Myles Standish first encountered the Indians on the bayside beaches. From Rte. 6, take a left on Samoset Road. At the bay a bronze marker commemorates the meeting. First Encounter Beach also holds (literally) a more recent historical artifact, the "target ship" *S.S. James Longstreet*. Grounded by the Navy in 1945, the ghostly ship suffered the battering of military target practice for 25 years, until 1970 when it was decidedly dangerous to continue such a practice only two miles from shore. The ghost ship now sits in the sand under the watchful eye of The Longstreet Preservation Society.

Back on Rte. 6, on your left is the "pride and joy" of the townsfolk, Windmill Park. The mill was built in Plymouth in the 1600s, making it the oldest wind-powered grist mill still in existence on the peninsula. Dismantled and shipped across the bay, it was reconstructed in 1793. Every autumn, the people of Eastham celebrate Windmill Weekend, a time of family fun, dancing, music, and games dedicated to community spirit. Visitors are cordially invited.

A short distance "down" Rte. 6 stands the Salt Pond Visitor's Center of the National Seashore, with ample parking, a shuttle bus to the beach (seasonal), rest rooms, and just about all the available information concerning the park areas.

Within walking distance is the School House Museum of 1869, now home of the Eastham Historical Society, easily identified by the whalebone jaw arch in front. The old school is a companion building to the 1741 Swift-Daley House on Rte. 6.

On the other side of the Visitor's Center is Eastham's famous Salt Pond, where shellfish of many varieties are suspended in floating nurseries. Hanging from the many rafts in the pond, the "babies" grow under near-perfect conditions, free from storm and predator alike, then they are used to seed the flats. Walk over with the kids and take a look.

When you return to the Center, the staff will answer any questions you may have about the National Seashore. Also for your viewing are dioramas depicting the early times of Nauset and a short film on how the Cape was formed geologically. Directly behind the center, there are a number of short marshside trails, a bike path to the beach, and a touch, smell, and "see" nature trail for the blind and visually handicapped, with descriptions in braille and large print.

When you leave the Visitor's Center turn right on Nauset Road, bear right at Doane Road to Coast Guard Beach, a supervised area with facilities, including lifeguard protection during summer. As you depart from the beach, follow the Ocean View Drive for one mile along the rolling hills to Nauset Light. The single lighthouse tops the bluff where the "Three Sisters" lights were lost to the erosion of the bluff, which occurs at an average of three feet per year. The beach at Nauset is also a supervised area; the light itself is one of the most photographed in the state.

Cable Road leads to Nauset Road from the ocean. Turn right to Rte. 6. Before leaving Eastham, you may want to wander through some of the back roads on the Bay side of Rte. 6 in search of the famed Eastham turnip sold at markets and roadside stands. This sweet, white and purple vegetable has become a delicacy associated with the town, and if you don't believe it, just ask one of the locals.

Wellfleet

Like so many of its neighbors, this small village is devoid of industry, save the ever-present fishermen. Art, leisure, oysters, and hospitality have replaced the whaling industry of the 1800s as an economic base. Fine art for serious collectors or those of high appreciation is an image cultivated by the proprietors and supporters of "gallery row." In the last decade, the small Bayside hamlet, population 2,000, has become the home of more than a dozen reputable galleries with special emphasis on conservative and traditional works of art. In keeping with the overall peacefulness of the town, a short stroll from Main Street to Commercial Street is suggested for viewing the sculptures, oils, watercolors, and scenes of the outer Cape. A leisurely pace is part of the personality of the town. You can hurry to Wellfleet, but you can't hurry in Wellfleet.

As you cross the boundary from Eastham, the Audubon Society welcomes you to the Wellfleet Bay Wildlife Sanctuary, situated on the left side of Rte. 6. The sanctuary has over 700 acres of moors, marsh, forest, wildflowers, and of course, wildlife. Audubon members are allowed camping privileges, while the general public is invited to explore during daylight hours year-round. A summer program for boys and girls is conducted by the Natural History Day Camp. Advance inquiries are necessary; Box 236, South Wellfleet, MA 02663.

When you leave the Sanctuary, follow Rte. 6 for two miles to the large sign indicating the National Seashore entrance to the Marconi Area on the Atlantic side. This is the second of the four major areas on the "backside" (the Atlantic side of the Lower Cape) maintained and supervised by the National Park Service. On this spot in 1903 Guglielmo Marconi transmitted the first wireless message from the United States across the Atlantic and ushered America into the age of electronics. At the ocean's edge is a model of the original wireless station, long since claimed by constant erosion. In addition, the Atlantic White Cedar Swamp nature trail, Marconi Beach, lifeguard supervision, and facilities are available to the public in season.

Back on the main highway, turn right again after a mile onto Lecount Hollow Road for a short ride along Ocean View Drive and a stretch of the backside beaches maintained by the town: Maguire Landing, Cahoon Hollow, and Newcomb Hollow. To return to Rte. 6, or Wellfleet Center, cross the narrow land on Gross Hill Road.

In town, you may want to stop at the Wellfleet Historical Society museum on Main Street. Society general meetings are held throughout the year in the Congregational Church, famous for its town clock, which strikes on the unfamiliar cadence of "ship's time," believed to be the only town steeple clock to do so.

At the town pier, ocean fish and shellfish are off-loaded and packed for market. Charter and party boats share the dock facilities, readily available for fishing enthusiasts. A number of forsaken boats in the tidal flats and marshes reflect the ravages of time and the elements, adding a salty flavor to the local legends of the sand and sea. They have been the subject of innumerable poems, paintings, and photographs.

From the pier, Chequesset Neck Road is the path to Wellfleet's most welcome surprises: a three-mile ride along Cape Cod Bay, a nine-hole oceanside golf course at Chequesset Yacht and Country Club (reservations required), an uncompromised view of the setting sun from the summit of "Sunset Hill," plus the nature trails and silent windswept dunes of Great Island. The island is really a peninsula connected by a long, narrow sand spit. Over seven miles of trails along the inner marshes and the water provide a meditative, peaceful backdrop to the wide expanse of the Bay. If the solitude and personal pleasures of beachcombing, walking, or hiking are what you seek, Great Island is a must.

Rejoin Rte. 6. A short distance on your right is the Museum of American Architecture, a most impressive collection of model homes in miniature including historically accurate detail and construction. JFK's birthplace, Mark Twain's study, Paul Revere's home, and the House of Seven Gables, are just four of the 35 models on display.

As you head for Truro you might like to flip a coin to decide how Wellfleet was named. One side of the coin says it was named after the Wallfleet section of the English coast made famous, as was its Cape counterpart, for oysters. The other version is attributed to the whaling ships that sailed from the harbor in search of the "blackfish" in the sea. Since the North Precinct of Eastham was incorporated in 1763, when the colonists were preparing to break the bonds that tied them to England, greater credence would have to favor the "whale fleet" version of the name. After all, consider the sharp inflections of the native New Englanders' tongue, and the slur of the two words when combined—"Whalefleet."

Over the Moors of Truro

There is no question as to the origin of the name given to the Pamet area of the Cape when it was incorporated in 1709. Truro was named after the region in Cornwall, England. Like the old country, the land is bounded by water, houses are sheltered in tiny valleys, estuaries and rivers back their way into the lowland grasses, and the moors rise and fall from the Bay to the Atlantic.

Look for a highway sign for Pamet Roads, a short loop-drive to Ballston Beach for a view of, or dip in, the ocean. Until recently you would return on the Pamet Road North section of the loop to cross the Cape to Truro Center, however shifting sands have appropriated the outer end of the road. The National Park Service has chosen to let nature take its course.

From the center, take Castle Road to Corn Hill Road. On Corn Hill itself is a tablet marking the spot where a party of men, led by Myles Standish, signalled the *Mayflower* of their safety after two days of exploring the Atlantic side and crossing through the hollows to the inside shore. Here on the hill, they found a buried cache of Indian corn, welcome foodstuffs on that cold day in November of 1620. Land's end, the ocean, and the bay are held in panorama on the horizon. To the south, Gull Island provides barrier protection to Pamet Harbor. The whaling industry was born in these waters. Packet ships from Boston anchored here and trading ships put to sea on Pamet winds. Many of the sons of Truro never saw the harbor again. This small seaside hamlet at one time lost 57 men in one infamous storm. The Paul Revere bell of the Congregational Church tolls in their memory and the old cemeteries bear witness to the loss of life extracted from Truro families by the caprice of the sea.

Back at Castle Road, turn left and enter Rte. 6 to Highland Road on the right. On a bluff overlooking the hazardous Peaked Hill Bars, the first Cape Cod Lighthouse, one of the most powerful beacons on the Atlantic, was erected to provide fair warning to the ships offshore. Rebuilt twice since, the present Highland Light continues its duty to the men who guide their ships around the backside of the outer Cape.

If you don't get mesmerized on the cliffs above the water, the Highland House Museum is open for viewing the exhibits of the Truro Historical Society.

Return to the South Highland road, turn right for Head of the Meadow Beach adjacent to Pilgrim Heights, the third major area managed by the National Park Service.

Pilgrim Heights designates the site of the first exploration route taken by the men of the *Mayflower* when they landed in the new world. Leaving the ship, they crossed the dunes to the Atlantic and turned back to the bay at the southeast side of what is now called Pilgrim Lake. Here, they found a freshwater spring, where they "drank our first new England water with as much delight as we ever drunk drink in all our lives." The area includes two short self-guided trails, a bicycle trail, picnic tables, and an interpretive shelter.

In departing, turn right on Rte. 6. The highway traverses the western meadows of Pilgrim Lake. As you pass, note the rising dunes lining the northeastern rim of the lake. Think about the forward progress of America from these tiny hollows and humble villages. Then cast your eyes along the contours of the hills. For all who come, this timeless beauty is preserved and secure. Ahead of you, the outermost region of the forearm envelopes the town of Provincetown in the protected palm of its hand.

At the Cape's End

If you asked a random number of people to describe "P-town" in one word, the answers would vary as much as the colors of the spectrum. Exciting, peaceful, artsy, remote, lively, inspiring, crazy, or eccentric would be some remarks, but not all.

From October to April, this small Cape colony is home for 4,000 permanent residents, mainly Portuguese fishermen and Yankee descendants who toil in the open seas, much as their ancestors have done for over 300 years. When the boats return to the docks, many of the mates retire to homes that stand watch over the harbor as in the 1700s. No matter what adjectives you use to describe it, Provincetown is a seafaring village, above all.

From the sand hills of Truro you cross the town line on one of two roads. Rte. 6 slips through the 60-foot dunes toward the open Atlantic, while the Rte. 6A extension runs parallel along the shore of Cape Cod Bay into town. For the most scenic approach, stay on the highway and turn right on to Race Point Road for the outermost region supervised by the National Park Service—the Province Lands.

Within the section designated as National Seashore, endless beaches of unbelievable beauty await townfolk and travelers alike. You can walk the shoreline for over 25 miles and never see a private home or commercial building. The outer reach is a favored place for surfcasters and solitude.

Three horseback riding trails are inside the perimeter of the park land. Sunset trail, West trail, and Herring Cove trail. Each is approximately two hours, round trip. Sunset rides are particularly popular. You can ride along the open beaches with no noise but the pounding of hooves and the pounding of the surf. Stables are located off Rte. 6 on Race Point and Nelson Roads and on Rte. 6A at Bradford Street Extension in the west end.

Just after entering the Province Lands on Race Point Road, note the Beech Forest and parking area on the left. Picnic tables, nature trails, and access to the eight-mile bicycle path are features of this particularly enjoyable section.

At the Province Lands Visitor Center you can acquire a listing and schedule of activities related to, or conducted by the Park Service. These include: self-guided trails, forest walks, bird-watching, bonfires, beach walks, lectures, films, and exhibits. Specimens of fish from local waters, historical notes, and environmental displays are on the first level. The upper level is an observation deck affording a 360-degree view of the dunes and the Atlantic. Ask for a peek through your neighbor's binoculars and you may be lucky enough to see whales gliding effortlessly in the outer waters. Watch for the spray blown into the air as the leviathans complete their breathing cycles. Looking back to the west you can see the landmark Pilgrim Monument that rises from the center of Provincetown. If you stop only once in the Province Lands, make it at the Visitor Center.

From the Visitor Center, the first right turn leads to the airport, with sightseeing, charter, and local flights. At the road's end, the Coast Guard Station and its forerunner, Old Harbor Station, flank the public beach at Race Point. Old Harbor Station stood at Chatham during the days of the U.S. Life Saving Service. A quirk of fate rescued it from the ravages of the Great Blizzard of 1978. During the storm, the Station rested in the safety of Provincetown

Harbor, where it had been towed by barge. In May of 1978, the structure, now on the National Register of Historic Places, was moved to its present site for restoration.

Provincetown

Back at the intersection turn right for a short ride to Herring Cove Beach, on the "Knuckles" of the Provincetown fist. From the cove road continue along the shore past Rte. 6A to the west end rotary at Commercial Street. Situated at this spot, the tip of the Cape, is a bas-relief plaque commemorating "the first landing spot of the Pilgrims" in 1620. To complete the loop of outer Provincetown, follow Rte. 6A back to the Pilgrim Monument on the hill above the Town Center.

From the top of the 255-foot monument you can survey the area as it appeared to the voyagers on the *Mayflower*—almost completely surrounded by water. One block toward the Bay, Commercial Street is the core of the town. At this point, walking is the recommended mode of travel. A bicycle is even more preferable for a leisurely investigation of the sights and sounds of this narrow main street. The pedestrians have literally claimed walking privileges on the one-way road and vehicles should be driven cautiously, if at all. Commercial and Bradford streets are like the tracks of a railroad with a number of short connecting "ties" as side streets, European in style.

In summer, Provincetown is part carefree. A blend of Greenwich Village and Sausalito, Commercial Street is dotted with craft shops, sidewalk cafés with a European flavor, specialty stores to suit every taste, wharf buildings converted to shops, and a constant street parade of people.

The east end of Provincetown is an art experience, most often described as the "quiet, charming side of town." Fine art, antiques, jewelry, and side-street restaurants are common. The galleries and guest houses share the same reputation for hospitality.

At 356 Commercial Street, you can visit the Provincetown Heritage Museum, owned by the town. Here you'll find the fishing boat *Charlotte* and a model of the schooner *Rose Dorothea,* plus a large collection of paintings evoke the seafaring tradition that has made P-town famous. A reading room from the old town library, antique fire apparatus, and a Victorian kitchen and parlor are also maintained.

A short walk will bring you to the center of town, where you can stop at the Chamber of Commerce information booth for inquiries. Or, take a dune buggy tour on the coastal sands, sail from MacMillan Wharf on one of the Grand Banks schooners, return to "whale watch" by the sea, or sign on a charter boat for a deep-sea

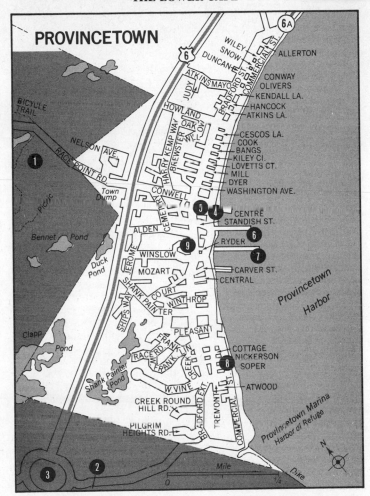

PROVINCETOWN

Points of Interest

1) Province Lands
2) Herring Cove Beach
3) First Landing Spot of the Pilgrims
4) Provincetown Heritage Museum

5) Chamber of Commerce
6) MacMillan Wharf
7) Fisherman's Wharf
8) Seth Nickerson House
9) Pilgrim Monument and Museum

excursion. MacMillan Wharf and the recently completed Fisherman's Wharf are the backbone of the marine facilities.

On the last weekend in June you can be a part of a traditional celebration. The Blessing of the Fleet starts with High Mass, then proceeds with a parade through the streets, which begins a festive tribute to the Patron Saint of Fishermen, Peter. A statue of Saint Peter is borne aloft by the procession, and at MacMillan Wharf, each individual boat, decorated for the occasion, passes before the local Bishop for the annual blessing and prayers for prosperous fishing in the next year. It is a fitting festival to initiate the circus atmosphere of the summer, but is really an illustration of the deep bond between the townspeople and the sea. During the rest of the "season" the local residents join in a visitor's common pastime, sitting on the benches downtown and watching other people as they cruise by. Don't be misled, P-town's outrageous, happy vitality is anything but dull.

From the Town Hall and docks to the west end of town, a profusion of eateries, sidewalk cafés, and specialty stores stand shoulder to shoulder. The "midway" atmosphere ends abruptly with a sharp left turn on Commercial Street.

The charm, quiet, and reserve of the east end reappears in the west end. Galleries, fine restaurants, inns, and guest houses mix with the established neighborhood of year-round homes. In addition to the Oldest House, the Seth Nickerson House (circa 1746) at 72 Commercial Street, a number of other historical points are included in the Historical Society's Walking Tour Guide, which is distributed at many locations throughout town.

Pilgrim plaque and the rotary are four blocks past the Nickerson house, a mere three miles from the other end of town. Yes, Provincetown is small town U.S.A., but the facets of P-town's personality and the faces of P-town's people offer more diversity than most cities.

PRACTICAL INFORMATION FOR THE

LOWER CAPE

HOW TO GET AROUND. By air: *Provincetown-Boston Airlines,* Provincetown Airport, all connections. 487-0240. *Nauset Airways,* Chatham Airport, charter service. 945-9000.

By bicycle: The suggested State bikeway is clearly marked on the highways and country roads of the Lower Cape. (See Trails for individual bike paths.) Rentals are available at numerous locations in all towns. Inquire locally or at the Chamber of Commerce.

By boat: Daily service between Provincetown and Boston, or Plymouth in summer. Weekends only to Boston off-season. For information call 487-1741.

By bus: Outer Cape towns are serviced by several major lines through the Hyannis terminal. For tickets and information, call 771-5524.

By car: Rte. 28 on the Southside and Rte. 6A on the Northside converge with Rte. 6 in Orleans and continue to Provincetown.

TOURIST INFORMATION SERVICES. *Brewster,* 1673 Rte. 6A, at Town Offices. 896-3701. *Chatham,* Main St. next to Town Offices. 945-0342. Winter, 945-1436. *Eastham,* Rte. 6 at Fort Hill Rd. 255-3444. *Harwich,* Rte. 28, Harwichport. 432-1600. Winter, P.O. Box 34, Harwichport, Massachusetts 02646. *Orleans,* Rte. 6A and Eldredge Parkway. 255-1386. Winter, 255-2700. *Provincetown,* 307 Commercial St. 487-3424. Winter, P.O. Box 1017, Provincetown, Massachusetts 02657. *Truro,* Rte. 6 at Head of the Meadow Rd. 487-1288. Winter, P.O. Box 26, North Truro, Massachusetts 02652. *Wellfleet,* Rte. 6 at Davis Corner. 349-2510. Winter, P.O. Box 571, Wellfleet, Massachusetts 02667.

RECOMMENDED READING. *Short Bike Rides on Cape Cod* by Jane Griffith and Edwin Mullen, published by Pequot Press, 1977. *Hiking Cape Cod* by J. H. Mitchell and Whit Griswold, published by The Eastwoods Press, 1978.

If you are visiting the Lower Cape, local periodicals and weekly newspapers are invaluable sources of current information. In addition, the First Encounter Press publishes a unique series of booklets containing pictures and prose about the Cape. Write: First Encounter Press, P.O. Box 946, North Eastham, Massachusetts 02651.

SEASONAL EVENTS. In addition to the annual town festivals, church fairs, bazaars, auctions, art exhibitions, and traditional holiday festivities of Christmas and Thanksgiving, the Lower Cape hosts an array of yearly events. For additional information, contact the Chamber of Commerce or Town Hall in the town you plan to visit.

June. *Blessing of the Fleet,* Cape Cod's biggest celebration; blessing of the fishing fleet in Provincetown, last weekend. The *Chatham Harbor Run,* road race over 6.2 miles along the seaside.

July. *Anheuser-Busch Half-Marathon* in Orleans; 13.1-mile road race with international field of runners. Annual *Arts and Crafts Fair* in Harwich and Harwich Port, exhibition and sale by local craftsmen. Annual *Arts and Crafts Sale* at Orleans Middle School, Rte. 28; exhibition and sale by local craftsmen. *Nauset Painters Outdoor Art Show* at various locations; limited schedule of public showings until Sept. *Village Fair* at Chase Park in Chatham; arts, crafts, food, and fun. *Strawberry Festival* at United Methodist Church on Main St., July 4.

August. *Annual Arts and Crafts Fair* sponsored by the Society of Cape Cod Craftsmen, Brewster Elementary School; exhibition and sale by local craftsmen. Annual *Craft and Art Show,* at Nauset Regional High School; exhibition and sale by local craftsmen. Annual *Lower Cape Tennis Open* in Orleans at Eldredge Park. Annual open *Tuna Tournament* in Provincetown. Annual *Women's Invitational Tuna Tournament* in Provincetown.

September. Annual *Harwich Cranberry Festival,* ten days of parades, exhibits, contests, tournaments, and fireworks. Lower Cape Arts and Humanities Council, *Fall Arts Festival in Provincetown.*

 HISTORIC SITES. Reminders of the past are present throughout the Lower Cape, from the handsome sea captains' homes of Brewster, to the Pilgrims' landing place in Provincetown.

Brewster. *Dillingham House,* Stony Brook Rd.; this saltbox is considered the second oldest house on Cape Cod. *Elijah Cobb House,* Lower Rd.; classic sea captain's home built in late 16th century. *Old Grist Mill,* Stony Brook Rd.; water-powered mill built in 1873; grounds open to visitors daily; migratory fish ladders, viewing in early spring; attendant miller in July and Aug., Wed., Fri., and Sat., 2–4 P.M.

Chatham. *Atwood House,* 347 Stage Harbor Rd.; built in 1752, the oldest house in Chatham is owned by the Historical Society; memorial stone and plaque dedicated to the Indian Squanto, plus the century-old reflector from Chatham Light are on the grounds; murals, memorabilia, and exhibits depicting Cape life; open June–Sept., Mon., Wed., and Fri., 2–5 P.M. *Stage Harbor,* landing of Samuel de Champlain in 1606, death of Squanto on a sloop in the harbor in 1622.

Eastham. *First Encounter Beach,* Samoset Rd.; Myles Standish and his party from the *Mayflower* first encountered the Native Americans on this shore in 1620. *Fort Hill-Captain Edward Penniman House;* beautifully restored French Empire style home, built in 1867 by one of the last great whalers. *Swift-Daley House,* Rte 6; built in 1741, period furnishings, antiques, and quilts; open July and Aug., Wed. and Fri., 2–5 P.M.

Harwich. Site of the first commercial *cranberry bog* in the U.S., a vital part of the Cape Cod economy; off Rte. 124 at Seymour Rd.

Orleans. *Nauset Spit,* along the Atlantic; the only part of the continental U.S. to take enemy fire (World War I). *Rock Harbor,* off Rte. 6A; after refusing to pay a ransom demand in the War of 1812, the Orleans militia turned back British invaders.

Provincetown. *Bas-relief plaque,* Bradford St.; commemorates the signing of The Mayflower Compact, the first document of democratic government in the U.S. *Pilgrim Plaque,* west end of Commercial St., landing place of Pilgrims. The *Seth-Nickerson House,* 72 Commercial St.; circa

1746, the oldest house in Provincetown is a nine-room Cape with antique appointments; open daily from June–Oct., 10 A.M.–5 P.M.; admission.

Truro. *Highland Light,* Highland Rd.; site of the first lighthouse on Cape Cod, erected in 1798.

Wellfleet. *Marconi Wireless Station,* off Rte. 6; site of original wireless station built in 1901, a pavilion contains a replica of Guglielmo Marconi's invention.

 MUSEUMS. Brewster. *Cape Cod Museum of Natural History,* Rte. 6A; environmental and marine exhibits, including outdoor nature trails. Daily in summer; Tues.–Sat. in winter; admission. *Drummer Boy Museum,* Rte. 6A; scenes from American Revolution with life-size figures. *Brewster Windmill* on grounds; guided tours from late May to mid-Oct.; admission. *New England Fire and History Museum,* Rte. 6A; early firefighting apparatus; daily from Memorial Day to mid-Sept., off-season tours by appointment; admission.

Chatham. *Old Godfrey Windmill,* off Shattuck Place; built in 1797, the working windmill is open July 1–Labor Day, closed Tues. *Railroad Museum,* Depot Rd.; railroad memorabilia and exhibits; open last week in June–Labor Day, Mon.–Fri., 1:30–4:30 P.M.

Eastham. *Old Grist Mill,* Rte. 6; the oldest windmill on Cape Cod, built in 1793, located at Grist Mill Park; open daily Memorial Day–Labor Day; free. *Eastham Historical Society,* off Rte. 6. *New England Schoolhouse Museum,* Indian artifacts and farming implements of historical significance; open June–Labor Day, Wed.–Fri., 2–5 P.M.

Harwich. *Harwich Historical Society* at Brooks Academy in Harwich Center; Indian artifacts, early tools, Sandwich glass, toys, and historical documents; Brooks Academy was the first school of navigation; open July and Aug., Mon., Wed., and Fri. 1:30–4:30 P.M.

Orleans. *Orleans Historical Society,* River and School Rds.; Indian and seafaring artifacts; Coast Guard memorabilia and assorted tools in Hurd Chapel; open July and Aug., Thu. and Fri., 2–4 P.M. *French Cable Station Museum,* Rte. 28 and Cove Rd.; terminal extension point for transatlantic cable; open July 1–Sept. 15, Tues.–Sun., 2–4 P.M.

Provincetown. *Pilgrim Memorial Monument,* Town Hill; exhibits commemorating first landing of Pilgrims in 1620; panoramic views from top of 255-foot tower; open daily, 9 A.M.–5 P.M.; admission. *Provincetown Art Association* and *Museum,* 460 Commercial St.; various media reflecting P-town's roots in the arts; open daily June–Oct., 12–4 P.M., 7–10 P.M.; admission. *Provincetown Heritage Museum,* Commercial and Center Sts.; varied displays reflecting P-town history and heritage; schooner *Rose Dorothea,* world's largest scale model ship; open daily in summer, 10 A.M.–10 P.M.; admission.

Truro. *Truro Historical Museum,* Highland Rd.; exhibits include firearms, ships, toys, farming implements, furniture, glass, and historical documents; Courtney Allen room—artist, model maker, wood carver; open daily June–Sept., 10 A.M.–5 P.M.; admission.

Wellfleet. *Wellfleet Historical Society,* Main St.; exhibits include early photographs, documents, marine and Indian artifacts, early implements, utensils, and clothing; open June–Labor Day, Tues.–Sat., 2–5 P.M.; admission.

TOURS. Aerial. A different way to see the Cape and surrounding waters; fares per person are about $6 for a minimum flight of 15 minutes. *Provincetown-Boston Airlines,* Provincetown Airport, 487-0240. *Nauset Airways,* Chatham Airport, 945-9000.

Bus. Organized day-trips to Chatham, National Seashore, and Provincetown are available. *Cape Cod Bus Lines,* 771-5165. The *Gray Line* of Cape Cod, 778-0182.

Boat. Whalewatching excursions depart from MacMillan Wharf in Provincetown, 4-hour tours of the harbor and Atlantic waters. *Cape Cod Princess,* 487-2274. *Dolphin Fleet,* 487-1900. *Ranger III,* 487-1582.

Sail on the *Hindu,* a two-hour excursion out of Provincetown aboard the 65-foot windjammer of Grand Banks schooner design; sunset sail, 7–9 P.M. On the *Olad,* 2-hour excursions out of Provincetown aboard the 55-ft. descendant of the Grand Banks schooners; sunset sail, 7–9 P.M.; 487-0659 or 487-9308.

Dune Taxi. Several sightseeing vehicles ferry passengers across the high dunes and beachfront. The trails are sometimes closed or restricted by the National Park Service as a protective measure. For information on the availability of tours, contact Provincetown Chamber of Commerce at 307 Commercial St.

Walking. *Cape Cod Bird Club* organizes 3–4 hour-long walks throughout the year. For information contact the Cape Cod Museum of Natural History, Rte. 6A, Brewster.

SHOPPING. The Lower Cape is a novel place to shop, whether you would just like a piece of homemade fudge, or a hand-carved decoy. You can buy your vegetables from a backyard garden in season, or browse around a converted barn full of toys and miniatures. Home-businesses, commonly called "cottage industries," are innumerable.

Quite frequently, a small roadside sign will announce someone's specialty—weaving, baskets, pottery, original clothing, sweet breads, Christmas ornaments, or dolls—something for any preference. Indian summer is a popular time of year to wander around visiting "shops" such as these. If you prefer a more familiar shopping atmosphere, the village and in-town stores will satisfy your needs.

ANTIQUES

Brewster. *Barbara Grant,* 1793 Rte. 6A; books, furniture, decoratives. *Breton House Antiques,* 1222 Stony Brook Rd. *The Brewster Rooster,* Rte. 6A and Old North Rd.; tools, cameras, paper. *Holly Hill of Brewster,* 1283

Main St.; chairs, furniture. *Marshlands Antiques*, 89 Main St.; tools, primitives, glass. *Sunsmith House Antiques*, Rte. 6A, East Brewster; toys, furniture, primitives.

Chatham. *The Cobweb*, Rte. 28 and Pond View Ave.; glass, miniatures. *Fred's Trading Post*, Rte. 28, West Chatham; furniture, primitives, weapons. *House On The Hill Antiques*, 17 Seaview St.; paper Americana. *Mildred Georges*, 447 Main St.; jewelry, Sandwich glass. *Suitsus II*, 490 Main St.; Chinese porcelains. *Ye Olden Times Antiques*, 585 Main St.; furniture, glass.

Harwich. *Misty Winds Antiques*, 571 Main St., Harwich Port; furniture, primitives. *The Solomon Thacher House*, Bank and Main St.; primitives, folk art. *South Antiques*, 7 South St., Harwich Port; jewelry, glass, prints. *Winstead Antiques*, 328 Bank St.; kitchenware, furniture.

Provincetown. *Selma Dubrin*, 423 Commercial St.; general. *September Morn*, 385 Commercial St.; Oriental art.

Wellfleet. *H. B. Watson, Jr. and Son*, 17 School St.; fine antiques.

ART

Brewster. *Aries East Gallery*, Rte. 6A; paintings.

Chatham. *McElwain-Falconer Art Studio*, 492 Main St.; oils, watercolors, artifacts. *Munson Gallery*, Main St.; paintings, prints. *The New England Gallery of Chatham*, 483 Main St. *The Bayside Gallery*, Lower Bank St., Harwich Port; paintings, graphics, sculpture. *Georgia Dearborn Gallery at Corner Card Gallery*, 7 Post Office Sq., Harwich Port.

Orleans. *Cove View Gallery*, Rtes. 6A and 28; watercolors, oils, photography. *Ethel Putterman Gallery*, Rte. 6A; paintings, crafts. *Orleans Art Gallery*, Rte. 28; paintings, drawings, graphics. *Peacock's Pride Art Gallery*, Rte. 28; crafts, paintings, photography.

Provincetown. *East End Gallery*, 424 Commercial St.; paintings. *Eva DeNagy Art Gallery*, 427 Commercial St.; African art, Oriental jewelry. *Graphics Etc. Gallery*, 355 Commercial St.; paintings. *Long Point Gallery*, 492 Commercial St. *Provincetown Group Gallery*, 286 Bradford St.; mixed media.

Wellfleet. *Blue Heron Gallery*, Bank St.; wildlife art. *Brehmer Graphics Gallery*, Commercial St.; etchings. *Cove Gallery*, Commercial St.; fine art. *Jacob Fanning Gallery*, Kendrick Ave.; painting, prints, sculpture. *Kendall Art Gallery*, East Main St. *Left Bank Gallery*, Commercial St.; paintings, sculpture, pottery. *Soroban Gallery*, Baker Ave.; Japanese woodblock prints. *Swansborough Gallery*, Main and School Sts.; fine art, sculpture.

CRAFTS

Brewster. *Brewster Pottery*, Rte. 124 and Tubman Rd.; pottery. *Sheep Pond Pottery*, 3 Jollys Crossing Rd.; pottery. *Town Ho Needleworks*, 1912 Main St.; needlepoint.

Chatham. *Fletcher III*, 255 Old Harbor Rd.; pewter jewelry. *Heller-*

Moore Stained Glass, 2092 Main St., South Chatham; stained glass. *Tom Odell*, 423 Main St.; jewelry. *Old Scrimshaw Leather Shop*, 616 Main St.; leather.

Eastham. *C & G Jewel Crafters*, Mill Rd.; jewelry. *Gigi Pottery*, Gigi Lane, North Eastham; pottery. *The Glass Eye*, Rte. 6, North Eastham, Rtes., 6A and 28, Orleans; stained glass. *Seascape House*, Rte. 6, North Eastham; needlepoint and crewel. *Serendipity*, Massasoit Rd., North Eastham; jewelry, prints.

Harwich. *Paradise Pottery*, 928 Main St., South Harwich; stoneware pottery.

Orleans. *The Artful Hand*, Main St.; scrimshaw. *Orleans Cove Gallery*, Rte. 6A; stained glass, pottery. *Quahog Hollow*, 14 Lower Cove Rd.; fabrics, custom clothes. *Yosemite At The Cove*, Rtes. 6A and 28; jewelry.

Provincetown. *Ann Lord Gallery*, 389B Commercial St.; pottery, sculpture. *Sign Of The Unicorn*, 208 Bradford St.; jewelry, sculpture.

Wellfleet. *Leeshore Craft Gallery*, Commercial St.; woodenware. *Salt Marsh Pottery*, East Main St.; pottery. *Secrest Gallery and Craftsmen's Barn*, West Main St.; contemporary crafts. *Wellfleet Pottery*, Commercial St.; ironstone ovenware.

SPECIALTY STORES

Brewster. *Brooks Cards*, 3732 Main St.; silkscreen Christmas cards. *The Cook Shop*, Rte. 6A; everything for the kitchen gourmet. *The Lemon Tree*, Rte. 6A; gallery, crafts, graphics. *The Spectrum*, Rte. 6A; crafts, graphics, paintings, sculpture, photography. *Sydenstricker*, Rte. 6A; glassworks, unusual and traditional items.

Eastham. *Seascape House of Cape Cod*, Rte. 6, North Eastham; needlepoint. *The Wildfowlers*, Oak and Massasoit Rds., North Eastham; gamebird prints, crafts, books, and antiques.

Orleans. *The Boardwalk*, Rtes. 6A and 28; courtyard cluster of specialty shops. *Goose Humock Shop*, Rte. 28; everything for the sportsman. *The Herbary*, Childs Homestead Rd.; herbs, teas, spices. *Tree's Place*, Rtes. 6A and 28; designer tiles, gifts.

Provincetown. *Marine Specialty, Inc.*, Commercial St.; surplus Marine and government merchandise. *Outermost Kites*, 240 and 315 Commercial St.; kites.

SPORTS. Baseball. The *Cape Cod Baseball League*, with over 30 graduates in the active Major League, consists of 8 teams. The *Chatham Athletics*, *Harwich Mariners*, and the *Orleans Cardinals* represent the Lower Cape. Information and game schedule can be obtained from P.O. Box 495, Hyannis, Massachusetts 02601, or call 775-0880.

Bicycling. (See Trails.)

Bowling. *Orleans Bowling Center*, Rte. 6A, Orleans Center; 14 candlepin lanes.

Golf. Golf on the Cape is one of the prime year round leisure sports. The

Indian Summer Pro-Am Tournament is an annual event; for information contact the Cape Cod Chamber of Commerce. Courses are located at: *Brewster Golf Club,* Rte. 6A; 9 holes, par 35, 2,825 yds.; 896-3785. *Chatham Bars Inn,* Shore Rd.; 9 holes, par 34, 2,400 yds.; 945-0096. *Eastward Ho!* in Chatham Port, Fox Hill Rd.; 18 holes, par 71, 6,300 yds.; 945-3825. *Cranberry Valley* in Harwich, Oak St.; 18 holes, par 72, 6,300 yds.; rated for excellence by *Golf Digest;* 432-6300. *Harwich Port Golf Club,* Forest St.; 9 holes, par 36, 2,700 yds. 432-0250. *Highland Golf Links* in Truro at historic Highland Light; 9 holes, par 36, 3,069 yds.; 487-9201. *Chequesset Yacht and Country Club in Wellfleet,* Chequesset Neck Rd.; 9 holes, par 35, 3,000 yds.; 394-3704.

Horseback Riding. *Deer Meadow Stable* in East Harwich, Rtc. 137. *Gale Force Stable* in Provincetown, Bradford St. Ext. *Nelson's Stable* in Provincetown, Rtc. 6 and Race Point Rd. *Seahorse Stable,* Provincetown, 38 Court St.

Hunting. Deer, rabbit, and wildfowl populate the entire Cape. Federal, state and local laws apply; resident sporting license for hunting and fishing, $16.50; non-resident, $23.25 (small game), $38.25 (big game); archery stamp, $5.10 additional; Ma. waterfowl stamp, $1.25 additional. (Fees subject to change.)

Regattas and Races. *Sail Boat Races;* every Tues., Thu., and Sat. at Pleasant Bay, Chatham; every Tues., Thu., and Sun. at Stage Harbor, Chatham; every Sun. at Orleans Yacht Club. *Sailboard Regatta* in Aug. at Wychmere Harbor, Harwich Port. All events are seasonal.

Soccer. The *Cape Soccer League* begins the first week of June. Games are played by Chatham, Wed. and Sun. at 8:30 P.M., at Veteran's Field. Orleans-Eastham, Wed. and Sun. at 8:30 P.M., at Eldredge Field. Nauset Sports, Wed. and Sun., at 6 P.M., at Middle School Field.

Surfing. Allowed at designated areas along the *Barrier Beach; Coast Guard Beach,* Eastham; *Nauset Beach,* Orleans.

Swimming. (See Public Beaches.)

Tennis. *Brewster:* Bamburgh House Tennis Club on Rte. 6A, 896-5023. Four Havens on Rte. 6A, 896-3367. *Chatham:* Chatham Bars Inn on Shore Rd., 945-3386. Jordan Village on Rte. 28. *Eastham:* Family Sports Center on Rtc. 6, 255-5697. *Harwich* Pleasant Bay Tennis Club, Rte. 28, 432-2500, Manning's Tennis Court, Rte. 28, 432-3958. *Provincetown:* Zen tennis instruction at Bissell's Tennis Courts on Bradford St. Ext., 487-9512. Host of *The Year-rounder's Tournament* in July, the Yacht and Tennis Club is at 286 Bradford St., 487-9574. *Wellfleet:* Chequesset Yacht and Country Club on Chequesset Neck Rd., 394-3704. Oliver's on Rte. 6, 349-3330.

FISHING AND SHELLFISHING. *Saltwater fishing* permits are not required. From May–Oct. gamefish are abundant, including striped bass, tuna, bluefish, swordfish, shark, and bonito. For bottom fishing, cod, flounder, haddock, halibut, perch, scup, and tautog offer the angler a wide choice for the catch of the day.

Harbors on the outer Cape providing *charter and party boat* services include; Chatham, Harwichport, Orleans, Provincetown, and Wellfleet. Party boat fares start as low as $10 per person for half-day trips. For charter information, contact Cape Cod Charter Boat Association, Box 668, West Yarmouth, Massachusetts 02673.

More than 40 miles of continuous sand beaches face the Atlantic on the outer Cape—a surfcaster's paradise. Access points are located in *Chatham:* Morris Island, Morris Island Rd. *Eastham:* Nauset Light, Cable Rd., and Nauset Beach North, Doane Rd. *Orleans:* Nauset Beach South, Beach Rd. *Provincetown:* Race Point, Rte. 6 at Coast Guard Station. *Truro:* Highland Light, Highland Rd. *Wellfleet:* Newcomb's Hollow, Cross Hill Rd. **On the Bay:** *Provincetown:* New Beach, Rte. 6 *Truro:* Pamet River, off Fisher Rd.

Licenses are required for all *freshwater fishing.* Fees for residents (six consecutive months) are $11.25; minors, ages 15–17, $6.25; non-residents, $17.25, seven-day permit, $11.25; alien status, $11.25. Check with local town clerk for license and regulations. Ponds vary in size from 17 to 700 acres. Trout, bass, pickerel, perch, salmon, and bullhead are most common. A complete listing of areas and facilities available can be obtained from the *Cape Cod Chamber of Commerce,* Hyannis, Massachusetts 02601, or call 362-3225. Request the "Sportsman's Guide to Cape Cod." Fees subject to change.

Local permits are required for *shellfishing.* Information is available through selectmen's offices. A permit can usually be purchased for under $10, but the rules and regulations vary greatly from town to town. Quahogs, bay scallops, and clams are readily available.

PUBLIC BEACHES. Brewster. Non-resident fees are: $1 per day, $5 for two weeks, or $15 for the full season. Permits are purchased through the Department of Public Works at Town Hall. All ocean beaches are on Cape Cod Bay and easily reached via Rte. 6A; locations at *Crosby Lane, Ellis Landing, Linnell Rd., Saint's Landing,* and *Robbins Hill.* **Freshwater sites** include *Long Pond, Pine Pond, Paine's Creek, Sheep Pond, Slough Pond,* and *Walker's Pond.*

Chatham. Non-resident fees are: $3 per day, $15 per week, $25 per season. Permits are purchased at the beaches. All ocean beaches are reached via Rte. 28; locations at *Cockle Cove, Harding's Cove,* and *Ridgevale Rd.* (permit necessary). Additional locations at *Oyster Pond* and *Schoolhouse Pond,* no charge.

Eastham. Non-resident fees are: $5 per day, $4 for seasonal renters. Permits are purchased at Town Hall. All beaches are reached via Rte. 6; on Cape Cod Bay, locations at *Campground, Cole Rd., Cook's Brook, First Encounter, Sunken Meadow,* and *Thumpertown.* **Freshwater sites** include *Great Pond, Herring Pond,* and *Wiley Park.*

Harwich. One-day permits are purchased for Red River Beach only, $3 fee. Renters in Harwich may purchase a $15 two-week, or $25 seasonal permit at Brook's Academy in Harwich Center. All ocean beaches are reached via Rte. 28; locations at *Bank St., Earle Rd., Pleasant Rd., Pleasant Bay,* and *Red River Rd.* **Freshwater sites** include *Buck's Pond, Long Pond,* and *Sand Pond.*

Orleans. On Cape Cod Bay, *Skaket Beach,* off Rte. 6A, $3 fee. On Atlantic side, *Nauset Beach,* off Rte. 6A or Rte. 28; surfing area; $3 fee, $4 on weekends and holidays. **Freshwater.** *Pilgrim Lake* and *Meetinghouse Pond* are free of charge. Renters in Orleans pay $10 for one-week privileges, $15 for two weeks, $20 for three weeks, $25 for four weeks, $30 for season. All others, $50 for season.

Provincetown. All supervised public beaches are under the jurisdiction of the National Seashore; $1 per day.

Truro. Non-resident fee is $30 per season. Seasonal renters pay $10 for one week, $15 for two weeks, $20 for four weeks, or $25 per season. Permits are purchased at Town Hall. All beaches are reached via Rte. 6. Ocean beaches are located at *Ballston, Coast Guard, Head of the Meadow,* and *Long Nook.* Locations on Cape Cod Bay are *Beach Point, Corn Hill, Fisher Beach, Great Hollow, Ryder,* and *Pond Village.*

Wellfleet. Non-resident fee is $3 per day at Cahoon Hollow and White Crest. Seasonal renters pay $10 per season. Permits are purchased at the Kendrick Avenue Beach house. All beaches are reached via Rte. 6. Ocean beaches are located at *Cahoon Hollow, Maguire's, Newcomb Hollow,* and *White Crest.* Locations on Cape Cod Bay are *Duck Harbor, Indian Neck,* and *Mayo Beach.* **Freshwater sites** are located at *Gull Pond, Great Pond,* and *Long Pond.*

Cape Cod National Seashore. All public beaches within the Seashore are on the Atlantic Ocean and are reached via Rte. 6. Locations include: *Coast Guard Beach* and *Nauset Light Beach,* Eastham; *Marconi Beach,* Wellfleet; *Head of the Meadow Beach,* Truro; *Herring Cove* and *Race Point Beaches,* Provincetown. Fee: $1 per day, except Coast Guard Beach, which provides no parking. (A free shuttle-bus service runs 9:30 A.M.–6 P.M. daily from the Salt Pond Visitor's Center on Rte. 6 in Eastham to Coast Guard Beach.) Ample parking is available at the center. A $10 Golden Eagle pass is good for the season at all Park beaches. Anyone 62 or over may request a free Golden Age pass.

Rules and Regulations. Most supervised beaches do not allow pets on the beach, restrained or otherwise. Glass objects, rafts, snorkels, masks, and ball playing are usually prohibited. Protection of the dunes is essential; unauthorized vehicles and foot traffic are also prohibited in most areas. Many other general rules apply. Check with Town Hall, National Seashore Centers, or at the beach for complete listings.

 BICYCLE TRAILS. A number of excellent trails are maintained on the outer Cape. **Eastham.** Nauset Trail, from Salt Pond Visitor's Center to Coast Guard Beach; rolling hills and views of Nauset marshes; two miles.

Truro. From Head of Meadow Beach to High Head Rd.; easy grades through Salt Meadow and Pilgrim Spring; two miles.

Provincetown. Province Lands Trail from Race Point Rd. to Race Point or Herring Cove Beach; varied grades, some steep; through the heart of the dunes, visitor center, beech forest, beaches, and Old Harbor Station; eight miles.

Nickerson State Park. Paths within the 1,750-acre park connect with ponds, rise and fall through pine and oak forests; eight miles.

Rail Trail of Cape Cod. The newest recreational pathway is constructed on the abandoned railroad lines. Beginning in South Dennis just over the West Harwich line, the trail continues east through Harwich, Brewster, Orleans, and into Eastham. A perfect way to enjoy the forests, ponds, bogs, waterviews, culture, history, and scenery of the Lower Cape. Including a couple of country roads connectors, the Rail Trail traverses 16 miles. Designed for pedestrians, equestrians, and bicyclists, the trail is easy riding.

HIKING AND NATURE TRAILS. Brewster. *Cliff Lake Trail,* Nickerson State Park, Rte. 6A; this three-and-one-half-mile trail rises and falls along the rim of the lake; pine-oak forests and view of the glacial waterhole; about two hours. *Wing Island Trail* at Museum of Natural History; two-mile tidal flats trail between Quivett Creek and Stony Brook; about one hour.

Eastham. *Buttonbush Trail,* Salt Pond Visitor's Center, off Rte. 6; a one-quarter-mile trail with guide rope and descriptive plaques in braille and large print; alternative nature and fragrance trail for the blind; 45 minutes. *Fort Hill Trail,* off Fort Hill Rd.; one and one-half miles of uplands, boardwalk through red maple forest, and along the bluff above Nauset marshes; recommended for scenic vistas; about one hour. *Nauset Marsh Trail,* Salt Pond Visitor's Center, off Rte. 6; a one-mile path along the edge of the north side marshes of Nauset Harbor; 45 minutes. *Nauset Spit,* three miles to Nauset Inlet and back; sand beach along the marshes; about two hours.

Provincetown. *Beach Forest Trail,* Race Point Rd. in Province Lands; a two-part loop trail of one mile from parking area through one of the last remaining beech forests in Provincetown; natural features along the trail are two lily ponds, azaleas, red maples, blueberries, inkberries; easy walking; about one mellow hour.

Truro. *Pilgrim Springs Trail,* Pilgrim Heights off Rte. 6. A one-mile companion trail to *Small's Trail,* the two can be done together as two halfs of a loop. The Pilgrim trail consists of gently rolling hills, sand dunes, and the Salt Meadow beside Pilgrim Lake. A small brook is designated as the source of the Pilgrim's first drinking water in the New World. Small's Trail descends into a seaside hollow of ground vegetation, azaleas, bayberries, and scrub pine. Either trail is easy walking, and about 30 minutes.

Wellfleet. *Atlantic White Cedar Swamp Trail* at Marconi area off Rte. 6; an excellent leisure walk into a lowland cedar forest, rimmed by sloping hills of pitch-pine and sand; a boardwalk allows for an unusual view of vegetation and forest; about 1.2 miles, one hour. *Great Island Trail,* Chequesset Neck Rd., eight miles to Jeremy Point and back; passes site of the 1690 Smith Tavern, from salt marshes and pine forests, along the bay beach and back; mixed terrain, about three hours; recommended only to hikers with stamina; check tides before going, since the final portion becomes submerged under higher tides.

Barrier Beach. Trail runs from Eastham to Provincetown 40 miles along the Atlantic; sand, dunes, and marshland; Thoreau's favorite.

CAMPING. *A word to the wise:* In season, accommodations of every kind generally display "no vacancy" signs. Many camp, tent, and trailer sites are filled to capacity. Advance reservations and inquiries are necessary to confirm arrangements. Most sites require reservations and/or deposits. Don't be disappointed; call first!

Brewster. *Henry's Camp Grounds,* Rte. 39, 255-3867; family tenting, 35 sites in pine-oak woods; showers, toilet facility, basic camp supplies; open June–Sept. *Shady Knoll Campground,* Rte. 137 and Rte. 6A, 896-3002; full hookups; 100 sites; showers, toilet facility, sanitary service, basic supplies; open May–Oct. *Sprawling Hills Park,* Rte. 124 and Rte. 6, 896-3939; family camping, full hookups, 300 trailer and tent sites in wooded area, on pond; showers, toilet facility, sanitary service, swimming, housekeeping cottages; open year-round. *Sweetwater Forest,* Rte. 124, 896-3773; family camping, full hookups, 250 sites in wooded area; showers, toilet facility, sanitary service, playground, swimming, children's beach, security patrol; open year-round. (See Nickerson State Park.)

Eastham. *Eastham Camps,* Rte. 6, 255-1437; family camping, full hookups, 55 sites in wooded area, showers, bathhouses; reservations necessary, families only, pet fee; open summer only.

Provincetown. *Coastal Acres Camping Court,* West Vine St. Ext., 487-1700; full hookups, 175 sites close to town, showers, toilet facility, basic supplies, dune buggy tours; open Apr.–Oct. *Dune's Edge Campground,* Rte. 6, 487-9815; family camping, electric hookup, 100 tent and trailer sites, showers, toilet facility, sanitary service, basic supplies; borders National Seashore; open May–Sept.

Truro. *Horton's Park,* South Highland Rd., 487-1220; family camping, full hookups, 222 camp and trailer sites on 40 acres within National Seashore Park; metered showers, toilet facility, basic supplies; adjacent to golf course, some waterviews, no pets; open Apr.–Oct. *North of Highland Camping Area,* Head of Meadow Rd., 487-1191; family camping, full hookups, 218 camp and tent sites on 60 acres; walk to beach; open May–Sept. *North Truro Camping Area,* Highland Rd., 487-1847; family camping, full hookups, 300 sites in native pine; showers, toilet facility, basic supplies; close to golf, National Seashore; open year-round.

Wellfleet. *Massasoit Hills Trailer Park,* Massasoit and West Rds., 349-2469; full hookups for mobile home and travel-trailers; wooded sites, showers; adjoining wildlife sanctuary; limited capacity, rentals for season or year only; open year-round. *Maurice's Campground*, Rte. 6, 349-2029; family camping, full hookups, 220 tent and trailer sites in wooded area, showers, toilet facility, sanitary service, basic supplies, no pets; open May–Oct. *Paine's Campground*, Old County Rd., 349-3007; electric and water hookups, 110 sites in wooded area, showers, toilet facility, security patrol, no pets; open May–Oct.

Nickerson State Park, Rte. 6A, Brewster, 896-7695. Basic camping, 420 sites on 1,750 acres; showers, toilet facility, water. No hookups, trailers limited by size to tent sites. Bicycle trails, freshwater beaches, hiking, stocked ponds (freshwater license at Town Hall), pine-oak forests. No reservations accepted, two-week maximum per site; no group sites; pets must be restrained. Fee $6 per day. Open Apr.–Oct.

National Seashore. Overnight camping is not allowed in the National Park; violators may be fined. However, self-contained campers are allowed overnight privileges at two sites on *Race Point Beach* in Provincetown. Certain restrictions apply and a 100-vehicle limit is in effect. For further information write to: National Park Service Headquarters, South Wellfleet, Massachusetts 02663, or call 349-3785.

WHAT TO DO WITH THE CHILDREN. Brewster. *Bassett Wild Animal Farm*, Rte. 124; a wide variety of animals in rural setting; petting area, picnic area; open daily, mid-May–mid-Sept.; admission. *Herring run at Stony Brook Mill;* migratory fish ladder, nature trail, viewing in early spring. *Sealand*, Rte. 6A; dolphin shows, sea lions, seals, and other marine attractions; picnic area; open year-round, closed Wed., Oct.–June.

Harwich. *Harwich Junior Theater,* Division St. Children's plays, limited schedule in July and Aug.

Provincetown. *Provincetown Aquarium,* Commercial St.; marine life and exhibits, limited summer hours.

General Information. There are several excellent summer camps for boys and girls; some provide special instruction in areas of interest such as nature studies, sports, or sailing. Consult the Cape Cod phone directory, or contact the Chamber of Commerce, W. Barnstable.

STAGE. The Lower Cape's theatrical atmosphere is centered around a number of small playhouses in rural settings. The production companies offer high-quality stage presentations throughout the summer season.

Chatham. *Monomoy Theater,* Main St. The Ohio University Players, long-established troupe; Broadway musicals and drama. Season begins in late June. The players were organized in 1958 and they traditionally present at least one play by Shakespeare each season.

Eastham. *First Encounter Coffee House,* Samoset Rd. Alternative entertainment. Summer schedule includes dramatic readings, poetry, and folk-oratory. Interesting fare.

Harwich. *Cape Cod Ballet,* Annual Spring Ballet performance at Harwich High School. *Harwich Junior Theater,* Division St., W. Harwich. For more than 30 years, the community-supported playhouse has presented quality theater, with an emphasis on children's plays. Children 10 years and over are urged to participate. Limited presentations in July and Aug.

Orleans. The *Academy of Performing Arts,* Main St. The Allegro Players perform a variety of live stage shows. Season begins in late June.

Provincetown. The famous *Provincetown Players,* the oldest theater group on the Cape, is rebuilding and reorganizing after fire destroyed the Playhouse. Formed in 1916, its association with Eugene O'Neill is part of the Provincetown heritage.

Wellfleet. *Outer Cape Performance Co.,* Main St. The recently formed group presents a limited schedule of live theater productions from poetry to drama. Season begins in July.

MUSIC. The *Cape Cod Conservatory Wind Ensemble* schedules engagements on the Lower Cape during the year. For information, contact the Conservatory on Rte. 132, W. Barnstable, Massachusetts 02668.

Chatham. The Town Band Concerts in Kate Gould Park are a major summer attraction every Fri. evening. Everyone is invited.

Harwich. The Town Band Concerts in Brook's Park are on Tues. evenings at 8 P.M. in July and Aug. Schedule may be expanded.

Orleans. Summer series of Meeting House Concerts performed Sun. and Mon. evenings in July and Aug.

Wellfleet. Summer Music series at First Congregational Church, Sun. evenings beginning in July.

HOTELS AND MOTELS. The Cape offers a wide variety of overnight accommodations, from deluxe seaside resort complexes to small inns, guest houses, and cottage colonies. Unless otherwise noted, listings are open year-round and prices are based on double occupancy, European Plan, in season. The word lounge indicates an establishment has liquor available. *Deluxe,* $60 and up; *Expensive,* $42–$60; *Moderate,* $30–$42; *Inexpensive,* $18–$30.

BREWSTER

Old Manse Inn. *Expensive.* 1861 Main St. 896-3149. Beautiful antique sea captain's home with 9 guest rooms, sunroom, and gardens. Complimentary continental breakfast. Walk to beach, tennis, restaurant, and shops.

Baywood Cottages. *Moderate.* Nauset Trail. 852-6512. Housekeeping cottages with fireplaces. Picnic area, 3-minute walk to private beach. Weekly rates.

Bramble Inn. *Moderate.* Rte. 6A. 896-7644. A restaurant and art gallery are located on the first floor of this restored 1861 Cape home. Complimentary continental breakfast. Beach and tennis nearby. Open May–Oct.

Inn of the Golden Ox. *Inexpensive.* Rte. 6A and Tubman Rd. 896-3111. A remodeled 1828 church, containing 6 guest rooms. Classic German cuisine served in restaurant on premises. Weekly rates available.

Winslow's Housekeeping Cottages. *Inexpensive.* Run Hill Rd. 665-6158. Family-size cottages on Lower Mill Pond. Free boats, fishing, lake swimming. Weekly rates. Seasonal.

CHATHAM

Chatham Bars Inn and Non-housekeeping Cottages. *Deluxe.* Shore Rd. 945-0096. Elegant resort on 65 acres, with views of Pleasant Bay and Atlantic Ocean. Private beach; golf, tennis, sailing, and fishing. Restaurant; cocktail lounge with dancing and entertainment. Walk to harbor. AP. Open late Apr.–Nov.

Queene Anne Inn. *Deluxe.* 70 Queen Anne Rd. 945-0394. Restored Victorian inn with 30 antique-filled rooms, all with private bath. Lounge, dining room, game room, garden. AP

Wequassett Inn. *Deluxe.* Rte. 28. 432-5400. 22-acre, 47-room resort complex overlooking Pleasant Bay. Beach, 5 championship tennis courts, pro shop, private dock, lawn games, rental boats, pool, restaurant, and night club. Service fees. Open late May–Sept.

Chatham Tides Motel. *Expensive.* 394 Pleasant St., South Chatham. 432-0379. Private Nantucket Sound beach. Lawn games; babysitters available. Efficiencies and cottages, some fireplaces, weekly rates available. Open late Apr.–Nov.

Chatham Wayside Inn. *Expensive.* 512 Main St. 945–1800. Colonial-style inn located in town. 24 rooms, some of which are motel units. Dining room, cocktail lounge, and entertainment. Open yr.-round.

Pleasant Bay Village Motel. *Expensive.* Rte. 28, Chathamport. 945-1133. 6 acres of landscaped grounds, efficiencies, studio apartments, and deluxe cottages. Heated pool, games, coffee shop. Open Apr.–Oct.

Town House Inn and Lodge. *Expensive.* 11 Library Lane. 945-2180. Restored 1881 Colonial inn. Family suites and cottage with fireplace available. Breakfast. Walk to beach and town attractions.

Dolphin of Chatham. *Moderate.* 352 Main St. 945-0070. Double and single rooms, kitchenette apartments, cottages. Walk to beach, restaurant and shops. Heated pool, whirlpool, play yard.

Ebb Tide Motel. *Moderate.* Rte. 28. 945-1095. 55 units on 17 acres. View of Oyster Bay and Atlantic Ocean. Heated pool, putting green, lawn games, coffee shop. Open Apr.–Oct.

Hawthorne Motel. *Moderate.* 196 Shore Rd. 945-0372. Overlooking Pleasant Bay. Private beach; efficiencies and cottages available on 4 acres. Open mid-June–Oct.

Moorings Motor Lodge. *Moderate.* 326 Main St. 945-0848. Victorian guest house, motel, efficiencies, and cottage. Picnic area, bicycles provided. Walk to beaches and historic sites. Weekly rates available.

North Chatham Motel. *Moderate.* Rte. 28. 432-1755. Central location to restaurants, beaches, and town. Pool, picnic area, patio. Open Apr.–Oct.

Reliance Motel. *Moderate.* Rte. 28. 945-0710. Close to beaches and restaurants. Heated pool, play area. Efficiencies and weekly rates available. Open Apr.–Oct.

Salt Acre. *Inexpensive.* 96 Water St. 945-0131. Furnished, housekeeping apartments for 2–4 persons in "old village" section of town. Walk to beaches. Full weeks only during season.

Surfside Motor Inn. *Inexpensive.* Holway St. 945-9757. Near Chatham Lighthouse and beach; walk to town. Family units available. Continental breakfast included. Open Apr.–Oct.

Whispering Pines by the Sea. *Inexpensive.* Harding's Beach Rd., West Chatham. 945-1581. Charming guest house with semi-private baths and kitchen privileges. Breakfast and lunch available. Walking distance to beach and Nantucket Sound. Seasonal.

EASTHAM

Sheraton Ocean Park Inn and Resort Spa. *Expensive.* Rte. 6. 255-5000. Large resort motel near Natl. Seashore. Heated indoor and outdoor pools, restaurant, lounge, entertainment, whirlpool, health spa, tennis.

Town Crier Motel. *Expensive* Rte. 6. 255-4000. Close to Natl. Seashore. Enclosed, heated pool; recreation room. Breakfast available.

Cove Bluffs Motel. *Moderate.* Rte. 6. 255-6514. Spacious grounds near Natl. Seashore. Pool, lawn games, picnic area. Housekeeping units available.

Cranberry Cottages. *Moderate.* Rte. 6. 255-0602. Overnight and housekeeping cottages on 6 acres. Close to fishing and boat rentals. Weekly rates available.

Eastham Motel. *Moderate.* Rte. 6. 255-1600. View of Nauset Bay. Close to Natl. Seashore beaches. Heated pool. Complimentary coffee. Seasonal.

Now Voyager Motel. *Moderate.* Rte. 6., North Eastham. 255-1159. Adjacent to Natl. Seashore Park. Restaurant, lounge, game room, picnic area, pool, and tennis on 23 wooded acres. Open May–mid-Oct.

Oak Grove Cottages. *Moderate.* Rte. 6, North Eastham. 255-3284. Housekeeping cottages and play area on wooded grounds. 2 miles to Bay or ocean, nature trails, and bike paths. Weekly rates. Seasonal.

Salt Pond Motel. *Moderate.* Rte. 6. 255-2100. Overlooking Salt Pond; near Natl. Seashore, nature walks, and bike trails. Private beach, fishing. Free boats and continental breakfast. Efficiency apartments available. Seasonal.

Whalewalk. *Moderate.* Bridge Rd. 255-0617. Captain's house restored to comfortable inn and housekeeping cottage complex. Guest parlor, library, game room and terrace. Breakfast available.

Eastham Country Cottages. *Inexpensive.* Rte. 6. 255-1437. Housekeeping cottages set in pine grove 1 mile from beaches. Weekly rates. Seasonal.

Saltaway Cottages. *Inexpensive.* Aspinet Rd., North Eastham. 255-2182. 1- and 2-bedroom housekeeping cottages on wooded grounds. Near Natl. Seashore. Seasonal.

HARWICH

Wychmere Harbor Club and Hotel. *Deluxe.* Snow Inn Rd., Harwich Port. 432-1000. Elegant 10-acre oceanfront resort estate. Poolside luncheons; private beach, and dock. Sailing, tennis, gourmet restaurant, dancing, and entertainment. MAP. Seasonal.

Harwich Port. *Expensive.* 558 Main St., Harwich Port. 432-2424. 40-unit motel close to restaurants, beach, golf, and shops. Heated pool. Seasonal.

Seader Inn. *Expensive.* Bank St. 432-0264. Inn and beach house overlooking Nantucket Sound. Buffet breakfast included. Walk to restaurants and shops. Open mid-May–Oct.

Coachman Motor Lodge. *Moderate.* Rte. 28, Harwich Port. 432-0707. Comfortable, 29-unit motor lodge. Restaurant for breakfast and lunch. Near beaches and marina. Pool, picnic area. Package plan available. Open mid-May–Sept.

Lion's Head Inn. *Moderate.* 186 Belmont Rd., West Harwich, 432-7766. Charming English-style guest house. 5 rooms, 2 cottages. Close to beach. Complimentary breakfast. Open Apr.–Dec.

Melrose Inn. *Moderate.* Main St., Harwich Port. 432-0171. Old-fashioned family inn. Restaurant, lounge, private beach, pool, launch. AP. (MAP, EP available.)

Moby Dick Motel. *Moderate.* Rte. 28, South Harwich. 432-1434. 22 inviting units set on 3 acres. Pool, picnic area, 9-hole putting green, lawn games. Close to Saquatucket Harbor, beach, tennis, and golf. Efficiencies and weekly rates available. Open Apr.–Nov.

Sound Side Court. *Moderate.* Rte. 28 and Bank St., Harwich Port. 432-1282. 5-minute walk to beach. Shuffleboard, croquet, restaurant. Open Apr.–Nov.

Stone Horse Motor Inn. *Moderate.* Rte. 28, South Harwich. 432-0662. On terraced hillside overlooking 4 landscaped acres. Heated pool, shuffleboard, game lounge, coffee shop. Near beach, marina, shops, tennis, and golf. Open mid-Apr.–Oct.

Troy Court. *Moderate.* 28 Sea St., Harwich Port. 432-1275. Motel and guest house overlooking Nantucket Sound. Continental breakfast. Walk to beach and shops.

Country Inn. *Inexpensive.* 86 Sisson Rd., Harwich Port. 432-2769. Charming old Cape Cod home with excellent restaurant. Pool, 3 tennis courts, lounge with fireplace.

Red River Motel. *Inexpensive.* Rte. 28, South Harwich. 432-1474. Comfortable motel operated by bird-watchers. Guided walks and efficiencies available. 1 mile to sandy beach.

West Pines Cottages. *Inexpensive.* 207 Division St., West Harwich. 432-1931. Housekeeping cottages in 5-acre pine grove. Children welcome. Play area, lawn games. 4 blocks to beaches. Open May–Oct.

Wishing Well Motel. *Inexpensive.* Rte. 28, West Harwich. 432-2150. Centrally located with 20 rooms. Efficiencies available. Complimentary continental breakfast. Heated pool, barbecue area. Seasonal.

ORLEANS

Governor Prence Motor Inn. *Expensive.* Rte. 6A at Rte. 28. 255-1216. Resort motel near Natl. Seashore and activities. 55 units, pool, coffee shop, lounge. Indoor pool, sauna, whirlpool available nearby. Package plans available. Seasonal.

Nauset Knoll Motor Lodge. *Expensive.* Beach Rd., East Orleans. 255-2364. 12 attractive oceanfront units on Nauset Beach. Swimming, fishing, dune walks. Open Apr.–late Oct.

Orleans Holiday Motel. *Expensive.* Rte. 6A and Rte. 28. 255-1514. Near Natl. Seashore Park and activities. Restaurant, heated pool. Open Apr.–Thanksgiving.

Seashore Park Motor Inn. *Expensive.* Canal Rd. at Rtes. 6 and 6A. 255-2500. Heated indoor and outdoor pools, jacuzzi whirlpool, saunas, health club. Complimentary coffee. 62 rooms, 24 with efficiency kitchenettes. Package plans available. Open Apr.–Nov.

Cove Motel. *Moderate.* Rte. 28. 255-1203. On Town Cove. Close to restaurants, 1 mile to Bay beach. Pool. Waterview apartments available.

Hillbourne House. *Moderate.* Rte. 28, South Orleans. 255-0780. Circa 1798 guest house and motor-inn with view of Pleasant Bay. Housekeeping units available. Complimentary continental breakfast. Private beach and dock. Open mid-May–mid-Oct.

Olde Tavern Motel. *Moderate.* Rte. 6A. 255-1565. Pool, private sundeck, and patio. Restaurant next door. Open Apr.–Nov.

Packet Landing and Sea Breeze Motel. *Moderate.* Beach Rd., East Orleans. 255-1550. Pool, sundeck, game room, restaurant, lounge, picnic area. Complimentary continental breakfast. Efficiencies available. Open Mar.–Nov.

Ridgewood Motel and Cottages. *Moderate.* Jct. Rtes. 28 and 39, South Orleans. 255-0473. Country location. Pool, play area. Refrigerator in each room. Complimentary coffee.

Skaket Beach Motel. *Moderate.* Rte. 6. 255-1020. Heated pool, picnic area, lawn games. Continental breakfast.

Nauset House Inn. *Inexpensive.* Beach Rd., East Orleans. 255-2195. Small country inn. Parlor, indoor garden room. Breakfast available. Open Apr.–Oct.

PROVINCETOWN

Bradford Gardens Inn. *Expensive.* 178 Bradford St. 487-1616. 8 attractive rooms and apartments, some with working fireplaces. Garden, barbecue area. Complimentary breakfast.

Buccaneer Motor Inn. *Expensive.* Rte. 6A. 487-1144. Modern units directly on the beach. Heated pool, play area. Seasonal.

Hargood House. *Expensive*. 493 Commercial St. 487-1324. 4 imaginatively remodeled Cape homes with 17 apartments overlooking the harbor. Private beach, garden patio. Weekly rates in summer; 2-day minimum off-season.

Holiday Inn. *Expensive*. Snail Rd. and Rte. 6A. 487-1711. Family motor-inn opposite swimming beach. Pool, dining room; lounge with entertainment. Open Mar.–Nov.

Provincetown Inn. *Expensive*. 1 Commercial St. 487-9500. Waterfront motel and inn. Private beach, dining room, lounge, heated indoor pool, and sauna. Tennis 1 block away. Bike trails, horseback riding, and dune tours nearby.

Sand Castle Motor Inn. *Expensive*. Rte. 6A. 487-9300. Private beach, indoor and outdoor pools, saunas, tennis, lounge. Open June–Sept.

Ship's Bell Inn and Motel. *Expensive*. 586 Commercial St. 487-1674. Across street from private beach on harbor. Barbecue patio. Efficiency apartments and fireplaces available. Open Apr.–Oct.

Surfside Inn. *Expensive*. 543 Commercial St. 487-1726. Convenient walk to town. Private beach, heated pool. Open Easter–mid-Oct.

Breakwater. *Moderate*. Rte. 6A. 487-1134. Motel and housekeeping apartments overlooking Bay. Private beach. Pool. Open mid-Apr.–Oct.

Kalmar Village. *Moderate*. Rte. 6A. 487-0585. Attractive motel and housekeeping-cottage colony on beach. Heated pool, laundry. Open mid-May–mid-Oct.

Masthead. *Moderate*. 31–41 Commercial St. 487-0523. Motel, cottages, and apartments, some with fireplaces, directly on the water. Private beach, sundeck on water.

Quality Inn Eastwood. *Moderate*. 324 Bradford St. 487-0743. In the heart of town, 1 block from beach. Heated pool, patio, barbecue, miniature golf, games, tennis. Open Apr.–Oct.

Tides Motor Inn. *Moderate*. Rte. 6A. 487-1045. Harborview rooms with balconies and patios on private beach. Heated pool, lawn games, laundry, coffee shop. Open mid-May–mid-Oct.

White Dory Inn. *Moderate*. 616 Commercial St. 487-0224. Comfortable inn located in the East End. Guest rooms, suites, and apartments. Private beach, guest living room, game room, sundeck, and gardens. Complimentary continental breakfast.

TRURO

Outer Reach Motor Resort (formerly Governor Prence Motor Hotel). *Expensive*. Rte. 6, North Truro. 487-0629. Hilltop family resort motel. Restaurant, lounge, pool, and tennis. Open May–Oct.

Seascape Motor Inn. *Expensive*. Shore Rd., Rte. 6A, North Truro. 487-1225. Overlooking Bay and Provincetown. Private beach, pool, fishing. Complimentary continental breakfast. Efficiency apartments available. Open May–Sept.

Cape View Motel. *Moderate*. Rte. 6, North Truro. 487-0363. Private balconies with views of Bay, ocean, and dunes. Pool, play area. Complimentary coffee. Open mid-Apr.–Nov.

Castle/Seascent Pines Cottages. *Moderate.* Castle Rd. 698-1835. 2-bedroom housekeeping cottages in wooded grounds. Play area. Near ocean and Bay beaches. Seasonal.

Cornwall House. *Moderate.* Pond Rd., North Truro. 487-1881. New England-style guest house with spacious suites. Continental breakfast. Walk to town beach and restaurant. Seasonal.

Fore N'Aft Motel and Cottages. *Moderate.* Rte. 6A, North Truro. 487-1257. Motel, cottages, and efficiencies with private beach. Pool. Seasonal.

Pilgrim Spring Motel. *Moderate.* Rte. 6, North Truro. 487-9454. Resort motel close to beaches, golf, and dunes. Pool, lounge, restaurant on premises. Open Apr.–Nov.

Seaside Village Motel. *Moderate.* Rte. 6A, North Truro. 487-1215. Motel, efficiencies, and housekeeping cottages on Bay. Private beach. Near Natl. Seashore, dunes and Provincetown. Weekly rates. Seasonal.

Whitman House. *Moderate.* Rte. 6, North Truro. 487-1740. 30 housekeeping cottages. Restaurant, bar, pool, play area. Weekly rates. Seasonal.

Anchorage. *Inexpensive.* Rte. 6A, North Truro. 487-0168. Motel and efficiency cottages and apartments on Bay. Private beach. Open Mar.–Nov.

Sea Song. *Inexpensive.* Rte. 6A, North Truro. 487-9227. Motel, housekeeping cottages, and beachfront apartments on Bay. Private beach. Seasonal.

White Caps Cottages. *Inexpensive.* Rte. 6A, North Truro. 487-0788. Housekeeping-cottage colony in garden setting. View of Bay. Close to Natl. Seashore and Provincetown. Weekly rates. Seasonal.

WELLFLEET

Billingsgate Motel. *Expensive.* Mayo Beach Rd. 349-3924. Near Wellfleet Harbor and marina. Refrigerators. Open June–Oct.

Southfleet Motor Inn. *Expensive.* Rte. 6, South Wellfleet. 349-3580. Near Natl. Seashore. Restaurant, lounge with seasonal entertainment, indoor and outdoor pools, saunas, game room.

Surf Side Colony. *Expensive.* Ocean View Dr., South Wellfleet. 349-2017. Oceanfront housekeeping cottage colony in Natl. Seashore. Fireplaces, porches. Golf and tennis nearby.

Wellfleet Motel. *Expensive.* Rte. 6, South Wellfleet. 349-3535. Across street from Audubon Bird Sanctuary. Heated pool, picnic area, lounge. Complimentary coffee.

Eventide. *Moderate.* Rte. 6, South Wellfleet. 349-3410. A-frame and Cape housekeeping cottages with fireplaces and picnic sites, in secluded settings. Play area, laundry.

Mainstay Motor Inn. *Moderate.* Rte. 6. 349-2350. Near Wellfleet Center. Heated pool. Complimentary continental breakfast. Open Apr.–Oct.

HOSTELS. *Mid-Cape Youth Hostel,* (Box 14OH), Bridge Rd., Orleans, 255-9762. *Little America Youth Hostel,* North Pamet Rd. (Ballston Beach), Truro, 349-3889.

DINING OUT. Whatever your fancy, from seven-course gourmet French cuisine to fish and chips picnic style, you will find a restaurant to accommodate your taste and pocketbook. On the Outer Cape many establishments close after the summer season, but a growing number now stay open year-round; phone inquiries are advisable. Our ratings are based on the average cost of a full meal, exclusive of alcoholic beverages, tax, and tip. *Deluxe,* $18 and up; *Expensive,* $15 and up; *Moderate,* $9–$15; *Inexpensive,* under $9.

BREWSTER

Chillingsworth. *Deluxe.* Rte. 6A. 896-3640. Elegant candlelit dining in Colonial home with 18th-century French appointments. Award-winning French cuisine and nouvelle cuisine. Two seatings only: 6–6:30 P.M. and 9–9:30 P.M. Sunday brunch.

Inn of the Golden Ox. *Expensive.* Rte. 6A and Tubman Rd. 896-3111. Gourmet German cuisine including Veal Schnitzels, Kassler Rippchen, and Sauerbraten. Home-baked tortes and kuchens. No credit cards. Closed Monday.

Bramble Inn. *Moderate.* 2019 Rte. 6A. 896-7644. Fine dining and an art gallery are highlights of this 1861 country inn. Continental menu, featuring Baked Stuffed Filet of Sole, Carbonnade Beef Bourguignonne, quiche, and crêpes. Seasonal beer and wine. Open June–Labor Day; closed Sundays.

Brewster Fish Market. *Inexpensive.* Rte. 6A. 896-7177. Informal café and picnic-table dining. Fresh fish and shellfish daily.

Brewster Inn and Chowder House. *Inexpensive.* Rte. 6A. 896-7771. Casual dining in the center of Brewster. Homemade chowder and soups. Seafood, chicken, and steaks. Fri. and Sat., prime rib nights. Bar. Nightly entertainment in adjacent *The Woodshed.*

Laurino's. *Inexpensive.* Rte. 6A. 896-3714. Informal Italian restaurant featuring lasagna and veal parmesan. Great pizza and grinders. Cocktail lounge with entertainment and dancing Thu.–Sun. No credit cards.

Michael's. *Inexpensive.* Rte. 6A. 896-5413. Comfortable country atmosphere with nightly entertainment. Varied menu of delicious deli sandwiches, salads, soups, and dinner specials.

CHATHAM

Christopher Ryder House. *Expensive.* Rte. 28, Chatham Port. 945-0608. Historic sea captain's home on Ryder's Cove, serving traditional New England fare. After dinner enjoy musical revues and dancing in the *Opera House.* Open mid-May–mid-Oct.

Earl of Chatham at the Queen Anne Inn. *Expensive.* 70 Queen Anne Rd.

945-0394. Elegant Victorian-style restaurant/inn serving New England seafood, continental cuisine, and Viennese pastries. Tuesday clambakes and Sunday brunch. Entertainment.

Wequassett Inn. *Expensive.* Rte. 28. 432-5400. 18th-century sea captain's house overlooking Pleasant Bay. Fresh native seafood served indoors or on the garden terrace. Music and dancing. Open late May–Sept.

Captain's Table of Chatham. *Moderate.* 578 Main St. 945-1961. Home-style chicken pie and fish dishes are the specialties of the house. Located in the town center. No liquor. Open Apr.–Oct.

Cranberry Inn. *Moderate.* 359 Main St. 945-9232. A wide variety of meats and seafood are offered in this 19th-century inn. Homemade clam chowder. Cocktail lounge.

Impudent Oyster. *Moderate.* 15 Chatham Bars Ave. 945-3545. Continental cuisine and native seafood, featuring Wellfleet oysters, served in an informal and relaxed atmosphere.

Northport Seafood House. *Moderate.* Rte. 28, Chatham Port. 945-9217. Nautically decorated dining room serving excellent seafood and steaks. Salad bar. Entertainment daily in season; weekends off-season.

Pate's. *Moderate.* Rte. 28. 945-9777. Warm colonial atmosphere. Lobster, steaks, Shrimp Scampi, Oysters Rockefeller, swordfish, and Key Lime Pie are house specialties. Cocktail lounge. Entertainment Wed.–Sun.

Via Veneto. *Moderate.* Rte. 28, West Chatham. 945-3720. Family dining in attractive setting. Italian cuisine in addition to steaks and seafood.

Chatham Squire. *Inexpensive.* 487 Main St. 945-9785. Located in Chatham Center. Dining room, raw shellfish bar, and deli. Fresh Chatham fish, steamers, and oysters the specialties. Entertainment.

Soup du Jour. *Inexpensive.* Main St. 945-2860. Art gallery/luncheon room featuring homemade soups, breads, and salads. Desserts a specialty. Beer and wine. No credit cards. Open Mon.–Sat., 11:30–2:30.

Sou'wester. *Inexpensive.* Rte. 28, West Chatham. 945-9705. Informal, relaxed dining. Seafood and Italian cuisine. Cocktail lounge with Country-western entertainment Fri. and Sat. nights.

EASTHAM

Demetri's Sandpiper. *Moderate.* Rte. 6, North Eastham. 255-9913. Casual eatery offering seafood, steaks, and chops. Homemade baklava and Greek salad are the house specialties. Cocktail lounge.

Eastham Lobster Pool. *Moderate.* Rte. 6, North Eastham. 255-9706. Casual family restaurant with a 1,000-pound lobster pool. Steamers, seafood platters, baked stuffed shrimp, and sole with Newburgh sauce. Children's menu. Thursday is Italian night. Cocktails.

Kings Colonial Restaurant and Pub. *Moderate.* Rte. 6, North Eastham. 255-4318. Northern Italian cuisine in addition to fresh seafood, veal and steaks. Home-baked breads. Cocktail lounge. Open May–Sept.

Ocean Garden Restaurant at Sheraton Ocean Park Inn. *Moderate.* Rte. 6. 255-5000. Large resort motel near National Seashore, serving breakfast and dinner. Veal Marsala, steaks, and a variety of seafood. Patio bar, cocktail lounge, entertainment.

Arnold's Lobster and Clam Bar. *Inexpensive*. Rte. 6. Casual, self-serve open-air patio dining. Fried seafood, lobster rolls, burgers, steamers. Beer and wine. No credit cards.

Helmsman. *Inexpensive*. Rte. 6. 255-3679. Casual new restaurant across from National Seashore Park serving typical New England fare. Lunch and dinner from 11:30 A.M. Liquor, entertainment. No credit cards.

Poolside Restaurant at Town Crier Motel. *Inexpensive*. Rte. 6. 255-4000. Bountiful breakfasts and brunches at poolside. Home-baked muffins and breads. Omelets, breakfast sandwiches. Open Mon.–Sat., 6–11:30 A.M. Sun., 6 A.M.–1 P.M.

HARWICH

Barnaby Inn. *Moderate*. Rte. 28, West Harwich. 432-6789. Charmingly restored inn with wide pine floors and colonial decor. Succulent seafood and charbroiled steaks. Homemade breads. Salad bar. Sunday brunch. Open Tues.–Sun. for breakfast and dinner.

Bishop's Terrace. *Moderate*. Rte. 28, West Harwich. 432-0253. Ornate French Provincial furnishings decorate this old New England home. Terrace dining. Varied menu. Luncheons, Mon.–Fri. Dinner, Mon.–Sat. Sunday brunch. Open mid-May–mid-Oct.

Brax Landing. *Moderate*. Rte. 28. 432-5515. Whether you dine on the garden patio, outdoor deck, or inside, you will enjoy a view of Saquatucket Harbor. Specialties include Shrimp Scampi and Steak Teriyaki. Raw bar. Sunday brunch.

Cape Half House. *Moderate*. Main St. and Silver St., West Harwich. 432-1964. Wide board floors and Sandwich glass windows are authentic details of this circa 1767 half-Cape. Varied menu. Luncheon buffet 12–2:30 P.M. Dinner, 5–10 P.M. Closed Sun.

Country Inn. *Moderate*. 86 Sisson Rd. Rte. 39, Harwich Port. 432-2769. Candlelit dining in an attractively restored Cape Cod home. Seafood, beef, and poultry. Home-baked breads and desserts a specialty. Closed Sun.

The 400 Club. *Moderate*. 429 Main St. 432-4636. Cozy, informal eatery offering deli-style sandwiches and a varied dinner menu. Daily specials. Sunday brunch, 12–3 P.M.

Harwich Restaurant. *Moderate*. Rte. 28, West Harwich. 432-5765. Antique seafarer's home offering intimate and relaxed dining. New England and continental cuisine featuring Viennese Goulash and Wiener Schnitzel. Dinner daily from 5:30 P.M.

La Grande Rue at Old Kemah Inn. *Moderate*. 551 Main St., Harwich Port. 432-1306. Intimate. candlelit French restaurant. Specialties include Chateaubriand Béarnaise, Oysters Parmesan, and Veal and Scallops Provençal. Dinner from 6 P.M.

The Smith House. *Moderate*. 31 Sea St., Harwich Port. 432-1147. Quiet elegance of a 1862 Cape home overlooking Nantucket Sound. Leisurely lunch, dinner, or Sunday buffet. Varied menu.

Thompson Brothers Clam Bar. *Moderate.* Snow Inn Rd., Harwich Port. 432-3595. Casual dockside dining on Wychmere Harbor. Fresh steamers, lobster, and seafood. Cocktail lounge. Children's menu. Seasonal.

Rexford Restaurant. *Inexpensive.* Main and Bank Sts. 432-9282. Informal family eatery. Homestyle cooking for breakfast and dinner. Steaks, seafood, home-baked desserts. No credit cards. Closed Mon.

Sword and Shield. *Inexpensive.* Main St., Harwich Port. 432-9763. In-town, casual family dining 11:30 A.M.–10 P.M. A varied menu of seafood, beef, and sandwiches. Cocktail lounge.

ORLEANS

Captain Linnell House. *Expensive.* Skaket Rd. 255-3400. Gracious dining in 1840 sea captain's mansion. Varied continental cuisine with an emphasis on seafood. Specialties Lobster Normandy and Sole New Orleans. Home-baked breads and desserts. Sunday champagne brunch. Cocktail lounge. Entertainment and dancing Wed.–Sun. in season

Adams Rib. *Moderate.* Rtes. 6A and 28. 255-2270. Casual family dining. Varied menu of seafood, beef, and poultry. Prime rib a specialty. Children's menu.

The Arbor. *Moderate.* Rte. 28. 255-4847. Comfortable dining room decorated with antiques and collectibles. Original and continental cooking. Flambée desserts a specialty. Cocktail lounge with entertainment.

Barley Neck Inn. *Moderate.* Main St., East Orleans. 255-6830. Victorian sea captain's house on the road to Nauset Beach. Varied continental menu specializing in Chicken Galliano, Shellfish Cioppino, and Beef Wellington. Sandwich menu and entertainment in the lounge.

The Cleaver. *Moderate.* Rte 28. 255-4860. Informal family dining for lunch or dinner. Charbroiled beef and Quahog Pie the specialties. Cocktail lounge.

Joy of Dining. *Moderate.* 222 Main St. 255-4021. Comfortable, classic Cape home serving lunch and dinner. Specialty of the house is Baked Stuffed Shrimp. Entertainment in lounge. Seasonal liquor. Closed Mondays.

Captain Elmer's Seafood Restaurant. *Inexpensive.* 18 Old Colony Way. 255-3350. Informal, family dining for breakfast, lunch, and dinner. Fish and chips, sandwiches, seafood. Raw bar. Year-round liquor.

Double Dragon Inn. *Inexpensive.* Rtes. 6A and 28. 255-4100. Chinese restaurant offering Polynesian and Cantonese cooking for lunch and dinner. Cocktail lounge.

Land Ho. *Inexpensive.* Rte. 6A and Cove Rd. 255-5165. Center-of-town location offering varied menu. Homemade soup and chowders, chili, fresh seafood. No credit cards.

Lobster and Clam Bar. *Inexpensive.* Rte. 6, East Orleans. Roadside, picnic-style eatery. Fried and broiled seafood, lobsters. Seasonal beer and wine. Children's menu. No credit cards.

Lobster Claw. *Inexpensive.* Rte. 6. 255-1800. Casual family dining for seafood, lobsters, steaks. Children's menu. Cocktails.

Lo Cicero's. *Inexpensive*. Rte. 6A, Orleans Shopping Plaza. 255-7100. Informal, private booths and tables. Italian specialties, Shrimp Scampi, Veal Scallopini, and pizza. Children's menu. Cocktail lounge.

PROVINCETOWN

Pepe's Wharf. *Deluxe*. 371 Commercial St. 487-0670. Rooftop and patio dining on Provincetown Harbor. Gourmet seafood for lunch and dinner.

Flagship. *Expensive*. 463 Commercial St. 487-1200. Elegant waterfront dining. Complete Continental menu featuring lobster and seafood. Jazz entertainment in the lounge.

Napi's. *Expensive*. 7 Freeman St. 487-9703. Oak, brick, and stained glass create an attractive Victorian setting. Varied menu. Liquor.

The Red Inn. *Expensive*. 15 Commercial St. 487-0050. Architecturally acclaimed New England country inn with greenhouse and fireplaces on Provincetown Harbor. Country cooking. Year-round liquor.

S'il Vous Plaît. *Expensive*. 186 Commercial St. Gourmet French cuisine in Victorian Cape home. Limited menu, featuring duck with tangerine sauce, Veal Marengo, Bouillabaisse.

Café at the Mews. *Moderate*. 359 Commercial St. 487-1500. European dining on the waterfront. Gourmet seafood served nightly from 6–11 P.M. Sunday brunch. Deck bar and bar with fireplace.

Cicero's. *Moderate*. 265 Commercial St. 487-3233. Restaurant and bakery offering varied seafood and beef menu. Superb deli sandwiches and pastries.

Ciro and Sal's. *Moderate*. 4 Kiley Court. 487-9803. Intimate wine-cellar atmosphere in quiet East End. Italian specialties and outstanding seafood—Scallopine Marsala, Lobster Louisiana. Open daily in season; weekends only Nov.–Apr.

Cottage Restaurant and Lounge. *Moderate*. 149 Commercial St. 487-9160. Home cooking for breakfast, lunch, or dinner. Seafood, steaks, and chops. Pot roast and blueberry muffins house specialties.

Everbreeze. *Moderate*. 429 Commercial St. 487-0465. Newly appointed, overlooking the harbor. Varied seafood menu including Portuguese Kale Soup, Seafood Strudel. Cocktail lounge.

Grand Central Café. *Moderate*. 5 Masonic Place. 487-9116. Intimate and rustic inside; outdoor garden. Steaks; seafood—Sole Florentine, Shrimp Scampi. Cocktails. Open Memorial Day–late Sept.

Landmark. *Moderate*. 404 Commercial St. 487-9319. Built in 1840 by captain Josiah Cooke. Scallops, lobster, duck, and chicken.

The Moors. *Moderate*. Bradford St. Ext. 487-0840. Informal nautical atmosphere. Specializes in Portuguese prepared seafood. Cocktail lounge. Entertainment.

Ocean's Inn. *Moderate*. 386 Commercial St. 487-0358. Rooftop and deck dining. Brook trout, Cortina duckling, Osso Bucco. Bar. Brunch.

Pilgrim House. *Moderate*. 336 Commercial St. 487-0319. Indoor and outdoor patio dining. Numerous meat and fish kabob entrees, Wellfleet oysters. Raw bar. Entertainment.

Poor Richard's Buttery. *Moderate.* 432 Commercial St. 487-3825. Candlelit garden atmosphere. "Chef's Pleasure" Quail and Duckling. Brunch. Seasonal.

Café Blasé. *Inexpensive.* 328 Commercial St. 487-3810. Sidewalk patio tables with flowers and umbrellas. Light fare—soup, sandwiches, quiche. Liquor. Seasonal.

Governor Bradford. *Inexpensive.* 312 Commercial St. 487-9618. Informal, family restaurant. Raw bar, game room, and lounge. Varied menu.

Papa's Place. *Inexpensive.* 296 Commercial St. 487-2320. Center-of-town location for light meals or full dinners. Specialties include scallops, teriyaki, scampi, Sole Stephen, and Chicken Cordon Bleu.

Plain and Fancy. *Inexpensive.* 334 Commercial St. 487-0147. Casual eatery with lounge downstairs. Beef Stroganoff, Chicken Kiev. Childrens' menu. Open mid-May–mid-Sept.

TRURO

Blacksmith Shop. *Moderate.* Rte. 6A. 349-6554. Rustic converted barn. House specialties Shrimp and Sole Mornay, Apricot Soufflé. Children's menu. Cocktails.

Mediterranee. *Moderate.* Pond Rd., North Truro. 487-1881. Garden cocktail terrace. Four-course gourmet dinners on weeknights. Specialties Paella Valenciana, duck pâté with truffles and cognac. Open daily.

Skipper II at Outer Reach Motor Lodge. *Moderate.* Rte. 6, North Truro. 487-0629. Enjoy a poolside lunch, light dinner, and entertainment in the lounge or formal dinner overlooking the Bay. Seafood and charbroiled meats. Children's menu.

Whitman House. *Moderate.* County Rd. North Truro. 487-1740. Established 1894. Three dining rooms with timbers and flagstone floors exude Cape charm. Seafood Newburg, Prime Ribs, Beef and Reef. Cocktail lounge.

Busted Shutter. *Inexpensive.* Rte. 6, North Truro. 487-9640. Roadside picnic-style eatery for fish and chips, sandwiches, ice cream. No liquor.

Cape Ender. *Inexpensive.* Rte. 6, North Truro. 487-1815. Casual family dining for breakfast, lunch, or dinner. Dancing nightly in the cocktail lounge.

Family Table. *Inexpensive.* Rte. 6, North Truro. 487-2026. As the name implies, this is a casual family restaurant serving Portuguese and Italian specialties. Cocktails. Entertainment. Children's menu. No credit cards.

Prince of Whales. *Inexpensive.* Rte. 6A, North Truro. 487-0567. Open for breakfast, lunch, and dinner featuring cranberry pancakes, homemade muffins, a variety of omelets, seafood, and steaks. Children's menu. Cocktails.

Top Mast. *Inexpensive.* Rte. 6A, North Truro. 487-3062. Informal poolside restaurant appointed with hanging plants and antiques. Seafood, veal, or poultry from a varied menu. Serving breakfast, lunch, and dinner. Cocktails.

WELLFLEET

Cielo Gallery and Café. *Expensive.* East Main St. 349-2108. Informal café atmosphere highlighted by gourmet cuisine. Serving 3-course lunches 11 A.M.–2 P.M. and 5-course dinners 4–6 P.M. Reservations required.

Wellfleet Oyster House. *Expensive.* East Main St. 349-2134. Circa 1750 Cape home decorated with antiques and art. Paella Costa Brava, Broiled Oysters with Celery Sauce, Steak Tartare. Homemade desserts, cappuccino. No credit cards.

Yesteryears. *Expensive.* Rte. 6, south Wellfleet. 349-9339. Unusual collection of antiques and memorabilia. Seafood specialties. Oyster bar. Cocktail lounge with entertainment daily July and Aug.; weekends June and Sept.

Aesop's Tables. *Moderate.* Main St. 349-6450. Restored sea captain's home decorated with tropical plants and art. Internationally flavored seafood. Homemade desserts. Cocktail lounge with entertainment. Closed Mon., June–Sept.

Captain Higgins Seafood Restaurant. *Moderate.* Across from Town Pier. 349-6027. Informal dining overlooking Wellfleet Harbor. Seafood, lobster, shore dinners. Salad bar. Cocktails. Open June–Labor Day.

Sweet Seasons at the Inn at Duck Creek. *Moderate.* East Main St. 349-6535. Overlooking Duck Pond. Seafood, Tenderloin Béarnaise, vegetarian dishes, Chocolate Mousse. Brunch, 9 A.M.–2 P.M. Dinner, 6–10 P.M. Entertainment in the *Tavern Room.*

VR's. *Moderate.* Rte. 6, South Wellfleet. 349-2127. Informal family dining for breakfast, lunch, and dinner. Seafood, prime ribs. Salad bar. Children's menu. Cocktails. Dancing on weekends.

Bayside Lobster Hutt. *Inexpensive.* Commercial St. 349-6333. Shingled oyster shack offering self-service, picnic-style dining. Lobsters, steamers, large variety of seafood. Raw bar. Salad bar. Bring your own beer or wine. Seasonal.

Bookstore Restaurant. *Inexpensive.* Kendrick Ave. 349-3154. Informal and cozy dining across from Wellfleet Harbor for breakfast, lunch, and dinner. Baked Stuffed Shrimp, Wellfleet Oysters, Chicken Cordon Bleu. Children's menu. Cocktail lounge.

Roodie's. *Inexpensive.* Rte. 6, South Wellfleet. 349-2688. Casual family eatery for Italian cuisine. Veal Parmesan, lasagna, pizza, seafood, and steaks. Liquor. Children's menu.

Serena's. *Inexpensive.* Rte. 6, 349-9370. Comfortable, informal family dining for lunch and dinner. Seafood and Italian specialties. Children's menu. Cocktail lounge.

Yum Yum Tree. *Inexpensive.* Rte. 6. 349-9468. Self-service indoor and patio dining. Specializing in a variety of seafood and Portuguese items. Open Memorial Day–Columbus Day.

NIGHT LIFE. The Lower Cape villages are for the most part "quiet" towns, but nightlife happenings are numerous enough to suit every taste. Every club is in full swing during summer. Call places of interest in advance during the off-season, since the majority are closed or limit entertainment nights. As a rule, year-round establishments reduce their activities to weekends only. Inquiries are welcomed.

Brewster. *Laurino's*, Rte. 6A; dancing and music from the 1940s and 1950s. *Michael's Black Rose*, 2377 Rte. 6A; contemporary music nightly. *The Woodshed*, Rte. 6A; contemporary music, shoulder-to-shoulder listening in the pub.

Chatham. *Christopher Ryder House*, Rte. 28; musical revues based on Broadway material, live in the Opera House. *Pate's*, Rte. 28; varied program of contemporary music. *Queen Anne Inn*, 70 Queen Anne Rd.; classical music. *Sou'wester*, Rte. 28; Country-western entertainment in lounge. *Wequasset Inn*, Rte. 28; dinner, dancing, and light listening music.

Eastham. *First Encounter Coffeehouse*, Samoset Road, off Rte. 6; folk and alternative entertainment. *The Helmsman*, Rte. 6; live entertainment, contemporary music. *Hose'n Hammer*, Rte. 6; live entertainment, contemporary music in the pub. *King's Colonial Restaurant*, Rte. 6; dance and sing-along favorites. *Sheraton Ocean Park Inn*, Rte. 6; listening music in lounge.

Harwich. *Bishop's Terrace*, Rte. 28; light piano music. *The Irish Pub*, Rte. 28; Irish music, popular songs. *Lincoln Lodge*, Lower County Rd.; popular music, guitar, and vocals. *Spinnaker's*, Rte. 28; blues and popular music.

Orleans. *Arbor Landing at the Binnacle Lounge*, Rte. 28; varied light entertainment in lounge. *Barley Neck Inn*, Beach Rd.; varied acoustic jazz, rock, and contemporary music. *Captain Linnell House*, Skaket Rd.; varied jazz entertainment. *Joy of Dining*, Rte. 6A; Happy Hour afternoon entertainment, periodic fashion shows, light contemporary dancing, and listening music. *Orleans Inn of the Yankee Fisherman*, Rte. 6A; varied live entertainment, usually based on Broadway material.

Provincetown. The circus atmosphere of summer offers the visitor a wide array of nightly entertainment. Many clubs cater to the male clientele. *Atlantic House*, 6 Masonic Place; recorded disco music for men. *Back Street*, Carver St.; recorded disco music. *Blitz*, 291 Commercial St.; varied program of recorded and live disco, rock, and new wave. *Cottage Restaurant*, 149 Commercial St.; piano and vocals. *Crown and Anchor*, 247 Commercial St.; recorded disco music, gay comics, and impersonators in The Back Room; varied sing-along, drink-along music in the Lobby Bar. *Flagship*, 463 Commercial St.; varied music program, jazz. *The Greenery at Howard Johnson's*, 350 Bradford St.; varied program of live entertainment. *La Disc* (known locally as Piggy's), Shankpainter Rd.; European disco atmosphere welcomes French-Canadians in particular. *Governor Bradford*, 312 Commercial St.; varied program of recorded and live Reggae, rock, and pop in the lounge. *Holiday Inn*, Rte. 6A; varied program of popular music for dancing. The *Moors Restaurant*, Bradford St. Ext.; piano bar in the Smuggler's Lounge. *Napi's*, 7 Freeman St.; varied program of jazz, popular, and country music. *Old Meeting House*, Standish and Bradford Sts.; varied program of country, bluegrass, and popular music. *Peter's at the Sandcastles*, Rte. 6A; late-night hot-spot. *Pilgrim House*, 336 Commercial St.; female impersonators, bawdy entertainment. *Post Office Cabaret*, 303 Commercial St.; vocals and piano, light listening. *Pied Piper*, 193A Commercial St.; recorded disco music for women, and "special event" nights. The *Surf Club* at MacMillan Wharf; generally headlines the famous Provincetown Jug Band for fun stuff. *Town House*, 291 Commercial St.; varied vocals and sing-along entertainment in the lounge. *Vorelli's*, 228 Commercial St.; varied program of comedy, singers, piano music.

Truro. *Mariner Lounge* at the Cape Ender, Rte. 6; recorded disco, rock, and pop for dancing. *Skipper II*, Rte. 6; varied program of pop music, guitar, and vocals in the lounge.

Wellfleet. *Aesop's Tables*, Main St.; varied program of jazz, piano, guitar, and vocals. *Beachcomber*, Cahoon Hollow; varied program of live and recorded popular and disco dance music. *Paddle's*, Main St.; varied musical entertainment. *VR's*, Rte. 6; varied program of dancing and listening music. *Yesteryears*, Rte. 6; live entertainment for dancing and listening, mainly jazz.

MARTHA'S VINEYARD

by

KEITH LIGGETT

Keith Liggett is a freelance writer who lives on Martha's Vineyard.

For generations the island of Martha's Vineyard has occupied a
singular position among the resort communities of the East Coast.
Well known by name but little known in fact, the island has
become a celebrated summer retreat. Visitors here are touched by
a sense of the past and by the quiet tranquility of island living—
qualities that attract many artists, musicians and writers, as well
as tourists, to the Vineyard's shores.

During its years as a prosperous seafaring community, Martha's
Vineyard experienced great growth. As the life of the sea lost
importance and summer visitors became the Vineyard's primary
economic boon, the importance of the island's early history was

recognized and preserved. Much of Martha's Vineyard today remains unspoiled. Waterfront development, common in larger oceanfront communities, is absent on the island, and many of the old homes built along the shores have been preserved and well maintained by their owners. In the towns, the original buildings and shops of the 1800s have been retained and converted to meet the needs of the present tourist trade.

This blend of past and present is exemplified in the island's transformation each summer when boats arrive carrying visitors and summer residents. For two months the Vineyard teems with life, much as it did in the days of the whalers when thousands of ships passed through every year. Then, in the early fall, the island rests, regaining an atmosphere reminiscent of the days of simple agriculture and fishing—until the first boat of the summer starts the cycle all over again.

A Brief Early History

Martha's Vineyard is a "terminal moraine," formed at the end of the last great glacial period. As glaciers moved down from the northern plains, they pushed large berms of rock and sediment in front of them. With the retreat of the glaciers, these large berms of debris were left isolated on the glaciated plains. Martha's Vineyard is part of the debris left as the glaciers retreated. Its hills and valleys were formed as the glacier melted, creating rivers that flowed over the land, cutting a path to the ocean.

The first visitors to the island were nomadic Native American hunters, who arrived soon after the glacier began to retreat. At this time the oceans were much lower than they are today and there was a land bridge connecting the Vineyard to the mainland. The hunters traveled across this bridge freely to hunt game. Several camps from this time have been found, along with bones of animals that carbon date the camps at about 4,300 years old. When the glaciers melted, the oceans rose, and Martha's Vineyard became a true island. There was plenty of game and the climate was rather mild, and a number of Native Americans settled on the island, forming the first villages.

The history of European contact with Martha's Vineyard is a little harder to trace. The "discovery" of the island is still a matter of some debate, even today. The debate revolves around current evidence that the Vikings traveled throughout the region in about A.D. 1000. Those who claim that Vikings discovered Martha's Vineyard cite oral history with its descriptions of the island and its residents and of the discovery of runes in Massachusetts. While there is little doubt that the Vikings were in the area in A.D. 1000, there is no hard evidence to demonstrate that they actually landed on the island.

The first cartographic record of Martha's Vineyard was made by the Italian Giovanni da Verrazano. As he sailed past the island he named it Louisa—the name did not stick. Neither did any of the other names used over the next few years. The naming of the island finally fell in 1602 to Bartholomew Gosnold. While charting the area for the queen of England, Gosnold named Martha's Vineyard in honor of his youngest daughter and the many wild grapes he found growing on the island.

In the early 1600s, a Massachusetts Bay Colony businessman, Thomas Mayhew, bought Martha's Vineyard, Nantucket, and the Elizabeth Islands from the Crown. He turned the care and governing of the islands over to his only son, the Reverend Thomas Mayhew, Jr., who, in 1642, founded the first European settlement on Martha's Vineyard. These early settlers named the new community Great Harbor for its fine protected deep water harbor. Today is is known as Edgartown.

The economy of the island flourished. The settlers learned fishing and whaling from Native Americans living on the island, and soon the settlers were building boats to use on their whaling and fishing voyages. Within a few years they were producing enough from fishing, whaling, and agriculture to enable them to export excess goods to the mainland.

This initial boom lasted until the Revolutionary War, when in a single raid the British took the majority of the cattle and sheep on the island and destroyed the fishing fleet. It was a blow from which the island would not recover until the new prosperity of the whaling days.

After the war, Martha's Vineyard became a stopover for outward- and inward-bound ships from New Bedford, on the mainland. The Vineyard's fine harbors made her a favorite of the captains of the day. Many seamen grew up on the island and as they earned their own ships they brought them home. With the rise of the whaling industry, the Vineyard's fortunes rose, too.

The prosperity of the whaling days brought new life to the island and its residents. The waterfront teemed with activity. The harbors were packed with ships provisioning for outward voyages and those come home from years at sea. The town of Edgartown in those days boasted a population greater than the island's total population today. Edgartown and Vineyard Haven were largely built during this time. Even today, the two towns retain the character of those early days, with their captains' mansions overlooking the harbors.

With the demise of the whaling industry in the 1860s, a new business emerged on the island—the tourist trade. Martha's Vine-

yard became a favorite summering spot during the Victorian era.
Ferries plied the waters between New Bedford and Vineyard Haven and Oak Bluffs. Large hotels rose on the water's edge. A
steam locomotive ran from Vineyard Haven to the steamship dock
in Oak Bluffs, and from there to the broad sandy ocean beach in
Katama (now called South Beach). These, too, were days of prosperity. Of the towns on the island, Oak Bluffs bears the mark of
this time most. Today, it boasts the largest collection of intact
Victorian houses in the country.

During these times of prosperity, the towns of West Tisbury,
Chilmark, and Gay Head remained relatively unchanged. New
houses were built and roads for wagons were laid, but most people
continued to settle in the towns of Vineyard Haven, Oak Bluffs,
and Edgartown.

Up Island and Down Island

When directing a visitor, an islander will use the expression "Up
Island" or "Down Island." There are two stories behind the use of
these terms. The first is that in the sailing days, to go from Edgartown or Vineyard Haven west to Gay Head, you sailed against the
prevailing winds, or "up wind." Thus, going to Gay Head you
sailed "Up Island" and coming back you sailed "Down Island."
The other explanation relates to navigation. As sailors moved from
east to west, away from the Greenwich Prime Meridian, they
moved up the degrees of longitude. When they went from west to
east, toward Greenwich, they moved down the longitude. This was
simply adapted to land travel. Going east to west on the island is
Up Island. Going west to east is Down Island. Today, the terms
are the common way of directing or referring to parts of Martha's
Vineyard. The Up Island towns are West Tisbury, Chilmark, and
Gay Head. The Down Island towns are Vineyard Haven, Oak
Bluffs, and Edgartown.

Martha's Vineyard Today

Most visitors to Martha's Vineyard land in Vineyard Haven,
considered by many cruising sailors to be the best port in the
region. Vineyard Haven has remained a sailing town over the
years. Behind the breakwater are sailboats of every size and age—
from classics built of wood 50 years ago to the latest in racing
designs hot off the drawing boards. Like any typical seafaring
community, the waterfront in Vineyard Haven is a mixture of
businesses: shops, next to boatyards, next to restaurants.

Visitors arriving by ferry will dock at the Steamship Authority
Terminal. Across the street from the terminal is the Seaman's

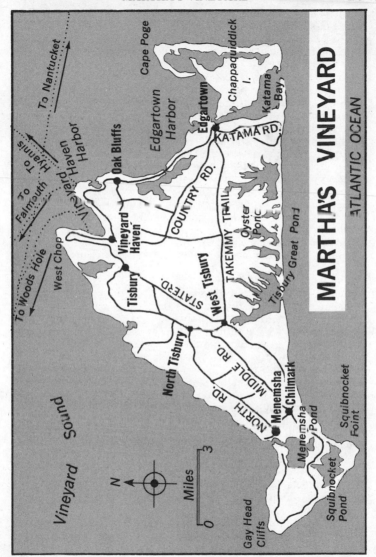

Bethel. Now a museum, it was originally built to meet the spiritual needs of sailors passing through the town.

The Main Street shopping area in Vineyard Haven is a short block up from the Steamship Authority Terminal and runs parallel to the waterfront. Most of the shops are open year-round, because Vineyard Haven is the economic center of the island.

The second busiest port on the island is Oak Bluffs, where boats arrive in the summer from Woods Hole, Falmouth, and Hyannis. The waterfront of Oak Bluffs is very different from that of Vineyard Haven. Oak Bluffs came to preeminence as a summer resort community. As such, the waterfront in Oak Bluffs is reserved for recreation. The town owns the beach, which is open to all. The last of the great hotels, Wesley House, stands between little Victorian cottages overlooking a harbor almost exclusively used by pleasure boats.

Back in the 1800s, Oak Bluffs was chosen by Methodists as the site for a summer meeting place. The first visitors stayed in tents. In later years the tents were set up on platforms, then finally replaced by Victorian cottages, which are still standing. This group of cottages is now called the Campground and is owned by the Campmeeting Association.

The main district for shopping and dining in Oak Bluffs is on Circuit Avenue, where the summer resort atmosphere emerges in the shops. Unfortunately, much of the town's activity dies down once the seasonal ferries stop arriving. With the cessation of the daily ferry service Oak Bluffs becomes quiet and reflective.

Edgartown has no commercial ferry service. If you want to arrive by sea here you must have your own yacht. Since Edgartown is considered to be one of the yachting capitals of the East Coast, many do arrive in this way. This lends a unique flavor to the town. The captains' homes that line the Edgartown harbor oversee the arrival and departure of thousands of boats every year.

The shopping and dining area in Edgartown is centered around the waterfront. As is true of Vineyard Haven, the shops in Edgartown are an interesting mixture—a store selling fishing tackle and live sand eels will be next to a fashion boutique, which is next to the take-out for fried clams. As you wander through Edgartown's narrow streets, you will also find antique stores, art galleries, and craft shops, often selling the works of local artists.

Many of the shops and inns in Edgartown are open year-round, but once the summer is over, the town returns to a relaxed old-fashioned pace. Quiet winter nights are filled with the smell of wood smoke and salt air.

On the eastern side of downtown Edgartown is the landing for the Chappaquiddick ferry. You can drive to Chappaquiddick, but you must have a four-wheel-drive vehicle.

The towns of West Tisbury, Chilmark, and Gay Head are still relatively rural. In the town centers are general stores that must meet the needs of summer residents by selling tennis balls but at the same time have the replacement hammer for the carpenter working Up Island.

Within Chilmark is the village of Menemsha. Menemsha is the only harbor on the Up Island end of the Vineyard and, as such, plays an important role for fishermen and yachtsmen. Most of the fishing boats unload their catches in Menemsha rather than steam the extra miles to Vineyard Haven. The fish dealers all have retail stores here, where you can be sure of getting the freshest of fresh fish. Typical of small fishing communities in the Northeast, Menemsha has remained unchanged for years.

Beyond Chilmark and Menemsha is the town of Gay Head. This is the westernmost tip of the island—an area of sand dunes, moors, and the famous Gay Head Cliffs. The cliffs are composed of clays and sediments left behind by glaciers in the last Ice Age. Today these clays are exposed in a brilliant array of yellows, reds, and oranges dropping right to the water's edge. From the top of the cliffs on a clear day you can see the twin towers of the Newport Rhode Island bridge.

Up Island does not have the lively atmosphere of the Down Island towns. The original character of Martha's Vineyard as a rural fishing and farming community has remained intact Up Island. The stone walls, New England farmhouses, barns and sweeping vistas of the Atlantic Ocean across a meadow of cattle grazing are a heritage preserved.

PRACTICAL INFORMATION FOR MARTHA'S VINEYARD

HOW TO GET THERE. There are two ways to get to Martha's Vineyard—by water and by air. While air is by far the quickest (the flight from New York takes about as long as the ferry ride from Woods Hole to Vineyard Haven), there is definitely more romance in arriving by "sea."

By Air. The island is serviced by regularly scheduled flights from New York, Newark, Boston, New Bedford, and Hyannis. Airlines providing service include: *PBA*, 1-800-352-3132; *Gull Air*, 1-800-352-7191; and *Northern Airlines*, 1-617-693-3653.

By Sea. Year-round ferry service between Woods Hole and Vineyard Haven is operated by the *Martha's Vineyard and Nantucket Steamship Authority* (known as the Steamship Authority). For information, write:

Box 284, Woods Hole, Massachusetts 02543, or call (617) 540-2022. Even in the slowest parts of the winter, several round trips are scheduled every day. They operate seasonal ferry service between New Bedford and Vineyard Haven and between Hyannis and Oak Bluffs. In the peak summer months, the Steamship Authority also adds several extra Oak Bluffs trips.

Other ferries with service to Martha's Vineyard are: *Cape and Islands Express Line,* Box J-4095, New Bedford, Massachusetts 02741, tel: 997-1688. *Hy-Line,* Ocean Street Dock, Hyannis, Massachusetts 02601, tel: 775-7185. *Island Queen,* 75 Falmouth Heights Rd., Falmouth, Massachusetts 02524, tel: 548-4800.

Although in the summer traveling to the island is a fairly easy proposition, in other seasons one must plan a little further ahead. If you are planning to bring a car, the only ferry handling cars is the Steamship Authority in Woods Hole. Reservations are best made as far in advance as possible. The big holiday weekends are booked far in advance, so plan your trip accordingly.

HOW TO GET AROUND. Although Martha's Vineyard is a large island—24 miles long and 10 miles wide—travel on the island is relatively simple. There are few main roads and these are all well marked. **By bicycle.** The most popular mode of transportation for visitors is the bicycle. Rental shops are close to each ferry terminal. The terrain of the island is perfect for bikes; it is mostly flat, with a few hills in Gay Head and Chilmark. On the heavily traveled roads, bike paths have been built to separate bikes from car traffic. On the other roads it is still quite safe to bike, since drivers on the island are very conscious of the bike traffic.

By car. For those wishing to forgo the physical exercise involved in bike riding, there are also mopeds and cars for rent on the island. Rental agencies are close to the ferry terminals.

By bus. *Island Transport* runs a shuttle bus from the late spring to the early fall. The bus travels a loop from Vineyard Haven to Oak Bluffs, then to Edgartown and back to Vineyard Haven. Trips run every half hour and the cost is small. The Vineyard Haven and Oak Bluffs stops are adjacent to the ferry terminals and well marked. The Edgartown stop is across the street from the police station on Church Street.

By taxi. Several taxi companies meet arriving boats and planes and provide reliable 24-hour-a-day service.

VISITOR INFORMATION. The Martha's Vineyard Chamber of Commerce will send prospective visitors a very complete information packet upon request. The Chamber's address is P.O. Box 1698, Vineyard Haven, Massachusetts 02568. The phone number is 693-0085.

For the benefit of visitors, the Martha's Vineyard Chamber of Commerce and the Edgartown Board of Trade maintain information offices on the island. The Chamber of Commerce office is on Beach Road, Vineyard Haven, a short walk from the Vineyard Haven Steamship Authority Terminal. The office is open weekdays year-round. The Edgartown Board of Trade Information Booth is at the junction of the Edgartown-Vineyard Haven Road and Beach Road (from Oak Bluffs). The booth is open every day from July 4 to Labor Day.

 SEASONAL EVENTS. Martha's Vineyard has quite a few seasonal activities, but there are also a number of cultural offerings throughout the year. *The Island Theater Workshop* produces four to six plays a year, covering a broad crosssection of theater—from musicals to Ibsen. *Katharine Cornell Theater* hosts a variety of classical concerts throughout the year. There are many summer concerts, and a series of chamber music concerts in the winter. *Nathan Mayhew Seminars* holds an evening lecture series. Past subjects have included philosophy, creative writing, photography, and the history of island boatbuilding. The seminars draw on the many talented individuals who have chosen to make Martha's Vineyard their home.

May. *Martha's Vineyard Road Race.* A benefit for the Community Services, the race is actually two races—a 3.1-mile race and an 8-mile race. The courses differ, but share a common start and finish. An exciting event for spectators and runners alike. The race takes place in early May, and draws many national class runners from off-island running clubs.

June. *Weekly Band Concerts.* Held in the Ocean Park Gazebo in Oak Bluffs, and in the band stand in Owen Park, Vineyard Haven, these concerts are a long-standing island tradition. Concerts take place each week from mid-June until Labor Day.

July. *Tisbury Street Fair.* In early July, Main Street Vineyard Haven closes and an old-time Street Fair takes over. Music, specialty foods, merchant specials, games, balloons, and lots of frivolity. *Vineyard Concerts, Inc.* Every summer Vineyard Concerts brings noted classical and semi-classical artists to the island in a series of concerts lasting through the summer. The first of the series is in early July with the last in late August. *Edgartown Regatta.* One of the premier yacht race series' on the East Coast. For a week in mid-July, the "big boats" converge on Edgartown Harbor and Yacht Club in a hotly contested series of races. At the same time, anywhere from 8 to 12 different one-design classes race daily just outside the harbor in Cow Bay. A fine week to get a taste of the racing side of yachting.

August. *Tabernacle Concert.* A concert is held each year in mid-August to add to the Oak Bluffs Tabernacle Improvement Fund. The Tabernacle is a wrought-iron structure built in 1879 by the Campmeeting Association in Oak Bluffs for revival meetings and is now listed in the National Register of Historic Places. *Oak Bluffs Fireworks.* A spectacular fireworks display over the waterfront at Ocean Park. Held in mid-August, as it always has been. *Illumination Night.* Once a year in mid-August, the Campmeeting Association dresses its cottages with lanterns. The evening begins with a band concert in the Tabernacle, and on the signal from the band leader, the lights go on. The traditional time for islanders to visit the campgrounds and socialize. *West Tisbury Agricultural Fair.* An Old Time Fair held late in the month. Fiddlers' contests, the Massachusetts Woodsman Championship, ox pulls, livestock shows, and equestrian shows. For a few days, the island returns to the times when this was the major social event of the summer season. *Edgartown Seafood Festival.* A time for island fishermen to show their catch and for people to see and taste the many varieties of seafood found in the waters around the island. Held in late August.

September. *Chilmark Road Race.* A 3-mile run down Middle Road, one of the most scenic of the Up-Island roads. Like the Martha's Vineyard Road Race, this race draws a strong field of island and off-island competitors. Held in early September. *Martha's Vineyard Striped Bass and Bluefish Derby.* One of the largest fishing derbys on the East Coast. Timed to coincide with the fall migration of the large game fish to the breeding grounds in the south. The derby draws fishermen from all over the country, and it is not unusual for world records to be broken in the course of the month. The big event for contestants and spectators is the morning and evening weigh-in of fish at Derby Headquarters. The Derby runs from mid-September to mid-August. *Tivoli Day.* Oak Bluffs' celebration of its Victorian heritage. The festivities include a nationally sanctioned bike race around the island, the blessing of the fleet, sailboat races, and a street dance/block party on Circuit Avenue. Held in mid-September.

October. *Island Craft Fair at Wesley House.* An annual showing of local crafts. Weaving, quilting, stained glass, and etched glass. Mid-October.

December. *Old Fashioned Christmas in Edgartown.* Shopkeepers and residents welcome the Christmas season with traditional New England vigor. Old-time caroling parties. Tours of the inns and some of the finer homes in Edgartown. Concerts in the Old Whaling Church. Continues from mid-December to Christmas Day.

 MOVIES. During the summer months, there are five active movie theaters on the island. Four show recent release movies—*The Edgartown Town Hall Theatre,* the *Capawock* in Vineyard Haven, and the *Island* and *Strand* in Oak Bluffs. The fifth theater is the *Movie Museum of Film Classics* in the Agricultural Hall, West Tisbury. The Movie Museum brings the classics of the film genre to the island for short runs. It is well worth the ride to West Tisbury.

The Edgartown Town Hall Theatre and the Capawock in Vineyard Haven are open all year and continue to show recent release movies in the off-season.

 MUSEUMS. As an old seafaring community, Martha's Vineyard has always maintained a strong historical awareness. Several museums on the island provide interesting, accurate glimpses of island life in the early days.

Dukes County Historical Society. School Street in the center of Edgartown. 627-4441. Open year-round Thurs.–Sat. afternoons. Open mid-June to mid-Sept. Tues.–Sat. 10:30 A.M. to 4:30 P.M. Admission, Adults $1.00; children $.50.

The Dukes County Historical Society offers island visitors the broadest and most detailed view of the history of Martha's Vineyard. Exhibits cover the major historical and economic facets of the island's past. The Society's library is a valuable resource for anyone researching the history of the island. It houses genealogical records, rare island books, and a large collection of ships' logs from the whaling days.

Hansel and Gretel Doll Museum. On New York Avenue, a short distance from the center of Oak Bluffs. 693-9285. Open daily 10:00 A.M. to 5:00 P.M., July and August. Other times only by appointment. Admission, $.75.

A private collection of dolls and toys. The collection, from the early 19th century, contains many rare items.

Mayhew Chapel and Indian Burial Grounds. Five miles from Vineyard Haven at the end of Christiantown Road. Leave Vineyard Haven on State Road. At the junction of Indian Hill Road and State Road turn right. In about ⅓ mile turn right on Christiantown Road. The Chapel is a little less than a mile on the left. Open Sunday, 2:00 P.M. to 5:00 P.M., from early June to mid-Sept. The grounds are open year-round. Admission is free.

In the 1600s the Reverend Thomas Mayhew, Jr., the son of the island's owner, converted a group of the American Indians to Christianity, and this chapel was their place of worship. Members were buried on the property. Today it is maintained by the Martha's Vineyard Garden Club as a bird and wildflower sanctuary.

Seaman's Bethel. Across the street from the Vineyard Haven Steamship Authority Terminal. 693-9317. Open 10:00 A.M. to 5:00 P.M. daily. Closed Tuesday.

The Seaman's Bethel was originally built to provide for the spiritual needs of the many sailors passing through Vineyard Haven in the days of the schooner trade. Today it is a museum and a chapel dedicated to those men it first served. The materials are all focused on the maritime history of the island.

The Tisbury Museum. Short walk from the Vineyard Haven Steamship Terminal on Beach Rd. Open afternoons mid-June to mid Sept. Closed Weds. Admission, Adults $1.25; children $.50.

The Tisbury Museum has six rooms of exhibits depicting life in Tisbury from 1800 to 1900. The museum building, *The Ritter House,* was built in 1796 and was the first building on Martha's Vineyard to be nominated to the National Register of Historic Places.

The Windfarm Museum. One-and-a-half miles from the town of Vineyard Haven on the Edgartown-Vineyard Haven Road. 693-3658. Open weekends June, Sept., Oct. Open daily 10:00 A.M. to 5:00 P.M. in July and August. Closed Weds. Admission to *Exhibit Building* free. Tours of the *Windfarm,* Adults $3.00; children $1.00.

The most unusual of the museums on Martha's Vineyard. The history of windmills is used to show their potential. The museum is appropriately located, since the island has steady year-round winds.

TOURS. The quickest way to get an overall feel for the island is to take a guided **bus** tour. The general tour takes about three hours and touches all the major points of interest. Three island companies offer bus tours—*Gay Head Sightseeing, Island Transport,* and *Martha's Vineyard Sightseeing.* At least one of the tour companies meets each boat as it arrives, so it is easy to arrange a tour.

For those wishing a more personal trip around the island, most of the **taxi** companies will arrange a private guided tour. The advantage of this alternative is flexibility. If you want to tarry a bit at one spot, you are not under the time constraint of a bus, which has a set route to cover in a set period. The taxis also meet the incoming boats and planes, so it is easy to arrange a small tour of the island upon arrival.

SPORTS. The opportunities for outdoor sports on Martha's Vineyard are endless. **Sailing** has been a part of the island's life since the first. Today it remains one of the most popular of the many outdoor activities. The winds are steady for most of the summer months, providing reliable and enjoyable sailing day in and day out. Sailboats can be rented at the *Harborside Inn* in Edgartown and at the *Selfin Sailing Center* in Vineyard Haven. Sailing lessons are offered by both businesses.

The fastest growing sport in the world today is **windsurfing.** The island is ideal for the beginner or expert. With the many bays and inlets, there is always a patch of protected water for the neophyte; the ocean side surf provides plenty of action for the expert. *Selfin Sailing Center* in Vineyard Haven and *Island Windsurfing* in Edgartown teach windsurfing and have rental windsurfers.

Hiking opportunities abound on Martha's Vineyard. There are miles of uninterrupted public beaches, and the wildlife refuges have well-marked trails showing hikers the many different types of ecological habitats established on the island.

And of course there is **swimming.** The island has waters to suit everyone's taste—from the booming surf on the Atlantic shore to the gentle waters of Vineyard and Nantucket sounds. See *Beaches,* below.

Both **tennis** and **golf** are long-time traditional summer activities. Golf was first brought to the island in the late 1800s, and today there are two fine public courses on the island. *Mink Meadows,* a 9-hole course on West Chop in Vineyard Haven and *Farm Neck Golf Club,* an 18-hole championship golf course on the shore of Sengekontacket Pond. Tennis courts are available in all the towns on the island. Many of the inns and hotels have their own or the guests are granted permission to use the town courts nearby. For hourly play, visitors should contact the *Farm Neck Tennis Club, Island Country Club Tennis,* or *Clark Leland Clark.*

Horseback riding is available at *Scrubby Neck Farm* and at *Misty Meadows.* Both have complete stable facilities, guided trail rides, and lessons.

FISHING. Fishing is both a way of life and a sport on Martha's Vineyard. Huge trawlers unload their catch daily at the docks in Vineyard Haven and Menemsha, attesting to the richness of the waters surrounding the island. One of the most popular spots for fishermen is *Wasque Point* on the southeast corner of the island. A steady producer of bluefish and striped bass, Wasque is often the site of bluefish blitzes. *South Beach* is another favorite spot. During the fishing derby many a big one is weighed in with South Beach in the location blank. Up-Island, the jetties at the mouth of *Menemsha Basin* are often good bets in the morning and evening.

For the party-boat fisherman, *Ranger* leaves the Oak Bluffs Harbor every day of the season, weather permitting.

Although no license is required for saltwater fishing, there are regulations concerning the size and number of striped bass a fisherman is allowed to take. Since the regulations are updated yearly, it is wise to pick up the current set at one of the tackle shops on the island.

SHELLFISHING

The saltwater ponds and the harbors of the island are rich in shellfish. Each town issues shellfish licenses for the waters under their jurisdiction. If you want to catch your own, contact the town hall of the town in which you wish to fish. There you may also obtain a list of the areas that are closed due to recent seeding projects.

BEACHES. Each island beach has a character of its own, from the clay cliffs of Lucy Vincent Beach in Chilmark to the broad sandy expanse of South Beach in Edgartown. Many of the beaches are open to all, but some are only open to residents of the town and their guests. The following listings will give you an idea of the beaches on the island of Martha's Vineyard and whether you will need a permit.

Tisbury. The *Owen Park Beach* is one block past the business district on Main Street, Vineyard Haven. The park and beach are open to all. There is a lifeguard on duty during the day in summer months. The *Tisbury Town Beach* is on the north side of the entrance to Lake Tashmoo and is open to all. To reach the beach go toward West Chop on Main Street to Daggett Avenue. Turn left on Daggett Avenue and continue until Daggett ends on Herring Creek Road-East. Turn Right on Herring Creek Road-East. The Beach is at the very end of Herring Creek Road. A note of caution: This road is dirt and not well maintained, therefore care should be taken when navigating it. The sandy beach is on Vineyard Sound with a view stretching from Woods Hole to the end of the Elizabeth Islands.

Oak Bluffs. The *Oak Bluffs Town Beach* extends from the mouth of the Oak Bluffs Harbor almost to the stone jettys that once were the entrance to Hart Haven. The beach fronts on Nantucket Sound, which rarely has large waves, making it a very good family beach. It is open to all and there are lifeguards on duty during the summer months. The *Joseph Sylvia State Beach* is on Beach Road between Oak Bluffs and Edgartown. A little less than two miles from either town, this barrier beach separates Nantucket Sound from Sengekontacket Pond. Wide and sandy, and fine for families since Nantucket Sound rarely has waves, the beach is open to all, with a lifeguard at the Edgartown end of the beach during the summer.

Edgartown. *Joseph Sylvia State Beach.* See description under Oak Bluffs Beaches. The *Lighthouse Beach* is at the Edgartown Lighthouse overlooking the entrance to the Edgartown Harbor. Very protected, it is a good beach for children. Open to all. *South Beach* is a sandy, wide beach on the Atlantic Ocean. To reach it, take the Edgartown Shuttle to Katama or turn right on Pease's Point Way as you come into Edgartown. At the fork take either road—they lead to both ends of the beach. This beach often has a heavy surf and a strong undertow. There are lifeguards on duty in the summer and the beach is open to all. The *East Beach* is a long barrier beach on the eastern side of Chappaquiddick Island. To reach it, take the Chappy Ferry and continue straight after landing. After two-and-a-half miles, the hard surface road makes a sharp right turn and a dirt road continues straight. Continue straight on the dirt road for a little more than one-half mile. The road ends at the Dyke Bridge. The beach is about a third of a mile from the bridge. Like South Beach, the East Beach is open water and often develops a good surf. There are no lifeguards. The beach is open to all. *Wasque Point* is the southeast corner of the island. After taking the Chappy Ferry, continue straight on the hard surface road and stay on it past the turn-off to East Beach. In about four-and-a-half miles, the road turns into a dirt road. Shortly thereafter is a sign marking the entrance to the Wasque Reservation of the Trustees of the Reservation. About one-half mile from the end of the hard surface a sign will direct you to parking. The beach is about a quarter of a mile from the parking area. This is an open water beach without a lifeguard, and recommended for strong swimmers. Open to all.

West Tisbury. The *Lambert's Cove Beach* is off Lambert's Cove Road about five miles from the town of Vineyard Haven. It is a wide cobble-and-sand beach on Vineyard Sound, with lovely views of the Elizabeth Islands. There is no lifeguard. The beach is only open to residents of West Tisbury and their guests. The *Long Point—Trustees of the Reservation* has a beautiful beach on the Atlantic Ocean. In addition to ocean swimming, there is swimming in a freshwater pond and a saltwater pond on the reservation. There is no lifeguard. Admission is to members of the Trustees of the Reservation and their guests, or by a daily fee. The Trustees are planning to build a new road in the spring of 1982. For directions call the Long Point Reservation: 693-1905. Adjacent to the Long Point Reservation is the *West Tisbury Town Beach*. There are no lifeguards. The beach is open to residents of West Tisbury and their guests.

Chilmark. The *Lucy Vincent Beach* is about one mile before reaching Bettlebung Corner in Chilmark. On the Atlantic Ocean, it is backed by cliffs similar to those at Gay Head. Open only to the residents of Chilmark and their guests.

Gay Head. The *Gay Head Town Beach* is a combination of cobble and sand on the Atlantic Ocean, backed by clay cliffs. The beach is only open to residents of Gay Head and their guests. The *Lobsterville Beach* runs along the last three-quarters of a mile of the Lobsterville Road. A broad, sandy barrier beach, it is a fine protected beach for children. Open to all.

WILDLIFE RESERVATIONS. *Cedar Tree Neck.* With rolling hills, small freshwater ponds, and a rough cobbled beach, Cedar Tree Neck is typical of the North Shore wooded area. A fine area for bird-watching. No picnics or swimming.

Felix Neck. A mix of oak woods and open meadowlands adjacent to Sengekontacket Pond, Felix Neck is a wildlife sanctuary, a feeding ground for wintering birds, and a nature museum. The museum often sponsors nature walks featuring local specialists in such areas as birding and wildflowers.

State Forest. The land in the center of the island is set aside as a State Forest. Over the last 20 years it has been reforested with pines and now is a tall pine forest mixed with oak. There are marked hiking and bike trails. The park headquarters is on Barnes Road between Edgartown-Vineyard Haven Road and Edgartown-West Tisbury Road.

Trustees of the Reservation

The Trustees of the Reservation is the oldest private foundation on Martha's Vineyard dedicated to the preservation of unique properties. On the island it maintains four very different properties: *Wasque Point and Cape Poge.* This area of delicate barrier beach extends from the southeast corner of the island, Wasque Point, to Cape Poge on the northeast corner of the island. The beach is an important migration stopover for many shore birds as well as a nesting area for those shore birds that do not go to the far north. The beach is open to four-wheel-drive vehicles, but they are required to stay on designated paths. *Long Point.* This 508-acre area in the center of the South Shore of the island encompasses a very diverse range of water habitats. It is bounded on the east by Long Pond, a large freshwater pond; on the west by West Tisbury Great Pond, a typical saltwater pond; and on the south by the Atlantic Ocean, and includes habitats ranging from barrier beach to freshwater marsh. An excellent place for birdwatching. *Mytoi.* A formal Japanese garden on the road to the Dyke Bridge. *Menemsha Hills Reservation.* A small 149-acre property, and rather difficult to reach, this reservation protects an unusual natural phenomenon—a sand cliff. To reach the reservation, park in the Menemsha parking lot and walk north along the shore. The sand cliff is about three-fourths of a mile from the parking lot. The rough boulder-and-cobble beach collects a lot of flotsam. Although the walk is long, it is very interesting.

CAMPING. There are no public campgrounds on the island of Martha's Vineyard. However there are two excellent private campgrounds—The *Martha's Vineyard Family Campground* (693-3772) and *Webb's*

Campground (693-0233). Both are completely equipped to handle trailers and tent campers. They have showers, laundromats, and hookups. With only two campgrounds on the island, it is wise to reserve a campsite prior to arriving on the island.

A last note on camping. There is no camping allowed on the public beaches. All the towns on the island have ordinances to this effect that are enforced throughout the year.

 CHILDREN'S ACTIVITIES. Kids will delight in the *Oak Bluffs Flying Horses,* reputedly our nation's oldest carousel. Located one-half block from the ferry landing, this is a truly old-fashioned carousel, with free rides for those who catch the brass ring. Little people—and big people too—should enjoy a visit to the *Hansel and Gretel Doll Museum.* Located on New York Avenue, this quaint museum houses a private collection of dolls and doll houses. $.75 admission.

 SHOPPING AND CRAFTS. Perhaps it's the quaint atmosphere that brings out the creative instinct in its inhabitants, but whatever the cause, the island is noted for its artisans and craftwork. To name a few: *C. B. Stark Silversmith, Inc.,* located on Water St., Vineyard Haven, specializes in handcrafted jewelry in gold and silver. *Caismer Michalczyk,* 28 Siloam Ave., Oak Bluffs, does wonderful sculpting in wood, stone, and bronze. For a more do-it-yourself touch, the *Silver Needle,* N. Summer St., Edgartown, sells unusual handpainted needlepoint, along with instruction kits. The island also houses various arts and crafts galleries. The *Edgartown Art Gallery,* located in the Charlotte Inn on S. Summer St., features the work of such artistic celebrities as Kib Bramhall and Andrew Wyeth. For more unusual pieces, try the *Red Barn Emporium,* on old Country Rd., West Tisbury. And if you time it right, you might catch the *Dukes County Fair,* held annually in Agricultural Hall, next to the Tisbury Elementary School. Usually held the third week in August, this fair gives a folksy flavor to Vineyard craftsmanship. Another worthwhile event is the *Annual Martha's Vineyard Craftsman Fair,* held in mid-July at the Wesley House Hotel, Harbor Front, Oak Bluffs. And for all of you antique lovers, or just those people who enjoy a good bargain, be sure to inquire about the island's summer assortment of flea markets and auctions.

 HOTELS, MOTELS AND INNS. Accommodations on the island of Martha's Vineyard are varied. From deluxe waterfront hotels to small guest houses on quiet wooded streets, the island has a special spot for everyone. The hotels, motels, and inns listed are grouped by towns, and within each town, facilities are grouped by price and amenities.

The peak season runs from mid-June to mid-September. Anyone wishing to visit Martha's Vineyard during those months should confirm reservations prior to arrival. The "off peak" seasons of the island are lovely in their own right. The pace is slower and the climate is milder than that of the mainland because the island is surrounded by water. For the budget-conscious traveler, this is the perfect time to visit—winter lodging is often half the peak season rate. Rates during the peak season, European Plan, double occupancy, run as follows: *Deluxe*, $60 and up; *Expensive*, $42–$60; *Moderate*, $30–$42; and *Inexpensive*; $18–$30.

VINEYARD HAVEN

Crocker Guest House. *Expensive.* Crocker Ave. 693-1151. On a quiet street, only a short walk from town and the beach, this is a guest house with classic charm and character. Open year-round.

Hanover House. *Expensive.* Close to town on the Vineyard Haven-Edgartown Rd. 693-1066. Newly renovated, with color TV and some housekeeping units. Open year-round.

Lothrop Merry House. *Expensive.* Directly on the Vineyard Haven Harbor. 693-1646. A typical, comfortable New England style inn. Fine views of the Sound. Open year-round.

Tisbury Inn. *Expensive.* A large inn on Main St., Vineyard Haven. 693-2200. Has a pool, health facilities, and restaurant (during the season). Open year-round.

Vineyard Harbor Motel. *Expensive.* Beach Rd. 693-3334. A modern motel with color TV, comfortable rooms, and a private beach on Vineyard Haven Harbor. Open year-round.

Waves Edge Motel. *Expensive.* Directly on the Vineyard Haven Harbor. 693-9695. A small, comfortable motel with a gift shop. Open mid-May to mid-Oct.

The Elms. *Moderate.* On the edge of the Main St. shopping district. 693-3767. A comfortable guest house of long standing. Open year-round.

Haven Guest House. *Moderate.* Main St. 693-3333. A quiet, comfortable house set back from the road on wooded land. Close to tennis. Open year-round.

High Haven House. *Moderate.* Summer St. 693-9204. Newly remodeled with both simple accommodations and apartments. Pool and TV. Open year-round.

OAK BLUFFS

Island Country Club. *Deluxe.* Overlooking Nantucket Sound and the Farm Neck Golf Club. 693-2002. Tennis, pool, golf, TV, dining room, and lounge. Open year-round.

Circuit House. *Expensive.* On Circuit Ave. 693-5053. Very comfortable, newly renovated and decorated rooms. Close to all the shops and restaurants in Oak Bluffs. Open year-round.

Island House. *Expensive.* 693-4516. Comfortable lodging in the center of Oak Bluffs. Dining room; lounge with excellent piano entertainment by owner. Open May to Sept.

Beach House. *Moderate.* Seaview Ave. 693-3955. Directly across the street from the town beach; close to tennis courts and Circuit Ave. Open mid-May to Oct.

Capricorn House. *Moderate.* On Beach Rd. across the street from the Oak Bluffs town beach. 693-2848. A large, comfortable house close to all the activities in town. Open year-round.

Martha's Vineyard Motor Inn. *Moderate.* Close to the Oak Bluffs Steamship terminal. 693-2500. Modern rooms with TV. Easy walk to all the restaurants and shops in town. Open mid-May to Oct.

Wesley House. *Moderate.* On the Harbor. 693-0135. This is the last of the great Victorian hotels that once graced the town of Oak Bluffs. Open May to Sept.

Captain's House. *Inexpensive.* On New York Ave. 693-9434. A large whaling captain's home that has been converted into a guest house. Five-minute walk to town and the beach. Open year-round.

EDGARTOWN

Chadwick House. *Deluxe.* 627-4435. Furnished with antiques, a carefully appointed inn in the town of Edgartown. Close to all the shops and restaurants. Open year-round.

Charlotte Inn. *Deluxe.* 627-4751. An atmosphere of quiet elegance and ease. The Edgartown Gallery and the Chez Pierre restaurant add to the fine character of this inn. Open year-round.

Harborside Inn. *Deluxe.* On the harbor. 627-4321. TV, pool, recreation room, sail and power boat rental, restaurant and lounge. One of the finest locations from which to watch the harbor activities. Open mid-May to Oct.

Harbor View Hotel. *Deluxe.* Overlooks the entrance to the harbor. 627-4333. The grande dame of the Edgartown hotels. A well-maintained, turn-of-the-century hotel with turn-of-the-century service and attention. Restaurant, lounge, pool, tennis. Open May to Nov.

Katama Shoes Inn. *Deluxe.* At South Beach (about 3 miles from town). 627-4747. A modern motel overlooking the Atlantic Ocean. Restaurant, lounge, pool, tennis, color TV. Open May to Oct.

Kelley House. *Deluxe.* 627-4394. One of the oldest inns on the island. Expanded in the 70s, yet has kept the old inn charm and character. Restaurant, bar service, pool; tennis close by. Open year-round.

Point Way Inn. *Deluxe.* 627-8633. In 1979 this old captain's home was converted to an inn. With antique and reproduction furnishings, every detail is in place. Eleven working fireplaces, gazebo, croquet. Open year-round.

Shiretown Inn. *Deluxe.* 627-4283. A renovated inn and carriage house only a block from the harbor. Fine restaurant, lounge, TV. Open mid-Apr. to Oct.

Victorian. *Deluxe.* 627-4784. A Victorian inn. Family run, one block from the harbor. Close to all the shops and restaurants. Open mid-Apr. to Nov.

Captain Henry Colt House. *Expensive.* 627-4084. In the center of town.

Very comfortable, with a congenial hostess. One housekeeping unit. Open year-round.

Colonial Inn. *Expensive.* 627-4711. A large inn, one block from the harbor. Two restaurants, lounge with entertainment; easy walk to all parts of town. Open May to mid-Oct.

Edgartown Inn. *Expensive.* 627-4794. An historic old inn one block from the harbor and close to all the shops. The restaurant serves a fine home-made breakfast. Open Apr. to Oct.

UP ISLAND

Beach Plum Inn. *Deluxe.* 645-9454. On the hill above Menemsha, the inn sets an island standard for excellence. The room rate includes breakfast and dinner. Restaurant, tennis; close to beach. Open mid-June to mid-Sept.

Lambert's Cove Inn. *Expensive.* Lambert's Cove Rd. 693-2298. Once the central house of the largest estate on the island, the inn retains the open "estate" feeling. Hiking, bird-watching. Short drive to Lambert's Cove Beach (open to guests). Restaurant. Open May to Oct.

Menemsha Inn and Cottages. *Expensive.* 645-2521. A small inn with several housekeeping cottages situated on the wooded grounds. Overlooks Vineyard Sound. Private beach, tennis, dining room. Open mid-May to mid-Oct.

Ochsmark. *Expensive.* 645-9876. On the Moshup Trail, overlooking the dunes of Gay Head and the Atlantic Ocean. Pets accepted. Open June to Aug.

YOUTH HOSTELS. *American Youth Hostel. Inexpensive.* Box 157, West Tisbury. 693-2665. For touring cyclists the hostel has dorm accommodations for 85. No motor vehicles. Evenings usually involve spirited games of volleyball. Open Apr. to Nov.

DINING OUT. The visitor to the island of Martha's Vineyard can choose from a very diverse group of restaurants. From French cuisine to the freshest broiled swordfish available, the choices are all interesting and worth exploring. The restaurants have been grouped alphabetically within four price categories: *Deluxe, Expensive, Moderate,* and *Inexpensive.* These refer to the cost of the average meal for one person exclusive of beverages and tip. *Deluxe* is over $18.00. *Expensive* is $15.00 to $18.00. *Moderate* is $9.00 to $15.00, and *Inexpensive* is below $9.00.

One last and important note: Only the towns of Edgartown and Oak Bluffs allow liquor to be served in restaurants or sold. Tisbury, West Tisbury, Chilmark, and Gay Head are "dry." It is perfectly acceptable and legal in the "dry" towns to bring your own bottle, and many of the restaurants will provide set-ups. It is just a little of the Puritan ethic that has survived unscathed.

EDGARTOWN

Andrea's. *Deluxe.* Main St. 627-5850. A gourmet Italian restaurant. Since the seatings are limited, reservations should be made in advance. Open for dinner year-round.

Chez Pierre. *Deluxe.* South Summer St. in the Charlotte Inn. 627-8947. French cuisine in a garden/greenhouse setting. Impeccable service and an extensive wine list. Reservations a must. Open for dinner and Sunday brunch year-round.

The Dunes. *Deluxe.* At the Katama Shores Inn, 3 miles south of Edgartown. 627-8972. Overlooking the dunes of South Beach and the Atlantic Ocean, The Dunes is favored both for its cuisine and its view. An excellent wine list with a broad range of choices and vintages. Open for dinner May to Oct.

The Harborside Boathouse Bar and Navigator Room. *Expensive.* Main St. 627-4321. The Boathouse Bar is a casual eating spot on the Edgartown Harbor. For lunch, they char-broil burgers and steaks outside. The Navigator Room is above the bar. More formal, with a spectacular elevated view of the full Edgartown Harbor, its menu features fresh seafood. Open Apr. to Oct.

The Harbor View. *Expensive.* Starbuck Neck (3 blocks from Main St. on North Water St.). 627-4333. The Harbor View Restaurant, in the Harbor View Hotel, overlooks the entrance of the Edgartown Harbor. The grand hotel character is carried over to dining. Attentive service, excellent cuisine, and a view that is hard to beat. Open May to Oct.

Martha's Restaurant. *Expensive.* Main St. 627-8316. With upstairs and downstairs porches, this restaurant has a touch of the French café. Its carefully decorated interior combines flowered prints with blond wood. The menu includes a number of dishes that have little unexpected touches in the garnishes. Open Apr. to Nov. for lunch and dinner.

The Seafood Shanty. *Expensive.* Dock St. 627-8622. The Shanty is known for its fine, fresh seafood, its view of the Edgartown Harbor, and its singing waiters and waitresses. The three combine to make any evening there memorable. Open May to Oct. for lunch and dinner.

Beeftender. *Moderate.* Upper Main St. 627-8344. The name says it all. Fine cuts of beef—with some seafood for those who must—and a great salad bar. Open for dinner year-round.

The Kelley House. *Moderate.* Kelley St. 627-4394. In the traditional manner of the inns of New England, the Kelley House serves excellent meals in a congenial way that makes you feel at home. Open year-round.

Lawry's Seafood. *Moderate.* Upper Main St. 627-8857. Operating their own fishing boats insures that Lawry's has some of the freshest seafood on the island. A comfortable, family-style atmosphere. Open for lunch and dinner Apr. to Oct.

Barbershop Deli. *Inexpensive.* North Water St. 627-8761. A New York-style deli, complete with spirited discussions of the latest political issue. Open year-round.

OAK BLUFFS

Anthony's. *Deluxe.* Beach Rd. (3/4 mile from Circuit Ave. on the road to Edgartown). 693-3330. Once the clubhouse and bar for the Island Country Club (now Farm Neck), Anthony's overlooks parts of the golf course and Nantucket Sound. Reservations suggested. Entertainment often on the weekends in season. Open for lunch and dinner year-round.

David's Island House. *Moderate.* Circuit Ave. 693-4519. With stained glass and lots of wood, the Island House re-creates the Victorian days of Oak Bluffs. The lounge has comfortable Victorian seatings around coffee tables. The owner, David Crohan, is a remarkable pianist and plays nightly during the season. Open for lunch and dinner May to Oct.

Ocean View. *Moderate.* Chapman Ave. (one block from the Oak Bluffs Harbor). 693-2207. "Generous" best describes the Ocean View. Thick-cut swordfish steaks, fresh sautéed scallops, and large sandwiches. Open year-round.

Orient Express. *Moderate.* Circuit Ave. 693-3634. The only Chinese restaurant on the island serves excellent dishes from several regions of China. A small restaurant, reservations are a good idea. Open for dinner Apr. to Dec.

Cozy's. *Inexpensive.* Circuit Ave. 693-2454. Cozy's "Hoagies" are an island sandwich favorite. Great ice cream for dessert. Open May to Oct.

Linda Jean's. *Inexpensive.* Circuit Ave. 693-4093. A family-style restaurant, Linda Jean's is well known among island residents for its home-style cooking and unpretentious atmosphere. Open year-round.

Papa John's Restaurant. *Inexpensive.* Circuit Ave. 693-1400. Made to order for families, Papa John's has something for everyone. Pizza, subs, and Italian dishes. Lots of large tables. Open for lunch and dinner year-round.

UP ISLAND

The Beach Plum Inn. *Deluxe.* Menemsha. 645-9454. The Beach Plum Inn is a small family inn that serves a very limited number of diners each evening. Reservations must be made well in advance. Open Memorial Day to mid-Sept. for dinner.

La Grange at the Cornerway. *Expensive.* Bettlebung Corner in Chilmark. 645-9098. A little French restaurant tucked in among the shops at the Cornerway. Excellent service and cuisine. Open May to Sept. for lunch and dinner.

The Home Port Restaurant. *Moderate.* Menemsha. 645-2679. On the water in Menemsha, with the fishing boats just out the window. Some of the freshest seafood on the island. Family-style dining. Reservations are suggested. Open May to Oct. for dinner.

Aquinnah Shop. *Inexpensive.* On the Cliffs at Gay Head. 645-9654. A small, family-run restaurant, the Aquinnah Shop has, perhaps, the most unspoiled view on the island. Overlooking the Gay Head Cliffs and the Atlantic Ocean, the simple menu is more than adequate. A spot from which to watch the sunset. Open May to Sept.

VINEYARD HAVEN

Le Grenier. *Deluxe.* Main St. 693-4906. Above the Patisserie Française on Main St. Le Grenier serves authentic French cuisine with classical continental flair. No credit cards. Open May to Oct. for dinner only.

Ocean Club. *Expensive.* Five Corners. 693-4763. An open, airy restaurant with huge potted palms. Specializes in the preparation of native seafood. Each seafood dish is offered with a variety of different sauces. A raw bar serves the full complement of local shellfish. Reservations for six or more. Open for dinner May to Oct.

The Black Dog Tavern. *Moderate.* Beach Rd. 693-9223. On the waterfront, the Black Dog Tavern is a local favorite. With a fine view of the harbor and imaginative food, this is a good bet. No reservations. Open year-round.

Patisserie Française. *Moderate.* Main St. 693-3037. A French-style sidewalk café, serving fresh pastries, omelettes, and simple sandwiches. No credit cards. Open May to Oct.

Martha's Vineyard Deli. *Inexpensive.* Main St. 693-3899. Fine deli with comfortable porch outdoors. Open year-round.

The Spaghetti Pot. *Inexpensive.* State Rd. (⅓ mile from Main St.). 693-3255. A casual, family-style restaurant with a wide selection of pizza and Italian food. Open for lunch and dinner year-round.

 NIGHT LIFE. The island of Martha's Vineyard is not noted for its wild nights. Most people come to the island to get away from the hustle and bustle of city life. There are several bars in Oak Bluffs and Edgartown that have low-key entertainment during the season. The easiest way to find out where there is entertainment is to look in the newspaper.

There is one club on the island, the **Hot Tin Roof,** at the Airport. The Hot Tin Roof brings in big name groups for concerts. Tickets are available at outlets in every town on the island and through the Hot Tin Roof, 693-1137.

NANTUCKET

by

GARY HOLMES

Gary Holmes is a native Nantucketer and a former reporter for Channel 3, Nantucket's cable television station, and the Inquirer and Mirror, *and island's weekly newspaper. He has published several stories about Nantucket in both* Cape Cod Life *and* Boston magazine.

All resort communities claim to be a ''world apart'' from the rest of civilization, but Nantucket, more than most, is truly something special. It is geographically isolated, well away from the rest of America; it is a place where history and the present exist in happy harmony and where man is constantly aware of his natural environment; it is a small town, a sophisticated playground, and a retreat all rolled into one.

Like the rest of Cape Cod, Nantucket has had its share of economic ups and downs. But because Nantucket is an island community located 20 miles out to sea, its swings between prosperity and depression have been more pronounced. At one point, because of its whaling industry, Nantucket was the third-richest seaport in Massachusetts, surpassed only by Boston and Salem. But later, the island's economy suffered such a deep and prolonged depression that it was in virtual hibernation, caught in a Brigadoon-like time warp. Finally, at the end of the 19th century, Nantucket developed a reputation as a genteel sort of summer resort. Nevertheless, because of its physical isolation, the island changed more slowly than the Cape. It wasn't until the end of World War II, when Americans had better transportation and more leisure time at their disposal, that Nantucket saw its dramatic rebirth and became one of the premier vacation spots in the Northeast.

It was that long hibernation that preserved Nantucket's character. For nearly 100 years, Nantucket remained unchanged and undeveloped, retaining its natural beauty and architectural charm. Through careful planning and good luck, Nantucket has remained a sort of living museum. Much of the island's downtown (although there are several villages scattered throughout the island there is really only one town) is the same as it was a century ago: the elegant mansions of the whaling captains still line the cobblestoned streets. Except for automobiles and electric streetlights, little of modern life is readily apparent; there are no traffic lights, parking meters, neon signs, or fast-food outlets on the island. On a fog-shrouded night, it is easy to visualize the Nantucket that existed in the 1840s when Herman Melville roamed the streets on his way to a whaleship.

Although Nantucket is now accessible by air, the first-time visitor really should travel to the island the way it's been done for centuries—by boat. You should take the slow ferry to Nantucket for the same reason you sip, rather than gulp, fine wine—to savor the experience. There's nothing like rounding Brant Point lighthouse, the Nantucket Harbor sentry, and seeing the tightly bunched gray-shingled or clapboard houses to realize what a different world you have entered. In the summer, ferries leave from Hyannis and Woods Hole (only Woods Hole in the winter). Unless the weather is bad and the seas are rough, the two- or two-hour-and-45-minute trip will be smooth enough for all but the weakest stomachs. The boats are fairly comfortable (get there early just to get a seat) and on a sunny day, travelers can sit on the deck and work on their suntans.

The Nantucket experience can be enjoyed on many levels—as a trip through a historical treasure; as a relaxing tour of a remarkable landscape of rolling moors, clean beaches, and calm ponds; or as an exciting experience in a popular and sophisticated resort, complete with lively nightclubs, tennis and golf clubs, and various water activities. Still, Nantucket's appeal is more subtle than it is practical. More than anything else, it serves as a reminder that human settlement does not have to be in conflict with the natural environment. There is little that is unattractive or out of proportion on this lonely, windswept island. Man and his surroundings are in a delicate balance that makes Nantucket one of the last true outposts of the civilized world.

Origins

What is now the island of Nantucket started out as the debris of the glacier that created Cape Cod 10,000 years ago. Nantucket marks the southernmost advance of the mass of ice and stone that covered the northern part of North America.

For hundreds of years, the only inhabitants of Nantucket were Indians, members of the Algonquin tribe. Historians now guess there were about 1,500 Indians on the island when white men arrived. The Indians were hunters and fishermen, peaceful, simple folk. None of them remain today. The last Nantucket Indian died in the 1840s, his tribe wiped out by disease, alcohol, and contamination by the European people. All that's really left of Nantucket's original inhabitants are some artifacts and the names they gave to the different parts of the island—*Wauwinet, Madaket, Quaise, Miacomet*. The word *Nantucket* is supposedly the Indian word for "far away island."

Bartholomew Gosnold discovered Nantucket in 1602 as he explored Cape Cod's outer waters. But it wasn't until 1660 that the island was actually settled. That year Thomas Macy sold most of his rights to the island to nine colonists who moved their families here for a variety of commercial and religious reasons.

The original settlement, then called Sherburne, was located near what has since become Capaum Pond, close to Dionis Beach on the north side of the island. But soon thereafter, the settlers moved their houses into the present town of Nantucket because what had been a harbor when they settled there had become a pond.

As would be expected of a group that would pick up and move to a nearly barren island, the original settlers comprised a hardy bunch—adventurous, ambitious, determined, and demanding. From the beginning, that drive and determination exhibited itself in factionalism and discord; there were many natural leaders in a community that needed only one. The island's first feud sprang from the community's legal structure. The island's political and economic system in the 1600s was based on the number of shares incorporated in the Proprietorship that governed it. Full shares had been awarded to the first settlers and each shareholder had one vote in community affairs. Later, half shares were created to induce tradesmen to move to the island, and eventually, the half-share men began to resent their lack of equal representation in town government.

Two men who are now remembered almost reverently for their other achievements were at the center of the first Nantucket feud. Leading what became Nantucket's landed gentry was the island patriarch, Tristram Coffin. Coffin and his descendents were a prolific clan; by 1820, there were over 10,000 Coffins on Nantucket and the mainland who could trace their lineage to this man. Coffin worked hard, using all his political, economic, and social power to gain control of the island. Among those who stood in his way was Peter Foulger, the grandfather of Benjamin Franklin. A respected artisan, poet, Indian interpreter, and preacher, Foulger was also Clerk of the Court. When he refused to give up the court records to Coffin and his faction, as the Governor of New York had ordered (the island was originally under New York jurisdiction), he was sent to jail and spent a year and a half awaiting trial. Folger's ally, John Gardner, finally succeeded in convincing the Governor to drop the charges and release the 61-year-old prisoner. The dispute was eventually resolved and the marriage of Tristram Coffin's grandson, Jethro Coffin, and John Gardner's daughter sealed the good will. As a wedding present, the Coffins donated wood from their New Hampshire saw mill and Gardner donated land on Sunset Hill and a house was built. That house still stands, and is, in fact, known as the island's oldest house. It is now owned by the Nantucket Historical Association and is open to the public in the summer.

Because Nantucket's land is sandy, the island was never a successful farming community. The islanders were forced to the sea. Nantucketers first became interested in whaling in the 1670s, when a whale strayed into Nantucket Harbor, where it was killed and its parts made into useful products. Nantucket's whaling skills developed slowly, but by 1730, Nantucket was the whaling capital of the world. Her men sailed the seven seas on voyages lasting up to three years, while the women stayed home, raising families, operating small businesses, and generally minding the island.

For Nantucket, whaling was a true community enterprise. Local tradesmen produced all the goods that were used on the ships and the ships themselves were completely self-sufficient. The whalers could catch, kill, and boil down their prey aboard the ships. Soon Nantucket began doing business directly with London, bypassing Boston and New York. It was a lucrative period.

It was also an adventuresome period. Even though Nantucket is located in the Atlantic Ocean, the two most prominent buildings on its Main Street—the Pacific National Bank and the Pacific Club—are named for a more distant body of water. That strikes no Nantucketer as odd since island ships made some of their greatest conquests in that ocean. In fact, the far-roaming Nantucket ships discovered many unchartered islands in the Pacific. And many of the most exciting American sea adventures were experienced by Nantucket men. In fact, the greatest sea tale of them all—Herman Melville's *Moby Dick*—is based on the true story of a whale that rammed a Nantucket ship, *The Essex*.

The Quaker Influence

Although whaling played a dominant role in the development of the Nantucket character in the 18th and 19th centuries, there was another influence that played as important a part—the Quaker religion. The original settlers were practically religious outcasts from the Puritan Massachusetts Bay Colony but they were not Quakers. Quakerism didn't take hold on Nantucket until several decades after the island was settled, but once it did catch on, it became a very strong force. By the end of the 18th century more than half the island's population belonged to the Society of Friends. On the whole, the Quakers were in the highest class of Nantucket society—the whaling captains, the merchants, the proprietors. They were very stern and humorless, but they did the hard work that had to be done to make Nantucket a prosperous community. As a social and moral force, Quakerism has pretty much died out on Nantucket. However, the Quaker Meeting House on Fair Street is still used for Sunday meetings during the summer.

Nantucket's prosperity was constantly in danger, despite the hard work of the Quakers. The island was under siege by the British navy during the American Revolution, for instance, and could not get whaleships in or out of the harbor. Because of the heavy influence of Quaker pacifism, the island remained neutral during the long war; those Nantucket men who fought on the side of the colonists were disowned by the Society of Friends meeting. Again, the island's population was split between the haves and have-nots, between the loyalists and the patriots, and meanwhile, everyone suffered economic losses.

The Decline of Whaling

But with the end of the war, Nantucket came into its real golden years. The mansions that line Main Street and Orange Street testify to the wealth of the whaling captains and merchants. Then, in the 1840s, several calamities struck and the island was suddenly as poor as it had been before whaling got off the ground. First, the town of Nantucket's waterfront and main business district were razed by fire in 1846. The Great Fire, as it came to be known, lasted several days and destroyed millions of dollars' worth of property. Then the gold rush of 1849 attracted many of the island's most ambitious men, who decided they'd rather pursue their fortunes on the land. Furthermore, the discovery of petroleum decreased the demand for whale oil. And to make matters worse, shifting sand bars partially closed Nantucket Harbor so only smaller boats could get to the island's wharves. Most captains then decided to ship out of deeper ports like New Bedford. Nantucket's last whaleship, the *Oak,* sailed in 1869, never to return. The island's economic decline was matched by a drop in population. In 1850, Nantucket boasted 8,000 citizens; by 1870, that number had dropped to 3,500. The island's year-round population stayed at 3,500 until the 1960s.

The swift decline sent the island into a state of suspended animation—still living, still breathing, but not growing or changing. Farming proved as unprofitable as ever. Islanders did have some success with sheep raising and cranberry growing, but neither industry could support the whole island. The island's eventual economic salvation—tourism—appeared in the mid-1870s, when rich mainland visitors started to stay for the summer. In the 1890s, Nantucket became a particularly popular spot for show people. In fact, one of the main streets in the village of 'Sconset still has the name Broadway in honor of the visitors who used to stay there. Except for the brief period when actors, directors, writers, and producers crammed 'Sconset, the "summer people" who came to Nantucket were for years and years rich but not flashy, and they enjoyed the slow-paced and close-knit qualities of the island. They bought and renovated old captain's homes or they built their own homes along the shore. The island was still very isolated, and, despite the yearly return of the well-to-do, property values were still low. Even in the early 1960s, 100-acre tracts of land in the undeveloped part of the island were sold for just a few hundred dollars.

All that changed dramatically in the mid-1960s, however. Americans as a whole were more affluent and transportation to the island became more convenient. Most importantly, Walter Beinecke's Sherburne Associates started buying hotels, business property, and the crumbling waterfront. A first-class marina was made out of the wharves that once serviced whaleships. The hotels were renovated and tourist-oriented shops opened all over town. As more and more tourists visited the island and decided they, too, would like to be a part of the summer community, property values sky-rocketed. Nantucket is no longer the sleepy summertime refuge it once was. Every year, old-timers and even some newcomers complain that over-commercialization and overcrowding have spoiled their vacation paradise. To combat overdevelopment, various conservation groups have attempted to purchase tracts of open space. The effort has succeeded to a certain extent; a quarter of the island's land is now owned by conservation organizations. So, while Nantucket might not be as undeveloped as it once was, it has fared better than most resort communities on the Cape. The charm, the simple elegance, the history, and the beauty are still there. In fact, Nantucket chauvinists have their saying: That Cape Cod is now as nice as the rest of New England used to be; that Martha's Vineyard is now as nice as Cape Cod used to be; but that Nantucket is still as nice as Martha's Vineyard used to be.

Exploring Nantucket

There is much for a tourist to do here. Depending upon your inclination, you can spend several days delving into Nantucket's past, you can view the scenic splendor of the island's moors, beaches, or ponds, or you can browse in the many shops and galleries located throughout the downtown area. There is no set length of time you should spend on the island. Many first-time visitors take a "day trip" from Woods Hole or Hyannis to get a quick taste of the island. Others stay for a weekend, a week, a month, or an entire summer. In fact, many day-trippers have immediately fallen in love with the island and decided to buy property, making Nantucket their permanent summer vacation home.

If you are coming to the island for the first time, you might consider taking a bus tour. Tickets can usually be purchased aboard the ferries on the trip over or on the dock itself. Smaller, more personalized tours are offered by guides who drive Volkswagen vans. The guides are usually parked in the downtown area and arrangements and reservations are made easily. Naturally, bus and van tours provide only a general overview of the island's history and geography, but within a few hours, you can see many sites that you might like to return to when you have more time.

The best way to explore Nantucket town is on foot. Start at the waterfront. Sometimes, especially in the off-season when a storm is brewing in the Atlantic, fishing boats will be tied at the docks. But mostly you will see very large, very beautiful, and very expensive yachts in the Nantucket marina. Straight Wharf, Old South Wharf, and Swain's Wharf were all built for the island's whaling fleet and all fell into disrepair before Sherburne Associates bought and reconstructed them. There is still some debate among

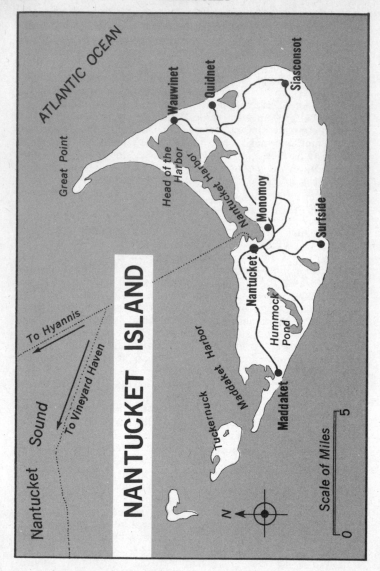

old-time Nantucketers about whether or not the conversion of the wharves into a tourist-oriented marina destroyed the character of the waterfront, but there is little doubt that the reconstruction had a major economic impact on the island. You can stroll up and down the wharves, looking at the boats and the people on them, or you can visit the shops and galleries located along the boardwalk. Clothes, gifts, crafts, food, and art are available at these shops.

Since Main Street leads right down to Straight Wharf, it is easy to walk to the island's main business district. Just follow the cobblestoned street up the slight hill. The island's Main Street is old-fashioned and charming; the buildings are brick and the street is lined with shady elm trees. Downtown is not as tourist dominated as the waterfront, but there are still plenty of stores and restaurants to enjoy.

Unless your visit is very brief, you should make an effort to visit the Whaling Museum on Broad Street. To get there from Main Street, follow South Water Street, which begins at the Pacific Club. The museum has a fabulous collection of scrimshaw, as well as many whaling artifacts and the skeleton of a whale that washed ashore in the 1960s. Next to the Whaling Museum is the Peter Foulger Museum, named after Benjamin Franklin's grandfather, which documents life on the island during the whaling days.

The Mansions

Walk back up Broad Street and take a left on Centre Street. During the whaling days, Centre Street was nicknamed "Petticoat Row" because many women ran shops there while their husbands were away at sea. The tradition persists. Although not all the stores on Petticoat Row are run by women, a good number of them are. Continue down Centre Street back to Main Street and turn right after passing the Pacific National Bank. Once past the bank, you are out of the central business district and into old-time Nantucket elegance. To get a good idea of Nantucket's wealth during its heyday, follow the cobblestoned street for a while and enjoy the captains' mansions. About a quarter of a mile along the street are some houses of note. On the right side of the street are three identical brick mansions built by whaling merchant Joseph Starbuck for his three sons. These "Three Bricks" were originally identical inside and out, but over the years changes have been made. Of the three houses, only the center one—the "Middle Brick"—is still owned by a direct descendent of Joseph Starbuck. Across the street from the Three Bricks are two Greek Revival mansions, also built by Joseph Starbuck. One of the mansions was donated to the Nantucket Historical Association and is open to the public.

The Main Street mansions are probably the most impressive architectural sights on the island, but wandering down the side streets is also a delight. One of the most impressive aspects of Nantucket is its architectural unity. More than 800 houses in the downtown area were built before 1840—the largest concentration of pre-Civil War construction anywhere in the country, with the exception of planned or controlled communities like Williamsburg and Sturbridge Village. What is remarkable about Nantucket is that it remains more than a living museum; it is a thriving, vibrant community. Laws have been made to protect the island's historical charm. In 1955, the island's downtown was designated an "Old Historic District" and since then, all architectural plans have to be submitted to an elected commission that is empowered to preserve the architectural unity of the town. The Historic District was expanded in 1971 to include the entire town.

Bicycling Around the Island

Another good way to see the island is by bicycle. Bikes can be rented at several locations throughout the downtown area or brought over on the ferry for a small fee. Moped rentals are becoming increasingly popular despite the opposition of local officials. Several years ago, the town tried to ban all moped rentals completely but was overturned in federal court. Although mopeds can now be rented legally, people should use them with caution. Nantucket roads are narrow and sandy and riders cannot control mopeds as easily as they can maneuver bicycles.

A visitor can see more of the town on a bike, since he can cover more ground than on foot, but he is not going so fast that he misses things, as so often happens in an automobile. All of the island's villages can be reached by a bicyclist in reasonably good shape, but there are three main destinations for the Nantucket pedaler: Madaket, Surfside, and Siasconset. Madaket is located at the western end of the island. To get there, follow Main Street to its end to a sign pointing to Madaket Road. This is probably the most arduous of the Nantucket bike trips because the six-mile road is very hilly. Also, there is no bicycle path, so you have to be careful of oncoming cars; the road curves quite a bit. Despite the difficulties, Madaket is a popular destination. The scenery along the way is beautiful and the Madaket Beach probably has the biggest surf on the island. There are also two ponds on Madaket Road where it is possible to catch crabs and eels.

Surfside is an easy bicycle trip away from town. The three-mile route is flat and a bicycle path is available most of the way. To get there from town, ride up Main Street to the white Hadwen-Satler mansion. Turn left on Pleasant Street and follow that road for a mile to the intersection known as five corners. Bear right on Atlantic Avenue and follow that street until you reach the bike path. Stay on the bike path until you reach the beach, which is located directly south of Nantucket town. Surfside is one of the island's most popular beaches. Not surprisingly, it also has substantial surf. You'll find a snack bar and a bath house at Surfside.

Biking to Siasconset (or "'Sconset" as it's known to islanders) is another ambitious task, but the round trip can be accomplished in an hour or two. To get there, take Orange Street, which intersects with Main Street across from the Pacific National Bank. At the first milestone (which indicates it is a mile from the bank), turn onto Milestone Road and get on the bikepath, following the signs to 'Sconset. There are some hills, but the six-mile trip is fairly easy. 'Sconset itself is the only real village on the island except for Nantucket town. There is a village square, a post office, a general store, a gas station, and several places to eat at this easternmost spot on the island. During the spring and early summer, 'Sconset is famous for its wild and cultivated roses. To return to town, bicyclists can either go back via the Milestone Road or take the longer scenic route along Polpis Road. To get to Polpis Road, go through the village square and turn right onto Broadway. Follow that road to the end, taking another left and following the signs that say Nantucket town. On the right you can see Sankaty Light, one of the three Coast Guard-operated lighthouses on Nantucket. The road will eventually bear to the left, so follow the signs to Polpis or to Nantucket. At one time Polpis was one of the island's agricultural centers. Only a few farms now remain, but the area is still beautiful. Also visible from Polpis Road are the island's moors, which can be seen on the south side of the road (the left as you are headed back to town). Nantucket is one of the few places outside Scotland where moors like this can be seen.

When to Visit Nantucket

Summer is the obvious time to visit Nantucket, but the island can be enjoyable in any season. It takes more imagination to appreciate Nantucket in the winter: it is cold and even more isolated than in the summer. Yet there is a brooding beauty to the island in the winter months and the community draws together. The wind howls over the closed-up grey-shingled and clapboard houses that seem to huddle together. The rough surf pounds the south shore of the island. If you have a romantic inclination and are prone to solitary walks, the island will hold great charm for you in the winter. For one thing, the town is virtually deserted; the summertime crush is gone and you can sightsee without having to deal with large crowds of people. It's easier to find a place to stay in the winter, to arrange travel plans, and to meet year-round Nantucketers. Also, wintertime is the only period except late fall when you can eat fresh Nantucket bay scallops. From November to April, Nantucket Harbor is filled with boats fishing for the small but succulent scallop that grows so abundantly in the island's waters. This shellfish is available at local restaurants throughout the summer; if they are cooked well, only the discerning palate can tell they've been frozen. Still, the true aficionado of Nantucket scallops will buy them only in the winter from a fisherman who has just finished shucking them in his shanty.

Spring is also a wonderful time to come to Nantucket. Because the winter is so severe, Nantucketers appreciate and celebrate the blossoming of the new season that much more. One by one, the restaurants and shops open, getting ready for the upcoming summer. People are the friendliest during the spring; they're not so busy yet that they can't smile, say hello, or stop to chat. Day-trippers begin coming to the island in May, but the numbers are manageable and comfortable. Spring also brings the return of the Nantucket flowers, especially the roses and daffodils.

By mid-June, the summer season is in full swing. There are parties every night, each bulging ferry unloads more cars and tourists, and prices for everything from lodging to food to gift items are sky high. But everyone who stays on the island for even the shortest time manages to find a special place away from the hustle and bustle of the crowds. That's why year after year, the rich, the famous, the socially ambitious, and the artistically inclined merrily pad down Main Street in get-ups so grubby you can't distinguish them from the old salts.

The crowds begin to thin out after Labor Day. Many people think September and October are the best months to visit the island; the weather is still warm but the intensity of the summer season is over. Most of the historical sites, restaurants, and other tourist attractions remain open until Columbus Day, so there is still plenty to see and do. Among the biggest promoters of visiting Nantucket in the fall is the Nantucket Island Chamber of Commerce. Although the organization has a vested interest in seeing that tourism increases in the off-season, what it writes in a brochure sent to potential visitors is none the less true: "As the fall gives way to Indian Summer, the Island becomes a rare place indeed. The air retains its warmth but has an added tang in morning and evening; the moors take on colorings not unlike the rich tapestries or weaves of an ancient carpet, and the beaches offer long stretches of seascape, with the surf breaking on the white sands or gently washing the more sheltered shore along Nantucket Sound. Rutted roads beckon on every hand and the changing hues of the blackberry, beach plum, and wild grape vines challenge each other as they blend with the green of the gnarled pines."

Hints on How to Appreciate the Island

Although many different crafts are offered for sale on the island, two are distinctively Nantucket. The first is scrimshaw—etchings, drawings, or carvings on ivory. This folk art developed among crewmen aboard whaling ships and has continued to the present day. Scrimshaw can be ornamental, with scenes etched on teeth, or jewelery, such as earrings, tie clasps, bracelets, or stick-pins. Most local gift shops carry some kind of scrimshaw. A second, increasingly popular, Nantucket craft is lightship basket making. These sturdy baskets were once made on lightships by crew members who had nothing better to do. For years, Nantucketers used them for everyday tasks. Then, someone decided to make them smaller, put a cover on them, and sell them as pocketbooks. The baskets are also often adorned with scrimshaw, adding to an already high expense. Partly because of their expense, and partly because they are so closely identified with Nantucket, the lightship basket pocketbook has become a status symbol and can be seen on the arms of women all over the world.

Nantucket also has its own disease—babesiosis. This malaria-like illness is transmitted by the bite of a deer tick and shows up several weeks later. For some reason, it has been diagnosed only on Nantucket and in the Balkans. Hardest hit by babesiosis, which strikes about half a dozen victims every year, are the elderly and those without spleens.

Among Nantucket's many traditions is a special tolling of the town clock every day at 7 A.M., 12 noon, and 9 P.M. At those times, the Unitarian Church bell tolls 52 times after ringing the time of the day. The origin of the tradition is obscure, but according to the man who last rang the bells by hand (it is now run electrically), the bells were struck for three minutes every day to awaken the town, tell the people to break for lunch, and to send them to bed.

To find out more about what's happening on Nantucket, turn to several sources: The *Inquirer and Mirror,* the local newspaper that is published every Thursday afternoon; Channel 3, a local origination cable television station that has morning and evening newscasts; the bulletin board outside the Hub newspaper store located at the intersection of Main and Federal streets; and several tourist-oriented magazines published in the summer, including *Nantucket Holiday* and *Nantucket Vacation Guide.*

PRACTICAL INFORMATION FOR NANTUCKET

HOW TO GET THERE. Because Nantucket is an island, there are special problems associated with getting there. And because it's so far out to sea, many visitors to Cape Cod never make it to Nantucket. But if you're willing to put up with a little inconvenience, it's certainly a worthwhile place to visit.

Most people travel to Nantucket by boat—the price is about one-third the cost of flying from Hyannis. During the summer, the *Steamship Authority* (540-2022) operates its ferries out of two locations, the Pleasant Street Dock in Hyannis, and the Steamship Authority dock in Woods Hole. In the dead of winter, the Hyannis terminal is closed and all Authority traffic runs from Woods Hole. Spring and fall traffic is variable from either location. The ride takes two hours from Hyannis and two hours and 45 minutes from Woods Hole. The large Authority vessels serve as the island's lifeline since they also bring in freight and cars. Vehicle reservations for the summer must be made far in advance. If you cannot get your car on the boat, you can leave it at the Authority parking lots. The *Hy-Line* boat line (775-7185) offers the only other boat service to Nantucket, from the Ocean Street Dock in Hyannis. The smaller Hy-Line boats run primarily in the summer and cater to day-trippers and short-term visitors. Hy-Line vessels do accept bicycles, but no cars.

The only other way to visit Nantucket is by air, which is much quicker than by boat. It takes 20 minutes from Hyannis, 45 minutes from Boston, and just over an hour from New York City by plane. However, the fare is much more expensive than the boat ride and many people are afraid to fly in the small planes that service Nantucket. Nantucket has been served off and on by several different commuter airlines, but the ones that have the longest track record are *Wills Air* (771-1470) *Gull Air* (800-352-7191), *PBA* (800-352-3132), and *New York Air* (516-454-0353).

Travel plans to Nantucket are often disrupted by the weather. Fog can ground flights, while heavy seas can prevent boats from reaching the island. Boat traffic is sometimes halted for up to two weeks in the winter if it's cold enough to freeze the water in the harbor. However, demand for limited boat and plane space, rather than weather, is the biggest worry facing island visitors. Make reservations early, especially if you plan to travel on a Friday or Sunday. Car reservations are tight all summer, but especially so near the end of the month. Even day-trippers, who buy boat tickets on the day of the trip, are well advised to arrive at the dock early to make sure they get on the excursion they want.

HOW TO GET AROUND. The town of Nantucket is compact enough that you don't need a car. In fact, Nantucket officials advise visitors, especially short-time visitors, to leave their cars on the mainland and either **walk** or **bike** about the island. There are only a few roads of any note on Nantucket: running west from town, *Madaket Road;* running south, *Hummock Pond* and *Surfside Roads;* and running east, *Milestone* and *Polpis Roads.* Bike paths run along the Milestone and Surfside Roads. While bicycling is an easy way to get around the island, stay on the asphalt roads. Dirt roads become rutted, sandy, and very difficult to negotiate after a while. Renting bikes is an old Nantucket tradition. Two island businesses located near Steamboat Wharf that have been renting bikes for generations are *Young's Bicycle Shop* (6 Broad Street, 228-1151) and *Cook's Cycle* (6 South Beach Street, 228-0800). Both places make reservations, especially for a large number of bicycles.

TOURIST INFORMATION. The *Nantucket Information Bureau* (22 Federal Street, 228-0925) provides walk-in service to tourists who need directions, advice, or answers to most questions about Nantucket. The bureau also keeps a list of last-minute cancellations from guest houses or hotels. For advance planning, the bureau prints a booklet listing guest houses, motels, hotels, and rental cottages. The *Nantucket Island Chamber of Commerce* (The Pacific Club, 228-1700) also provides walk-in service and sells a more comprehensive book than the Information Bureau.

RECOMMENDED READING. The romance of Nantucket has inspired writers for years. There are perhaps more books written about Nantucket than any other small town in America. The list starts with *Moby Dick,* Herman Melville's well-known tale of a Nantucket whale ship and her captain's quest for the white whale. Book lovers will find two stores on Nantucket that offer a wide variety of books, including a complete list of Nantucket publications. For summer reading, or any other reading, check out *Mitchell's Book Corner,* at the intersection of Main Street and Orange Street, and *The Bookworks,* at the intersection of Easton Street and Beach Street. Among some of the selections to browse through:

Sweet Anarchy, Benchley, Nathaniel, 1979. Although Nantucket is not mentioned by name in this satirical novel by year-round resident Benchley, Nantucketers have no problem recognizing the similarities between the activities in the book and their own unsuccessful attempt to secede from the state during the late seventies. *Nantucket Island,* Gambee, Robert, Hastings House, 1978. A collection of black-and-white Nantucket photographs. *Nantucket: the Life of an Island,* Hoyt, Edwin, Stephen Greene Press, 1978. Informal, anecdotal history of Nantucket. *Nantucket in the Nineteenth Century,* Lancaster, Clay, Dover Publications, Inc., 1979. A collection of Nantucket photographs taken during the 1800s. *Nantucket! Nantucket! Nantucket!* Mackay, Dick, Sankaty Head Press, 1981. Self-styled "insider's guide" to Nantucket that pulls no punches in telling one man's openion about what's right and what's wrong with Nantucket. *The History of Nantucket,* Macy, Obed, reprinted by Research Reprints, Inc.,

1970; first published in 1835. *The Nantucket Way,* Mooney, Robert, and Sigourney, Andre, Doubleday and Company, Inc., 1980. Two lawyers take a fond and often humorous look at the legal tradition on Nantucket. *Nantucket Then and Now,* Williams, Winston, Dodd, Mead, and Company, 1977. Concise and to-the-point history of the island.

 SEASONAL EVENTS. April. *Daffodil show* and *antique car parade.* The first big weekend of the year welcomes the much-needed spring to the island. Islanders compete for best daffodil and best daffodil arrangements in a two-day flower show. The weekend climaxes with an antique car parade from town to 'Sconset and a community picnic.

July. *Rose Sunday* at the Congregational Church; the church is decorated with wild roses for services that are very well attended. *House and Garden Tour;* island homeowners spruce up their fancy mansions and open them to the public for the benefit of the Nantucket Garden Club. *Independence Day* is the occasion for fireworks and old-fashioned family events.

August. *Carnival;* annual event behind the Finast store on Sparks Avenue. *Sand Castle Contest;* sponsored by the Chamber of Commerce, for families, kids, and mixed groups; at Jetties Beach. *Billfish Tournament;* boats from all over New England enter this Nantucket Angler's Club contest for the biggest swordfish. *St. Paul's Church Fair;* Fair Street is closed off for this large church fundraiser. *Sidewalk Art Show;* island artists set up paintings along the sidewalk for three-day sale; proceeds go to the Chamber of Commerce's scholarships for budding Nantucket artists.

September. *Nantucket Seafest,* at Steamboat Wharf; thousands of people attend for the chance to taste fish not normally eaten, like squid and monk fish.

December. *Christmas Shoppers' Stroll;* Main Street is blocked off for this event as Nantucket tries to re-create an old-fashioned small-town shopping atmosphere. *Annual candlelight service* at the Congregational Church; impressive musical display and dramatic presentation of the Christmas story.

 HISTORIC SITES AND MUSEUMS. The *Nantucket Historical Association* has a wide variety of museums, restored houses, and special exhibitions that are open every day in the summer and at reduced rates during the spring and fall. Among the sites:

The Whaling Museum, on Broad Street. Extensive collection of whaling memorabilia.

The Peter Foulger Museum, next to the Whaling Museum. Exhibitions on island life during the whaling days.

The Old Mill, on Mill Hill. Built in 1746, this restored mill still grinds corn with its original wooden machinery. The ground flour is for sale.

Lightship Nantucket, on Straight Wharf. This floating lighthouse is now permanently docked on Straight Wharf and is open to the public, displaying what life was like on the Nantucket Shoals.

The Oldest House, on Sunset Hill. Medieval-looking structure built in 1686 exhibits the life and architecture of the original settlers.

Macy Christian House, on Liberty St. Architecture of the early whaling days (1723).

The 1800 House, on Mill St. Former home of Nantucket's High Sheriff.

Hadwen Satler House, on Main St. Greek Revival house built in the 1840s. Opulent living during Nantucket's most prosperous whaling days.

The Greater Light, on Howard St. Originally a pig barn, this interesting house was converted into a comfortable home by two sisters during the Roaring Twenties.

The Friends Meeting House, on Fair St. The building is still used as a Quaker gathering place.

The Old Jail, on Vestal St. Summer only. Open at irregular times.

Other buildings and exhibits of interest, not operated by the Historical Association, are: The *Maria Mitchell House*, 1 Vestal St., the birthplace of America's first woman astronomer and discoverer of Mitchell's comet; the adjacent *Observatory and Mitchell Memorial Library;* and the *Lifesaving Museum* on Polpis Rd., with an extensive collection of nautical memorabilia in a replica of a 19th-century lifesaving station.

TOURS. *Barrett's Tours*, 20 Federal St., and *Island Tours*, at Straight Wharf. *Taxi drivers* will also give personalized tours. The island's taxi stands are at the airport, Steamboat Wharf, and beside the Pacific Club on Main St. Most of the tours take in the local historical sites and the outlying areas of the island. They usually last two or three hours.

SHOPPING. Antiques. *Island Attic Industries*, 99 Washington St., *Sylvia Antiques*, 12 Main St., *Tonkin of Nantucket*, 33 Main St.

Art Galleries. *Artists Association of Nantucket*, Kenneth Taylor Gallery, Straight Wharf; most local artists submit a painting to the weekly show. *The Main Street Gallery*, 50 Main St.; exhibits one artist at a time; show changes weekly. *South Wharf Gallery*, Old South Wharf; one or two artists on display each week.

Baked Goods. *The Nantucket Bake Shop*, 79 Orange St. *Something Natural*, 8 Federal St.; 228-0607; doubles as natural foods store. *The Upper Crust*, 7 West Creek Rd.

Clothing Stores. *Murray's Toggery Shop*, 60 Main St.; well-known home of the Nantucket Reds trousers; listed in the *Official Preppy Handbook* as "must" shopping. The *Nobby Shop*, 17 Main St.; casual clothes. *Upstairs/Downstairs*, 21 Main St.; Irish and English imports.

Gift Stores. *Coffin's Gift Shop*, 49 Main St.; open year-round. *The Crow's Nest*, Harbor Sq., Straight Wharf; games, posters, and jewelry. *The Seven Seas*, 46 Centre St.; rooms and rooms of souvenirs and gifts.

Handicrafts. *The Crafts Centre*, Quaker Rd.; needlework, baskets, carvings, and ceramics. *Craftmasters of Nantucket*, 7 India St.; leathercraft.

Nantucket Kiteman, Old South Wharf; world-renowned kites. *Nantucket Looms*, 16 Main St.; 228-1908; handwoven fabric.

Nantucket Lightship Baskets. *Four Winds Craft Guild*, Straight Wharf; *Michael Kane*, 18½ Sparks Ave.; *Tonkin of Nantucket*, 33 Main St.

Needle Arts. *Nantucket Needleworks*, 11 South Water St.; *Erica Wilson Needleworks*, 25 Main St.

Retail Stores. *Nantucket Ship's Chandlery*, Old South Wharf; nautical goods. *Nantucket Model Tees*, 22 Centre St.; tee shirts. *Penny Patch*, The Courtyard, Straight Wharf; penny candy. *Robinson's Five-and-Ten*, Lower Main St.; housewares, toys, beach accessories, souvenirs.

Scrimshaw. *Nancy Chase*, off Surfside Rd.; custom-made jewelry (rings, necklaces, tie clasps, key chains, etc.). *Whales World Gifts*, 33 Centre St.; also sells lightship baskets.

SPORTS. Nantucket offers few recreational sports in the winter, but during the summer, a wide variety of athletic opportunities are available. Except for high school sports in the off-season, however, there are no spectator sports.

Golf. *Miacomet Golf Club*, off Somerset Rd., public 9-hole golf course; bar, light lunch. *Siasconset Golf Club*. Milestone Rd.; 9 holes.

Sailing. *Erickson's Marine*, Steamboat Wharf; boat rentals. *Nantucket Sail, Inc.*, Swain's Wharf; lessons, boat rentals, harbor sail with captain.

Running. Nantucket's many dirt roads make it an ideal running location. The *Nantucket Easy Striders*, a group of local running enthusiasts, sponsor numerous races and even less formal "fun runs."

Tennis. *Nantucket Tennis Club*, off Cliff Rd.; four clay courts, individual instruction; membership available. *Raymor Raquet Club*, Field Ave. *Sea Cliff Tennis Club*, Beach St.; 9 Har-tru clay courts; instruction available; pro shop.

Windsurfing. *Island Windsurfing*, Jetties Beach; rentals.

FISHING AND SHELLFISHING. Surfcasting off the Nantucket beaches for bluefish and bass is the most popular type of fishing on Nantucket. The first bass of the year is usually landed in mid-May and the first bluefish arrives about two weeks later. By June, blues and bass are so abundant that several fishermen actually make a living casting for them. Although the fish can be caught from virtually any beach during the summer, the best locations are generally thought to be along the south shore, especially near Madaket. No license is required to fish from the Nantucket beaches. For more information on Nantucket fishing, or to rent equipment, contact *Fisher's Tackle Shop* on New Lane or *Barry Thurston's Tackle Shop* at Harbor Square. Sport fishing trips can also be chartered from *Gibby Nickerson*, on Straight Wharf.

Freshwater fishing is not as popular on Nantucket as ocean fishing, although there are several freshwater ponds where fish are available, such as Sesachacha Pond in 'Sconset, where white and yellow perch are caught.

During the right seasons, fishermen also catch eels and crabs from the Nantucket ponds, especially from the two small bridges on the Madaket Road. Because all the ponds are owned by the town of Nantucket instead of the state, no license is required to fish in them.

Shellfishing can be a worthwhile pastime on Nantucket with a little hard work and luck. Scallops, quahogs, soft-shell clams, oysters, and mussels are all available in the Nantucket waters. However, different rules and regulations apply to each type of shellfish and a license is required. The Selectmen publish a list of rules concerning the length of the season, allowable size, and amount of catch for each shellfish. That list can be obtained from the *Selectmen's* office in the Town Building, or from the *Shellfish Warden*, who has an office at the town pier on Washington Street.

PUBLIC BEACHES. Nantucket is blessed with miles and miles of beautiful beach. Islanders and long-time summer residents know out of the way and secluded spots where they can bathe and swim in privacy. But those locations are usually on private property and until the visitor becomes familiar with the ins and outs of Nantucket, he should stick with the public beaches, where lifeguards provide protection and bath houses or concession stands are available. Furthermore, going to a Nantucket public beach could not be easier; no stickers are required and there is no charge for parking. There are basically three types of beaches on Nantucket: the *harbor beach* where the water is shallow, warm, and very calm, therefore an ideal spot for children; the beaches on the *north shore* of the island, which are deeper and less protected but still very calm; and the *surf beaches* on the south shore, which have strong undertow and high waves.

There are two public beaches within Nantucket Harbor: the *Washington Street Beach*, on Washington Street Extension, and *Children's Beach*, on Harbor View Way. Both beaches have swings for children, while Children's Beach has public bathrooms and a concession stand.

On the north shore of the island are *Jetties Beach*, at the end of Beach Street, and *Dionis Beach*, on Dionis Road. Both have bath houses, but a concession stand is available only at Jetties Beach.

The surf beaches on the south side of the island are *Madaket Beach*, at the end of Madaket Road; *Cisco Beach*, at the end of Hummock Pond Road; *'Sconset Beach*, in Codfish Park; and *Surfside*, at the end of Surfside Road. Only Surfside has a bath house and a food stand.

PARKS AND FORESTS. Although there are two tracts of land on *Milestone Road* designated as state forest, the island offers little in the way of forest or park recreation. No picnic benches or cook-out grills are provided and in fact, during many summers the forest is closed to the public because of dry conditions. Furthermore, camping is *absolutely prohibited* on Nantucket. Campers are subject to arrest and fine under a town by-law that is strictly enforced.

WHAT TO DO WITH THE CHILDREN. Although there are only a few events specifically designed for children, Nantucket is an ideal place for them to visit. Children can appreciate any of the historical attractions on the island, enjoy exploring the town and outlying areas on their bikes, or play on the beaches under the supervision of the town's lifeguards. The *Nantucket Atheneum* (the town's library) on lower India Street, offers a children's program during the summer in its children's room. For more information, call 228-1110. The local Red Cross gives *swimming lessons* on Children's Beach weekday mornings. And a *day-care center* is operated by the Quaise Children's Day Care Center (228-4147).

 STAGE AND MUSIC. *Nantucket Theatre Workshop* presents four or five amateur stage productions during the winter. However, for one reason or another, summer theater has not taken root on the island since the former Straight Wharf Theatre burned down in 1975. Similarly, there is little professional music available on the island during the summer except for occasional concerts in the *Unitarian Church* or *Performance Center* in the Methodist Church. The *Nantucket Arts Council* offers an extensive concert season in the winter, however.

 HOTELS, MOTELS AND GUEST HOUSES. The Nantucket hotel tradition is more informal than it is on the mainland. There are no hotel or motel chains on the island; in fact, when Holiday Inn wanted to build a motel at the local airport, it was soundly turned down by the town. Almost none of the rooms anywhere on the island are air-conditioned. Unless otherwise noted, all the establishments listed below do not have televisions in the individual rooms. However, all are within easy walking distance of the harbor or some beach.

Guest houses are another popular type of overnight accommodation on Nantucket. They are usually located in big old houses that now rent rooms. In a guest house, the bathroom is down the hall and shared with the other guests, and the television is in the living room. Although staying at a guest house is slightly more inconvenient and less private, it is less expensive and a friendlier experience. For both hotels and guest houses, call well in advance for reservations. The summer is booked early. The following categories are based upon average summer rates for double occupancy, European Plan (room only): *Deluxe*, $60 and up; *Expensive*, $42–$60; and *Moderate*, $30–$42. For a complete listing of hotels, motels, guest houses, and cottages, call the *Nantucket Information Bureau* at 228-0925 for its annual booklet.

Beachside Motel. *Deluxe*. North Beach St. 228-2241. Televisions in each room. Nantucket's only real motel, if a motel is a facility where you park your car outside your room. However, since the motel is located within walking distance of the town and the beach, only about a third of the guests actually bring cars. Open all year; reduced rates in mid-Sept. through the rest of the year.

The Harbor House. *Deluxe.* South Beach St. 228-1500. Televisions, pool, restaurant, bar, meeting room facility. Located close to town. Complex resembles typical Nantucket street. Open April through Dec.; rooms slightly less expensive after Labor Day.

The Jared Coffin House. *Deluxe.* Broad St. 228-2400. Some televisions in rooms. Restaurant and bar. Located in the center of town in the mansion of a whaling merchant. Famous for "Twelve Days of Christmas"—special dinner every night for twelve nights. Open year-round; no off-season rates.

The White Elephant. *Deluxe.* Easton St. 228-2500. Televisions, restaurant, bar, pool, private dock in Nantucket Harbor. The most expensive hotel on Nantucket but a first-class operation. Located on Nantucket Harbor, with a good view. Within walking distance of town. Open mid-spring to mid-fall; reduced rates in the off-season.

The Gordon Folger Hotel. *Expensive.* Easton St. 228-0313. Restaurant and bar. Within walking distance of center of town. One of the last surviving big hotels built around the turn of the century. Open mid-spring to Columbus Day; reduced rates in off-season.

Hussey House. *Expensive.* 15 North Water St. 228-0747. Typical guest house, located downtown. Open May 1 through Oct. 25; reduced rates off-season.

Ships Inn. *Expensive.* Fair St. 228-0040. Restaurant and bar. Located on site of birthplace of early feminist Lucretia Coffin Mott. Open Easter to Thanksgiving, with reduced rates in off-season.

Stone Barn Inn. *Expensive.* North Beach St. 228-0723. Located near Jetties Beach in roomy stone building. Probably too far out of town to walk. Open spring to fall.

Wade Cottage. *Expensive.* 'Sconset. 257-6308. Guest house, with separate cottages available. Located out of town in village of 'Sconset. Spectacular view from 'Sconset Bluff. Open spring to Columbus Day; reduced rates off-season.

Nesbitt Inn. *Moderate.* Broad St. 228-0156. Guest house, located in center of town. Open year-round; no off-season rates.

For convenient and comprehensive listings of rooms still available, call *Nantucket Accommodations* at 228-9559. They have a lsit of last-minute cancellations and can make reservations at most hotels and rooming houses on Nantucket.

DINING OUT. Nantucket is blessed with a large number of very fine restaurants. As in most resort communities, however, dining out on Nantucket can be expensive. Nevertheless, it is still possible to get a decent meal at a reasonable price. Price categories are based on the average cost of a full meal, not including alcoholic beverages, tax, or tip. The categories are: *Deluxe,* $18 and up; *Expensive,* $15 and up; *Moderate,* $9–$15; and *Inexpensive,* under $9.

Company of the Cauldren. *Deluxe.* 7 India St. 228-4016. Serves a *prix* *fixe* menu nightly at 7 and 9:15 sittings. Intimate atmosphere accompanied by live harp music. Specializes in Northern Italian cuisine. No credit cards accepted; reservations requested. Closed Mon.

The Chanticleer. *Deluxe.* 'Sconset. 257-6231. Acknowledged to be the fanciest restaurant on Nantucket. Specializes in French cuisine. Elegant lunch in the garden from noon to 2:30. Dinner from 6:30 to 10. Closed Wed. Dinner reservations required.

The Opera House. *Deluxe.* 4 South Water St. 228-9755. A long-time Nantucket favorite. French food served in fine French ambiance. Lunch served from noon to 3 on the patio. Dinner served from 6:30 to 10:30. Reservations are required. Open from end of May to Columbus Day.

The Boarding House. *Expensive.* 12 Federal St. 228-9622. Two restaurants really. Upstairs features à la carte serving from 6 P.M. and has a piano bar. Downstairs has à la carte lunch daily from noon to 2:30, and dinner nightly from 6. Menu changes nightly. Lunch and cocktails served on the patio. Reservations accepted.

The India House. *Expensive.* 37 India St. 228-9043. Probably the best breakfasts on Nantucket, 8:30–11, Tues. to Sat.; 8:30–1, Sundays. Dinner 6:30–9:30. Menu changes weekly. The restaurant is located in a lovely old island home and the individual rooms are simple but elegant serving areas.

Obadiah's. *Expensive.* 2 India St. 228-4430. Specializing in seafood native to the Nantucket waters. Try the quahog pie as an appetizer. Dinner served 7 days a week, 6–11. Courtyard and raw bar open daily at 5:30 for dinner patrons only. Reservations accepted.

The Thistle Restaurant. *Expensive.* 20 Broad St. 228-9228. Intimate dining in a converted home. Fresh seafood and international cuisine. German chocolate cake is excellent dessert. Open Apr. through Dec. Dinner served from 6. Patio with raw bar opens at 6 P.M. Reservations accepted.

The Lobster Trap. *Moderate.* 23 Washington St. 228-4041. Lobster, scallops, fried clams, and other typical seafood fare in bright atmosphere with wooden tables and benches. Cocktails and raw bar on patio. Reservations not required.

The Mad Hatter. *Moderate.* 72 Easton St. 228-9667. A guaranteed good meal at reasonable prices (by Nantucket standards). Open 7 days a week year-round. Breakfast 8–10:30, summer only. Lunch from noon to 2, Mon. through Sat. Dinner from 6 every day. Sunday brunch popular. Reservations accepted.

The Skipper. *Moderate.* Steamboat Wharf. 228-4444. Restaurant on converted boat hull in Nantucket Harbor. Beautiful view of Old North Wharf. Menu features fish exclusively. Open 7 days a week for breakfast, 8–11:30, lunch from 11:30–2, dinner from 5:30–9:30. Open summer only. No reservations accepted.

The Brotherhood. *Inexpensive.* 23 Broad St. A Nantucket institution and probably the island's best-known restaurant. Located in the basement of a house, with exposed beams and bricks. Good sandwiches and chowder. Shoestring fried potatoes a must. Full meals during the winter. No credit cards or reservations. Open 7 days a week, year-round, Mon. through Sat., 11:30 A.M. to 12:45 A.M., Sun. noon to 12:45 A.M.

Morning Glory Café. *Inexpensive.* Old South Wharf. 228-2212. Small outdoor café, also with 5 or 6 tables inside. Good breakfast, lunch, and light dinners. Try the spinach cheese puff and Morning Glory Muffins. Wine and beer license. Complete take-out service. No credit cards or reservations. Open 7 A.M. to 10 P.M. in the summer.

The Upper Crust. *Inexpensive.* 9 West Creek Rd. 229-2519. Bakery and coffee shop. Excellent breakfasts and lunches. Open Tues. through Sat., 7 A.M. to 5 P.M., Sun. 8 A.M. to 1 P.M. Closed Mon. No liquor. No credit cards or reservations.

 NIGHT LIFE. For a small isolated island, Nantucket has a broad spectrum of club music; only country and western music is missing from the Nantucket scene. By law, all nightclubs close at 1 A.M.

The Atlantic Café, South Water St.; open year-round; no live music, but has loud taped background music; the closest thing to a singles bar on Nantucket. *The Brotherhood*, Broad St.; open year-round; live folk music in whaling-tavern atmosphere. *The Chicken Box*, Dave St.; open year-round. Nantucket's "funkiest" club features New York City fusion bands; dancing, pool tables, and video games. *The Skipper*, Steamboat Wharf; open only during the summer months; after dinner, your college-student waiter or waitress becomes your entertainer, performing Broadway show music. *The Harbor House*, North Water St.; closed in the winter; "middle of the road" music. *The Jared Coffin House Tap Room*, 29 Broad St.; open year-round; piano music, sometimes with singer. *The Muse*, Atlantic Ave.; open year-round; rock-and-roll or new wave bands; dancing, pool tables, video games. *The Rose and Crown*, South Water St.; open May–Oct.; sophisticated jazz. *The White Elephant Shell Lounge*, Easton St.; open during the summer months; air conditioned; synthesized organ or guitar music; some dancing.

CRUISING CAPE COD

by

KEVIN FIELDING

Cape Cod and its surrounding sounds and bays is one of the finest cruising areas on the East Coast, perhaps in the world. The following chapter will serve as a cruising guide to Cape Cod Bay, as far north as Plymouth; Nantucket and Nantucket Sound; Martha's Vineyard and Vineyard Sound; and Buzzards Bay, west of Marion.

The waters of Vineyard Sound, Nantucket Sound, and Buzzards Bay are a real test if you are used to predictable tidal currents, such as in Long Island Sound. Here it is essential that you have an understanding of—and use—the Tide Tables, Tidal Current Tables, and Tidal Current Charts, or you're going to have some unpleasant surprises. It's also recommended that you have detailed nautical charts when entering some of these harbors—they can be tricky.

You will have plenty of breezes; you can count on fog. Some of these harbors will be crowded, but there always seems to be room for one more.

CAPE COD BAY

Cruising Cape Cod Bay can be delightful, but it's a large body of water and the yachtsman will be wise to prepare fully before venturing out. The winds of the Bay may be fine for sailing, but you'll encounter more frequent calms than in Buzzards Bay. There are often varying wind patterns at the same time. Open from the north and northeast, strong winds are capable of making up heavy seas. If a northeaster blows up, get into a harbor.

Fog is possible in all Cape waters, but you'll experience less north from the Canal in Cape Cod Bay.

Concerning tides, the flood generally sets south into the Bay, the ebb north out of the Bay. Currents are generally less strong in the Bay than on the Cape's south side. Mostly under one knot. The heights of tides are important in all harbors on Cape Cod Bay. Typical mean ranges: Barnstable—9.5 feet, Wellfleet—10 feet, P'Town—9.1 feet. Buzzards Bay tidal ranges are less than half this height, accounting for the strong currents in the Cape Cod Canal.

While cruising Cape Cod Bay, whether under sail or power, it becomes necessary eventually to return to a safe harbor to replenish stores. Allow plenty of time, for the harbors on the Bay are often widely separated, shallow, and difficult of access.

Plymouth Harbor

This harbor provides the only deep-draft shelter between Scituate and the Cape Cod Canal. A major tourist attraction and quite crowded in summer, it is still a popular refuge for cruising yachtsmen. It's not the best harbor for visiting but you'll find ample gas, diesel fuel, water, ice, showers, and repair facilities. All necessaries can be procured at stores in the town, a short walk from the docks. There is a long approach channel, a yacht club, and one marina. The anchorage area is extensively dredged and protected by a breakwater. Still, it's a tight anchorage situation, as is true of all the harbors on Cape Cod Bay. As fast as new boating facilities are built, boats fill them up.

Plymouth Marine is a good choice to pull in if you want to be dockside, but it is wise to check the present channel depth if you draw over three feet. Reservations should be made.

Plymouth Yacht Club has a few guest moorings and is prominent on shore with its seven-pillared portico.

If you choose the anchorage area, the State Pier is the best place to leave your dink when you go ashore. The float is too small for cruising boats to tie up, but the water is deep enough to pull up and discharge passengers. Here the *Mayflower II,* an exact replica of the original *Mayflower,* is tied up. For a small fee, visitors may board her from spring to early autumn. Also close by is Plymouth Rock and the 1749 Courthouse, which displays exhibits describing government in colonial times. The Plymouth National Wax Museum, the Antiquarian House Museum, and the Pilgrim Museum all have small admission charges. One can easily spend two days visiting sights in this old harbor.

Cape Cod Canal

If you are leaving Cape Cod Bay, the Canal provides a painless passage for pleasure boaters to cruising in Buzzards Bay, Nantucket Sound, and Vineyard Sound. The passage is an eight-mile land-cut, but the Canal is actually twice that length when going all the way to the Cleveland East Ledge Light.

Traffic lights are located at Wings Neck for eastbound traffic, and at the Sandwich jetty for westbound traffic. Boats over 25 feet must get permission to go through whether by traffic lights, radiophone, or the Corps of Engineers patrol boat. The radiotelephone in the Canal office is continuously monitored on Channel 16, call letters WUA 21. Channel 16 is used only to establish contact. Transmissions are then switched to Channels 12 or 14 to pass information. Boats under 65 feet may proceed against the red light to the East Mooring Basin while awaiting the green light or radiotel clearance. Entering from the western end, you may proceed against the red to the West Mooring Basin at Hog Island. Minimum speed limits are set in times for the passage, as follows: Against Head Tide—60 min., With Fair Tide—30 min., Slack Water—45 min.

The administration building in Buzzards Bay can monitor each boat's passage by TV cameras. They're mounted in pairs at three locations along the land-cut, as well as Wings Neck and Sandwich at each end of the Canal. The cameras are remotely controlled and equipped with zoom lenses; a vessel can be viewed at any time during its passage. The cameras work at night and are, in fact, monitored 24 hours a day to divert traffic around any hazardous situation. Once a boat starts through the land-cut from either end, the Engineers require a complete passage be made.

Although sailboats are required to use power, sails may be kept up. No fishing from boats in the land-cut or in the channel of the Canal is permitted.

High tide occurs approximately three hours earlier at the Buzzards Bay end of the Canal than at the Cape Cod Bay end. The mean range of tide is 3.5 feet at the Railroad Bridge, and 8.8 feet at the Canal's east end. When the tidal current is with you, passage is speedy. It is well to consult the tide charts before entering the Canal. If you time it right, you can go through with the lowest-powered boat in less than an hour. If you have to buck the tide, the trip may take several hours. If you have little power, it might be wise to pull in to the East Basin Harbor at the Cape Cod Bay end or into Onset or Monument Beach on the west end until the tide changes or at least becomes slack.

The scenery through the Canal is beautiful and thousands of pleasure boats go through each season. Three bridges cross the Canal—the Sagamore Highway Bridge (Route 6), the Bourne Highway Bridge (Route 28), and the ConRail Lift Bridge (or Railroad Bridge). The highway bridges have a clearance of 135 feet, the lift bridge has seven feet clearance with the span down and 135 with the span up. The span remains up until a train must cross, then two long blasts announce it is lowering.

Entering the Canal from Cape Cod Bay is much easier than from the west because of the short approach. The electric power plant at Sandwich makes a fine landmark for the entrance.

East Basin Harbor (Sandwich)

The Sandwich East Basin, a harbor of refuge, is located on the east side of the entrance to the Canal and is a good spot to overnight if you come off the Bay late in the afternoon. The commercial fish houses here can make your mooring odoriferous if there's a north wind; however, the Cape Cod Canal Marina is a clean, modern facility with slips, some of which are reserved for transients. Gas, diesel fuel, ice, and showers are available. The best place to anchor, if you choose to do so, is in the northern half of the basin. Be careful not to block access to the docks. Picnic tables and rest rooms are nearby. A good seafood restaurant offers takeout service. Bikes may be rented at the Sandwich Bike Shop for a sightseeing trip around town. Taxi service is also available.

The East Basin is the only way to reach Sandwich by boat; both Sandwich Harbor and Scorton Harbor are bare at low tide. In the town of Sandwich, there are several fine restaurants, as well as fascinating museums. Neither the Glass Museum or the Doll Museum should be missed.

Barnstable Harbor

Barnstable is a quiet little village with a picturesque harbor but, unfortunately, little space for overnight stays. Gas, showers, restaurants, and repair services are available, but the few slips are seasonally occupied, and a transient is usually asked to stay with his boat while attending to needs.

The Barnstable Marine Service has no overnight space since most boats from this harbor make only day fishing trips.

Millway Marine and the Barnstable Yacht Club also have limited facilities for visitors. If you can stop for a few hours, the Mattakeese Wharf Restaurant has good food and a fine view of the harbor to enjoy while having lunch on the porch.

This harbor is a little difficult to enter, but you can see 20 to 30 feet down and the sandy shoals are visible. Following the five buoys marking the long stretch of shoal water is not really that tough. This is the only harbor for a larger boat between the Canal and Wellfleet.

Sesuit Harbor (East Dennis)

This tight little harbor has a short easy approach, but keep watching your depth finder. Some scoop-dredging was done in 1979 but the shoal has become extensive. Plans have been in the works for more dredging.

When entering the harbor, it's best to line up on the east breakwater and watch the color of the water.

The Dennis Yacht Club has its boats moored inside the west breakwater. Sesuit Marine Services has slips and moorings. Gas, diesel fuel, ice, engine repairs, marine hardware, charts, and supplies are available. Again, there are very limited facilities for visitors.

The Town Dock also has slips and you can use the dink dock at the Town Landing. You'll find a shopping plaza for groceries, a pharmacy, a liquor store that also sells ice cubes, and a laundromat close by.

Sightseeing is rewarding, but you'll want to rent a bike or be ready for a good walk. Scargo Hill, one of the highest spots on the Cape, is about 1½ miles from the Town Dock. A stone tower on the hill allows a magnificent view of Cape Cod Bay.

The famous Cape Playhouse is about two miles from the harbor.

Rock Harbor (Orleans)

This is a little creek and a high-tide-harbor with an eight-foot tide range. Using the tide tables you should have no problem, but remember to check plus or minus tides for the day you're entering.

Although at the Town Wharf all the space is taken by fishing boats and the charter fleet, you should be able to tie up in a vacated space. Consult the people in the charter information booth. Gas and diesel fuel is available at the wharf east of the asphalt launching ramp.

Rock Harbor Creek is the dividing line between Orleans and Eastham, and the Town of Eastham maintains floats north of the bend in the creek. One berth is reserved for transients. No facilities are available there. A seafood restaurant is right at the dock and, nearby, bikes can be rented. The Orleans Shopping Plaza with shops for every need is about a mile from the harbor.

Wellfleet Harbor

Probably the best harbor for visitors on the bay side of Cape Cod. Its large, modern Town Marina has over 200 slips, and should accommodate the transient visitor. As with most of the harbors on Cape Cod Bay, however, the transient slips are often booked solid a month ahead. The harbormaster is located two-thirds the distance down the slips at the gas dock. They also have diesel fuel, ice, marine supplies, and rental boats.

The anchorage is at the head of the 125-foot-wide, 10-foot-deep channel, which extends for about a mile from deep water.

Bay Sails Marine has moorings in the anchorage basin. Not far from the docks, cars and bikes can be rented. With a supermarket nearby, as well as restaurants, shops, and art galleries, most needs are available within a short distance.

Pamet Harbor (Truro)

A very small harbor in constant need of dredging. Current depths should be checked before going in. It becomes more shallow every year. There is perhaps one guest mooring near the Pamet Yacht and Tennis Club. The Town has no guest moorings and very little room to anchor. The small yacht club has very limited facilities. You can explore up the river in your dink. About one mile up is a grocery store, a laundry, and the Truro Post Office. Not too much available here, but it's a charming spot to anchor.

Provincetown Harbor

You can't miss the leading landmark for this harbor. The Pilgrim Monument stands 255 feet high. Plenty of anchorage space is available in this interesting port. Thanks to a new breakwater, completed in 1972, the anchorage is now well-protected. Other than this feature, the harbor has poor facilities for visiting boats. Dockside space is scarce. Sometimes a space is available at the wharves, but rarely. Most spaces are taken up by party boats and commercial fishermen. There are no commercial marinas or yacht clubs with any moorings. Gas and diesel fuel are available between the Town (MacMillan) Wharf and Cee-Jay Pier. You tie alongside pilings to take on fuel. The dockmaster must be consulted before you use any space.

You can land your dink at the little beach next to the West End Racing Club off Commercial Street.

Provincetown has everything you might need; fine restaurants, old museums, plenty of night life. There are lots of gift shops to visit, and the three large art galleries and the Provincetown Playhouse shouldn't be missed.

The town is best seen on foot, but bikes or cars can be rented if you want to explore the nearby Cape Cod National Seashore.

NANTUCKET SOUND

Nantucket Sound has good summer sailing breezes, and, although the southwest winds prevail, there are some westerlies and southerlies. The Sound is open from the east and portions of it from the south, so strong winds and heavy seas are not out of the question. Although a northeaster is not common in the summer, if one does occur, the waters of Nantucket Sound can be quite dangerous for small craft. Fog, too, is always possible.

The tide in the Sound generally sets eastward on the flood, and westward on the ebb. The time of the change becomes later as you proceed westward. The strength of the current is normally one to two knots.

On the outer shore of Cape Cod, the flood sets north, the ebb south. It is not recommended here that you try to circumnavigate Cape Cod unless you have a large boat. To reach Nantucket Sound from the north, the Cape Cod Canal is the safest and easiest route. The combination of fog, rough shoal waters, complex tide sets, the absence of harbors, and a very inhospitable shore can make the trip around the Cape an uncomfortable passage.

Nantucket Sound and the South Shore of Cape Cod is one of the world's great cruising areas. Everything is excellent—the visual variety, the inviting beaches, the well-protected harbors.

Nantucket Harbor

The island of Nantucket, roughly 30 miles at sea, is a good test of your seamanship and navigation. Approach from the west via Cross Rip Lighted Horn. There are virtually no reefs, but there are shallows which change with the storms. Your first landmark will be standpipes sticking up like masts at a distance. Next you will pick up Great Point Light and Sankaty Head Light. Finally, Tuckernuck Island and the cliffs west of the harbor. You should watch your Tidal Current Charts, because the set varies depending on where you are as you approach.

The harbor entry is well marked and it is easy to locate the Nantucket Boat Basin. There are almost 200 slips, gas, diesel fuel, ice, pump out station, propane, showers, laundromat, marine supplies, restaurants, and a supermarket. The only problem, it's all spread out. Commercial Wharf is Pier A, Old South Wharf is Pier B, the middle of the three piers, and Straight Wharf is Pier C.

If you should choose the anchorage area, it is a long dink ride to town. For dockside, it is really necessary to reserve ahead. The availability of TV and phone hookups indicates that many boats stay for extended periods.

The marina office is in a two-story building on the dock. Detailed maps of the marina area are available. Close by are numerous gift shops, art galleries, and souvenir shops. Although there are several good restaurants, Nantucket is rather quiet—there isn't much nightlife.

East of the basin is the Nantucket Shipyard, which has moorings, a few slips, gas, hull, and engine repairs. The Nantucket Yacht Club has guest moorings in the anchorage area. You should check at their launch dock. Members of other recognized yacht clubs are accorded full club privileges.

The Nantucket Information Bureau in the center of town can provide you with a map.

Since the island is only 15 miles long by about 3½ miles wide—and few hills—bikes are the popular way to get around. In fact, they outnumber the cars.

Madaket Harbor is the only possible alternate choice to Nantucket Harbor. It is not as convenient, but there is room to anchor and services are available. At the Hither Creek Boat Yard there are slips, gas, engine repairs, and small boat rentals.

Nantucket is indeed a "far-away place," as the Indian name indicates, but a cruise of Nantucket Sound would be incomplete without visiting this beautiful, austere island.

Stage Harbor (Chatham)

Heading for Stage Harbor, sailing north from Nantucket, you will pass by Monomoy Island. This eight-mile sandy length is now a National Wildlife Refuge. Since 1970, it has been a designated National Wilderness.

Stage Harbor is a good deep-water harbor and you should have no difficulty with water depths. There are two good anchorage areas as you enter the harbor. One is behind Harding Beach Point, the other and more popular is north of Stage Island. Stage Harbor Marine rents moorings at the latter. They also have some slips for transients, and offer gas, diesel fuel, ice, engine repairs, and row-boat rentals. As with all the marinas on the Cape, it is essential that you call ahead and make reservations.

It is possible to go further up the channel through a hand-operated bridge to anchorage in Mill Pond and Little Mill Pond if your boat isn't too large. This would shorten the walk to the town of Chatham.

Oyster Pond River, which shoots off of Stage Harbor, is too shallow for most cruising boats. There is only two feet controlling depth at mean low water. However, if you can go up the river, the Chatham Yacht Basin has some transient slips. If they are full, you could at least tie to their bulkhead. They have gas, engine repairs, marine supplies—a full service boatyard.

The town of Chatham is very beautiful and unspoiled. There is a good shopping district with stores for all your needs, five art galleries, sports, theater.

Chatham Harbor

Shielded from the ocean by the Nauset Marsh, Chatham Harbor is a long stretch of water. It was once more accessible from the ocean. Entry to this harbor is difficult from the ocean side since the channel shifts with each storm. It is wise to get advice before attempting entry, since even the charts can't help you. The fishing fleet goes in and out everyday, but even they have trouble. These waters are all tidal, and the current runs very strong in Chatham Harbor. It also can be very choppy. Time your arrival to take advantage of the tide. Once inside, you will discover that it is all worthwhile.

As you proceed up the harbor you will come to Tern Island and the Chatham Fish Pier off your port side. Between the two is good anchorage. At the pier, gas and diesel fuel are available. On the dock is Nickerson's, a retail fish market with take-out service and outdoor tables.

Pleasant Bay (Chatham and South Orleans)

As you continue north in this long Chatham Harbor, you will be heading toward Pleasant Bay. Rounding Allen Point you should be watching your fathometer. All these channels south of the Bay are constantly shifting, but they are pretty well marked and there are good anchorages up in Crows Pond and Ryders Cove. The Ryders Cove Boat Yard has floating slips, and moorings—a full service boatyard. They accommodate transients.

Pleasant Bay really is just that, a beautiful body of water with good depths and plenty of room.

Going still farther north through the Narrows you will enter Little Pleasant Bay. The clearly marked channels up here are much more stable than south of Pleasant Bay.

South Orleans is a good place to get provisions. It is best to pull in to Paw Wah Pond, where the Orleans town ramp is located with dockage for up to two hours. The South Orleans General Store is about a mile away.

Through another small channel off of Little Pleasant Bay you will find Arey's Pond. It looks small and impossible to reach, but there are moorings and services at the Arey's Pond Boatyard.

Farther north is Meeting House Pond, which is reached through a narrow creek with about three feet of water. Nestled in this little pond is the East Orleans Boat Yard, as well as the town dock. You will be amazed at the size of the boats here so far from the ocean. The boatyard has slips, some for transients, and moorings, engine repairs, and a marine supply store. Nearby, there are a variety of stores for shopping.

This whole area of coves, ponds, and rivers that run off of Pleasant Bay and Little Pleasant Bay is perfect for exploring. Dredging eventually will make it much easier to navigate.

Saquatucket (Harwich Port)

Back at the ocean and heading west from Stage Harbor, you first come to Cape Cod's newest harbor, Saquatucket. The entry looks difficult on the chart, but it isn't. The deep water is visible across the shallows. Controlling depth is 3½ feet at mean low water, four feet in the basin, and six feet at the slips.

The Saquatucket Municipal Marina has floating slips, gas, diesel fuel, ice, showers, and laundromat. There is no room to anchor in the basin, so telephone ahead to reserve a slip. Keep in mind that on a regular basis there is a waiting list for slips, so the transient must plan ahead. Route 28 passes near the dock; there are stores for all needs a short distance in both directions.

Wychmere Harbor (Harwich Port)

This harbor is close to Saquatucket Harbor—about one quarter-mile apart. Actually, the two harbors share a common entry across the bar, but they have separate buoys. Wychmere is a little closer to Harwich Port. The narrow entry channel has a depth of about five feet at mean low water. The harbor is small, about 300 yards across, but it is beautiful with lots of moorings.

The Stone Horse Yacht Club is on your starboard as you enter and has guest moorings for members of other recognized clubs. The Harwich Port Boat Works has slips and moorings. Gas, diesel fuel, engine, and hull repairs are all available. They have some designated guest moorings. Also, the Harwich Port Town Dock might have a slip available for the night. A few fishing boats tie up here. Harwich Port, just to the west on Route 28, has a number of stores for marketing.

Yachtsmen are always interested to know that one of the buildings at Brooks Academy—where the Harwich Historical Society now resides—was the first school of navigation in America (1844).

Allen Harbor (Harwich Port)

Down the coast a couple of miles heading west is Allen Harbor. A word of caution: When you are harbor jumping on the South Shore, be prepared to detour well off shore to avoid fishing weirs. There are many stakes broken off below the water.

The entrance to Allen Harbor is not easy to see from out in Nantucket Sound. The spire on the Pilgrim Congregational Church in Harwich Port will help you get to the outer pair of entry buoys. From the breakwater you follow Doane's Creek to the harbor. The controlling depth is only four feet at mean low water. After winding through a marsh you pop out into the harbor. There are quite a few moorings in here but there is anchorage room in seven feet at the south end.

Allen Harbor Marine Service caters to transients. They have floating slips and some moorings, gas, ice, a marine supply and gift store, as well as complete engine and hull repairs. Town slips are up the creek, east of the Harwichport launching ramp. A supermarket is close by, as is a good laundry and cleaners. By heading east you will come to all the services mentioned for Wychmere Harbor.

Herring River (Harwich Port)

This harbor has another hard-to-find entry. However, there are any number of motels along the shore, a decided help as a landmark. The entrance is not marked well and you must line up the jetties carefully. This river is fairly quiet and there are anchorage possibilities, but you must use your dink to get around. Controlling depth in the river is four feet at mean low water. The first fixed bridge going up river has ten feet vertical clearance, the second has seven feet. This second bridge is Route 28 and a short distance away is West Harwich, with stores for all necessities. Good restaurants and plenty of recreational possibilities abound. This is a very busy part of Cape Cod.

Bass River (South Yarmouth and West Dennis)

Farther west on the southern coast is Bass River, one of the most popular boating harbors in this part of the Cape.

Although there are constant shoaling problems, the controlling depth should be three feet at mean low water. The shallowest part is beyond the first pair of buoys and you should hug the east side from the breakwater in.

There is a concrete launching ramp on the north side with piers and landing floats. Up a little further you will come to Windmill Park, which has a landing. From here it is just a short walk to the Bass River Store.

The Bass River Yacht Club might have a guest mooring. The only other marine facility south of the Route 28 fixed bridge is Ship Shops. They have dockside slips, and moorings. Gas is available; diesel fuel, ice, complete engine and hull repairs, plus a marine supply store.

If you are cruising in a powerboat, you have other options beyond the fixed bridge. Merry Mill Boat Rentals has slips at floating finger piers. They have gas and can accommodate a boat up to 22 feet. Also beyond the bridge and near Merry Mill is the Bass River Marina, which has a dredged channel leading to it. Here are more than a hundred slips, gas, ice, showers, engine repairs, and a good marine supply and gift shop. This is a busy area. If you want to go farther up the river, you can travel all the way to South Dennis. At Kelley's Bay there is a large marina, the Mayfair Boat Yard, which also has slips. Follins Pond is the end of the line.

South Yarmouth, back at the beginning of Bass River, has a small shopping area with good restaurants, antique shops, art galleries, a laundry, liquor store, bike rentals—all within walking distance of the Bass River Marina.

Parkers River (West Yarmouth)

Just a creek, but deep enough for good-sized boats. Parkers River is to the right of Sea Gull Beach as you enter. There is a drive-in movie screen, which makes a fine landmark from the water. Gateway Isles Marina and Restaurant is up the river on the right, just before the bridge. They have slips at floating finger piers, gas, diesel fuel, ice, party and charter boats. The lounge and dining room overlook the marina.

Near the mouth of the river is the Red Jacket Beach Motor Inn, which has a pier and float suitable for your dink or daysailer. They have a good dining room open to visiting yachtsmen.

Hyannis Port, Lewis Bay, Hyannis

The harbor of the largest town on Cape Cod actually consists of three harbors: Hyannis Port, Lewis Bay, and the inner Hyannis Harbor. It is a complete supply and refurbishing port for cruising boats.

The approach is well marked and whether you are coming from the east, south, or west you should have no problem entering. The harbor is very large and apt to be choppy when the wind blows.

The first anchorage possibility is off the Hyannis Port Yacht Club. It's a good spot with plenty of room.

In Lewis Bay there are several good anchorage areas. Guest moorings are available at the Hyannis Yacht Club for members of other recognized clubs. For a marina, you should go into the Hyannis Inner Harbor. The Hyannis Marina appears first on your right. It has floating slips, gas, diesel fuel, ice, showers, laundromat, propane, complete repairs, marine supply and gift shop, and more. It can handle deep draft yachts up to 130 feet.

The Lewis Bay Lodge Marina is next door and has slips for transients. They also offer services for most of your needs, including a good restaurant and a dockside bar.

At the Pleasant Street Wharf, two other marinas, the Bradbury Marine and Anchor Outboard, have slips and the usual services.

The Ocean Street Wharf should be avoided. It's very busy with ferries, sightseeing boats, and commercial fishermen.

East Bay (Centerville and Osterville)

Heading west toward Falmouth, the south shore of the Cape offers numerous bays and rivers for gunkholing. Generally, they are larger than east of Hyannis, but the approaches have been dredged through shallows and are consequently subject to shoaling. East Bay is one of these gunkholes and accessible if you don't draw over four feet. No facilities, but great beaches and some quiet anchorages.

West Bay (Osterville)

The entry channel should have adequate depths for most boats. The Wianno Yacht Club is up the bay near the village of Osterville. Plenty of anchorage space for smaller boats; tight for deep-draught vessels. They have moorings and dock space for members of other recognized yacht clubs. No fuel is available.

Two of the largest ship yards on Cape Cod are just north of the Grand Island Bridge: Chester Crosby Co., Inc. and Crosby Yacht Yard, Inc. Both cater to transients. They have guest slips, gas, diesel fuel, ice, showers, engine repairs—full service marinas. The town is close by.

Cotuit Bay (Cotuit)

You can reach this bay from West Bay via the Seapuit River. As long as you don't draft over four feet, you should be able to explore all these interconnecting waterways.

Should you wish to stay overnight in Cotuit, you might inquire at the Town Dock about guest moorings. Otherwise, the Town Landing is perhaps the best place to stop and visit.

North Bay (Osterville and Marstons Mills)

An adequate-depth channel connects Cotuit Bay with North Bay. There is also another channel coming from Osterville, but it is not as deep. There are many moored boats up in this bay, but there are good anchorage possibilities for the transient. Prince Cove, located still farther north off North Bay, is really only for shallow draft boats. Prince Cove Marina, however, has most services.

All through these interesting bays and coves are many fine beaches, marinas, good gunkholes, convenient restaurants—satisfying all your needs without retreating to the principal harbors on Nantucket Sound.

Waquoit Bay (Mashpee and East Falmouth)

The next harbor following the coast west is big and beautiful. It is shallow at the beginning, but the channel is well marked. There is a channel on the east side of the bay that leads to the Little River Boat Yard, which has about a dozen slips and room for transients. They have gas, ice, showers, and a repair service. It is about three miles to the nearest store. Little River and nearby Hamblin Pond have anchorage room, although Waquoit Bay itself affords excellent anchorage. There are good picnic grounds nearby.

At the northern end of the bay is the Waquoit Bay Yacht Club. From there you can walk to a variety store for ice cubes, newspapers, and some groceries. If you are really exploring, you might make it all the way to the Childs River and Edwards Boat Yard. There is four feet of water. Complete facilities and moorings for transients if you get this far from the ocean.

Eel Pond (East Falmouth)

A small harbor with very limited facilities but some good anchorage possibilities. Watch the water depths at the entrance.

This is the location of the Menauhant Yacht Club. There are some good beaches here but not much ashore for the visitor.

Green Pond (East Falmouth)

Many moored boats in here but room to anchor off the channel. The Green Pond Yacht Services has slips and moorings, gas, diesel fuel, ice, complete repairs, and marine supplies. With room for transients, they can handle a boat up to 60 feet.

Green Pond Tackle serves hotdogs and quahogs, has slips for boats up to 24 feet, but they are beyond the fixed bridge, which has a clearance of only seven feet.

Not too much ashore. You would have to walk two miles to get to a general store. However, the marina is good, the water depths are fine, and it's a good overnight stop.

Falmouth Inner Harbor

After all the gunkholing from Hyannis, you may be ready for a good supply harbor. Easy access here; no shoal problems. However, this is one harbor where you really must reserve ahead; there is no room to drop anchor. The Falmouth Harbor Marina is the town marina and a good spot for dockside. Here are showers, but no gas or ice. Between pilings, slips with finger piers.

The Falmouth Yacht Club is a good host if you belong to another recognized yacht club, but their space is limited. The Falmouth Marine Railways is the largest facility in the harbor. They have both slips and moorings, gas, diesel fuel, ice, propane, complete repair service, and a nautical gift shop. This is also the location of the great Flying Bridge Restaurant.

Across the harbor is MacDougall's Cape Cod Marine Service, which is a full service yacht yard—slips, moorings, fuel, and ice. There are other smaller marinas here, as well as good restaurants and stores within walking distance. A visit to the famous Falmouth Playhouse, however, would require transportation. There's a lot to see and do in Falmouth.

VINEYARD SOUND

Martha's Vineyard has an enormous variety of scenery, shoreline, and towns. There is something for everyone on this beautiful 15-by-eight-mile island. The entire south shore is one long spectacular beach.

Menemsha

This picturesque port has been expanded in recent years with many slips in the basin reserved for noncommercial boats and transients. Inquire about a space at the Menemsha Marine Service, which also has gas, diesel fuel, ice, and a small store.

It is crowded in the basin, but it's charming and everything you might need is close by, including groceries and a Post Office.

If you should wish a little privacy and want to anchor, you can negotiate with care the channel up Menemsha Creek to Menemsha Pond. The tide runs fast and there is some shoaling. Here you will find plenty of room and the water is deep. Nashaquitsa Pond is off of Menemsha Pond, but they don't encourage overnight visitors. Also, water depths are questionable. But Menemsha Pond is beautiful, a peaceful gunkhole, and completely protected.

While in Menemsha, it is possible to take a bus to Gay Head. These magnificent clay cliffs shouldn't be missed. It's only about three miles and it's one of the main attractions of Martha's Vineyard.

Lake Tashmoo

A landlocked lake and a beautiful anchorage. There is an entrance channel between two short breakwaters and some care is required entering. Watch water depths, it may be only two to two-and-one-half feet at mean low water. Once inside, it is a perfect gunkhole for the night. There is a Town Dock and beach to land your dink if you wish to go ashore.

Vineyard Haven

Inasmuch as the year-round ferry service from Woods Hole comes to this port, it is really the commercial center of the island. It boasts the largest shopping area and is an excellent supply port for cruising yachtsmen. Also, everything is close to the harbor.

The Vineyard Haven Yacht Club is just outside the harbor, but they have limited transient moorings. Inside, the Town of Tisbury has set out some guest moorings on a first-come, first-served basis. The town pier is available for a limited tie-up at no charge—no overnights.

The Coastwise Wharf Company has gas, ice, showers, and a laundry. They have room for quite a few boats to tie up alongside the dock. The Pilot House Machine & Marine Service has complete facilities and can accommodate about 30 boats dockside.

The largest shipyard on the island is the Martha's Vineyard Shipyard. Here again are gas, ice, propane, and a pump-out station. They have an excellent marine supply and gift shop; NOS charts are available. Close by you can rent bikes and cars or take sightseeing tours. There are stores and little shops for just about everything. Be advised that Vineyard Haven is a dry community. Some restaurants do allow you to bring your own liquid provisions.

Lagoon Pond runs off of Vineyard Haven and is a wonderful gunkhole. A little difficult to enter but worth it. There is a draw bridge that is manned and the controlling depth at the entry is three feet. Inside is the Massachusetts State Lobster Hatchery & Research Station.

West of Cedar Neck is Burt's Boatyard, a well-protected marina. Burt's has about a dozen slips, a few moorings, gas, engine, and hull repairs, a canvas shop, and sailmaker. This pond is a very beautiful and secluded anchorage.

Oak Bluffs

On the northeast corner of Martha's Vineyard and usually crowded. However, it's well-protected, supplies are handy, and it is interesting.

This was a lake opened to the sea. Easy to enter through a narrow cut, Oak Bluffs is filled with moorings; there is no room to anchor. The town does set out some guest moorings for a small fee. They also have some reasonable guest slips if you check with the harbormaster. Paul Rousseau's has a few slips, gas, diesel fuel, ice, and showers. Church's Pier has a dozen slips and offers the same. The East Chop Yacht Club is in the north corner of the harbor with slips and moorings, but they are small and limited. The ferry terminal is at the Oak Bluffs Wharf.

Unlike Vineyard Haven, there are a lot of bars at this port. Fascinating sightseeing at the Camp Meeting Association and surrounding area. It's an interesting place for a cruising yachtsman.

Edgartown

Surely this is the yachting capital of the entire area. As usual, it too is crowded in the summer and the boat traffic in the harbor is considerable. If you want to get to a mooring immediately, the Edgartown Marine will be on your starboard side just inside the harbor. They have only a few slips but there are some moorings for transients at reasonable rates. Gas, diesel fuel, ice, showers, laundromat, marine hardware, and gifts are all available.

A little farther on the right is the well-known Edgartown Yacht Club, which is limited to members and their guests.

Visiting yachts are permitted to tie up at the Town Dock if there is room, though it's very busy here. You may wish just to go to a quiet anchorage in the direction of, and perhaps into, Katama Bay. There is also a good anchorage before you enter the harbor at Cape Poge Bay. It is secluded and great if you can manage the narrow entry. Check your chart for location of rock in channel.

There are many and varied restaurants at Edgartown. The Harborside Inn is one with a spectacular view. All the windows look out over the boats and the dock scenes. They have a dinghy dock, but no overnight tie-ups.

You cannot pass up a stroll through the center of town. Sightseeing, specialty shops, art galleries—it's a beautiful place! The Edgartown Regatta is the oldest annual regatta on the East Coast.

It is difficult to do descriptive justice to the harbors covered here; there is so much to see and do. Whether you ride on mopeds or horses, prefer golf, tennis, or sightseeing, it's all available. Whether you stay between Hyannis and Falmouth, or cruise out to the magnificent Martha's Vineyard ports, it's all prime cruising.

BUZZARDS BAY

There are, of course, no buzzards in Buzzards Bay. British explorers around 1750 looked up at the large fish-eating hawks, ospreys, and thought them to be buzzards. They look similar in the air. "Buzzardet" was the first term used, and later became just "buzzard." Consequently, Buzzards Bay.

Because of the common four- and five-foot waves, some mariners over the years have called Buzzards Bay "a place for the birds" and other less-refined expletives. However, in 1602, an early explorer, Bartholomew Gosnold—who gave the area the name Cape Cod—called Buzzards Bay "Gosnold's Hope" and spoke of it as "the stateliest sound I was ever in."

The summer southwest wind blows with such regularity in Buzzards Bay it might almost be called a trade wind. This sou'wester will be slight in the morning but by early afternoon usually reaches 15 knots or more. It, along with the shallow water depths at the funnel-shaped NE end, accounts for the heavy chop as you come out of Cape Cod Canal heading southwest into the bay.

Although rough sailing can be experienced in all bodies of water around the Cape, it will most often occur in Buzzards Bay.

The fog usually dissipates by noon, but is common in the bay and at the entrance to Cape Cod Canal. Not as bad perhaps as some "downeast" fogs, but severe enough.

Tides in Buzzards Bay are difficult to predict; the best advice to a yachtsman cruising this body of water is to be familiar with, and consult, the Tide Tables, Tidal Current Tables, and Tidal Current Charts.

Woods Hole

This harbor is headquarters for a sizable fleet, including vessels of the Oceanographic Institute and the Marine Biological Laboratory.

Although there are alternate routes into this harbor, the main Woods Hole Passage is a very tricky two-mile channel with some reefs, rocks, and a strong tidal current. In short, it is not for the unskillful. It is recommended that you get detailed advice before entering and never attempt it in a fog.

The Woods Hole Yacht Club has limited facilities, but there is anchorage room while you visit town. They have a dink dock and a place to dump refuse. For overnight anchorage, behind Penzance Peninsula or Ram Island would be a good choice. Eel Pond and Little Harbor have moorings and there is some room to anchor at the latter. (We should note here that the lift bridge at Eel Pond is unmanned after September.)

There is only one marine facility, the Woods Hole Marine Railway and Supply Co., Inc., with some moorings for transients, some dock space, gas, ice, showers, laundromat, and a marine supply store.

In town a few stores sell groceries, liquor, ice cubes, newspapers, and other needs.

Despite the difficulties of entering Woods Hole, it is an interesting harbor with interesting people and well worth the challenge.

Quissett Harbor

Heading north along the west shore of Cape Cod you will come upon a truly beautiful little port. Seldom used by transients, Quissett does have facilities and good anchorages. The harbor is easy to enter, since the west shore has no shallow, sandy shoals, but deep water, close in; a good change from the south shore.

Quissett Harbor Boat Yard has a few transient moorings, a dink dock, gas, ice, engine, and hull repairs, and marine supplies. There are two good anchorages, one south of the entrance and the other in the inner harbor. Not much ashore within walking distance, but taxis can be called from the pay phone.

West Falmouth

With the sandbar near the entrance, this harbor's entry looks more difficult on the chart than it is. The channel should be a fathom deep at mean low water.

The town dock at the east end has gas, but no slips. There are many moored boats, but there should be room to anchor here or south of the channel.

A grocery store is within two blocks of the dock. Some good restaurants are close by. From the late 1600s through the next two centuries, this area was a Quaker settlement. There are, consequently, many historical sightseeing opportunities.

Wild Harbor—Silver Beach Harbor

Still farther north lies a harbor infrequently used by transients. No gas is available, but you can get ice and groceries. Although Wild Harbor is pretty exposed, the tight channel to Silver Beach Harbor should have a fathom at mean low water and is well protected. Among the many moorings there is usually room to anchor. This harbor is an interesting alternative.

Megansett Harbor (North Falmouth)

The outer harbor is exposed to winds except behind Scraggy Neck, but a dredged basin, known as Fiddler's Cove, lies on the harbor's south side. Inside is Fiddler's Cove Marina, with gas, ice, engine, and hull repairs, and a marine supply store.

The inner Megansett Harbor is behind the breakwater and here you will find the Megansett Yacht Club, where there should be room for a visiting cruiser.

For supplies, land at the town dock in the inner harbor. About a half-mile away is a market and, a little further on, an apothecary and a laundry.

A channel leads from the inner harbor around a bend into Squeteague Harbor. Check water depths before attempting entry. This is a landlocked gunkhole, a lovely spot for the night.

Pocasset Harbor—Red Brook Harbor

The west side of Pocasset Harbor is too exposed for anchorages, but behind and around Bassett's Island there are at least five little harbors and coves. Red Brook Harbor, one possibility, has two good marinas: Parker's Boat Yard has slips and moorings, gas, diesel fuel, showers, self-service ice, and complete engine and hull repairs. They cater primarily to auxiliary sailboats up to 42 feet. Launch service to the dock is also offered. Next door is Kingman Marine with hundreds of slips and moorings. Some dockside space is reserved for transients. They have gas, diesel fuel, ice, showers, complete engine, hull, and electronics repairs, a marine supply, and gift shop as well as a laundromat.

If you want to get off by yourself, Hen Cove runs off Red Brook Harbor and has deep water but is somewhat exposed to the wind. Around the bend is another good anchorage, Barlow's Landing. A lot of boats are moored here; if you have a shallow-draft boat you should be able to get in and find room to anchor. This is the closest point to Pocasset village.

Pocasset River

After cruising north on the west side of Wings Neck, you will find this snug harbor. It isn't easy to enter, but there are six-foot depths. Barlow's Boatyard on the south bank has just a few slips but gas and engine repairs. The Town of Bourne Marina is opposite with some slips and moorings. Just a short walk to Pocasset stores.

Phinney's Harbor—Monument Beach

If you are going to wait for a tide change in Cape Cod Canal, this is a good jumping off spot.

Behind Toby's Island is Monument Beach Marina in the southeast corner of the harbor. They have slips and moorings and welcome transients. Gas is available along with ice, showers, boat rentals, and a snack bar. Monument Beach, close by, has a variety store, liquor store, and a Post Office.

Just north is Perry's Boat Yard with several dozen moorings, engine repairs, and marine hardware.

Three excellent gunkholes are across the northern end of Phinney's Harbor.

Buzzards Bay (Village)

Not to be confused with the body of water, the village of Buzzards Bay (Town of Bourne) is located on the northside of the canal entrance and the eastside of Cohasset Narrows. A long well-marked channel leads in to Buttermilk Bay. Two fixed bridges at the entrance to the bay, however, limit passage to boats that can clear six feet at mean high water. Two small marinas between the bridges cater to outboards, offering gas and fishing equipment.

If you can't get under the bridges, there is one anchorage to port just before them. This is Butler Cove, with five-foot depths in the outer part. It is a short walk to village stores for almost everything. Seafood restaurants and fish markets cluster around the bridges.

Not a terribly attractive spot to spend the night, but it's adequate.

On Taylor Point at the canal entrance is Massachusetts Maritime Academy, where visitors are welcome on weekends.

Onset

Because of its fine facilities, cruising yachtsmen are apt to go into this harbor after coming out of the canal, even though it's farther down the bay.

It has a long channel going in, similar to Buzzards Bay, with good anchorages before you get to Onset; if you just want to wait for the tide to change in the canal, drop your hook between Hog Neck and Burgess Point.

Independence Yacht Club, a large marina on your starboard as you come up the channel, has guest moorings and slips, gas, ice, showers, and a laundromat. On the second floor, the bar is usually open on weekends.

The Onset Bay Marina, next door, has slips, moorings, gas, diesel fuel, ice, showers, complete engine and hull repairs, marine supplies, and a small grocery store. They cater to transients. Most power boats take slips, and sailboats use moorage.

Jones Marina, beyond the fixed bridge heading into Broad Cove, deals more with the outboard fleet, since the bridge has only about nine-foot clearance.

In an emergency, and if nothing else is available, some boats do get permission to tie-up at Onset Pier, but not generally. The Onset Cash Market, just a mile away, is the best place for groceries. They will deliver to your boat.

Wareham River

Heading southwest down Buzzards Bay, you will soon see a two-mile-long sandy strip of beach, the Stoney Point Dike. You must go around the dike and head northwest for channels leading to Wareham and Weweantic Rivers.

There should be a fathom of water all over the Wareham River. Adequate water depths make possible good anchorage at Mark's Cove, Broad Marsh River, and off Long Beach Point. If you need supplies, go all the way up river to Warr's Marina. Next to the town and stores for most necessaries, Warr's Marina has more than a hundred slips and almost as many moorings, some for transients, gas, diesel fuel, ice, showers, and complete repairs, as well as a supply store with NOS charts.

Once, free berths were provided by the town, but they deteriorated and were ripped-out a few years ago.

Weweantic River

This is a beautiful place to pull in for the night. Lots of gunkhole possibilities. On the other side of the fixed bridge are two marinas with gas and other offerings but, unfortunately, the clearance is so low, only outboards can get to them.

Sippican Harbor (Marion)

Easily entered, this harbor is very popular among yachtsmen. Beverly Yacht Club has a few guest moorings and, if not, there is fine anchorage close by. Otherwise, there are two good marinas.

Barden's Boatyard is a full-scale marina. It has limited dock space but many moorings, gas, diesel fuel, ice, propane, complete engine, and hull repairs, and a good marine hardware and gift shop.

Burr Brothers Boatyard is at the head of the harbor with a channel that has three-and-a-half feet at mean low water. They have slips and moorings, gas, diesel fuel, ice, propane, engine, and hull repairs—they are boat builders—and stock marine supplies and nautical gifts.

Marion is a good supply port with many interesting shops and stores for all your basic needs and pleasures. A quiet town with few restaurants and no night life; but this is what many cruisers look for. After some of the busy ports, you're apt to welcome a quiet, peaceful, snug harbor.

The shoreline of Buzzards Bay is so varied and interesting, it is well-worth dealing with rough water, strong tidal currents, and occasional fog. The towns are fascinating, each harbor is one-of-a-kind, and there is no end to the delightful gunkhole possibilities. Sail into Buzzards Bay and experience it. It is, indeed, a stately sound!

INDEX

(*Index continues on page 264*)

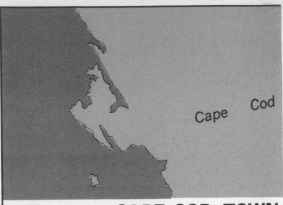

CAPE COD TOWN

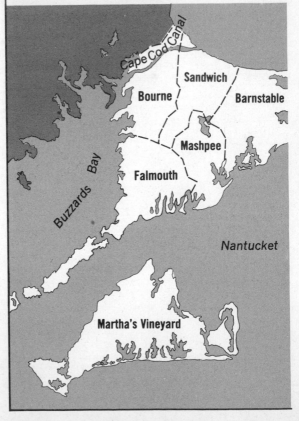

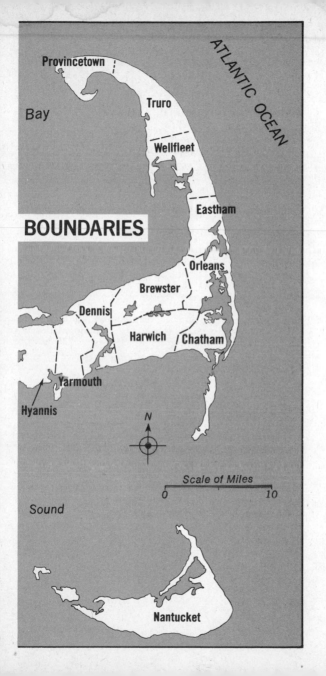